THE NEW WINDS OF CHANGE

The Evolution of the Contemporary
American Wind Band/Ensemble
and Its Music

FRANK L. BATTISTI

Published by
Meredith Music Publications
a division of GIA Publications, Inc.
7404 S. Mason Ave., Chicago, IL 60638
giamusic.com

MEREDITH MUSIC PUBLICATIONS and its stylized double M logo are trademarks of
MEREDITH MUSIC PUBLICATIONS, a division of GIA Publications, Inc.

Cover image by Dorothy Gaziano/Shutterstock.com

International Standard Book Number: 978-1-57463-473-0
Cataloging-in-Publication Data is on file with the Library of Congress.
Library of Congress Control Number: 2018952024
Printed and bound in U.S.A.

22   21   20   19   18   PP   1   2   3   4   5

To Charlotte,
my love and companion on our journey together.

品

Contents

PART I   THE AMERICAN WIND BAND/ENSEMBLE 1

Foreword

Why are you reading this book? Are you a researcher, a student, a wind band historian, or someone with the luxury of reading this fascinating chronology purely for pleasure? This book is full of valuable information tracking the progression of the wind band from its roots in the sixteenth century to the second decade of the twenty-first century, and identifies the movement's important personnel—composers, conductors, pioneering pedagogues, researchers, and commissioning bodies; and wind band/ensemble associations and organizations. *The New Winds of Change* is an update of the two earlier publications—*The Winds of Change* and *Winds of Change II*. The latter third of this most recent edition is all new material, with lists of the premieres and commissions that fomented the creative milieu of the last two decades. Frank Battisti has written the perfect hybrid of a research publication and an historical read. Feel free to use the extensive index to cherry-pick data and to track down the who, what, when, and where of all things wind band; read it from the beginning and reflect on the long centuries of band development and the amazing explosion of activities in the last fifty years. What an amazing timeline, stretching from the vellum of Gabrieli to the airwaves of NPR's Composer Datebook!

In my "Forward—it's not a typo, it's an imperative" to Frank Battisti's 1996 *The Twentieth-Century American Wind Band/Ensemble: History, Development, and Literature*, I asked readers to consider where their own experiences intersected with events outlined in the twentieth-century wind band/ensemble history. Now, twenty-two years later, most readers in the "band business," including students, will have a personal connection with many of the things and people discussed in this book. Indeed, when I read the sections about the conventions and premieres that I had attended, I had an unexpected visceral response! I recalled who I sat with at the premiere of John Corigliano's settings of Bob Dylan's poems, remembered the smell of the room and the electricity in the air, and how I sat weepy eyed as it ended. Frank Battisti's narrative is a kind of historical communal diary, in that so many of us share personal connections and involvement with many of the events that he chronicles. This latest volume also serves as a kind of proceedings for the many professional organizations identified within; there is great detail about the wind band/ensemble pieces that were presented at their national meetings—details that identify several composers at their beginnings who have more recently come into great prominence.

So delve in. And be inspired. And maybe, with hard work and good fortune, you may find your name and successes in the index of Frank Battisti's next book on the wind band/ensemble world of the third and fourth decades of the twenty-first century!

Thomas C. Duffy
New Haven, Connecticut
June 20, 2018

Acknowledgments

I am deeply indebted to many people who have helped me in the writing of *The NEW Winds of Change*. The individuals below furnished me with information and numerous documents that were needed to trace and write about the development and evolution of the American wind band/ensemble, especially about its development during the last decade and a half (2000–2015). I thank all of them for their generous help and assistance.

Glen Adsit, William L. Berz, Marcellus B. Brown, Brendan Caldwell, Thomas Caneva, Scott Casagrande, Richard Clary, Patricia Cornett, Paula Crider, Steven Davis, Thomas Duffy, Thomas Dvorak, Richard L. Floyd, Robert M. Floyd, Lowell E. Graham, Roby George, Michael Haithcock, Frederick Harris, Felix Hauswirth, Paula Holcomb, William V. Johnson, Jerry Junkin, Brian Lamb, Robert Margolis, Stephen C. Massey, Linda Moorhouse, Gabe Musella, Andrew Pease, Charles Peltz, Stephen Peterson, Nikk Pilato, Paul Popiel, Malcolm W. Rowell, Scott Rush, Timothy Salzman, Mark Scatterday, Mary Schneider, Kevin Sedatole, Scott Stewart, Kerry Taylor, Mallory Thompson, Cynthia Johnston Turner, Jess Turner, Thomas E. Verrier, David A. Waybright, Matthew Westgate, Chris David Westover, and Chris Wilhjelm.

I also wish to express special thanks and gratitude to five other people.

Thomas Duffy and I have been friends and colleagues for many years. In 1995 Tom penned a wonderful Foreword for my first book, *The Twentieth Century American Wind Band/Ensemble*. Responding to my request to write the Foreword for this book, Tom created a brilliant and insightful Foreword that graces the pages of this book. *Molte grazie*, Tom!

Garwood Whaley is president of Meredith Music Publications. We have known each other since 1995 when he published my first book. During the two decades we have worked together, Gar has been a constant source of support and encouragement for which I am most grateful and appreciative.

Russ Girsberger's contributions to the creation of this book are immense. He has helped and accompanied me through three drafts of the book, researched and discovered information I needed but couldn't find, wrote the informative end notes, and compiled the book's extensive and comprehensive index. Without his many contributions this book could not have been written. He is truly the indispensable person. I extend to him my deepest appreciation and gratitude—Russ, you are "the best!"

The book's design and layout artist is Shawn Girsberger. Shawn and I have worked together on all of my books. She is a dedicated professional and wonderful artist whose work I greatly appreciate.

And finally, I thank Charlotte, my wonderful wife of 63 years, for her patience in enduring many lonely days and evenings when I was "down the hall" writing this book. For this—but not for this alone—this book is dedicated to her.

Frank Battisti
Leverett, Massachusetts
July 9, 2018

Introduction

The historical timeline followed in *The NEW Winds of Change* is the same as that followed in the original version of the book but extended to include the first two decades of the twenty-first century (through 2015). In the Preface of the first edition of *The Winds of Change* I wrote, "I have rowed over the great ocean of wind band/ensemble material and information accumulated over my 48-year career, dropped a bucket into it and brought to the surface items and treasures that hopefully reveal the growth and development of the American Wind Band/Ensemble in the twentieth century. At the beginning of the twentieth century the wind band was primarily an organization providing music for entertainment purposes and/or civic/public functions/celebrations. By century's end the "contemporary American wind band/ensemble" had developed into a viable expressive musical medium with an increased presence in the professional artistic musical world." This also describes what I have done in *The NEW Winds of Change* but with two exceptions: 1. I have accumulated materials and information for over 65 years (instead of 48), and 2. the "contemporary American wind band/ensemble," in addition to continuing to develop as a viable expressive artistic medium, is also striving to increase its relevance in a rapidly changing and diversified society.

This book contains much new information. For example, in 2015 a lost large wind work by Igor Stravinsky, *Chant funèbre*, was discovered at the St. Petersburg State Conservatory. This is a work Stravinsky wrote in 1908 to honor the memory of his teacher Rimsky-Korsakov. Stravinsky stated that it was the best of his works before the *Firebird*. *Chant funèbre* provides an important missing link between Stravinsky's *Fireworks* and *Scherzo Fantastique*. It is a welcomed and valuable addition to wind band/ensemble literature.

When writing a one-volume book about a subject that has a long history, one is forced to make choices about what to include. I have chosen composers, compositions, events, initiatives, and happenings, that, in my opinion, best illuminate the overall development of the American wind band/ensemble. For compositions, I selected pieces that are representative of the various styles of music created for the medium during specific periods of time. I avoided rendering critical judgment on recently composed pieces (those written in the twenty-first century) since doing so from such a short perspective would, in my opinion, be unfair and premature. Time and the scrutiny of conductors, players and audiences will determine the worth and destiny of these works. I hope readers of *The NEW Winds of Change* will take time and listen to the pieces identified in the pages of this book. Doing so will increase their knowledge, understanding and appreciation of the wind band/ensemble and its literature.

Part I of my book focuses on "The American Wind Band—Development, History and Literature" from the canzoni of Gabrieli to the present time; Part II focuses on "The American School Band Movement and Other Important Wind Band/Ensemble, Music Education Issues," including the need for wind band/ensemble conductors/directors to establish and solidify a repertoire. The final chapter of the book includes suggestions for advancing the medium in future years.

I hope others in the future will continue to study, explore and write books about the history of the American wind band/ensemble and its music. It is a subject that has been neglected far too long by musicologists and historians.

Frank L. Battisti
Leverett, Massachusetts
June 18, 2018

Definitions

I want to clarify two terms used in this book: *literature* and *repertoire*. When I use *literature* I'm referring to the total body of music available for performance by wind bands/ensembles. When I use *repertoire* I'm referring to the selective body of literature that is actually being performed regularly on concerts by wind bands/ensembles.

My use of the term "wind band/ensemble" is deliberate. Today many wind groups perform concerts that include works written for both the full wind band and wind ensembles of varying instrumentation. "Wind band/ensemble" is, for me, a more precise description of these ensembles.

When I refer to a composer as being a *major* or *world-class composer* I am referring to one whose works are performed by great artists and musical ensembles that command the attention of important critics and leaders in the greater musical world.

Choice of Literature

The literature commented upon in this book consists of:

- works that have advanced the image of wind bands/ensembles as an expressive musical medium,

- masterpieces of wind music (Stravinsky, *Symphonies of Wind Instruments*; Varèse, *Ionisation*; Messiaen, *Et exspecto resurrectionem mortuorum*; Husa, *Music for Prague* 1968, etc.),

- works which, when viewed collectively, convey the breadth of musical styles found in wind band/ensemble literature at a given time.

Conductor and music historian David Whitwell has stated that anyone contemplating writing about the history of wind bands/ ensembles faces two alternatives:

1. The band's cultural forebearers were the military bands, and the works of Mozart, Berlioz, Gounod, Strauss, etc., were peripheral to that history; or

2. The band's cultural forebearers were Mozart, Berlioz, Gounod, Strauss, etc., and the military bands were peripheral to that history.

As I did in the first edition of *The Winds of Change*, I again choose to pursue Whitwell's second alternative in writing this second edition of the book. In the original version of *The Winds of Change* and also in *Winds of Change II*, I traced the evolution and development of the American wind band/ensemble from the 16th century to the end of the first decade of the twenty-first century. In this book I extend it to the middle of the second decade of the twenty-first century (2015).

PART I

The American
Wind Band/Ensemble

Development, History, and Literature

CHAPTER 1

Beginnings—16th through the Early 20th Century

From Gabrieli to Vienna Octet School to Strauss •
Early European and American Bands • Patrick Gilmore
• Sousa's U. S. Marine and Professional Bands • Wind
Societies/Ensembles in Paris, Boston, and New York

Roots: Early European Wind Music

The early Italian composer Giovanni Gabrieli (1557–1612) is often called the "father of orchestration." Gabrieli employed wind instruments brilliantly in the sophisticated, highly developed antiphonal music he composed for performances in Venice's Cathedral of St. Mark. Later, in France, Jean-Baptiste Lully (1632–1687) provided music for King Louis XIV's infantry bands of oboes and bassoons. Across the channel in England, Henry Purcell (c. 1659–1695) used trumpets, trombones, and timpani in the music he wrote for the funeral of Queen Mary, and, still earlier, Matthew Locke (c. 1630–1677) used wind instruments in music composed for the coronation of Charles II. George Frideric Handel (1685–1759) created the *Music for the Royal Fireworks* in 1749 for the celebration of the Peace of

Aix-la-Chapelle. This festive music is scored for a huge band of woodwind, brass, and percussion instruments which totaled 40 trumpets, 20 French horns, 16 oboes, 16 bassoons, 8 pairs of timpani, and 12 side drums.

In the eighteenth century, Haydn (1732–1809), Mozart (1756–1791), Beethoven (1770–1827), and Krommer (1759–1831) wrote "Harmoniemusik" for wind octets in and around Vienna, Prague, and Budapest (1780-1830). Included in this literature were original wind works (i.e., serenades, divertimenti), opera arrangements/transcriptions, and concerti for various instruments with wind ensemble accompaniment. Wind music authority David Whitwell describes the activity of this Octet School as "unique in wind history ... these ensembles existed primarily to perform concerts and served no functional, military, or entertainment purpose. This is rare in any period of wind music, but especially so in the eighteenth century."[1]

European Band Development

Richard Franko Goldman (1910–1980) suggested that the modern wind band began with the French Revolution and the organization of the French National Guard Band by Bernard Sarrette (1765–1858). French bands were fortunate to have music written for them by such composers as Cherubini (1760–1842), Gossec (1734–1829), Catel (1773–1830), and Méhul (1763–1817). In the period from 1795 to 1810, French bands became the best in Europe.[2]

During the first half of the nineteenth century, improvements in woodwind and brass instruments by Boehm, Klosé, Buffet, Heckel, Blümel, and Stölzel, along with the invention of new ones by men such as Adolphe Sax (1814–1894), inventor of the saxophone and saxhorns, increased the expressive and technical potential of wind instruments and the wind band. The outline on pages 5 and 6 tracks important developments in the evolution of wind instruments in parallel with those of the violin and orchestra.

Wilhelm Wieprecht (1802–1872), celebrated leader of military music in Prussia, made many important recommendations about the instrumentation and section proportions of bands. He articulated the advantages to be gained through the use of French horns and trumpets with valves. His transcriptions of Mozart and Beethoven symphonies, Classic and Romantic era overtures, operatic excerpts, national airs, etc., expanded the nineteenth-century band literature.

The primary function of European bands in the nineteenth century was furnishing music for local and national civic ceremonies and social occasions. The repertoire performed by these bands consisted principally of transcriptions and arrangements of popular, folk, and light music. Very little original music was composed for or performed by these wind bands.

In 1826, Felix Mendelssohn (1809–1847), while at the Spa (Kurort) of Bad Dobberan on the Baltic Sea, composed his *Notturno* for "harmoniemusik" (1 flute, 2 clarinets, 2 oboes, 2 bassoons, 2 French horns, 1 trumpet, and 1 bass horn). Later he rescored the piece for a larger wind orchestra which was published by Simrock in 1839 as the *Overture for Wind Band, Op. 24*. Carl Maria von Weber (1786–1826) and Hector Berlioz (1803–1869) expanded the role of wind instruments in the orchestra by assigning them important expressive solo parts. Berlioz composed his *Grand Symphonie Funèbre et Triomphale, Op. 15* in 1840 for the 10th anniversary of the July Revolution of 1830 and, in 1844, Richard Wagner (1813–1883) composed his *Trauersinfonie* for ceremonies marking the re-interment of Carl Maria von Weber's body in Dresden after its return from London. Both the Berlioz and Wagner pieces were written for outdoor performances and are scored for large wind band.

Berlioz's *Treatise on Orchestration* (*Grand Traité d'instrumentation et d'orchestration modernes*) (1843) provided composers with important mechanical and technical information about the instruments in the orchestra, especially wind instruments. His comprehensive knowledge of orchestration led conductor Felix Weingartner (1863–1942) to proclaim Berlioz as the "creator of the modern orchestra."

1467	Tieffenbrucker builds a true violin
1542–1610	Gasparo de Salò established the form of the violin
1608	Monteverdi wrote Orfeo (orchestra established)
1644–1737	Birth and death dates of Stradivarius
1677	A key is finally added to the flute
1690	First clarinet (by Denner) appears
1770	Basset horn appears
1793	Bass clarinet appears in an early form
1808	Woodwind key-ring is patented
1810	Ivan Müller brings out a 13-key clarinet

1810	Keyed bugle appears
1815	Piston valve invented
1830	First three-valve brasses appear
1832	Boehm conical-bore wooden flute appears
1840	Saxophone is invented
1843	Saxhorns are invented
1843	Klosé and Buffet improve the clarinet (Boehm system)[3]

During the second half of the nineteenth century, several pieces for small chamber wind ensemble were written by major composers. Antonín Dvořák (1841–1904) composed his *Serenade in d minor, Op. 44* in 1878, Charles Gounod (1818–1893) his *Petite Symphonie* in 1883, and Richard Strauss (1864–1949) his *Serenade in E-flat, Op. 7* in 1881 and *Suite in B-flat, Op. 4* in 1884.

American Wind Band Development

The development of bands in the United States began in 1798 when President John Adams signed an Act of Congress establishing the United States Marine Band. Starting as a "drum major, fife major, and 32 drums and fifes," the Marine Band has, over the past two plus centuries, developed into what *The Washington Post* describes as "...not only the best [band] in the land, but, very likely, the best in the world." The band's first White House performance was on New Year's Day 1801, two months after President John and wife Abigail Adams moved into the still-unfinished structure. It has performed at every Presidential Inauguration since that of Thomas Jefferson in March 1801.

Among the first bands organized in the United States were the Salem (Massachusetts) Brigade Band (1806), which consisted of five clarinets, two bassoons, one trumpet, and a bass drum; the Militia Band of Bethlehem, Pennsylvania; and the Eleventh Regiment Band of New York, established in 1810. The instrumentation of these early bands consisted of assorted combinations of woodwind and brass instruments. They were largely civilian groups, often associated with local militia. Their primary activities were presenting concerts (mainly out-of-doors) and participating in parades, military drills, and civic and patriotic ceremonies.

The English band was the model for early American bands. Pieces published by Boosey and Company and William Chappell for the

British band market often appeared in the repertoire performed by American bands, along with newly printed band pieces by American composers such as Alexander Reinagle (*Jefferson's March*—1805) and Samuel Holyoke (*Massachusetts March*—1807). The country's first completely professional band, the Independent Band of New York, was formed in 1825 and three years later (1828) the nation's first community band, the Allentown (Pennsylvania) Band, came into existence.

Thomas Dodworth and his sons Allen Dodworth and Harvey Dodworth, all conductors, composers, music publishers, and instrument dealers, introduced and implemented new concepts in instrumentation and performance as members of the Independent Band of New York in the 1830s. Eventually Thomas Dodworth changed the band's instrumentation to all brass and renamed it "Dodworth's Band" (1836). It was considered the finest band in New York until Patrick Gilmore arrived on the scene in the 1870s.

Many bands embraced the change to all brass. These bands performed a repertoire consisting of arrangements of overtures by composers such as Daniel Auber, Luigi Cherubini, Gioachino Antonio Rossini, and Giuseppe Verdi, plus polkas, galops, quadrilles, waltzes, and popular music. Included on the next page is a typical mid-19th century brass band program.

From the 1830s through the start of the Civil War, brass bands were especially active in New England states. One of the best was the Providence Brass Band, later renamed the American Brass Band, organized in 1837. Woodwinds were added later, in 1853, and again the band was renamed and incorporated as the American Band of Providence, Rhode Island. When David Wallis Reeves, one of America's great bandmasters, became its leader in 1866, it developed into one of the nation's foremost bands.

In 1853, the talented French musician and supreme showman-promoter Monsieur Louis Antoine Jullien (1812–1860) arrived in the United States. He organized and presented dazzling and spectacular concerts and became enormously popular and famous. His extravagant productions fired the imagination of Patrick Sarsfield Gilmore (1829–1892), an Irish immigrant musician and cornet virtuoso, who eventually became the father of the modern American concert band.

American Brass Band Concert
February 3, 1851

Part I

Elfin Quick Step—Band	W. F. Marshall
Song of America	Carl Lobe
Miss Carpenter	
Cornet Solo—(accompaniment by orchestra)	Romaine
Mr. J. C. Greene	
Pas de Fleurs—Band	Max Maraetzek
Romanza—"Sounds so entrancing"	Andreas Randel
Miss Carpenter	
Overture—La Donna del Lago—Band	Rossini

Part II

Grand Wedding March	Mendelssohn
from Mendelssohn's Opera – "Midsummer Night's Dream"	
Arranged expressly for the Band by W. F. Marshall	
Song—"Let the bright Seraphim"	Handel
Miss Carpenter	
With Trumpet Obligato by Mr. J. C. Greene	
Septette—From Amille—("Rest Spirit, Rest")	Rooke
Miss Carpenter	
Polka—Band	A. Dodworth
Cavatina—"Twas no vision"—From I Lombardi	Verdi
Miss Carpenter	
Evergreen Galop—Band	Labitsky

Shortly after arriving in the United States, Gilmore was appointed the leader of the Boston Brigade Band, quickly transforming it into a professional ensemble and renaming it "Gilmore's Band." Under his leadership it developed into America's first great concert wind band. When the Civil War broke out, Gilmore and his players enlisted as a unit and served one year with the Twenty-fourth Massachusetts Volunteer Regiment, after which they returned to Boston, performing concerts for the remainder of the war as part of the home front effort to bolster morale.

Lawrence Levine points out "… that the most popular and ubiquitous instrumental organization in nineteenth-century America was the band, over 3,000 of which, containing more than 60,000 musicians, existed on the eve of the Civil War. It is...essential to understand that the clear distinction we tend to make today between bands and orchestras did not obtain for much of the nineteenth century. For most Americans the distinction, in so far as it existed at all, was more a functional than an aesthetic one.... Nineteenth-century bands and orchestras shared musicians, who moved easily and regularly between the two, often earning money by belonging to both types of organization simultaneously. They also shared repertories: overtures, operatic arias, waltzes, polkas, fantasies, and of course marches, which were the common fare of both."[4]

Gilmore became the P. T. Barnum of American bandmasters, organizing three gigantic musical events between 1864 and 1872. The first took place in New Orleans for the inauguration of Louisiana Governor Michael Hahn and featured a band of 500 musicians and a chorus of 5,000 school children. The second event, the National Peace Jubilee, was held in Boston in 1869. Here Gilmore doubled the number of his performing forces, creating a band of 1,000 and a chorus of 10,000 voices plus soloists. The culmination of his extravaganzas was the 1872 World Peace Jubilee, again held in Boston, that featured performances by an orchestra of 1,000, a band of 2,000, and a chorus of 20,000. Gilmore invited several European bands to perform at the World Peace Jubilee, among them the Band of the Grenadier Guards, the Kaiser Franz Grenadier Regiment Band, the National Band of Dublin, and the Garde Républicaine Band. The high performance standards demonstrated in the concerts performed by these visiting bands proved to be an important event in American band history. It stimulated improvement in the performance level, instrumentation, and repertoire of American bands.

Gilmore next became leader of the Twenty-Second Regiment Band of New York (1873), renaming it the "Gilmore Band." He immediately expanded the band's repertoire by adding transcriptions of orchestra music by composers such as Beethoven, Mozart, and Wagner. He also brought innovation to the band's instrumentation, shifting the emphasis from the brasses to the woodwinds, especially the clarinets. In 1878, Gilmore's Band consisted of 35 woodwind, 27 brass, and 4 percussion players (see list below). Under his inspired leadership the ensemble became the greatest band in America.

Instrumentation of Gilmore's Band (1878)

2 piccolos	2 bassoons
2 flutes	1 contrabassoon
2 oboes	1 E-flat soprano cornet
1 A-flat sopranino clarinet	4 B-flat cornets (1st & 2nd)
3 E-flat soprano clarinets	2 trumpets
16 B-flat clarinets (8, 1st; 4, 2nd; 4, 3rd)	2 fluegelhorns
1 alto clarinet	4 French horns
1 bass clarinet	2 E-flat alto horns
1 soprano saxophone	2 tenor horns
1 alto saxophone	2 euphoniums
1 tenor saxophone	3 trombones
1 bass (baritone?) saxophone	5 bombardons (basses)
	4 percussion

Total 66 players[5]

In addition to being a conductor, Gilmore was also a prolific composer. He reputedly composed *When Johnny Comes Marching Home* (1863), which was published under the pseudonym of Louis Lambert. When Gilmore died in St. Louis in 1892, Sousa wrote, "He [went] into the highways and byways of the land, playing Wagner and Liszt, and other great composers, in places where their music was absolutely unknown, and their names scarcely more than a twice-repeated sound."[6]

John Philip Sousa (1854–1932), the "March King," is generally considered to be the greatest bandmaster who ever lived. He assumed leadership of the Marine Band in 1880 and during his 12-year tenure molded it into the world's most famous band. In 1892, Sousa resigned his position with the Marine Band and organized the Sousa professional band. Sousa's goal as a conductor was to present band concerts that would entertain people—"Entertainment is of more value to the world than technical education in music appreciation." He saw no inconsistency in programming "...tinkling comedy with symphonic tragedy or rhythmic march with classic tone-picture." Sousa "entertained" audiences by creating programs featuring transcriptions of orchestral works, solo performances by famous artists (singers and instrumentalists), arrangements of national airs and popular music, novelty numbers, and his own compositions, especially his marches.[7]

The Sousa era (1880–1925) was the "Golden Age" of the American professional band. Bands and band music became the nation's favorite popular form of entertainment. The Sousa Band, performing in parks, resort areas, and concert venues, became the most popular and successful of the many professional bands touring the country and the world. Frederick Fennell describes Sousa as "the god of the American concert band world.... the imperishable repertory of marches he composed...[was]...his most important contribution to the development of the band in America."[8] Sousa described his marches as "music for the feet instead of the head" and said they should "make a man with a wooden leg want to step out."[9] He knew that writing a good march was a challenging task. "[T]he march speaks to a fundamental rhythm in the human organization and it is answered. A march stimulates every center of vitality, wakens the imagination.... But a march must be good. It must be as free from padding as a marble statue. Every line must be carved with unerring skill. Once padded, it ceases to be a march. There is no form of musical composition where the harmonic structure must be more clean-cut. The whole process is an exacting one. There must be a melody which appeals to the musical and unmusical alike. There must be no confusion in counterpoints."[10]

In his book, *Music in a New Found Land*, Wilfrid Mellers states that Sousa's marches "...will continue to be played, wherever a public occasion calls for communal rejoicing or even for mass hysteria. They are a necessary part of the experience of all common men (and of some uncommon ones), for they fulfill our most primitive instincts at the same time as they cage them in conformity. They are at once Revolutionary and Established!"[11] Besides composing marches, Sousa wrote other types of band music, mostly of a lighter character, including suites, waltzes, novelty, and solo numbers.

One does not associate contemporary music with John Philip Sousa. However, in 1968 Richard Franko Goldman stated that, "On the subject of contemporary music...we must give honor where it is due, and remember that both Gilmore and Sousa played Wagner transcriptions at a time when Wagner's music was considered daring, if not outrageous; and before we pat ourselves on the back for our courage in playing Schuman's *Chester Overture* or even the Hindemith *Symphony for Band*, let us remember that these works are not really as "modern" as was Wagner in the days of Gilmore. So again, the difference is not one of kind, but merely one of advancing time and changing names."[12]

Other important bandmasters of the era were Thomas Preston Brooke, Patrick Conway, Giuseppe Creatore, Mace Gay, Frederick Innes, Bohumir Kryl, Allessandro Liberati, Jean Missud, Arthur Pryor, and D. W. Reeves, who Sousa called "the Father of Band Music in America."

Wind Societies/Ensembles in France and the United States

Coinciding with the development of the American professional band was the formation of four societies dedicated to the performance of serious wind music. In France, Paul Taffanel (1844–1908), father of the modern school of French flute playing, founded the Société de Musique de Chambre pour Instruments à Vent in 1879. This ensemble, consisting of many of the leading wind players in Paris, made a significant contribution to wind literature by premiering works by composers such as Gounod, d'Indy, and Pierné. When Taffanel became conductor at the Paris Opera, the ensemble disbanded. Shortly after its demise Georges Barrère (1876–1944), another flutist living in Paris, formed a similar ensemble, naming it the Société Moderne pour Instruments à Vent. This ensemble presented concerts for sixteen years, performing over 100 new works composed by 50 composers.

Georges Longy (1868–1930) (who tried to continue the Société de Musique de Chambre pour Instruments à Vent when Taffanel left) came to the United States in 1898 to become the principal oboist of the Boston Symphony Orchestra. In 1900, he organized a wind ensemble in Boston patterned after Taffanel's Société de Musique de Chambre pour instruments à Vent, naming it the Longy Club. David Whitwell in his book, *The Longy Club: A Professional Wind Ensemble in Boston (1900–1917)*, states that "This ensemble...gave regular concerts in Boston and throughout New England. It was an ensemble that enthusiastically supported contemporary music and performed all its concerts with the very highest level of artistic integrity. This is all the more extraordinary given the musical climate and in particular the social role relegated to traditional wind bands of that era."[13]

Longy's public announcement of his intention to found a Boston ensemble of professional wind players reads, "I propose to give a series of public concerts in Boston, at which a number of works especially written for wind instruments will be performed. The public hitherto has had very little opportunity to hear such works performed.... There is no lack in the number, the variety, or the excellence of the pieces, but the difficulty in organizing a company of artists of homogeneous talent has naturally caused this form of concert to be of infrequent occurrence...."[14] The Longy Club gave its first concert on December 18, 1900, in Boston's Association Hall. Included on the program were the Beethoven *Quintet, Op. 16* and the Bernard *Divertissement, Op. 36*

Even though Longy's concerts offered new music and exciting music-making to Boston audiences, attracting a sizable audience was a challenge. The *Boston Transcript's* review of the concert of December 26, 1910, states that "the audience, while responsively appreciative, should have been larger. The individual skill of the members of this club and their painstaking and brilliant ensemble should have a more attentive response from a supposedly discriminating public." The Longy Club continued to give concerts for seventeen years through the 1916–1917 season. However, on November 22, 1918, the *Boston Transcript* reported that the Longy Club wind ensemble had been, "disbanded as a consequence of the recent reorganization of the [Boston Symphony Orchestra]."[15] David Whitwell speculates that its demise was probably due to a number of factors including aging members, members wishing to return to France at the end of World War I and lack of financial support. At the beginning of the 21st century, attracting audiences for performances of contemporary wind band/ensemble music continues to be a challenge.

Five years after Longy came to America, Georges Barrère arrived (1905) to become principal flutist in Walter Damrosch's New York Symphony Orchestra, and immediately formed the New York Symphony Quintet. Six years later (1911) he expanded the quintet to an ensemble of eleven winds (2 flutes, 2 oboes, 2 clarinets, 2 bassoons, 2 French horns, and 1 trumpet) and named it the Barrère Ensemble. The first concert performed by Barrère's Ensemble (February 28,

1911) included the Beethoven *Octet, Op. 103*, and the Haydn *Octet*. The repertoire performed by both Longy's and Barrère's ensembles consisted of music composed by 18th- and 19th-century masters (Haydn, Mozart, Beethoven, Dvořák, Strauss, etc.) and new works by contemporary composers such as Charles Gounod, Arthur Bird, and Georges Enesco.

ENDNOTES

1 David Whitwell, "The Incredible Vienna Octet School—Part I," *The Instrumentalist* 24 (October 1969): 33.
2 Richard Franko Goldman, *The Wind Band: Its Literature and Technique* (Allyn and Bacon, 1961), 25–26.
3 Kenneth Berger, *The Band in the United States–A Preliminary Review of Band Research and Research Needs* (Band Associates, 1961), 33.
4 Lawrence W. Levine, *Highbrow/Lowbrow: The Emergence of Cultural Hierarchy in America* (Harvard University Press, 1988), 104.
5 Richard Franko Goldman, *The Wind Band: Its Literature and Technique* (Allyn & Bacon, 1961), 59, 62.
6 John Philip Sousa, *Marching Along: Recollections of Men, Women, and Music* (Hale, Cushman & Flint, 1928; rev. ed. by Paul E. Bierley, Integrity Press, 1994), 133.
7 Ibid.
8 Frederick Fennell, *Time and the Winds* (Leblanc Publications, 1954), 38–39.
9 Paul E. Bierley, *John Philip Sousa, American Phenomenon*, rev. ed. (Integrity Press, 1973), 123.
10 Sousa, *Marching Along*, 359–360.
11 Wilfrid Mellers, *Music in a New Found Land* (Oxford University Press, 1987), 257–258.
12 Richard Franko Goldman, "Fifty Years of Band Programs and Audiences," *The Instrumentalist* 22 (June 1968): 42.
13 David Whitwell, *The Longy Club: A Professional Wind Ensemble in Boston (1900–1917)* (WINDS, 1988), 6.
14 Ibid.
15 Ibid., 192.

CHAPTER 2

Beginning of Modern Wind Band Literature (1900–1940)

I *British Composers of Band Music • Percy Grainger* **I**

British Composers and Band Music

Music found on band programs during the first quarter of the twentieth century consisted primarily of transcriptions of orchestral literature, opera excerpts, light music (waltzes, polkas, patriotic, and popular tunes, etc.), and marches. No significant body of original music for the wind band existed at this time.

Gustav Holst composed the twentieth-century's first important original band work, *First Suite in E-flat for Military Band*. Holst was a composer, performer, conductor, and teacher. In 1905, he began teaching music to students at four schools in London, including St. Paul's Girls School in Hammersmith. A significant portion of Holst's life was spent teaching, composing, and arranging music for amateur music makers (students and adults).

During the first decade of the twentieth century, British military bandmasters appealed to composers to write original works for the military band. George Dyson, in an article entitled "The Composer and the Military Band," wrote, "It has often been remarked, and often deplored, that composers of serious aims ignore the military band. The bandmaster who would raise the standard or extend the scope of his repertory can find little or nothing to help him so far as music written specifically for the military band is concerned. Such original music as exists is of doubtful or commonplace character."[1]

In 1895, Holst and Ralph Vaughan Williams met at the Royal College of Music in London. The two quickly became friends and were soon celebrating their fabled "field days" together. During these "field days" they studied and critiqued each other's latest works with a "frankness that would have caused offence to acquaintances of less mutual sympathy."[2] Vaughan Williams grew to rely on Holst's philosophical stimulation and advice about his compositional development. Between 1906 and 1916, the creative endeavors of both men were influenced by the work being done by Cecil Sharp and his associates in the collection of English folksongs. Holst was soon creating harmonizations and accompaniments for many of Sharp's newly discovered folk melodies. Using a compositional style that was direct and economical, "Holst arranged many of these songs effectively for unaccompanied chorus, for amateur string orchestra, and for bands."[3]

Gustav Holst (1874–1934)

When Holst composed his *First Suite in E-flat for Military Band* in 1909, he was probably responding to military bandmasters' appeal for new original band works or the Worshipful Company of Musicians' first ever band composition contest. Having played in "civic" military and summer resort bands as a trombonist from 1895 to 1903, Holst possessed excellent knowledge of the band medium. The *First Suite in E-flat for Military Band* is an outstanding piece in which Holst achieves a classic balance between musical content and form through the use of efficient and traditional compositional devices and block scoring. Excluding Sousa marches, the *First Suite* is probably the most-played composition in wind band literature. The entire piece is based on a three-note melodic motive found in the first movement's opening theme. When Holst was composing the *First Suite*, he was also studying the music of Henry Purcell. This could account for his decision to use the "chaconne" form for the *Suite's* opening movement. Holst employs a new style of writing for military band in both the first and startling scherzando-like second movement of the

Suite. It is characterized by clear, defined textures and imaginative development of thematic material. In the final "March" movement, Holst creates music that captures "... the whole spirit of the military band combination."[4] The folk-like melodies used in this work are all original tunes created by the composer. Holst authority Jon Mitchell states that an examination of the first page of the manuscript score of the *First Suite* "... indicates that Holst was writing for a medium that was in a state of flux. Saxophones, relative newcomers to the military band, were gradually replacing the alto and bass clarinets; likewise, B-flat trumpets were replacing those in E-flat. It was partially in response to these changes, but also the result of years of offering optional instrumentation—a practice that had started as far back as the 1880s with the cueing in of missing instruments for his father's orchestra at the Montpellier Rotunda—that Holst's [First Suite] manuscript full score offers several options in the instrumentation of the work. Of the thirty-eight instrumental parts listed, some sixteen—over 40% of the total—are listed as "ad Lib."[5]

When was this piece premiered? According to Jon Mitchell, "What is generally considered to have been the first concert performance of the *First Suite in E-flat for Military Band* took place at Kneller Hall on June 23, 1920 ... [performed] by the 165 member Royal Military School of Music Band."[6] The *Suite* received many more performances during the 1920–21 season. An article in the *Richmond Times* following a subsequent performance of the piece at Kneller Hall states, "... a notable contribution was Gustav Holst's *Suite in E-flat*, a virile and arresting composition. Mr. Holst, who is a force to be reckoned with in modern music, takes a keen interest in the work at Kneller Hall to the extent of personal visits when any of his music is being rehearsed for performance."[7] A more substantial review of the work appeared in the *Birmingham Post*, following a performance by the Birmingham Police Band in November 1920. "Mr. Holst's suite is a successful attempt to provide for a work of serious musical interest in which the characteristic qualities of the combination have dictated the lay-out of the music. It is in three short numbers. They are unified not only by the force of the contrasts between them, but also thematically.... The writing exploits to good purpose the natural angularities of the combination, and has the admirable clarity of construction that is a feature of Mr. Holst's music. A modal flavour is lent to the work by the prominence of the super-tonic in its subjective melodies. The march has the rhythmic fascination of the true march, although it has rather of the quick-step variety."[8]

Boosey & Hawkes's initial publication of the *First Suite* (1921) contained only a two-line condensed score. An examination of the original manuscript reveals that Holst created a full score of the work plus a condensed two-line score (located at the bottom of each page of the manuscript). In 1948 (twenty-seven years after the original publication), Boosey & Hawkes issued a new edition of the *Suite* in which the instrumentation of the piece was expanded. Additional instruments were added to make the piece more compatible with the instrumentation of American school, college, and university bands. This edition, constructed from a set of parts without reference to the original score, contains many misprints. Boosey & Hawkes' most recent publication of the *Suite* was issued in 1984. In this edition, editor Colin Matthews corrects the misprints in the 1948 edition and the instrumentation is once again adjusted to better match that found in contemporary wind bands.

The title page of Holst's manuscript score contains important informational notes for conductors regarding the performance of the *First Suite*. These were included in Boosey & Hawkes' first edition compressed score of the piece (1921) but, for some unknown reason, omitted in the full score edition published by Boosey & Hawkes in 1948. The first note is of particular importance, "As each movement is founded on the same phrase it is requested that the Suite shall be played right through without a break." Traditionally the *First Suite* has been performed with pauses between movements. When this happens, the formal structure of the piece is weakened. Only when the three movements are performed without pauses separating them, does the piece have the expressive form envisioned by Holst when he created the work. Fortunately, this important instructive note was reinstated in the Boosey & Hawkes edition published in 1984.

Richard Franko Goldman proclaimed that the Holst *First Suite* was the "... first available and universally recognized original band work of the century.... This credit belongs to the work for reasons other than simply priority of time. For this work ... together with his *Second Suite in F Major* of 1911, established an altogether new style of idiomatic band writing and, one might say with all justice, a new conception of band sound and of the kind of forthright music most suited to the performing medium ... no more effective pieces have been written for band."[9]

Holst's *Second Suite in F for Military Band, Op. 28, No. 2*, was composed in 1911. Again the reason why Holst wrote this piece is not clear. Imogen Holst, his daughter, speculates: "I think it is unlikely that Holst would have written it in 1911 unless it had been asked for, with a performance in mind. It is possible that it was first played during the Festival of Empire which was held at the Crystal Palace (London) from May to October 1911 as part of the celebrations for the coronation of George V."[10] This work is scored for a smaller instrumentation (no "ad lib" parts) than used by Holst in the *First Suite* and all the melodies are authentic English folk music, most of them from Hampshire county. The first movement is in ABA form and is the longest of any of the movements in either suite. The second movement is a beautiful lyrical statement based on the folk song, "I'll Love my Love." The robust, energetic third movement is a rhythmical setting of "Song of the Blacksmith" in which Holst employs mixed meters (often adding up to Holst's characteristic seven beats), an anvil, and a surprise ending—a brilliant D major chord! The final movement, "Fantasia on the 'Dargason'," shows Holst at his compositional best. Imogen Holst states that "the six-eight tune travels lightheartedly with time to notice all that happens on the way, and when he combines it with 'Greensleeves,' ... [he] achieves the perfect of contrasted folk tunes. It is difficult to believe the two tunes were not especially intended for each other; they live their own lives, each leaning to the other instead of fighting for independence."[11] The work, published in 1922, is "Dedicated to James Causley Windram," a bandmaster of the Coldstream Guards, who was instrumental in getting Holst's *First Suite* published.

As with the *First Suite*, the *Second Suite* was premiered by the Royal Military School of Music Band on a concert presented in association with the British Music Society at Royal Albert Hall in London on June 30, 1922. The objective of the concert was to show that the military band had become a "... far more important factor in the nation's musical life than it used to be."[12] A review appearing in *The Daily Mail* (London) on July 1, 1922, stated that "A new *Suite in F* of

English folk songs for military bands, by Mr. Gustav Holst, carried the audience off its feet. It is perhaps the most notable piece of music ever written for military bands." Another review proclaimed, "The example of Mr. Holst ought to bring about a change in securing band works from composers, for his *Suite in F* ... is a most effective piece of serious music and at the same time a proof that a composer gifted with inspiration and understanding can obtain from a military band effects of sounds entirely novel and beautiful."[13] Due to the excellent press coverage and glowing reviews, the *Second Suite* was quickly published by Boosey & Hawkes two months after its premiere.

On December 3, 1927, Holst received a letter from the British Broadcasting Corporation (B.B.C.) requesting that he compose a one-movement piece "for Military Band ... lasting from twelve to fifteen minutes ... in the form of a Concert Overture, or Fantasy, or Symphonic Poem." Two days later (December 5, 1927) Holst responded stating that he "should be delighted to write a piece for military band" but requested a postponement in order that he might "first arrange one of Bach's Organ Fugues for military band." The postponement was agreed upon and Holst immediately proceeded to arrange Bach's *Fugue in G major (BWV 577)* calling it *Fugue à la Gigue*. Holst conducted the premiere performance of this arrangement on the B.B.C. Wireless Military Band's radio broadcast concert of July 22, 1928. It was during this time that Holst also made a military band version of the "Marching Song" (from *Two Songs without Words*), which was published by Novello in 1930.

In 1929, Holst started working on the large single-movement piece requested two years earlier by the B.B.C. The B.B.C. Military Band was an excellent ensemble made up of many of London's better wind players and several college professors. Holst was at the height of his compositional powers and was determined to write a substantial work for these professional players. What he created was *Hammersmith—Prelude and Scherzo*, a masterpiece for wind band and one of Holst's greatest works. While writing the piece, Holst constantly sought advice and suggestions from B.B.C. conductors Adrian Boult (Symphony Orchestra) and B. Walton O'Donnell (Wireless Military Band) as well as Ralph Vaughan Williams, who found the work very puzzling—a "very different kind of band piece." As Holst neared the completion of the piece, discussions were undertaken in hopes of arranging a public concert by the B.B.C. Wireless Military Band which would feature the premiere performance of *Hammersmith* (the band's performances were almost exclusively confined to radio broadcast concerts). Negotiations for the concert proceeded very slowly and soon stalled, putting the premiere of Holst's piece on hold. However, the B.B.C. Wireless Military Band did arrange a reading of *Hammersmith* on May 19, 1931, after which Holst made revisions in the piece.

It was at this time that Adrian Boult, conductor of the B.B.C. Symphony Orchestra, approached Holst, suggesting that he consider writing an orchestra piece or possibly making an orchestra version of *Hammersmith*. Holst immediately proceeded to compose the orchestra version of *Hammersmith*, which was premiered by the B.B.C. Symphony, Adrian Boult conducting, in London's Queen's Hall on November 25, 1931. In the program note provided by the composer for this performance, Holst states, "as far as the work owes anything to outside influences it is the result of living in Hammersmith for thirty-five years on and off and wanting to express my feelings for the place in music.... The only two things that I think were in my mind were 1) a district crowded with cockneys which would be overcrowded if it were not for the everlasting good humour of the people concerned, and 2) the background of the river, that was there before the crowd and will be there presumably long after, and which goes on its way largely unnoticed and apparently quite unconcerned."[14]

Holst continued to make slight revisions in the band version of his piece as he waited for its premiere performance. When it became necessary for him to leave the UK in 1932 to take up a six-month residency at Harvard University, the band version of *Hammersmith* still had not received its premiere performance.

Arriving in the United States, Holst was contacted by Edwin Franko Goldman and invited to conduct *Hammersmith* at the American Bandmasters Association (ABA) convention in Washington, D.C. on April 17, 1932. Holst, aware that the premiere performance of *Hammersmith* still belonged to the B.B.C., contacted them. Since all attempts by the B.B.C. to arrange a public concert for the premiere of Holst's piece had resulted in failure, Holst requested permission from them to conduct its premiere at the ABA Convention. Permission was granted and Holst anticipated traveling to Washington, D.

C. to conduct his piece at the ABA Convention. Unfortunately Holst became ill late in March and was unable to travel to the convention. It therefore fell to Captain Taylor Branson to conduct the U. S. Marine Band in the premiere performance of the original version of *Hammersmith* at the 1932 ABA Convention. Holst's work was one of a number of new pieces performed at the Convention, which also included the world premiere performance of Ottorino Respighi's *Huntingtower Ballad*.

Boosey & Hawkes planned to publish *Hammersmith* in April of 1932, however, this never came to pass. It lay dormant and forgotten until 1953 when Robert Cantrick, director of the Carnegie Institute of Technology Kiltie Band, wrote to Boosey & Hawkes requesting a copy of the original band score. In their response they stated that they did not have the score. Cantrick next wrote to Imogen Holst in hopes that she might assist him in finding one. He was overjoyed when he received news from her that she had located the original manuscript score and was sending it to Boosey & Hawkes. Boosey & Hawkes quickly produced a copy and sent it to Cantrick, who copied out a set of parts and began rehearsing it with his band. Cantrick's subsequent performance of *Hammersmith* on April 14, 1954, brought this great work to the attention of American wind band conductors. Boosey & Hawkes finally published *Hammersmith* in 1956 and two years later (1958), the piece received still more exposure via a recording by Frederick Fennell and the Eastman Wind Ensemble. *Hammersmith* is one of the masterpieces of wind band/ensemble literature.

Robert Cantrick, writing in *Music and Letters* in 1956, stated, "In 'Hammersmith' Holst turned to the band to express musically a profound philosophical problem, one which was deeply rooted in his nature all his life: the paradoxical interplay of the humane and mystical in man's experience.... This tension never resolved itself in Holst's personal life ... but this very unresolved tension is the essence of 'Hammersmith.' Here he finally found adequate musical means for expressing the paradox in a one-movement work—the mood of the Prelude other-worldly, non-human, unemotional, spiritually serene, cool, withdrawn, self-contained and inward looking; the mood of the Scherzo raffish, vulgar, worldly, excited, warm, emotional, and extroverted."[15]

Ralph Vaughan Williams (1872–1958)

Holst's colleague and friend, Ralph Vaughan Williams, composed three pieces for military band: the *English Folk Song Suite* and *Sea Songs* in 1923 and *Toccata Marziale* in 1924. The thematic material in the *English Folk Song Suite*, like Holst's *Second Suite in F*, consists of folk songs (this time from Norfolk and Somerset counties). It was composed for the Royal Military School of Music at Kneller Hall and received its premiere performance on July 4, 1923. Frederick Fennell states that "... according to his wife ... Vaughan Williams had been particularly happy to undertake the *Suite* as he enjoyed working in a new medium."[16] "A military band was a change from an orchestra, and in his not-so-far off army days he had heard enough of the 'ordinary monger's light stuff' to feel that a chance to play real tunes would be an agreeable and salutary experience for Bandsmen."[17] The original *English Folk Song Suite* had four movements (I. "Seventeen Come Sunday," II. "Sea Songs," III. "My Bonnie Boy," and IV. "Folk Songs from Somerset.") According to Jon Mitchell, "'Sea Songs' was later removed (probably by Boosey & Hawkes) and published as an independent composition in march-size format."[18] David McBain, Director of Music at Kneller Hall in the 1950s, added that the publisher felt the four-movement work was too long, wouldn't fit neatly on the allotted pages, and welcomed the opportunity to extract the march for separate publication.

Vaughan Williams's *Toccata Marziale* is a piece with great rhythmical energy. Everything in the piece is original. Technically, it is a much more difficult work than the *English Folk Song Suite* and needs players with advanced skills for performance. An examination of the original manuscript of the piece reveals both a 21-line full and a 3-line condensed score. It is a virtuoso piece, contrapuntal in nature and with a sophisticated-but-clear harmonic sequence. The themes are juxtaposed between various-sized choirs of woodwinds and brasses, and marked with numerous dynamic changes and contrasting articulation styles. Its symmetrical march-like rhythms give the work a "Victorian flavor."

In 1986, scholar Robert Grechesky found a lost work by Vaughan Williams, *Adagio for Military Band*, in the manuscript room of the British Museum. He speculates that the *Adagio* is "the second movement of a *Concerto Grosso for Military Band* which Vaughan Williams was apparently working on when he was commissioned to write [a work for the commemoration of the British Empire Exhibition of 1924].... The first movement of the concerto became the *Toccata Marziale* and was submitted for the commission; the second movement 'Adagio' was forgotten; and the third movement was never completed."[19]

Sea Songs, as a separate piece, was probably premiered at the British Empire Exhibition at Wembley in 1924. It is in typical march form, incorporating three well-known sailing songs as melodic material. The tempo throughout remains constant but the piece has good contrast because of the variety of styles found in the themes, which move from bright and lively to slower and lyrical. It was published in 1924 simultaneously for military and brass bands and later, in 1942, rescored for full orchestra.

Commenting on how folk music had influenced him as a composer, Vaughan Williams stated, "The knowledge of our folksongs did not so much discover for us [Vaughan Williams and Holst] something new, but uncovered for us something which had been hidden by foreign matters.... Our composers are much too fond of going to concerts. There they hear the finished product. What the artist should be concerned with is the raw material.... For instance, the lilt of the chorus at a music-hall joining in a popular song, the children dancing to a barrel organ, the rousing fervour of a Salvation army hymn."[20] "Folksong(s) contributed something profound to Vaughan Williams' style ... His discovery of the dignity and vitality of his national heritage helped him define his own character."[21]

In 1938, Vaughan Williams composed music for a pageant organized to preserve the English countryside. His *Music for the Pageant, "England's Pleasant Land"* for military band and SATB chorus is a noble and majestic work. Grechesky states that, "This music is of great interest ... because it contains much material that was later used in the Fifth Symphony. The 'Funeral March' opens with an exact statement (but in a different key) of the principal material of the first movement of the Fifth Symphony."[22] Another often-performed wind band piece by Ralph Vaughan Williams is *Flourish for Wind Band*. It was originally composed as an overture for the pageant "Music and People," and first performed in London's Royal Albert Hall on April 1, 1939.

Gordon Jacob (1895–1984)

Gordon Jacob's two most important works for wind band are his *William Byrd Suite* and *An Original Suite*. Jacob studied composition with Ralph Vaughan Williams and, while he did not think him particularly helpful as a teacher, was definitely influenced by his music. Vaughan Williams acknowledged Jacob's skills as an orchestrator and suggested to his publisher, Boosey & Hawkes, that Jacob be invited to transcribe his *Folk Song Suite* from military band to orchestra. Jacob latter acknowledged that doing this transcription put him on the track of writing band music.

In 1924, "Adrian Boult urged Gordon Jacob to arrange his orchestral work, *William Byrd Suite*, for the massed bands [which would be performing as part of] the Festival of Britain [to be] held at Wembley Stadium."[23] Jacob's orchestral version of *William Byrd Suite*, composed in 1922, consisted of three movements, "The Earle of Oxford's Marche," "Pavana," and "The Bells" (from Byrd's *Fitzwilliam Virginal Book*). Jacob added three new movements for the band suite, "Jhon Come Kisse Me Now," "The Mayden's Song," and "Wolsey's Wilde." The tercentenary celebrations of William Byrd's death in 1923 were probably the motivation for Jacob to compose his new *William Byrd Suite* for wind band. Boosey & Hawkes published a three-line compressed score in 1924 and 26 years later (1960), a new edition with a full score.

Jacob composed his second work for military band, *An Original Suite*, in 1928 when he was a student at the Royal College of Music. The piece's strange title is an indication of how unusual original works for military band were at the time. The work was renamed *An Original Suite* (its original name was *Suite for Band*) to identify it as an original work and not an arrangement. The piece sounds like a folk song suite but all the melodies are original. In 1951, Jacob composed *Music for a Festival*, which is a long eleven-movement work for wind band and brass choir. It was commissioned by the Arts Council of Great Britain and performed at the Festival of Britain the same year.

Jacob also composed two delightful works for small wind ensemble (double woodwind quintet with ad lib parts for double bassoon and two trumpets), *Old Wine in New Bottles* and *More Old Wine in New Bottles*, in 1960 and 1981, respectively. Both works consist of four beautifully orchestrated arrangements of English folk songs. Jacob's final work for full wind band is the *Symphony A.D. 78*. Written in 1978, the work was commissioned and dedicated to Arthur Doyle (hence the A.D. in the title of the piece). The piece is Jacob's largest for winds and is more difficult and chromatic than most of his other pieces for the medium.

The works of Gustav Holst, Ralph Vaughan Williams, and Gordon Jacob are often referred to as "British Military Band Classics." All three of these composers believed that creating music that could be sung and played by amateurs, based on melodies from the folk culture of their country, contributed to an increased sense of national identity. Their music for wind band is evidence of their commitment to this belief.

Percy Aldridge Grainger (1882–1961)

In 1902, Percy Grainger (1882–1961), celebrated Australian-born concert pianist, dedicated collector of English folk music, and composer, composed his unusually orchestrated *Hill Song No. 1* (for 2 piccolos, 6 oboes, 6 English horns, 6 bassoons, and contrabassoon) and five years later (1907), his shorter *Hill Song No. 2*, based on music borrowed from *Hill Song No. 1*. Grainger had a great interest in and fascination for wind instruments, especially those with a nasal, reedy tone. "I was in love with double-reeds (oboes, English horns, etc.) as the wildest & fiercest of musical tone-types. In 1900 I had heard a very harsh-toned rustic oboe (piffero) in Italy, some extremely nasal Egyptian oboe players at the Paris Exposition, and bagpipes in the Scottish Highlands. I wished to weave these snarling, nasal sounds (which I had heard only in single-lined melody) into a polyphonic texture as complex as Bach's, as democratic as Australia (by 'democratic', in a musical sense, I mean a practice of music in which each voice that makes up the harmonic weft enjoys equal importance & independence—as contrasted with 'undemocratic' music consisting of a dominating melody supported by subservient harmony). In this way I wished to give musical vent to feelings aroused by the soul-shaking hill-scapes I had recently seen on a three days tramp in Western Argyleshire."[24] Grainger considered the Hill-Song No. 1 "... by far the best of all my compositions."[25] It is one of the most unique works of the twentieth century.

In composing *Hill Song No. 1* Grainger was attempting to write music free of a basic pulse. An explanation of the work's unusual meter signatures and barring is included in the notes found on the first page of the autograph score: "The dividing of this piece into bars does not imply that the first beat of each, or a bar shall receive greater pulse or accent than the beats inside the bar. The divisions are made only for the sake of facility in reading."

The first performance of *Hill Song No. 1* in its original scoring did not occur until 1969 (sixty-seven years after Grainger wrote it!). Professor Alan Stout of Northwestern University prepared and edited a score and set of parts for a performance at the university, conducted by Professor Fred Miller. Because of its rhythmic complexities and technical challenges, *Hill Song No. 1* is Grainger's most difficult piece for wind instruments. In 1987, R. Mark Rogers created a new version of *Hill Song No. 1* employing an instrumentation similar to the one used by Grainger in *Hill Song No. 2,* which makes the work more compatible with the instrumentation generally found in present day wind bands/ensembles.

In 1904–05, Grainger decided to expand his knowledge of wind instruments. He contacted Boosey & Hawkes, London, and entered into a contract that allowed him to borrow and study different woodwind and brass instruments. Drawing on the knowledge of wind instruments gained through this experience, Grainger composed the *Hill Song No. 2* in 1907. The metrical plan and instrumentation of *Hill Song No. 2* is much more conventional than that of *Hill Song No. 1.* In this piece Grainger begins the practice of scoring for complete families of wind instruments, using families of flutes, double reeds, and clarinets, plus two cornets and two French horns. The first public performance of *Hill Song No. 2* took place on July 25, 1929, at the Festival of British Music in Royal Hall, Harrogate, England. After the premiere performance, Grainger made revisions of the piece in 1940, 1942, and 1946. It was published in 1950 by Leeds Music.

Percy Grainger left England in 1915, came to the United States, and quickly became an American citizen. A few months after Woodrow Wilson declared war on Germany (April 1, 1917), Grainger purchased a soprano saxophone, practiced on it for a short time, and then enlisted in the army as a bandsman. About a year later (June 1918) he was assigned to the U.S. Army Music Training School on Governor's Island (New York City) where he conducted and composed for the band. The pieces composed during this period (*Irish Tune from County Derry, Shepherd's Hey, Children's March—Over the Hills and Far Away*) show a growing sensitivity to the sonorities of the wind band medium. Prior to being demobilized in 1918, Grainger was offered the position of conductor of the St. Louis Symphony Orchestra which he "declined on the grounds that he would be obliged to conduct so many items from the classical German, Austrian, and Russian repertoire and he felt that no one would want to listen to the kind of programs he wished to present."[26] "Grainger ... with an almost evangelistic fervour ... was already nursing a growing dislike of the inflexibility of the symphony orchestra [because of the] inherent imbalance between strings and wind instruments with the best tunes almost always given to the violins.... his own musical output was increasingly becoming a one-man crusade ... [against] the domination of the world of composition by the symphony orchestra."[27] Nineteen years later (1937), in the preface of the score of his masterpiece, *Lincolnshire Posy*, Grainger wrote of the "special morality incumbent upon those who composed for, those who lead and those who played in bands.... He would never talk to students in universities or in high schools, for example, about a desirability of 'graduating' from wind bands to a 'nobler' symphony orchestra because he did not believe in its musical or moral superiority himself."[28] The wind band became the "vehicle for many of what he considered to be his loftiest and most profound musical utterances."[29]

Grainger composed *Lincolnshire Posy* (1937) as the result of a commission from the American Bandmasters Association for two works. The ABA proposed that the premiere of both pieces, with the composer conducting, would be given at their annual convention to be held in Milwaukee, Wisconsin, in March 1937. Grainger responded to the commission by composing a new version of *Lads of Wamphray* (originally arranged for wind band in 1905) and *Lincolnshire Posy*, a suite of six folk-song arrangements for band.

Grainger realized that *Lincolnshire Posy* would challenge and even confuse many band directors. He included information and advice in the first pages of the score that he hoped would help and encourage conductors who might be daunted by the complexities of this score.

> Bandleaders need not be afraid of the two types of irregular rhythm met with in the "Lincolnshire Posy": those conveyed by changing

time-signatures in "Rufford Park Poachers," and those (marked "Free Time") left to the band leader's volition in "Lord Melbourne." Both these types lie well within the powers of any normal high school band. The only players that are likely to balk at those rhythms are seasoned professional bandsmen, who think more of their beer than of their music.[30]

Later in the program notes, Grainger reflects on the lack of interest by composers for composing for the wind band.

With the exception of military marches almost all the music we hear played by wind bands (military bands) was originally composed for other mediums (for orchestra, for piano, for chorus, as songs for voice and piano) and afterwards arranged for wind band—and as good as never by the composer. (Notable exceptions are: Wagner's "Huldigungs-marsch"; Henry Cowell's "Celtic Set"; R. Vaughan Williams' "Folksong Suite" and "Toccata Marziale"; Gustav Holst's two "Suites for Band" and "Hammersmith" [author's note: not yet published or publicly performed in the band version when Grainger wrote these words]; Hindemith's "Concert Music for Wind Band"; Ernst Toch's "Spiel"; Florent Schmitt's "Dionysiaques"; Respighi's "Hunting-Tower Ballad"; several compositions by Leo Sowerby).

Why this cold-shouldering of the wind band by most composers? Is the wind band—with its varied assortments of reeds (so much richer than the reeds of the symphony orchestra), its complete saxophone family that is found nowhere else (to my ears the saxophone is the most expressive of all wind instruments—the one closest to the human voice. And surely all musical instruments should be rated according to their closeness to man's own voice!), its army of brass (both wide-bore and narrow-bore)—not the equal of any medium ever conceived? As a vehicle of deeply emotional expression it seems to me unrivalled.[31]

"Lincolnshire Posy" ... was conceived and scored by me direct for wind band in early 1937. Five out of the six movements of which it is made up existed in no other finished form, though most of these movements ... were indebted, more or less, to unfinished sketches for a variety of mediums covering many years (in this case the sketches date from 1905–1937).... This bunch of "musical wildflowers" (hence the title "Lincolnshire Posy") is based on folksongs collected in Lincolnshire, England ... and the work is dedicated to the old folk-singers who sang so sweetly to me. Indeed, each number is intended to be a kind of musical portrait of the singer who sang its underlying melody.... For these folksingers were kings and queens of song![32]

David Tall describes *Lincolnshire Posy* as "... a compendium of many of [Grainger's] established techniques welded together with mature insight. The blatant parallel major triads of the opening could have come from the earliest days of willful experiment; the second movement is melody supported by dissonant harmony, with a profound bitter-sweet quality that only comes from great experience. The third movement is astonishing in its aural imagery, opening and closing with strict canons in irregular rhythms; Grainger is here using a classical formula but on his own terms, with widely spaced instrumental texture that adds a new dimension to the form. Irregular rhythms of a different kind occur in the fifth movement, with block chords to be played at the rhythmic whim of the conductor."[33]

Today everyone recognizes Percy Grainger's enormous contribution to the wind band repertoire. *Lincolnshire Posy* and his other works for the medium (*Colonial Song, Gumsucker's March*, and *Molly on the Shore*, etc.) expand the bounds and exploit the potential of wind band sonorities. Grainger's band orchestration achieves a unique resonance that is both startling and beautiful. He employs instruments such as the English horn, bass clarinet, bassoon, contrabassoon, and saxophones (soprano to bass) in a manner that reveals new textures and colors. Grainger made liberal use of changing meters (*Marching Song of Democracy, Lincolnshire Posy, Hill Songs No. 1 and 2*) and "Free time" (*Lincolnshire Posy*) to achieve "irregular rhythm" in his music.

In a Symposium on Memorizing Music, Grainger stated that he thought that conducting was not a difficult art. "The orchestra plays the notes, and all the conductor has to do is to listen to the orchestra, follow along with it and look inspired. (I can get up and conduct a piece of mine I haven't thought about for twenty years, without the least preparation. But I couldn't play the same piece on the piano, without preparation, to save my life.) That is why so many famous pianists have become conductors—to escape the endless misery and unreliability of keyboard memorizing into the comparative easiness and laziness of conductor-memorizing!"[34] Later, as he became more involved in conducting, Grainger came to realize that directing players in the performance of complex music (changing meters and complex rhythms, etc.) was a challenging and difficult task.

In addition to performing and composing, Grainger was also a passionate folk song collector who pioneered the use of the phonograph in capturing the folk singers singing their favorite songs in their natural environments. He recorded his first folk songs in 1905 and "... between the years of 1905 and 1908 ... was able to collect over five hundred songs on wax cylinders ... [and composed] a series of British folk-music settings which would eventually number over fifty-eight works."[35]

ENDNOTES

1   George Dyson, "The Composer and the Military Band," *Music and Letters* 2 (January 1921): 58.
2   James Day, *Vaughan Williams* (J. M. Dent & Sons, 1975), 13.
3   William H. Austin, *Music in the Twentieth Century* (W. W. Norton, 1966), 95.
4   *Birmingham Post*, October 15, 1928.
5   Jon C. Mitchell, "Gustav Holst: An American Perspective" (Unpublished paper, 2000), 75.
6   Jon C. Mitchell, *From Kneller Hall to Hammersmith: The Band Works of Gustav Holst* (Ars Ventorum, 1985), 31.
7   *Richmond Times*, July 17, 1920.
8   "City Police Band: Holst's Suite in E-flat," *Birmingham Post*, November 6, 1920.
9   R. F. Goldman, *The Wind Band*, 225.
10 Imogen Holst, *A Thematic Catalogue of Gustav Holst's Music* (Faber Music, 1974), 99.
11 Imogen Holst, *The Music of Gustav Holst* (Oxford University Press, 1968), 34.
12 "Military Band Concert: Music Society's Project to Encourage Composers," *The Times* (London), July 2, 1922.
13 *The Daily Telegraph* (London), July 1, 1922.
14 Jon C. Mitchell, "The Premieres of Hammersmith," *CBDNA Journal* 1 (Spring 1984): 22.
15 Robert Cantrick, "'Hammersmith' and the Two Worlds of Gustav Holst," *Music and Letters* 37 (July 1956): 219–220.
16 Frederick Fennell, "Vaughan Williams' Folk Song Suite," *The Instrumentalist* 30 (June 1976): 45.
17 Michael Kennedy, *The Works of Ralph Vaughan Williams* (Oxford University Press, 1964), 224.
18 Mitchell, "Holst, American Perspective," 266.
19 Robert Grechesky, "The Wind Music of Ralph Vaughan Williams" (Unpublished paper, 1989), 4.
20 Austin, *Music in the Twentieth Century*, 95.
21 Ibid., 489–490.
22 Grechesky, "Ralph Vaughan Williams," 5.
23 Mitchell, "Holst, American Perspective," 76.
24 Percy Grainger, "Percy Aldridge Grainger's Remarks About His Hill-Song No. 1 (September 1949)," in Teresa Balough, ed., *Percy Grainger: A Musical Genius from Australia* (University of Western Australia, 1997), 82.

25 Ibid.

26 John Bird, *Percy Grainger* (Oxford University Press, 1999), 189.

27 Ibid., 189–190.

28 Ibid., 190.

29 Ibid., 191.

30 Percy Grainger, *Lincolnshire Posy* (Schott, 1940), Full score, page 1.

31 Ibid., 2.

32 Ibid.

33 David Tall, "Traditional and Folk Settings." *Grainger Centennial Volume* No. 16 (1982): 27.

34 Bird, *Percy Grainger*, 189, quoted from James Francis Cooke, ed., *How to Memorize Music* (Theodore Presser, 1948), Chapter 6.

35 "Folk Song," in Balough, ed., *Musical Genius*, 17.

CHAPTER 3

Twentieth Century Expansion (1900–1953)

American and European Composers of Wind and Wind Band/Ensemble Music • Dr. Edwin Franko Goldman and the Goldman Band • American Bandmasters Association

In 1907, at approximately the same time Holst was composing his *First Suite in E-flat for Military Band* and Grainger his *Hill Song No. 2*, one of America's most original and unique creators, Charles Ives (1874–1954), was composing two radical works for woodwinds and brass—*Scherzo: "Over the Pavements"* and *Calcium Light Night* (which also employs two pianos and percussion). *Scherzo: "Over the Pavements,"* composed between 1906–1913, is written for piccolo, clarinet, bassoon, trumpet, trombones, bass drum, cymbal, and piano. Ives composed the piece when he and a friend, George Lewis, lived in a front bedroom on Central Park West in New York City. "In the early morning, the sounds of people going to and fro, all different steps, and sometimes all the same—the horses, fast trots, canter, sometimes slowing up to a walk (few if any autos in those days)—an occasional trolley throwing all rhythm out (footsteps, horse and man)—then back again. I was struck with how many different and changing kinds of beats, time, rhythms, etc. went on together."[1]

Calcium Light Night had its origins in Ives's college experiences at Yale. It is a "march-like" piece consisting of six college melodies that are introduced one at a time and then played simultaneously in the middle section of the work. The second half of the piece is a mirror-version (retrograde) of the first half.

One year after Ives wrote his two small wind pieces, Igor Stravinsky (1882–1971) composed *Chant funèbre* (1908) in memory of his teacher Rimsky-Korsakov, who had recently died. The score and parts of the piece were lost for over a hundred years until a set of parts was discovered at the St. Petersburg State Conservatory in 2015. Conductors and scholars have searched for this piece for many decades. Robert Craft recalled Stravinsky telling him that *Chant funèbre* was "the best of my works before the *Firebird*, and the most advanced in chromatic harmony."[2] Following the assembly of a score from the discovered parts, conductor Valery Gergiev conducted the modern premiere performance of the piece on December 2, 2016—107 years after its first performance on January 17, 1909—with the Mariinsky Opera Orchestra. *Chant funèbre* provides an important missing link between Stravinsky's *Fireworks* and *Scherzo Fantastique*. Natalya Braginskaya, Russian Stravinsky scholar, describes the piece as a "slow unvarying processional with contrasting instrumental timbres: a dialogue of sonorities."[3]

Stravinsky also composed four additional works for wind instruments: the *Symphonies of Wind Instruments* (1920) for orchestra wind section instrumentation, *Octet* (1922–1923) for flute, clarinet, and pairs of bassoons, trumpets, and trombones, and the *Concerto for Piano and Wind Instruments* (1923–24) for solo piano, and orchestra wind and brass sections plus three double basses and timpani. All three of these works were later revised in 1947, 1952, and 1950, respectively. In 1920, Stravinsky composed a suite from the music he wrote for *Histoire du Soldat* for four wind instruments plus violin, string bass, and percussion, and in 1918, a *Ragtime* for five wind and four string instruments plus cimbalom and percussion. His *Symphony of Psalms* for chorus, winds, brass, and low string instruments, was composed in 1930 for the celebration of the fiftieth anniversary of the Boston Symphony Orchestra. Two decades passed before Stravinsky composed another work for woodwind, brass, and percussion instruments. Ringling Brothers and Barnum & Bailey Circus commissioned him to write a piece for their elephant ballet, which was to be choreographed by George Balanchine. The piece, *Circus Polka* (1942), is a satire on band transcriptions of orchestra works which incorporates musical quotes from Tchaikovsky, Shostakovich, and most prominently Schubert's *Marche Militaire*.

Three years later (1945), Stravinsky composed the *Ebony Concerto* for Woody Herman's band, and seven years later the *Concertino for 12 Instruments* (1952) for flute, oboe, English horn, clarinet, 2 bassoons, 2 trumpets, and 2 trombones, with violin and cello obbligato. The latter piece is a rescored version of an earlier work, the *Concertino* for string quartet (1920). The great body of works Stravinsky composed for winds, along with the important roles assigned to them in his orchestral music, is clear evidence of his abiding enthusiasm for wind instruments.

Stravinsky dedicated his masterful *Symphonies of Wind Instruments* "to the memory of Claude Achille Debussy." It is arguably the most significant work to be composed for winds since Mozart's *Serenade No. 10, K. 370a* (formerly K. 361). Harrison Birtwistle, the distinguished English composer, stated, "I think that the *Symphonies of Wind Instruments* is one of the great masterpieces of this century ... and certainly one of the most original, in that it's to do with juxtaposition of material without any sense of development.... If someone had said to me, what's the biggest influence on your life as a composer, I would say this piece."[4] Conductor James Levine states that the *Symphonies of Wind Instruments* is "the biggest beast of a piece to do from memory ... the score ... recycles the same music again and again but barred differently each time. If I conduct [the] piece and take my eye away from connecting what is in the score to the pattern of the beat I will make a mistake and we will have a train wreck."[5]

In 1920, Stravinsky was in the midst of a transition, moving away from the music of his Russian period (*The Firebird*, *The Rite of Spring*) towards a neo-classical style of composition. He was progressing towards smaller dimensions, greater control, and more precision regarding color and shapes in form, harmony, rhythm, and instrumentation. It was at this time that a Paris publication, *La Revue musicale*, asked him to contribute a short piece for a memorial issue they planned to publish in memory of Claude Debussy, who had died in 1918. Stravinsky contributed a short piano piece, *Chorale*, which he ultimately used as the final section of the *Symphonies of Wind*

Instruments. Stravinsky described the *Symphonies* as "... an austere ritual which is unfolded in terms of short litanies between groups of homogeneous instruments."[6]

The *Symphonies of Wind Instruments* exists in two versions—the original 1920 and the revised 1947 versions. For the 1947 version (begun in 1945 but not published until 1947) Stravinsky changed the instrumentation by eliminating the alto flute and alto clarinet in F, substituting three clarinets in B-flat for the original two clarinets, and substituting three trumpets in B-flat for the original two in C. This change in instrumentation led to some rescoring and modification in the music (changed note values, rebarring, etc.). Robert Craft felt that Stravinsky's third proof revision of the 1920 score, was the best and most interesting version of the piece.

Stravinsky continually urged performers to perform his music exactly as notated. He identified "tempo" as the principal challenge in the performance of his works. "Tempo is the principal item. A piece of mine can survive almost anything but wrong tempo or uncertain tempo."[7] He also stated that, "The stylistic performance problem in my music is one of articulation and rhythmic diction."[8]

In 1950, Vincent Persichetti (1915–1987) was a respected and important composer who was enthusiastic about "... the band medium and recognized the artistic potential of what many viewed as only a source of popular entertainment."[9] More than any other major American composer, Persichetti poured his talents into literature for wind band. From the *Serenade for Ten Wind Instruments, Op. 1* to the *Parable IX for Band, Op. 121*, he provided performers and audiences with a body of works of unparalleled excellence. Of his fourteen band works, four are of major proportions: *Masquerade, Parable, A Lincoln Address*, and *Symphony for Band*.

Persichetti was a champion for bands and persuaded other composers, including two of his colleagues at the Juilliard School of Music—William Schuman and Peter Mennin, to compose music for band. Persichetti's orchestration created a refreshing new kind of band sound, sparse in texture and clear in colors and timbre. He seldom used full wind band scoring and his innovative use of percussion instruments added a new textural fabric to the wind band. Persichetti's music has been described as "remarkable for its contrapuntal compactness, in a synthetic style, amalgamating the seeming incompatible idioms of different historical epochs; the basis is tonal, but the component parts often move independently, creating polytonal combinations; the rhythmic element is always strong and emphatic; the melody is more frequently diatonic than chromatic or atonal."[10]

The Goldman Band premiered Persichetti's first piece for band, *Divertimento for Band*, in 1950. The eleven-minute long work consists of six short movements ("Prologue," "Song," "Dance," "Burlesques," "Soliloquy," and "March") and is Persichetti's most performed band piece. The University of Louisville (Kentucky) Band premiered his *Psalm for Band*, commissioned by Pi Kappa Omicron fraternity, in 1952. One year later (1953) his third work for band, *Pageant*, was premiered by the University of Miami (Florida) Band with the composer conducting.

Conductor Ainslee Cox stated, "There is no more honored and respected American composer than Vincent Persichetti. His works, in virtually every form and all media, are played throughout the world. Lovers of band music are especially indebted to him because he—of all the leading American composers—has most often turned his attention to the band, bringing to his many compositions for band all the originality, skill, taste, and spontaneity which mark his other works."[11] Writing in the Autumn 1964 issue of *The Journal of Band Research*, Persichetti stated, "Band music is virtually the only kind of music in America today (outside the pop field) which can be introduced, accepted, put to immediate wide use, and become a staple of the literature in a short time."[12] That is exactly what happened to his band pieces—he composed them, they were premiered, and quickly became part of the basic repertoire of the wind band.

The Donaueschingen Music Festival began in 1921. This chamber music festival was intended to be a forum for performances of innovative works by young German and Austrian composers. Composer Paul Hindemith (1895–1963) became the festival's director and headed the music selection committee. In 1925, the fifth year of the festival, Hindemith decided to embark on a new venture, namely to spotlight genres that were being overlooked by composers. The first to be featured was "a cappella" music. The next year, 1926, Hindemith and his committee decided to organize a concert of "military band" music and then proceeded to commission four composers to write new works. Hindemith wanted to improve the literature that was available for performance by "military wind bands."

On July 24, 1926, a concert took place at the Donaueschingen Festival which featured premiere performances of Hindemith's *Konzertmusik für Blasorchester, Op. 41, Drei lustige Märche, Op. 44* by Ernst Krenek (1900–1991), *Kleine Serenade für Militärorchester* by Ernst Pepping (1901–1981), and *Spiel für Blasorchester, Op. 39* by Ernst Toch (1887–1964). The works by Hindemith, Krenek, and Toch were soon published and later enjoyed numerous performances. Ernst Pepping's piece disappeared but was rediscovered in the late 1980s and received occasional performances. In 1926, "serious works" for military band were of no interest to German and Austrian bandmasters, who preferred to continue performing the standard repertoire of transcriptions, arrangements, and marches. Critics, after hearing these new works remained convinced that the military band would never become a medium of artistic musical expression. One critic stated that he felt the second movement of Hindemith's new piece "to be as worthy as any variations produced during modern times—he only regretted that it was for band and suggested that it be rescored for another medium."[13]

In 1990 John C. Carmichael and the Mostly Modern Chamber Music Players recreated the 1926 Donaueschingen Music Festival Military Band Concert on a CD recording. In the CD's liner notes Carmichael wrote, "The qualitative importance of this festival has only recently begun to be understood ... today the wind band is enjoying increased recognition as an ensemble of serious music ... As far as projecting the possibilities for the band ensemble, the efforts of Hindemith and the Donaueschingen Music Selection Committee were prophetic.[14]

Hindemith was unique among the "advanced" composers of this era. He believed in and worked very hard to establish a relationship between composers and amateur musicians. In composing "Gebrauchsmusik," he strove to create excellent music that could be understood and performed by student musicians and amateurs. Hindemith, in his 1952 book, *A Composer's World*, explains:

> In former times the broad phalanx of those participating in music consisted predominantly of a vast middle field of amateurs; people who made music their hobby in the form of singing and playing but did not

practice it professionally. At their right wing there was a relatively small group of professionals, and at the left, an equally small number of mere listeners. The amateur ... played in the orchestras together with the professional, he sang in the choirs, and for him all chamber music was written. Haydn's, Mozart's and Beethoven's quartets, even Brahms's chamber music counted mostly on the amateur. Today, with the number of participants ... swollen from thousands to millions, their make-up has changed ... once you join an amateur group, you are a member of a great fraternity, whose purpose is the most dignified one you can imagine: to inspire one another and unite in building up a creation that is greater than one individual's deeds. Amateurs of this kind, when listening to music, will not be the stupid receivers, the targets of virtuosity, the idle gourmands of which our audiences predominantly consist.... the composer ... would have to provide the music needed and appreciated by the amateur.... Certainly, writing such music will not be the only means, but it will be the form in which the desire for replacing external brilliancy with genuine musical values finds its clearest expression. Once a writer's technique and style is organized in this direction, so that music which satisfies the amateur's wishes can be created, his approach to his entire work will inevitably undergo a radical change: the emphasis on moral aspects will now become recognizable also in his works written for the concertizing professional, and now he will talk with a different spirit to the general audience.[15]

In the late 1920s, Hindemith composed two concerto-type works for keyboard instruments and wind orchestra, the *Concerto for Organ and Wind Instruments, Op. 46, no. 2 (Kammermusik No. 7)* (1927) and the *Konzertmusik für Klavier, Blechbläser und Harfen, Op. 49* (1930).

Florent Schmitt (1870–1958) composed a massive, elaborate, romantic, and brilliantly orchestrated work, *Dionysiaques*, in 1913 for the 100-member Garde Républicaine Band of France. After a delay of twelve years the work was finally premiered by the band, conducted by Guillaume Balay, at a concert presented in the Jardin de Luxembourg on June 9, 1925. The title refers to Dionysius, the Greek god of drama, wine, and fertility. "*Dionysiaques* is a romantic tone poem in the mold of Liszt and Richard Strauss, but with a distinctly French tonal language which in its more tender moments is reminiscent to Ravel and in its more boisterous moments has vigor similar to Stravinsky's *Le Sacre du printemps*. However, the weight and power of Wagner are always in the background with a healthy dose of César Franck thrown in for good measure."[16]

Other works composed for the band in the 1930s included *Huntingtower Ballad* (1932) by Ottorino Respighi (1879–1936), *Athletic Festival March* (1937) by Sergei Prokofiev (1891–1953), *La Marche sur la Bastille* (1936) by Arthur Honegger (1892–1955), *Le Palais Royal* (1936) by Georges Auric (1899–1983), and *Prélude du deuxième acte* (1936) by Albert Roussel (1869–1937). The latter three pieces were part of a commission for incidental music to be used in *Le Quatorze Juillet*, which was to be a spectacular civic celebration, organized by French Minister of National Education Jean Zay in 1936, in an effort to rekindle the spirit of the French Revolution. The other three composers contributing music to this pageant were Jacques Ibert, Charles Koechlin, and Daniel Lazarus. The music, which consists of preludes and finales, is scored for military band. Its significance is more for its place in the history and development of French military band literature than as a model of high quality composition.

Edgard Varèse (1883–1965) is one of the most innovative and influential composers of the twentieth century. He was born in France and studied mathematics, engineering, and music before coming to the United States in 1915. Between 1923 and 1931 he created four revolutionary pieces for woodwind, brass and percussion, *Octandre* and *Hyperprism* in 1923, followed by *Intégrales* in 1925, and his masterpiece for percussion ensemble, *Ionisation*, in 1931. All are complex, bold, and highly original compositions and reflect his determination to rethink western musical aesthetics. Central to Varèse's aesthetics of music was the proposition that all sound was inherently intelligent, and hence, in his thinking, all available sounds qualified for use in creating music. Varèse's revolutionary works confused most musicians, critics, and listeners in the 1930s.

In selecting the instrumentation for his pieces, Varèse favored woodwind and brass instruments because they could produce clear sounds, relatively free from clouding factors such as vibrato and approximate pitch, as well as neat and varied attacks and timbres that could either be blended or used to produce bold contrasts. He embraced percussion instruments because of their lack of pitch, which made possible limitless rhythmic development outside the tempered scale. Sirens and the lion's roar allowed him to create an infinite curve of pitches (glides). Compositionally he employed vertical (harmonic) and horizontal (melodic) material (intervals) to create music that exploited sound, dynamics, range and rhythm. Varèse referred to his music as "organized sound" and developed a technique that he called "transmutation." According to Varèse, "transmutation" is what happens when the attributes of a sound or sound-mass are transferred to (penetrates) another changing the attributes of each sound or sound-mass. With a single pitch it describes the changing of color by imperceptible degrees over a wide range. Later he applied this technique to the music he composed for electronic music-making equipment with instruments (*Déserts*, 1951–54) and alone without instruments (*Poème électronique*, 1957–59).

In an interview with Gunther Schuller in 1965, Varèse discussed things that influenced him as a composer. "I was not influenced by composers as much as by natural objects and physical phenomena. As a child, I was tremendously impressed by the qualities and character of the granite I found in Burgundy, where I often visited my grandfather.... I used to watch the old stone cutters, marveling at the precision with which they worked. They didn't use cement, and every stone had to fit and balance with every other. So I was always in touch with things of stone and with this kind of pure structural architecture—without frills or unnecessary decoration. All of this became an integral part of my thinking at a very early stage."[17]

When Varèse composed the works listed above, he orchestrated them for traditional musical instruments but his creative mind was imagining sounds that one day he hoped could be produced by electronic sound machines. Therefore, when conductors/players interpret and/or perform Varèse's music, it is essential that they imagine sounds that lie beyond the colors and textures normally associated with traditional musical instruments.

Alban Berg (1885–1935) wrote his great *Chamber Concerto for Piano and Violin with Thirteen Wind Instruments* to honor Arnold Schoenberg, his former teacher, on his fiftieth birthday. Composed during the years 1923–25, this is a three-movement work linked together and played without pause. The first movement is scored for the piano and wind ensemble, the second for the violin and wind ensemble and the third for the violin, piano, and wind ensemble. Because of its demanding musical and technical challenges, this piece receives very few performances.

In the mid-1920s, Kurt Weill (1900–1950) was recognized as one of the most significant German composers of his generation. He composed his *Concerto for Violin and Wind Orchestra* in 1924 and, four years later (1928), the *Suite for Wind Orchestra from "The Three-penny Opera"*. His *Concerto for Violin and Wind Orchestra* is scored for violin, 2 flutes/piccolo, oboe, 2 clarinets, 2 bassoons, 2 French horns, trumpet, timpani, percussion, and was premiered on June 11, 1925, at the International Society for Contemporary Music (ISCM) Conference in Paris. Marcel Darrieus was soloist with the Orchestre des Concerts Walter Straram. Formally, Weill develops each of the movements primarily through continuous variation, giving the first and third movements, in particular, an almost rondo-like quality and shape. The middle movement consists of three interlinked nocturnes. T. W. Adorno wrote the following about the *Concerto*: "In this piece, the lines of Weill's development intersect: the Busoni-esque lucidity is still there, playfully avoiding both dense polyphony and indeed the melodic plasticity which Weill was later to round out so strikingly. There is a strong trace of Stravinsky to be found in the classical, masterly clarity of the sound and in much of the wind writing. The later Weill can be heard in the dramatic pungency which often enough contradicts the classical balance, but most remarkable of all is a Mahlerian quality, at once garishly expressive and painfully laughing, which calls everything playful and secure into question. Weill thus relinquishes objective realism in favour of the dangerous, surrealistic realm he inhabits today. The piece stands isolated and alien: this is, in the right place."[18] In the 1920s, this *Concerto* was Weill's most performed instrumental work.

In the decade following World War I, social and economic confusion swept through Germany. Bertolt Brecht (1898–1956), revolutionary poet-dramatist and disillusioned World War I veteran, was in Berlin singing his simple ballads (accompanying himself on the banjo) and writing plays and incidental music. Brecht and Weill met in 1927 and were soon collaborating and creating works that boldly depicted contemporary themes. Their most famous collaborative creation is *The Threepenny Opera (Die Dreigroschenoper)*. In *The Threepenny Opera*, Brecht and Weill succeed brilliantly in transforming John Gay's 1728 satire on English life, *The Beggar's Opera*, into a startling, new kind of opera. Hans Heinsheimer (later president of

G. Schirmer music publishers) describes the premiere performance of the opera:

> When the curtain went up over the first performance of *Die Dreigrosche-noper* in the little Theater am Schiffbauerdamm, on August 31, 1928, it revealed to the brilliant audience what was perhaps the high point of these tremendous years—a perfectly beautiful production, with the best actors and singing actors that could be found within the boundaries of the German language. A new, daring, shockingly direct language by a great poet, strikingly different, utterly unexpected music, that was both popular and sophisticated, a little band of ten players which utterly denied the lush patterns of accustomed musical fare, a story that reflected eerily the political and social tensions which, together with all the brilliant achievements of the period, were ever present in the sharp, biting, never-tiring air of the city.[19]

Conductor Otto Klemperer of the Kroll Opera in Berlin was one of the first musicians to recognize the brilliance of Weill's score and commissioned him to prepare a concert suite from the opera's music. This was a continuation of the practice started during the Classical era—the composing of suites from successful operas. In composing the *Little Threepenny Music* suite (*Kleine Dreigroschenmusik*), Weill choose an instrumentation similar to, but not exactly the same as the one used for the opera's orchestra. The suite is scored for 2 flutes/piccolo, 2 clarinets, alto sax, tenor sax, 2 bassoons, 2 trumpets, trombone, tuba, guitar/banjo, piano, accordion, timpani, and 2 percussion. Due to its unusual instrumentation and unique musical style (being both "serious" and "light"), the suite received few performances during Weill's lifetime. This author can recall contacting the publisher of this work, Theodore Presser, in 1973 to request the score and parts for *Little Threepenny Music*. I was informed by the publisher that the piece was not in their catalog. However, after a search, they discovered the materials. The piece had evidently "disappeared" due to the total absence of requests for the "non-published but available on rental" score and parts. As conductors gradually discovered the piece, the number of performances grew and soon the score and parts were published.

Two other works that are not entirely wind pieces, but ones in which wind instruments figure prominently, are Erwin Schulhoff's *Concerto for String Quartet and Wind Orchestra* and William Walton's

Façade. Erwin Schulhoff (1894–1942) was a Czech composer who was very much influenced by the music of Dvořák, Debussy, and Reger. His *Concerto for String Quartet and Wind Orchestra* was written in 1930 and is an interesting and unique work. It is fashioned in the traditional three-movement concerto form with an energetic Hindemith-like first movement, a slow torchy second movement, and a final third movement with jazz references, including a tempo marking of "slow fox," as in fox-trot. It was premiered in 1932 on a concert by the Czech Philharmonic conducted by Václav Talich. Ten years later, during World War II, Schulhoff died in a German concentration camp.

In 1923, English composer William Walton (1902–1983) composed *Façade, An Entertainment. Façade* is a series of poems written by English poet Edith Sitwell, eighteen of which Walton uses in his work. A speaker narrates Sitwell's poems (often through a hole in a curtain) over music being made by an ensemble of four musicians (clarinet, cello, trumpet, and percussion). Walton wanted the poems and music to be enjoyed purely for their sound—their meanings unclear and abstract. He achieves a wonderful integration of words and music. This is a work of great wit and humor. "The general atmosphere of the music is one of incisive, yet not cruel, parody; virtuosity in the use of rhythms and tones epitomizes the taste of a decade."[20]

Other composers writing music for wind instruments during the 1920s and 30s included Austrian Ernst Krenek (1900–1991)—*Symphonie, Op. 34* (1924–25); French composers Darius Milhaud (1892–1974)—*Dixtuor (Little Symphony No. 5)* (1922); Francis Poulenc (1899–1963)—*Suite française* (1935); Charles Koechlin (1867–1950)—*Quelques chorals pour des fêtes populaires* (1935); and Russian composer Nikolai Miaskovsky (1881–1950)—*Symphony No. 19, Op. 46* (1939). Miaskovsky's *Symphony* is a conservative work in four movements. It was the first major symphony composed for the wind band since Berlioz's *Grand Symphonie Funèbre et Triomphale, Op. 15*. The composer stated that he wanted to produce a work "which would be equally appreciated by experts and by the general public."[21] The first wind band symphonies of the twentieth-century written by American composers were those of James R. Gillette (*First Symphony, "Pagan"*—1932), Ernest Williams (*First Symphony for Band*—1938), and Robert Saunders (*Symphony for Band*—1944).[22]

Dr. Edwin Franko Goldman and the Goldman Band

One professional band director who survived the end of "the Golden Age of Bands" was Dr. Edwin Franko Goldman (1878–1956). When Edwin was nine years old (1887), his father died and it was necessary for him and his brother to enter the Hebrew Orphan Asylum in New York City while their mother worked to establish herself as a piano teacher. Edwin learned to play the cornet and while still in his teens earned a scholarship to the National Conservatory of Music, then under the leadership of Antonín Dvořák. By 1895 (age 17) he was an established cornet virtuoso and a member of the Metropolitan Opera Orchestra, playing under famous conductors such as Gustav Mahler and Arturo Toscanini. He started conducting in 1905 and six years later (1911), formed the New York Military Band which he considered to be the beginning of the Goldman Band. The New York Military Band performed summer concerts on "the Green" at Columbia University from 1913 through 1922. In 1921 Goldman changed the name of the band to the Goldman Concert Band and a year later (1922), to just the Goldman Band. Beginning in 1936 the Goldman Band performed its summer concerts on The Mall in New York's Central Park and at Brooklyn's Prospect Park. Its programs consisted mostly of transcriptions, marches, and light and popular music.

In 1920, Goldman inaugurated the first American competition for new serious band works in an effort to expand the original literature for bands. Victor Herbert and Percy Grainger served as judges and awarded the $500.00 prize to Carl Busch for his *A Chant from the Great Plains*. Unfortunately, there was never a second Goldman Band Competition. However, for the remainder of his life, Goldman constantly tried to persuade composers to take an interest in the wind band. He was painfully aware that the band "... had so little music of its own [and that] ... great composers of the past had not written for the band, dismissing it as a military necessity."[23] He concluded, "... [we can] either work half-heartedly with what we [have], or ... patiently and by planning, we could develop, side by side, both the repertory and the audience understanding of the music."[24]

In 1941 Edwin Franko Goldman invited Aaron Copland (1900–1990) to compose an original work for the Goldman Band. Copland responded positively but indicated that due to time constraints he might have to compose a band version of one of his already composed works. That is exactly what he did, creating a band version of *An Outdoor Overture,* which he had composed in 1938 for the orchestra of New York City's High School of Music and Art in hopes that it would serve as a vehicle to introduce good contemporary American music to young school instrumentalists.

An Outdoor Overture represents a turning point in Copland's compositional life. His music in the 1920s and early 1930s emphasized complex and harsh sonorities influenced by the rhythmic language of jazz and Stravinsky. In *An Outdoor Overture,* Copland composed an optimistic, vibrant, fresh piece—"youthful in spirit"—with diatonic melodies and simple counterpoint. Elliott Carter, in a review of the piece, commented, "The *Outdoor Overture* ... contains some of [Copland's] finest and most personal music. Its opening is as lofty and beautiful as any passage that has been written by a contemporary [composer]. It is Copland in his 'prophetic' vein ... Never before, though, has he expressed it so simply and directly."[25] In the program note for a 1954 orchestra performance of the work by the London Philharmonic Orchestra, Cecil Smith wrote, "Youth and freedom and tireless energy are the subject matter of the *Overture* ... It is music without a care in the world. Could any composer anywhere have written it after 1938?" Following the Goldman Band's premiere of the band version of the piece in 1942, Copland made minor changes in the orchestration to strengthen the work. It was published by Boosey & Hawkes in 1958.

The Goldman Band performed its first complete program of original works on June 21, 1942. While it is not a "great" program by today's standards, it constitutes a historically significant event in wind band/ensemble development.

PROGRAMME

PART I

1. Christmas March	Edwin Franko Goldman
2. Overture Spring	Leo Sowerby
3. Canto Yoruba	Pedro Sanjuán
4. Rhapsody, Jericho	Morton Gould
5. Legend	Paul Creston

PART II

6. News Reel	William Schuman
7. First Suite in E-flat for Band	Gustav Holst
8. Fantasie Caprice—San Soucci	Edwin Franko Goldman
9. Festive Occasion	Henry Cowell
10. a. A Curtain Raiser and Country Dance	Richard Franko Goldman
b. Lost Lady Found	Percy Grainger
11. Folksong Suite	Ralph Vaughan Williams[26]

By 1943 the literature available for wind bands to perform had been expanded and the quality elevated. Prominent composers such as Holst, Vaughan Williams, Jacob, Schmitt, Grainger, Respighi, Prokofiev, Cowell, Gould, Creston, Copland, Schuman, Hanson, Harris, and Sowerby all had written works for the medium. Goldman continued his dedicated work to entice major composers to write works for band. He was extremely disappointed when Elgar, Sibelius, Prokofiev, Britten, Poulenc, and Richard Strauss turned him down. Ravel, however, did promise to write a piece, but his death prevented him from doing so.

On January 3, 1948, the League of Composers presented a concert by the Goldman Band in honor of Dr. Goldman's seventieth birthday. All the pieces on the program were conducted by Walter Hendl except *The Power of Rome and the Christian Heart* which was conducted by the composer, Percy Grainger.

The League of Composers
25th Anniversary Season
presents
A Program of Contemporary Music
Written for Symphonic Band
in Honor of the 70th Birthday
of Edwin Franko Goldman
January 3, 1948

Toccata Marziale (1924)	Ralph Vaughan Williams
Suite Française (1945)	Darius Milhaud
Shoonthree (1941)	Henry Cowell
Canto Yoruba (1941)	Pedro Sanjuán
The Power of Rome and the Christian Heart (1947)	Percy Grainger

(First performance, conducted by the composer)

Theme and Variations for Wind Band, Op. 43a (1942)	Arnold Schoenberg
Three Pieces written for "Le Quatorze Juillet"	Romain Rolland
a. La Marches sur la Bastille	Arthur Honegger
b. Prelude	Albert Roussel
c. La Palais Royal	Georges Auric

(First performance in America)

Symphony No. 19 for Band (1939)	Nicholai Miaskovsky[27]

In sponsoring this concert, the League of Composers hoped it would motivate other bands to perform more original band music. Richard Franko Goldman, Edwin's son, stated that the event represented "a turning point" in concerts presented by bands in America.[28] Kirby R. Jolly added that "it was the first band concert that based its appeal on serious contemporary music and … it was presented for an audience of winter concert-goers."[29] In his review of the concert, Virgil Thomson commented:

> This writer has long preferred band music in a military vein to the more ambitious efforts in that medium of orchestral composers. But last night revealed to him a justification for Dr. Goldman's effort to found a more thoughtful repertory. When composers like Cowell and Roussel and Schoenberg can express themselves as fully through the wind ensemble as they have done in these works, we have the beginnings of a new and noble repertory for what has always been a noble assemblage of instruments.[30]

The following year (1949) Goldman instituted a formal program of commissioning original band works under the auspices of the League of Composers. This was the first commissioning series established in the United States. It is interesting to note that "although Edwin and Richard Franko Goldman were responsible for instigating much new literature, the Goldman Band as an organization, never commissioned a piece."[31] From 1949 until his death in 1956, Edwin Franko Goldman was responsible for securing the funds needed to commission the following works:

1949—*A Solemn Music* by Virgil Thomson
1950—*Tunbridge Fair* by Walter Piston
1951—*Canzona* by Peter Mennin
1952—*Mademoiselle*, Ballet for Band by Robert Russell Bennett
1953—*Pageant* by Vincent Persichetti
1954—*Chorale and Alleluia* by Howard Hanson

1955—*Celebration Overture* by Paul Creston
1956—*Santa Fe Saga* by Morton Gould[32]

On June 22, 1953, a special Jubilee Concert was held "on the Mall" in New York City's Central Park to commemorate the Goldman Band's 2,000th concert performance at the site. This program consisted entirely of original works and was conducted by Dr. Edwin Franko Goldman and four guest conductors. Conducting their own compositions were Aaron Copland—*An Outdoor Overture*; Morton Gould—the second movement of his *Symphony for Band*; Vincent Persichetti—*Pageant for Band*, and Percy Grainger—two of his folk song settings, *Ye Banks and Braes O' Bonnie Doon* and a new version of *Country Gardens*. The concert program included messages from important musical figures. The one from William Schuman stated that "Through the vigorous and creative leadership of Edwin Franko Goldman, the serious contemporary composer has been encouraged to write for band and not limit his output to orchestral music." Henry Cowell praised the Guggenheim Foundation and conductor Edwin Franko Goldman for their efforts to interest "outstanding serious composers of America and Europe [to write] directly for the symphonic band, thus producing a new and valuable musical literature."

H. W. Schwartz, in his book, *Bands of America* (published in 1957), praised Goldman and the Goldman Band for their contributions to music in America: "... for three decades it [the Goldman Band] ... stood as America's foremost symbol of what a modern concert band should be."[33] Even though it was a "local" band, it reached millions of Americans through its radio broadcasts. During the mid-part of the 20th century it was the most important and listened-to band in America.

Besides being a conductor, Edwin Franko Goldman was also a prolific composer, writing over 150 pieces including 129 marches, 35 cornet solos, and other lighter works. 121 of these works were included on the 1,474 concerts he conducted with his band between 1919 and 1955.

Goldman's ideas concerning program planning was very pragmatic.

> "I find it appropriate to start a concert with a march—preferably a grand march. After this, perhaps we perform an overture, and then perhaps an Ave Maria or a chorale. There should not be two very slow

pieces in succession; there should be contrast. The concert should end with something thrilling that will arouse the audience. Listeners should always be sent away demanding more. No program should last over two hours. In fact, a program lasting only about an hour and three quarters, including an intermission of fifteen minutes and all extra numbers, would be ideal. If a program is carefully planned, with plenty of contrast, it should never be interrupted with encore or extra numbers or with music that is out of keeping with what was played or what was coming next."[34]

When Edwin Franko Goldman died in 1956, his son, Richard Franko Goldman, succeeded him as conductor of the Goldman Band. As assistant conductor of the Band under his dad, he had conducted many of the contemporary works performed by the band including the world premiere performance of Schoenberg's *Theme and Variations, Op. 43a* in 1948. He also "discovered" and conducted the first American performance of Hector Berlioz's *Grand Symphonie Funèbre et Triomphale, Op. 15* on June 23, 1947. Richard was also an educator, music critic, composer and author of four books, including *The Wind Band* (published by Allyn and Bacon), as well as numerous articles and reviews that were published in some of the world's most prestigious musicological journals. With the passing of Richard Franko Goldman in 1980, Ainslee Cox became conductor of the Goldman Band which he conducted until 1988. After the Band was renamed the Guggenheim Band, it was led by Gene Young from 1990 to 1997, and David Eaton in 1998. The Band was disbanded in 1999 due to the lack of funding.

Founding Of the American Bandmasters Association

Edwin Franko Goldman founded the American Bandmasters Association (ABA) in 1929. He believed there was a need for an association, made up of the best band directors in the country, that could provide the leadership needed to improve and elevate the performance and musical standards of American bands. The Constitution of the Association stated that "The object of this organization shall be mutual helpfulness and the promotion of better music ... [for] ... the concert band." In the early years of the Association, membership was limited to band directors who were nominated by one of the charter members of the Association. However, in 1931 it became possible for any member of the Association to nominate individuals for membership. All nominees were required to take and pass an examination that covered Musical Form and Analysis, Musical History, Harmony, Instrumentation, and Scoring. Listed below are three questions from the examination regarding Musical Form and Analysis:

1. Name the composers of the following:

    Overtures: (1) *Jubel.* (2) *Die Fledermaus* (The Bat). (3) *Italiana in Algeria.* (4) *The Marriage of Figaro.* (5) *Tannhauser.* (6) *Le Roi d'Ys.* (7) *Masaniello.* (8) *Fidelio.* (9) *In Springtime.* (10) *Coriolan.*
    Write a short description of any one of the above Overtures.

2. What is a Motive? Write a few words about its Value in Music. You may quote examples if you wish.

3. State a Characteristic of the Music of Wagner. His style in Music Writing was in vivid contrast to that of Mozart. Write a short essay on the contrast between the two composers.

This examination requirement remained in effect until 1940, when it was waived.

ENDNOTES

1   John Kirkpatrick, "Scrapbook," in *Charles E. Ives: Memos* (W. W. Norton, 1991), 62–63.
2   Igor Stravinsky and Robert Craft, *Memories and Commentaries* (University of California Press, 1960, 1981), 59.
3   Phillip Huscher, "Discovery of a Lifetime: 'Funeral Song,' Stravinsky's Salute to Rimsky-Korsakov," Chicago Symphony Orchestra, CSO Sounds and Stories, March 22, 2017, accessed April 8, 2018, https://csosoundsandstories.org/discovery-of-a-lifetime-funeral-song-stravinskys-salute-to-rimsky-korsakov/.
4   Jonathan Cross, *The Stravinsky Legacy* (Cambridge University Press, 1998), 6.
5   Robert C. Marsh, *Dialogues & Discoveries—James Levine: His Life and His Music* (Scribner, 1998), 87.
6   Igor Stravinsky, *An Autobiography* (W. W. Norton, 1962), 95.
7   Robert Craft, *Conversations With Igor Stravinsky* (Doubleday, 1959), 135.
8   Ibid.
9   Donald Morris and Jean Oelrich, "Vincent Persichetti Remembered: Music From Gracious to Gritty," *The Instrumentalist* 47 (November 1992): 30.
10 Nicolas Slonimsky, ed., *Baker's Biographical Dictionary of Musicians*, 5th ed. (G. Schirmer, 1958), 1231.

11 Ainslee Cox, quoted at The Guggenheim Memorial Concerts; cited in Frederick Fennell, *A Conductor's Interpretive Analysis of Masterworks for Band* (Meredith Music Publications, 2008), 25.

12 Vincent Persichetti, "Symphony No. 6 for Band," *Journal of Band Research* 1 (Fall 1964): 17.

13 Furman Wind Ensemble, *Music for Winds*, Contemporary Record Society CRS 9051, 1990, Liner notes, "Donaueschingen, Hindemith, and Music for Winds," by John C. Carmichael.

14 Ibid.

15 Paul Hindemith, *A Composer's World: Horizons and Limitations* (Harvard University Press, 1953), 214–219.

16 United States Marine Band, *American Games: Twentieth Century Classics for Winds*, USMB-CD-13, 1997, Liner notes by Frank Byrne.

17 Gunther Schuller, "Conversation with Varèse," *Perspectives of New Music* 3 (1965), 34. Quoted in Robert Erickson, *Sound Structure in Music* (University of California Press, 1975), 49.

18 Kurt Weill, *Kleine Dreigroschenmusik/Violin Concerto*, London Sinfonietta, David Atherton, conductor, Deutsche Grammophon DG 2740 153, 1976, Liner notes by David Drew.

19 Kurt Weill, *Die Dreigroschenoper*, Lotte Leyna/Wilhelm Brückner-Rüggeberg, conductor, Columbia Masterworks O2L 257, 1958, 2 LPs, Liner notes by Hans W. Heinsheimer.

20 Frank Howes, *The Music of William Walton*, 2nd ed. (Oxford University Press, 1974), 21.

21 R. F. Goldman, *The Wind Band*, 231.

22 Ibid., 232.

23 Edwin Franko Goldman, "Facing the Music" (typescript document, 1942), 270.

24 Ibid.

25 Elliott Carter, "Forecast and Review: Once Again Swing; Also 'American Music,'" *Modern Music* 16 (January-February 1939): 103.

26 The Goldman Band, Programs of Summer Concerts, 1942.

27 Kirby Reid Jolly, "Edwin Franko Goldman and the Goldman Band." (Ph. D. diss., New York University, 1971), 150.

28 Richard Franko Goldman, "Band Proves Its Right to the Concert Hall," *The New York Times*, December 28, 1947.

29 Jolly, "Goldman and the Goldman Band," 148.

30 Virgil Thomson, "Music," *The New York Herald Tribune*, January 5, 1948.

31 William D. Nicholls, "Factors Contributing to the Commisioning of American Band Works Since 1954." (D.M.A. diss., University of Miami, 1980), 10–11.

32 Jolly, "Goldman and the Goldman Band," 158.

33 H. W. Schwartz, *Bands of America* (Doubleday, 1957), 309.

34 Edwin Franko Goldman, "Program Repertory of the Concert Band," *Music Journal* 11 (January 1953): 70–71.

CHAPTER 4

Development (1939–1959)

Size and Instrumentation of Wind Bands • Wind Band/Ensemble Works Composed 1939–1959 • Literature performed on Band Concerts • First Midwest National Band Clinic • College Band Directors National Association Founded

In 1939–40, Walter Duerkson surveyed 351 college band directors in an attempt to determine the sizes of bands. His findings, published in the MENC Yearbook (1939–49) and *Etude* magazine (November 1941), revealed that the average size of college bands in 1939–40 was 50.4. Through information gathered at school music contests in 1940, it was determined that the average size of bands competing in these contests was 61.[1]

Listed below are the instrumentation of four of the America's best bands in the late 1940s:

The Goldman Band
1 piccolo
3 flutes
2 oboes (2nd doubling on English horn)
1 Eb clarinet
19 Bb clarinets (1st, 2nd, 3rd)
1 bass clarinet

United States Air Force Band
6 flutes (all doubling on piccolo)
3 oboes (one doubling on English horn)
1 Eb clarinet
14 Bb clarinets
1 alto clarinet
1 bass clarinet

The Goldman Band (continued)
2 bassoons
3 saxophones (1 alto, 1 tenor,
    1 bari)
4 cornets
3 trumpets
4 horns in F
6 trombones (4 tenor, 2 bass)
2 euphoniums
4 tubas
1 string bass
1 harp
3 percussion
Total: 60 players

University of Michigan Band
8 to 10 flutes
2 to 4 oboes (English horn)
24 to 28 Bb clarinets
3 alto clarinets
3 bass clarinets
3 to 4 bassoons
5 to 6 saxophones (alto, tenor, bari)
6 to 8 cornets
2 trumpets
6 to 8 French horns
6 trombones
4 baritones or euphoniums
6 tubas
2 string basses
1 or 2 harps
4 to 6 percussion
Eb clarinet and 2 fluegel horns are
    occasionally added
Total: About 100 players

United States Air Force Band (continued)
4 bassoons (one doubling on contra
    bassoon and one on bass sarrusophone)
5 saxophones (2 alto, 2 tenor, 1 bari)
11 cornets and trumpets
8 horns in F
6 trombones (4 tenor, 2 bass)
3 baritones
4 tubas
4 violoncellos
4 string basses
6 percussion
Total: 81 players

Lenoir (NC) High School Band
6 flutes in C
2 flutes in Eb
2 oboes
24 Bb clarinets (4 solo, 5-1st, 9-2nd, 6-3rd)
2 alto clarinets
3 bass clarinets
3 bassoons
6 saxophones (4 alto, 1 tenor, 1 bari)
12 cornets or trumpets (4 each on 1st, 2nd
    and 3rd parts)
7 horns
4 trombones
4 baritones
4 tubas
6 percussion
Total: 85 players

Source: Richard Franko Goldman, *The Concert Band* (Rinehart, 1946)

Except for the Goldman Band, which had 60 players, these bands were very large ensembles with players numbering between 81 and 100. The development of the large or "symphony band" concept was motivated, in part, by the desire to imitate the symphony orchestra in sound and size. The literature performed by these large bands consisted of pieces that fit the dimensions of their large instrumentation. This ruled out performances of selectively instrumented works written by composers such as Stravinsky, Varèse, Weill, and Walton, which were discussed in Chapter 3.

Some of the original works for wind band composed between 1939–44 included:

Roy Harris	Cimarron Overture (1941)
William Schuman	Newsreel (1939)
Morton Gould	Jericho (1940)
Paul Creston	Legend (1942)
Philip James	Festal March (1942)
Leo Sowerby	Spring Overture (1941–42)
William Grant Still	Old California (1941)
Henry Cowell	Festive Occasion (1942)
John Alden Carpenter	Song of Freedom (1941)
Wallingford Riegger	Passacaglia and Fugue (1942)
Samuel Barber	Commando March (1943)
Joseph Wagner	American Jubilee Overture (1941–42)
Arnold Schoenberg	Theme and Variations, Op. 43a (1943)
Darius Milhaud	Suite Française (1944)
Nikolai Miaskovsky	Symphony No. 19, Op. 46 (1939)
Henry Cowell	Hymn and Fuguing Tune No. 1 (1943)
Alfred Reed	Russian Christmas Music (1944)

Arnold Schoenberg (1874–1951) created his uncompromising and tonal *Theme and Variations, Op. 43a* in 1943. Carl Engel, president of G. Schirmer and Schoenberg's publisher, requested that the composer write a piece for high school/amateur bands. Engel felt that these bands played an important role in the development of music appreciation in America and that the music they played, mostly marches and not very good arrangements of orchestra works, needed to be upgraded. Engel's directive to Schoenberg suggested he write a work that contained "many different characters and moods." The completed piece, scored for full wind band/ ensemble, turned out to be a quasi "concerto grosso" cast in the form of a theme with seven contrasting variations in which individual instruments functioned as soloists (for example, in Variation V the canon between the solo clarinet and solo baritone horn). The performance of this mature work requires an ensemble of instrumentalists that possess excellent technical and expressive skills.

Schoenberg's scoring for brass instruments in the piece features conical bore instruments (cornets, flügelhorns, French horns, and baritone/euphonium) against cylindrical bore trumpets and trombones. Schoenberg stated that the *Theme and Variations, Op. 43a* was not one of his main works. "As everybody can see . . . it is not a composition with twelve tones. It is one of those compositions which one writes in order to enjoy one's own virtuosity and, on the other hand, to give a certain group of music lovers—here it is the bands—something better to play."[2]

The work proved to be too challenging for average high school/amateur band players and too sophisticated for band audiences. In hopes of increasing performances of the work, Schoenberg made an orchestra transcription of the piece (Op. 43b) which was premiered by the Boston Symphony Orchestra, Serge Koussevitzky conducting, on October 20, 1944. Schoenberg, responding to a letter from Fritz Reiner (then conductor of the Pittsburgh Symphony Orchestra) concerning Koussevitzky's performance of the piece wrote, "You are perfectly right in your criticism about Koussevitzky's performance of my *Variations, Op. 43b*. Some of the shortcomings . . . derive from his disregard of my metronomical indications. Why he did this is unimaginable to me."[3]

Schoenberg's work, for all intent and purpose, is really a "chamber music piece" for the fully instrumented wind band. Only when conductors and ensemble players respect and adhere to all instructive and notated information found in the score and parts (stylistic instructions; metronome, dynamic, and tempo markings) can Schoenberg's piece of "different characters and moods" be realized. The band version of the work was published by G. Schirmer in 1944 and premiered on a concert performed by the Goldman Band, conducted by Richard Franko Goldman, in New York's Central Park in 1946.

Darius Milhaud composed his first work for full wind band, *Suite Française*, in 1944. He had previously written a work for ten winds, *Dixtuor d'instruments à vent (Little Symphony No. 5)* (1922), and a Harlem jazz-inspired orchestra work, *La Création du monde* (1923), in which wind instruments play prominent roles. *Suite Française* was commissioned by the Leeds Publishing Corporation who requested that he write a piece for high school band students which wouldn't be "too difficult to perform, but representative of the characteristic idiom of the composer." The thematic material of the five-movement work is based on folk tunes from French provinces where fathers and brothers of American school students had fought to defeat the German invaders in World War II. Like Schoenberg's *Theme and Variations*, *Suite Française* proved to be too difficult for most high school bands to play, so Milhaud also composed an orchestra version of the piece in hopes of getting more performances for the work.

Another piece composed in 1944 was *Russian Christmas Music* by Alfred Reed (1921–2005) The story behind this composition is very interesting. During World War II, Reed was a member of the 529th Army Air Force Band stationed in Colorado. He was asked to compose a piece for a Christmas holiday performance by a special 85-piece band that would be made up of musicians from the five service bands in the Denver area. However, on December 16, 1944, the German Army launched an offensive that became known as the Battle of the Bulge. General Dwight Eisenhower, Supreme Allied Commander, decided more troops were needed to halt the German advance into Belgium. As a result, 35 members of Reed's band were immediately sent to Europe (they were assigned to duty as military police). The diminution of the band from 85 to 50 players made it necessary for Reed to revise the work. This he did and his *Russian Christmas Music* was performed and broadcast over the NBC national radio network on Christmas day 1944.

Following the war in 1946, Reed returned to New York City and enrolled at the Juilliard School of Music where he studied composition with Vittorio Giannini. Upon learning of a new concert band music contest, sponsored by Columbia University, Reed submitted his *Russian Christmas Music*. The piece was selected as one of the three prize-winning works. Harwood Simmons, one of the judges for the contest, performed Reed's piece with his Syracuse University Band in April 1948. In 1949, Walter Beeler conducted another performance of the work with the Ithaca College Concert Band which was greeted with great enthusiasm. I can personally attest to this because I was a 17-year old high school student in the audience at the concert.

As enthusiastic reports about *Russian Christmas Music* began to circulate among band directors, Reed began receiving inquiries about the piece from people whose names meant absolutely nothing to him: William D. Revelli, Glenn Cliffe Bainum, Frederick Fennell, etc. Looking for a publisher, Reed submitted the piece to Boosey & Hawkes who expressed great interest but declined publication of the piece because "it was too long and too difficult for the average high school band." For the next twenty years the piece was available only through rental from the composer and when Reed became an editor at Hansen Publications, through that company. After Reed did another revision of the piece, *Russian Christmas Music* was acquired and published by Sam Fox Music in 1968. It is interesting to note that the "climate" in the band world in the late 1950s was such that publishers were reluctant to publish lengthy and technically challenging pieces like *Russian Christmas Music* because it was financially too risky.

Russian Christmas Music is a musical portrait of the jubilant celebration of Christmas in old Russia. The single movement work has four distinct sections, each of which were originally titled "Children's Carol," "Antiphonal Chant," "Village Song," and "Cathedral Chorus." The melodic material used by Reed includes an old Russian carol ("Carol of the Little Russian Children"), some motivic material derived from the Eastern Orthodox Church liturgy, as well as original melodic material.

The programs that follow are typical of those performed by bands in the mid-1940s. They only include thirteen original works for wind band. Due to the shortness of the pieces, the average number on each program is 11.5.

A typical program presented by the Goldman Band (on the Mall in Central Park, New York), under the direction of Edwin Franko Goldman:

Grand March, "America"	Edwin Franko Goldman
Suite from "The Water Music"	George Frideric Handel
An Outdoor Overture	Aaron Copland (arranged by the composer)
First Suite for Band, in E-flat	Gustav Holst
Finale, "The New World Symphony"	Antonín Dvořák
Festal March	Philip James
Fantasie for Cornet Solo	Del Staigers
Russian Dance from *Petrouchka*	Igor Stravinsky
"Lads of Wamphray"	Percy Grainger
March, "Anniversary"	Edwin Franko Goldman
Waltz, "Liebeslieder"	Johann Strauss

A typical program presented by the University of Michigan Concert Band (for its appearances at the university auditorium in Ann Arbor), conducted by Dr. William D. Revelli:

Overture, *Il Matrimonio Segreto*	Domenico Cimarosa
Prelude to Act I from *Lohengrin*	Richard Wagner
"Bravada," Paso Doble	Frederick Curzon
Trombone Solo	Arthur Pryor
Frühlingsstimmen Waltzes	Johann Strauss
Rhythms of Rio	David Bennett
Capriccio Italien	Piotr Tschaikowsky
Three Chorales	J. S. Bach
March "Varsity"	Earl Vincent Moore
Mannin Veen	Haydn Wood
The Stars and Stripes Forever	John Philip Sousa
The Yellow and Blue	(University Song)

A typical program presented by the United States Army Air Forces Band (while the band was on tour in Canada), conducted by Captain George S. Howard:

Overture, *Il Guarany*	Antonio Carlos Gomez
Pavane	Morton Gould
Trombone Solo	Arthur Pryor
Dance of the Amazons	Anatoli Liadov
Horn and Flute Duet: Serenade	Anton Titl
Finale from Symphony No. 4	Piotr Tschaikowsky
Melody of Popular Airs	
Polka from *The Golden Age*	Dmitri Shostakovich
Russian Sailors Dance	Reinhold Glière
Saxophone Solo	Eric Coates
Waltz, "Voices of Spring"	Johann Strauss
Vocal Solo, "Danny Deever"	Walter Damrosch
Rhapsody in Blue	George Gershwin

A typical program by the High School Band of Lenoir, North Carolina, James C. Harper, director:

Symphonic March	Silvio Mancini
Elsa's Procession to the Cathedral from *Lohengrin*	Richard Wagner
The Sorcerer's Apprentice	Paul Dukas
Entrance of the Bojaren	Johan Halvorsen
Southern Roses Waltz	Johann Strauss

Il Guarany Overture	Antonio Carlos Gomez
Ballet Suite, *La Source*	Léo Delibes
Tannhäuser March	Richard Wagner
Woodwind Ensemble	
"Ballet Egyptien"	A. Luigini-Holmes
Overture to *The Merry Wives of Windsor*	Otto Nicolai

Source: Richard Franko Goldman, *The Concert Band* (Rinehart, 1946)

Many of the published pieces for band at this time (both original works and transcriptions) came only with a condensed score. (This applies to a number of works included on the programs above.) For quick-step-sized marches, the conductor's score often consisted of a Solo Cornet or Solo Clarinet part with small cue notations to indicate what other instruments were playing. The lack of full scores made it impossible for a conductor to acquire the information and knowledge needed to effectively rehearse and conduct a piece.

Concern about the quality of literature for wind bands continued to grow among band directors. Two influential university band directors spoke to this issue at CBDNA Conferences in the final years of the 1940s. In 1946 Dr. William D. Revelli, Director of Bands at the University of Michigan, urged colleges and university band directors to "... devise ways and means of motivating our better composers to [write] masterpieces of original music."[4] Three years later (1949), Bernard Fitzgerald echoed Revelli's message and added a warning, "College and university bands must assume the responsibility for developing the concert band repertory. Since professional bands are almost nonexistent and high school bands usually lack either resources or musical maturity, leadership is therefore in the hands of the colleges and universities. The burden of proof is upon us, the directors.... We cannot afford to perpetuate the concert band in the musical tradition of the town band of several years ago unless we are willing to accept the musical reputation that was associated with it."[5]

A number of original wind band/ensemble pieces were composed between 1949–1957. Among them were the following:

Morton Gould	Ballad for Band
	Symphony for Band (West Point) (1952)
H. Owen Reed	La Fiesta Mexicana (1949)

Virgil Thomson	A Solemn Music (1949)
Robert Russell Bennett	Suite of Old American Dances (1950)
	Symphonic Songs (1957)
Walter Piston	Tunbridge Fair (1950)
Paul Hindemith	Symphony in B-flat (1951)
Peter Mennin	Canzona (1951)
Vincent Persichetti	Divertimento for Band (1949–50)
	Psalm for Band (1951)
	Pageant (1953)
	Symphony No. 6 for Band, Op. 69 (1956)
Gordon Jacob	Music for a Festival (1951)
William Schuman	George Washington Bridge (1951)
Darius Milhaud	West Point Suite (1952)
Clifton Williams	Fanfare and Allegro (1956)
	Symphonic Suite (1957)

William Schuman (1910–1992) composed *George Washington Bridge*, subtitled "An Impression for Band," in 1950. In the work Schuman attempts to capture the image of the bridge acquired during his many years of "driving and walking across it, sailing under and flying over it." Like all of Schuman's wind band pieces, *George Washington Bridge* is a work of high aesthetic value that is technically playable by amateur instrumentalists. Schuman believed that writing band music offered composers an excellent opportunity to introduce young American instrumentalists and audiences to contemporary music.

A year after Schuman composed *George Washington Bridge* (1951), Paul Hindemith composed his *Symphony in B-flat* for the United States Army Band. This three-movement work is a masterpiece of contrapuntal technique and thematic integration, a "breakthrough piece" in the development of wind band literature. It also helped convince other first-rank composers that the band was a legitimate vehicle for serious musical expression.

Another important composer of wind band/ensemble music at this time was Clifton Williams (1923–1976). His *Fanfare and Allegro* and *Symphonic Suite* won the first and second ABA Ostwald Composition Prizes in 1956 and 1957, respectively. Composer W. Francis McBeth felt that these two works did "… much to grease the way for true 20th-century band literature. There were important works before, but these two seemed to have just the right level of contemporary composition coupled with the traditional to achieve acceptability by so many. It was Williams who was the major evangelist for the coming new literature among the composers."[6] McBeth relates how Williams "would alternate bringing in Vincent Persichetti and Paul Creston [to his Southwestern Symposium at the University of Texas] because [he believed] they were the major composers with true band interest in those days. John Barnes Chance and I were students at the University of Texas during that time, and we wrote mainly for orchestra. Williams convinced us ... of the necessity of writing for band. One noon at an Austin restaurant, Williams said, 'The orchestra is the Cadillac; I know that, but they don't want you. They don't want anything past Debussy and truly dislike 20th-century music. The winds are where you want to go because they want new music.'"[7]

Many of the works composed during the mid-decades of the twentieth century received hundreds of performances by school and college/university bands and were quickly incorporated into the band repertoire. The longer (multi-movement) and technically more difficult works such as Milhaud's *Suite Française* and *West Point Suite*, Gould's *Symphony for Band*, Hindemith's *Symphony in B-flat*, H. Owen Reed's *La Fiesta Mexicana*, and Giannini's *Symphony No. 3* received fewer performances, most by the better university/college wind bands/ensembles.

Some composers created wind band versions of pieces originally written for orchestra, among them *An Outdoor Overture* (1942) and *Variations on a Shaker Melody* (1956) by Aaron Copland, *Three Japanese Dances* (1954) by Bernard Rogers, and *When Jesus Wept* (1959) and *Chester* (1957) by William Schuman.

William D. Revelli founded the College Band Directors National Association (CBDNA) in 1941. He believed there was a need for a leadership organization devoted to the professional concerns of the college band director. As founder and first president of CBDNA from 1941–1945, he led the association through its challenging formative years (World War II). CBDNA's Declaration of Principles defines its purpose—the advancement of "the college band as a serious and distinctive medium of musical expression."[8] Throughout its seventy-seven year history, CBDNA has championed the commissioning and performance of new works and sponsored conducting seminars and courses which have provided wind band/ensemble conductors with opportunities to improve their conducting skills and expand their knowledge of wind band/ensemble literature.

Neil Kjos Sr., Howard Lyons, and H. E. Nutt founded the Midwest National Band Clinic in Chicago, Illinois, in 1946. They envisioned a clinic where band directors and music educators could find "counsel, support, and inspiration." Their idea became hugely successful and after more than seventy years it attracts thousands of band and orchestra directors from around the world. Now it is called the Midwest International Band and Orchestra Clinic. Early Midwest Clinics featured performances of newly published works performed by visiting school bands and an exhibition area populated by numerous musical instrument and music publishing companies. During the past two decades clinic offerings have expanded and now include a broad spectrum of demonstrations and presentations.

In addition to the numerous works written for the full wind band/ensemble in the 1950s, many world class composers wrote pieces for smaller combinations of woodwind, brass, and percussion instruments. Included among them were the following:

Richard Strauss	Symphony for Winds (1945)
Paul Hindemith	Septett für Blasinstrumente (1948)
Willem van Otterloo	Symphonietta for Wind Instruments (1948)
Leonard Bernstein	Prelude, Fugue and Riffs (1949)
Ingolf Dahl	Concerto for Alto Saxophone and Wind Orchestra (1949—revised 1953)
Gunther Schuller	Symphony for Brass and Percussion, Op. 16 (1949–1950)
Wallingford Riegger	Music for Brass Choir (1949)
Edgard Varèse	Déserts (1954)
Easley Blackwood	Chamber Symphony No. 2 (1955)
Olivier Messiaen	Oiseaux exotiques (1955–1956)
Robert Kurka	The Good Soldier Schweik Suite, Op. 22 (1956)
Ned Rorem	Sinfonia (1956–1957)
Alan Hovhaness	Symphony No. 4, Op. 165 (1958)
Peter Maxwell Davies	St. Michael: Sonata for 17 Winds (1959)
Walter Hartley	Concerto for 23 Winds (1957)

French composer Olivier Messiaen (1908–1992) wrote *Oiseaux Exotiques* (*"Exotic Birds"*) in 1955–56. It is a work for piano, winds, and percussion that is cast in a Baroque-like form. Messiaen employed bird calls from North and South America and Asia for his melodic material. Messiaen also used bird calls in other works. He wrote the following about bird calls and freedom.

> If you want symbols, let us go on to say that the bird is the symbol of freedom. We walk, he flies. We make war, he sings. Among birds most fights are settled by tournaments of song. Finally, despite my deep admiration for the folklore of the world, I doubt that one can find in any human music, however inspired, melodies and rhythms that have the sovereign freedom of bird-song.[9]

Messiaen had a profound and powerful influence on twentieth-century music as a composer and as a teacher. Among his most famous students were Pierre Boulez, Luigi Nono, Karlheinz Stockhausen, and Alexander Goehr.

Prelude, Fugue and Riffs was composed by Leonard Bernstein (1918–1990) in 1949. It is one in a series of jazz-inspired works Woody Herman intended to commission for his band (Stravinsky's *Ebony Concerto* was the first). When Herman suddenly disbanded his band, the performance of Bernstein's piece was cancelled. The piece lay dormant until 1952, when Bernstein incorporated it into a ballet sequence for his musical, *Wonderful Town*. Unfortunately the music did not survive out-of-town tryouts. The premiere performance of the work finally took place on October 16, 1955, when Bernstein programmed it on one of his *Omnibus* telecasts, "What is Jazz," with Benny Goodman as soloist.

Robert Kurka's (1921–1957) opera, *The Good Soldier Schweik*, was inspired by the novel of the same name by Czech journalist and novelist Jaroslav Hašek. It is a story of a common man who is forced to become a soldier and fight for a cause for which he has no sympathy. In 1957, Kurka interrupted his writing of the opera to compose a suite based on music from the opera. Scored for piccolo, flute, oboe, English horn, clarinet, bass clarinet, bassoon, contrabassoon, three French horns, two trumpets, trombone, percussion, and timpani the suite portrays different episodes in Schweik's life. The music ranges from a soulful "Lament" to an aggressive, violent "War Dance."

In 1957, Walter Hartley (1927–2016) composed his *Concerto for 23 Winds* for the Eastman Wind Ensemble. It was premiered in 1958 at the school's annual Festival of American Music. The four-movement concerto is essentially a large chamber work in which various soloists and groups of soloists function against each other and the whole ensemble. The work's instrumentation is identical to that used by Stravinsky in his *Symphonies of Wind Instruments*.

Contained in the 1950 CBDNA Conference Book of Proceedings is a "Bibliography of Recorded Band Music." It was compiled by Bryce Jordan and lists 603 items, summarized as follows:

Quickstep marches	61 percent
Serious music (a general category that includes all works designated as overture, suite, tone poem, etc.)	16 percent
Patriotic music	6 percent
Concert marches	5 percent
Folk music (straightforward treatment of folk melodies without any developmental treatment)	4 percent
Novelties	3 percent
Waltzes (other than symphonic works such as Rosenkavalier waltzes); ensembles and solos (with band accompaniment); descriptive works; opera selections; fanfares	5 percent

Source: David Whitwell and Acton Ostling Jr., "The Concert Band and Its Music," in *The College and University Band* (Music Educators National Conference, 1977), 2.

An examination of Jordan's summary, reveals that the music performed by bands at the mid-point in the twentieth century still consisted primarily of transcriptions, arrangements of popular melodies, operatic excerpts, marches, and various types of light music.

During the second quarter of the twentieth century many of the world's great composers (among them Stravinsky, Ravel, Copland, and Schoenberg) exploited the virtuosic and expressive potential of woodwind and brass instruments in their orchestral works. Band directors at the time were either unaware or uninterested in what they were doing and did not ask/commission any of these great composers to write a work for the wind band. Imagine how much more enriched the literature for wind bands/ensembles would be had they done so.

ENDNOTES

1   Kenneth Berger, *The Band in the United States—A Preliminary Review of Band Research and Research Needs* (Band Associates, 1961), 14–15.
2   *Arnold Schoenberg Letters*, ed. Erwin Stein, trans. E. Wilkins and E. Kaiser (Faber and Faber, 1964), 221.

3   Ibid.

4   David Whitwell and Acton Ostling Jr., *The College and University Band* (Music Educators National Conference, 1977), 7.

5   Ibid., 13.

6   W. Francis McBeth, "The Evolving Band Repertoire," *The Instrumentalist* 50 (August 1995): 21.

7   Roger Rocco, "Band Music and the Paper-Plate Mentality: An Interview with W. Francis McBeth," *The Instrumentalist* 46 (December 1991): 14.

8   College Band Directors National Association (CBDNA) National Conference Program, Ohio State University, Columbus, Ohio, February 1993.

9   Antoine Goléa, *Rencontres avec Olivier Messiaen*, (Juilliard, 1961), 19; quoted in Austin, *Music in the Twentieth Century*, 395.

CHAPTER 5

Innovations (1952–1960)

> *Fennell creates the Eastman Wind Ensemble • West Point Sesquicentennial Celebration Commissioned Works • Boudreau creates the American Wind Symphony Orchestra • MENC/Ford Foundation Young Composers Project*

An important event took place in Rochester, New York, in September 1952 that had a profound effect on the evolution and development of the wind band and its literature—Frederick Fennell founded the Eastman Wind Ensemble. In the early years of its existence, the ensemble was identified as the Eastman Symphonic Wind Ensemble, a name given to it by Howard Hanson, Director of the Eastman School of Music at the time. Mercury Records used this name on the Ensemble's first recording, *American Concert Band Masterpieces*, because they thought inclusion of "Symphonic" would "upgrade" the group's image. Fennell was decidedly opposed to its use because he perceived the wind ensemble as an entirely new wind group and wanted it recognized as such. His determined opposition finally won out and the "Eastman Wind Ensemble" became the official name of the group. Composer W. Francis McBeth (1933–2012) felt that Fennell's decision to call his "new wind band" a "wind ensemble" was one of the most ingenious acts of the 20th century. "Fennell saw into the future. He saw a coming repertory for winds. He was well aware that the name band was a four-letter word to many serious musicians. He wanted to present serious wind literature to audiences, but realized that the term wind band was an albatross around the neck of many people because of the past."[1]

The formation of the Eastman Wind Ensemble came about as the result of a concert of wind music organized by Fennell at the Eastman School of Music in the winter of 1952. In an article that appeared in the March 1953 issue of *The American Music Teacher* entitled "The Wind Ensemble," Fennell described this concert:

> This evening of music began with a *Ricercare* for wind instruments by Adrian Willaert (1480–1562), and ended ten compositions later with the *Symphonies for Wind Instruments* by Igor Stravinsky.... The wonderful effect this concert had upon the discriminating audience and the press is a pleasure to recall, as is the reaction of the players which was positive, articulate, and enthusiastic in the extreme. The direct result of this evening of original music for wind instruments was the establishment in the Fall of 1952 of the Eastman Wind Ensemble.[2]

In a letter to Percy Grainger on July 8, 1952, Fennell wrote, "The concert was one of the best I have had among all I have both heard and conducted here, and as an event of practical musical value and a glimpse into the future, it was without parallel."

Later, in the April 1987 issue of *The Instrumentalist*, Fennell discussed the formulation of the instrumentation of his new ensemble. "[I started with] ... the basic format of the British military band ... increasing it to allow for triples among the reeds required for Stravinsky's *Symphonies*, each player would be the soloist his private teacher always taught him to be.... I could hear how clean this sound was going to be ... We would sit in the straight rows of orchestral seating.... I wanted a carefully-balanced instrumentation capable of performing styles from the 16th-century brass music and moderate-sized chamber music to Paul Hindemith's new *Symphony in B-flat*."[3]

The following is the instrumentation of Fennell's new ensemble.

Reeds	Brass
2 flutes and piccolo and/or alto flute	3 cornets in B-flat or 5 trumpets in B-flat
2 oboes and English horn	2 trumpets in B-flat
2 bassoons and contrabassoon	4 horns

1 E-flat clarinet	3 trombones
8 B-flat clarinets or A clarinet	2 euphoniums
(divided as demanded by	1 E-flat tuba
composers)	1 BB-flat and 2 BB-flat tubas if desired
1 E-flat alto clarinet	Other instruments—percussion, harp,
1 B-flat bass clarinet	celesta, piano, organ, harpsichord,
2 alto saxophones	solo string instruments and choral
1 tenor saxophone	forces if desired
1 baritone saxophone	1 string bass

Commenting on his choice of this modest instrumentation Fennell stated, "... it was my primary intention to keep the instrumental forces as simple as possible. Its instrumentation is simply that of the orchestra for which Richard Wagner scored his *Ring of the Nibelung* ... plus a section of saxophones and one alto clarinet, and minus one bass trumpet. This is the same wind section which Stravinsky later used for *The Rite of Spring*."[4] (See chart on page 70.)

The exact instrumentation was far less important than Fennell's reason for adopting it. His intention was to create a "sound resource" available to composers wishing to write music for the wind ensemble. Decisions concerning instrumentation, how many players on each part, etc., would be made by the person writing the music—the composer. Fennell's idea about instrumentation and its use was completely opposite that advocated by the American Bandmasters Association and the College Band Directors National Association, who sought to identify and establish an "ideal" standard instrumentation for wind band compositions (more about this in Chapter 6).

Fennell believed there was a genuine need for another wind instrument organization which would combine the appropriate features of the symphony orchestra, military band, and concert band with regard to performance, composition, and music education. In the program note for the concert given by the Eastman Wind Ensemble on March 20, 1960, Fennell wrote:

> Our decision to establish this new group was made after twenty years of careful study and performance by the Eastman School Symphony Band of the significant musical literature for the wind band, both original and transcribed. In establishing the Wind Ensemble as an adjunct to the Symphony Band, it has been our desire to strike out in new directions which would begin from the premise that we could make music with the

	Wagner	Stravinsky	Eastman Wind Ensemble
Flute and Piccolo	4a	5b	2
Oboe and English Horn	4c	5d	2
Bassoons and Contrabassoon	4e	5f	2
Clarinets	3g	4h	9i
Alto Clarinet	—	—	1
Bass Clarinet	1	2	1
Saxophones	—	—	4
Trumpets, soprano	3	5j	5k
Bass Trumpet in E-flat	1	—	—
French horns	8m	8n	4
Trombones	5o	3	3
Euphonium	—	—	2
Tuba	1 (in F)	2	2p
Percussion	q	r	s
Harp	6	—	—
	—	—	—
	40	39	37

Comparison of Wind Instruments used in Wagner's *Ring of the Nibelung*, Stravinsky's *Rite of Spring* and the Eastman Wind Ensemble

a-piccolo and 3 flutes, 3rd flute doubles 2nd piccolo. b-piccolo and 3 flutes, 3rd doubling 2nd piccolo, and one alto flute in F. c-3 oboes and one English horn which doubles 4th oboe. d-4 oboes and English horn, with 4th oboe doubling 2nd English horn. e-3 bassoons and contrabassoon. f-3 bassoons and 2 contrabassoons. g-1 doubles E-flat Clarinet. h-1 in D and 3 in B-flat or A. i-1 E-flat plus 8 in B-flat or A. j-1 in D and 4 in C with 4th doubling E-flat bass trumpet. k-3 cornets and 2 trumpets or 5 trumpets in B-flat. m-4 double on 2 tenor tubas in B-flat and 2 double bass tubas in F. n-2 double tenor tuba in B-flat. o-3 tenor, 1 bass, and a contrabass trombone which doubles bass trombone. p-1 E-flat and 1 BB-flat or 2 BB-flat. q-2 pairs of timpani, triangle, cymbals, snare drum, bells. r-5 timpani (2 players), bass drum, triangle, cymbals, gong, tambourine, guiro, and antique cymbals in A-flat and B-flat. s-percussion, harp, piano, organ, harpsichord, etc. as desired.

Source: Kenneth Berger, *The Band in the United States—A Preliminary Review of Band Research and Research Needs* (Band Associates, 1961), 29

minimum rather than with the maximum number of players, that we would confine our rehearsals and performances to the study of the original music written for the massed wind medium, and that we should embark upon a most active program to stimulate the composition of music for the Wind Ensemble by contemporary composers everywhere.

We do not call our group a band simply because we do not believe that it is a band. To qualify for that distinguished classification a group should be uniformed in the tradition of the band, should be able to march and perform in the open air in the tradition of that band, should perform the traditional musical literature of the band, and maintain those time-honored traditions and associations to which the public and its institutions have become so rightfully accustomed.

With the full knowledge of what has gone before in the history of composition and performance, and with due respect for the existence of the symphony orchestra, military band, and concert band, there is validity in the premise that their contributions to the arts of public performance, composition, and musical education may be supplemented by an ensemble which combines the appropriate features of those three established mediums of musical art.[5]

In the summer of 1952, Fennell sent letters to approximately 400 composers informing them of his plan to organize a new ensemble comprised of the specific instrumentation listed on pages 68–69.

My letter stated in part that it was our hope that composers would look upon this instrumental establishment as the basic instrumentation from which they could deviate should a particular score require more or less instruments than were listed. It was further stated that they might consider this in the same manner as one does the *tutti* orchestra, the full organ, or the complete seven-plus octave range of the piano keyboard— a sonority resource to be utilized *only* when desired. My correspondents were informed that the Eastman School would have one annual symposium for the reading of all new music written for the Wind Ensemble, and that there would be no "commissions" save those of a performance that was prepared with skill and devotion.[6]

Among the first composers to respond to Fennell's letter were Percy Grainger, Vincent Persichetti, and Ralph Vaughan Williams. It is interesting to note that Grainger's response listed only four pieces, *The Duke of Marlborough Fanfare*, *The Power of Rome and the Christian Heart*, *Ye Banks and Braes O'Bonnie Doon*, and *Children's March*. He did not include *Lincolnshire Posy*. In an accompanying letter, Grainger stated that he had "... always loved the band and wind ensemble ... and [had] composed steadily for the band since 1905. My first *Hill-Song* (No. 1) was scored for 24 double reeds in 1902." He inquired if Fennell would like to see "some of my transcriptions (rather than arrangements—since I have altered no notes, nor added any) of pre-Bach music, such as *Two Bach Fugues* for four (six) saxophones, *Prelude in the Dorian Mode* for band (or four saxes) by Antonio de Cabezón, *When Yuletide Comes* for four saxes by S. Olsen, *First Five Part Fantasia* by John Jenkins for Clarinet Choir, and *The Four Note Pavan* by Alfonso Ferrabosco for brass choir." In Fennell's reply to Grainger's letter (July 8, 1952), he expressed delight in the good response he had received from composers. "The daily mail brings response that is amazing. Much of it simply confirms the existence of already known material, but does so in the composer's hand." Ralph Vaughan Williams, in a brief note to Fennell, promised to contact him "if ever I write music for that combination [again]."

In an essay entitled "The Wind Ensemble Concept," Donald Hunsberger points out that Fennell began a process that was in opposition to standardized practices at the time.

> Fennell [placed] a primary emphasis upon the development and support of composers on behalf of the wind band. Since the early days of the century, with the highly successful Sousa Band as a model, the quality and quantity of original works, other than occasional pieces, suites, solos, and marches, was sparse, compared to the vast amount of music for band transcribed from orchestral, operatic, and keyboard sources. This imbalance of transcribed versus original music for the band had its origin during the middle of the previous century when Military Band Journals were beginning to be published both in the United States and in England. The arranger and the transcriber held a position of importance in the eyes of band directors, especially during the first half of this century.[7]

Fennell was hopeful that band conductors would find the wind ensemble concept interesting and exciting.

> I sincerely wish that my colleagues would give the Wind Ensemble a whirl. I know it will be a success here and it could be so in any city in America. I must also be frank to say that I am banking quite heavily on simple terminology. The word band is death to too many people. So they are blind and stupid and narrow and prejudiced. Well, I can't say that those who conduct most bands have been able to do much to alter those

opinions. But I do not think there are many people who would doubt the success that would attend the following fictional illustration: "*The New York Times* announced today a projected series of 6 concerts of music for wind instruments to be played in Town Hall by the wind-brass-percussion section of the New York Philharmonic Symphony Orchestra under the direction of its conductor, Dimitri Mitropoulos. Music by Monteverdi, Josquin des Pres, Vivaldi, Mozart, Strauss, Stravinsky, Grainger, Berg, Schoenberg, Toch, Krenek, Schuman, Hindemith, and Mennin will be played on the first Tuesday of the month beginning in September. Concerts are open to subscription by the public." I am certain they would be sold out. But I am equally convinced that if the announcement said that Mitropoulos was organizing a band, that people who think it strange and unorthodox—(even for Mitropoulos!) and would stay away in droves. I wish Mitropoulos would try it! But regardless of others, I want to see this idea get a proper development here. We have every facility with which to create and maintain it. We must not fail.[8]

In 1961, nine years after Fennell formed the Eastman Wind Ensemble, Richard Franko Goldman stated that, "It [the wind ensemble] becomes, in effect, the realization of what a concert band aims for in its most musically serious moments ... its appeal should be very great for those who feel that ... the wind band can exist on a somewhat more sophisticated level than is commonly attained."[9]

In creating programs for the Eastman Wind Ensemble, Fennell selected one-third of the music for woodwinds, one-third for brass, and one-third for the reed-brass-percussion combination. The inaugural Eastman Wind Ensemble concert program was a perfect example of Fennell's programming philosophy: Mozart—*Serenade No. 10 in B-flat, K. 370a*; Riegger—*Nonet for Brass*, and Hindemith—*Symphony in B-flat*.

Fennell's wind ensemble concept and Eastman Wind Ensemble recordings stimulated questions and concerns in band circles— "what is a "band?"—what is a "wind ensemble?" Many viewed the wind ensemble as a "small band in tails or tuxes performing wind band literature." Fennell's detractors could point out that the Eastman Wind Ensemble's first recording, *American Concert Band Masterpieces*, contained six pieces, four of which had the word "band" in the title or sub-title (Persichetti's *Divertimento for Band*, Gould's *Ballad for Band*, Schuman's *George Washington Bridge—An Impression for Band*, and Piston's *Tunbridge Fair—Intermezzo for Band*). Kenneth

Berger, writing in his research report, *The Band in the United States*, states "... few would not agree that the Eastman (Band) group has been a good and major influence in the contemporary band world. [But] without twisting logic we might admit that if the Eastman Symphonic Wind Ensemble is not really a Band then it has been playing for its recordings a repertoire of transcriptions!"[10]

What Fennell's detractors failed to grasp was that his new concept was not about the size of the group but about the flexible use of sound resources (instruments) included in the wind band constituency. The "wind ensemble concept" allowed conductors to select music from a broader and expanded body of quality literature including traditional band literature. No longer were conductors of wind groups restricted to selecting pieces that employed "all the players in the band"—they could select excellent pieces composed over the last five centuries for various complements of woodwinds, brass, and percussion instruments.

Another of Frederick Fennell's important contributions to the wind band/ensemble profession was his book, *Time and the Winds*. Published by the Leblanc Company in 1954, it is a short history of the use of wind instruments in the orchestra, band, and wind ensemble from Gabrieli to the Eastman Wind Ensemble. In addition, Fennell also authored a series of sixteen articles for *The Instrumentalist* from 1975 through 1984. Published later under the title "Basic Band Repertory," it was what Fennell called the "... indestructible masterpieces for band that have survived the ravages of time and many an inept conductor."

Captain Francis E. Resta, Commanding Officer and Conductor of the West Point Academy Band, was also well aware of the need for more and better original works for the wind band. To commemorate the 1952 Sesquicentennial Celebration of the United States Military Academy at West Point, Resta commissioned a series of works by leading world composers (Darius Milhaud, Morton Gould, Charles Cushing, Erik Leidzén, Henry Cowell, Roy Harris, Robert Russell Bennett, William Grant Still, Francis Resta, H. Lynn Arison, Robert Dvorak, Douglas Gallez, and Barry Drewes). His commissions were really "invitations" since he could not promise them any financial compensation. Every composer except Ernest Bloch accepted Resta's request. In a letter to Resta, Bloch explained why he turned down his invitation.

As much as I would like to comply with your request, I am sorry to say that it will not be possible for me to compose a work for your celebration. I am a very slow worker, and it takes me sometimes years of meditation before I am able to give shape to my ideas. Furthermore, I see that the medium needed is not for symphonic orchestra, but for military band, and I am completely unfamiliar with this medium. If I were much younger, and in better health, I certainly would devote the time to study it carefully, as it deserves.[11]

A letter from Roy Harris provides insight into how one composer viewed the challenge of composing a work for the wind band at this time.

The writing of this work has been extraordinarily difficult for me because I hoped to achieve a work of symphonic breadth for your noble West Point Symphonic Band. My attention has been given, for many years, to writing for symphony orchestra wherein one can draw heavily on the sustaining quality of the strings. The problem of writing for wind instruments is much more difficult in that one must make proper allowance for breathing. At this time, it seems to me that a symphonic band is like a cross between a pipe organ and a chorus; yet it has a great deal more agility than a chorus and more expressive control than a pipe organ.[12]

Harris's concept of the sound of a "symphonic band" seems to be based on the sound of a symphony orchestra. He expressed concern for the difficulty a composer would have in achieving the "sustaining quality of the strings" with wind instruments. However, composers such as Vincent Persichetti, William Schuman, and Ingolf Dahl viewed the wind band as a completely new medium. In their works they explored the unique possibilities of wind instruments regarding color, texture, technique, and style, as opposed to approaching it as "a cross between a pipe organ and a chorus."

The premieres of the West Point Band's commissioned pieces took place on six special concerts performed by the Band between January 5, 1952 (Carnegie Hall) and May 30, 1952 (West Point Army Theatre). These new works were:

Darius Milhaud—*West Point Suite*
Morton Gould—*Symphony for Band, "West Point"*
Charles Cushing—*Angel Camp*
Erik Leidzén—*USMA Suite*
Henry Cowell—*Fantasie*
Roy Harris—*West Point Symphony*

Robert Russell Bennett—*Choral Overture*
William Grant Still—*To You, America*
Francis Resta—Overture, *100 Days*
H. Lynn Arison—Tone Poem, *Israfel*
Robert Dvorak—*Symphony No. 2, "West Point"*
Douglas Gallez—Cantata, *From These Gray Walls*
Barry Drewes—*West Point Suite*

Two works stand out among these thirteen pieces. Morton Gould's *Symphony for Band, "West Point"* is an outstanding piece that has been performed many times over the past sixty-six years. It is a work in two extended movements, entitled "Epitaphs" and "Marches." The melodic material recalls things associated with military life, including march-like tunes and bugle calls. Gould's knowledge and command of the resources of the modern wind band are evident throughout the work.

The other is *Angel Camp* by Charles Cushing (1905–1982), a piece that has been almost totally overlooked by wind band/ensemble conductors. Cushing was Director of Bands and Professor of Music at the University of California, Berkeley. He received Bachelor and Masters Degrees from the University of California and in 1929 traveled to Paris to study composition with Nadia Boulanger. His music generally exhibits characteristics associated with French impressionism. In 1961, his symphony, *Cereus*, was commissioned and premiered by the San Francisco Symphony Orchestra. When Ernst Bloch declined Resta's invitation, he recommended that he contact Cushing about writing a piece. Bloch's recommendation of Cushing was enthusiastically supported by Darius Milhaud. Based on the recommendations of these two composers, Resta invited Cushing to compose a piece for the celebration. Cushing's piece, *Angel Camp*, is an interesting and imaginative piece cast in a theme and variations form. Although composed for the standard symphonic band instrumentation, much of the work is transparently scored and chamber music-like in character. It is a very expressive work by an overlooked composer.

The West Point Sesquicentennial Commissioning Works Project was a spectacular example of what a single imaginative, committed band director can do. Through Resta's initiative, thirteen new works were added to wind band literature for only the cost of having scores and parts copied and produced.

In the same year that Fennell created the Eastman Wind Ensemble and Resta commissioned his series of West Point pieces, members of the University of Louisville Band were becoming dissatisfied with most of the music they were playing. They had performed Vincent Persichetti's *Divertimento for Band* in 1952 and liked it very much They found the piece interesting and exciting. This prompted them to ask Persichetti to compose a work for them. Persichetti accepted and composed *Psalm for Band*, which the Band premiered the following year. Following their performance, the students formed a publishing company (Pikaron) and published the piece. The Louisville band commissioned another work—this time from William Schuman, who was just finishing composing his *New England Triptych* for orchestra. To fulfill the Louisville commission, Schuman borrowed material from the third movement of *New England Triptych*, expanded it, and composed *Chester (Overture for Band)*. The money needed to fund these commissions was raised by band members who formed jazz bands and played dance jobs to pay for them.

Something else of great significance also occurred in Louisville during this same period. It concerned the commissioning and recording of contemporary music in the United States. In April 1953, the Rockefeller Foundation awarded the Louisville Orchestra $400,000 for the "composition, performance and recording of new works by living composers." This grant-funded commissioning project ran concurrently with a city-funded project in which approximately six new works were premiered each year. During the next three years, over one hundred new works for orchestra were premiered by the Louisville Orchestra, conducted by Robert Whitney. Most of them were also recorded by the Orchestra on its own label, "First Edition Records."

In 1953, Kappa Kappa Sigma and Tau Beta Sigma, national band fraternity and sorority, respectively, began commissioning works. The idea originated with Grand President Hugh E. McMillen, who saw the National Intercollegiate Band (sponsored by the fraternity and sorority) as the perfect performance vehicle for newly composed works for band. By the end of the twentieth century more than two dozen works had been commissioned and premiered by the National Intercollegiate Band. The composers commissioned included Alfred Reed, David Maslanka, Robert Russell Bennett, Paul Creston, Vaclav

Nelhybel, Gunther Schuller, Norman Dello Joio, Francis McBeth, Martin Mailman, and Karel Husa. In most cases, the composer conducted the premiere performance of their piece.

In 1957, five years after Fennell created the Eastman Wind Ensemble, Robert Boudreau (b. 1927) founded the American Wind Symphony Orchestra (AWSO). At first Boudreau recruited players for his Orchestra from colleges, universities, and conservatories in the United States and later, from countries throughout the world. The Orchestra's original instrumentation was very unique. It consisted of 6 flutes, 2 piccolos, 6 oboes, 2 English horns, 6 clarinets, 2 bass clarinets, 6 bassoons, 2 contrabassons, 6 French horns, 6 trumpets, 6 trombones, 2 tubas, percussion, harp, keyboards, and string bass. Saxophones and euphoniums were not used. Whereas Fennell choose the British Military Band as the point of departure in choosing the instrumentation for the Eastman Wind Ensemble, Boudreau used the woodwind, brass, and percussion sections of the symphony orchestra for his. The AWSO traveled up and down waterways in the United States, Caribbean, and Northern Europe performing concerts on a floating art gallery, Counterpoint II, which was designed by American architect Louis Kahn.

During the almost seven decades of its existence, Boudreau and the AWSO commissioned and premiered over 400 works composed by composers from the United States and throughout the world, especially from Europe, Mexico, and Central and South America. One of Boudreau's earliest commissions went to Alan Hovhaness (1911–2000), a very prolific composer who wrote over 400 pieces including 9 operas, 2 ballets, 60 symphonies, and 100 chamber pieces. Hovhaness was very interested in Western and Asian musical styles, particularly the giant melody of the Himalayan Mountains, Armenian and South Indian classical music, the orchestra music of the Tang Dynasty, and Handel's operas and oratorios. *Symphony No. 4*, the piece he composed for the AWSO, is a three-movement work in which various instrumental choirs play chant-like hymns interrupted by exotic solo passages for bass clarinet, contrabassoon, and percussion instruments.

Below are two American Wind Symphony Orchestra programs which were performed during the 1969 season. The Vivaldi transcription and works by Penderecki, Badings, Nelson, Somers, and Amram are all AWSO commissioned works.

American Wind Symphony
Concert of July 10, 1969

A. Vivaldi—Concerto for Two C
  Trumpets
K. Penderecki—Pittsburgh Overture
H. Badings—Symphony in C
O. Nelson—Concerto for Xylophone,
  Marimba, Vibraphone and Wind
  Orchestra

American Wind Symphony
Concert of August 3, 1969

A. Dvořák—Serenade in D minor,
  Op. 44
H. Somers—Symphony for
  Woodwinds, Brass and Percussion
D. Amram—Concerto for French
  Horn and Wind Orchestra
O. Messiaen—Et exspecto
  resurrectionem mortuorum [13]

Other composers commissioned by Boudreau included: Samuel Adler, Samuel Akpabot, Alexander Arutiunian, Georges Auric, Robert Russell Bennett, Warren Benson, Elmer Bernstein, William Bolcom, Eugène Bozza, Henry Brant, Leon Brouwer, Chou Wen-Chung, Paul Creston, Ton de Leeuw, Luboš Fišer, Jean Françaix, J. J. Johnson, George Kleinsinger, Norman Lloyd, Nicolai Lopatnikoff, Ivana Loudová, Toshiro Mayuzumi, Colin McPhee, Akira Miyoshi, Juan Orrego-Salas, Joaquín Rodrigo, Bernard Rogers, Ned Rorem, Ramón Santos, Lalo Schifrin, Hale Smith, Carlos Surinach, Erkki-Sven Tüür, Ivan Tcherepnin, Heitor Villa-Lobos, and Patrick Zuk. More information about Boudreau's commissioning project can be found in Chapter 7.

In 1957, the Ford Foundation undertook a study that investigated the relationship between the arts and American society. One of the recommendations emanating from the study was made by composer Norman Dello Joio who suggested that talented young composers be placed in public school systems throughout the United States to compose music for students performing in school bands, orchestras, and choirs. In 1959, the Young Composers Project (YCP), funded by the Ford Foundation and administered first by the National Music Council and later by the Music Educators National Conference, was established for that purpose. From 1959–1968 seventy-six composers (under the age of 35) were placed in public schools as composers-in-residence where they composed music for school music groups. Included among the young composers who were participants in this project were Stephen Albert, Donald Erb, Arthur Frackenpohl, Charles Fussell, Peter Schickele, and Philip Glass. The YCP proved to be a "win-win situation" for everyone involved. School band, orchestra, choir directors, and students grew in their understanding and appreciation of contemporary music and the composers became aware of the opportunities available to them in writing music for young musicians.

In 1957, William Tarwater conducted a survey among the CBDNA membership to determine what they considered to be the ten best original works for band. Below are the results of his survey:

1. Holst—Suite in E-flat (1909)
2. Hanson—Chorale and Alleluia (1954)
3. Holst—Suite in F (1911)
4. Jacob—Music for a Festival (1951)
5. Persichetti—Divertimento for Band (1950)
6. H. Owen Reed—La Fiesta Mexicana (1949)
7. Milhaud—Suite Française (1944)
8. Vaughan Williams—Folk Song Suite (1923)
9. Hindemith—Symphony in B-flat (1950)
10. Jacob—An Original Suite for Band (1928)[14]

Four of the above works were composed between 1909–1928 and the remaining six between 1944–54. Five were composed within an eight-year period prior to the survey which supports Vincent Persichetti's belief that a piece for band can be "... introduced, accepted ... and become a staple of the literature in a short time."[15] No wind band pieces composed between 1920–1948 were selected by CBDNA members. This might indicate that band directors during these years were not motivated and/or lacked interest in expanding the literature for the medium.

In August 1958, *The Instrumentalist* published a listing of "The Best in Band Music." Thirty-one of the magazine's columnists, which included many of the leading bandmasters of the time, selected what they considered "the finest selections available for performance by band." Of the 118 compositions selected, 67 (over 57%) were transcriptions. At the close of the 1950s transcriptions were still the dominant type of music performed by bands. However, six of the ten top-rated compositions were original works for wind band.

Holst	First Suite in E-flat
Vaughan Williams	Folk Song Suite
Wagner/Cailliet	Elsa's Procession to the Cathedral
Hanson	Chorale and Alleluia
Holst	Second Suite in F
Fauchet/Gillette	Symphony in B-flat
Milhaud	Suite Française

Bennett	Suite of Old American Dances
Bach/Leidzén	Toccata and Fugue in D minor
Weinberger/Bainum	Polka and Fugue from Schwanda[16]

Of the 118 pieces included on this list, only a few were marches and none were Sousa marches! In a letter to *The Instrumentalist* following the publication of this list, Gabriel Kosakoff, band director at the High School of Music and Art in New York City wrote, "Since, apparently, there is not an over-abundance of good original band music, it is up to us, the band leaders, to do something about it. I am encouraged by the organizations and schools commissioning original band works, and the bandmasters who enable composers to have a hearing of their compositions ... Let's all band together, and plan at least one entire program this season of original band music."[17]

The period from 1952–60 was a very interesting and productive one in the evolution of the wind band/ensemble and its literature. A growing number of conductors began embracing Fennell's wind ensemble concept; publishers were publishing and bands were performing works written by major composers; "What music should be played" and "how it should be played" became the primary concern of wind band/ensemble conductors.

ENDNOTES

1   W. Francis McBeth, "Assessing the Wind Ensemble," *The Instrumentalist* 46 (March 1992): 28.

2   Frederick Fennell, "The Wind Ensemble," *The American Music Teacher* 2 (March–April 1953): 12.

3   Frederick Fennell, "Growing as a Conductor," *The Instrumentalist* 41 (April 1987): 51.

4   Fennell, *Time and the Winds*, 52.

5   R. F. Goldman, *The Wind Band*, 138–139.

6   Fennell, "The Wind Ensemble," 12.

7   Donald Hunsberger, "The Wind Ensemble Concept," (Unpublished paper, University of Rochester, Eastman School of Music, 1994), 29.

8   Frederick Fennell, Letter to Percy Grainger, July 8, 1952.

9   R. F. Goldman, *The Wind Band*, 141–142.

10 Berger, *The Band in the United States*, 28.

11 Larry D. Harper, "The Sesquicentennial Celebration: Wind Band Commissions of the United States Military Academy at West Point (1952)" (Ph.D. diss., Michigan State University, 1987), 111.

12 Ibid., 29.

13 American Wind Symphony Orchestra, Concert Programs, 1969 Season, 13, 15.

14 William Harmon Tarwater, Jr., "Analyses of Seven Major Band Compositions of the Twentieth Century" (Ph.D. diss., George Peabody College for Teachers of Vanderbilt University, 1958); Cited in Berger, *The Band in the United States*, 54.

15 Vincent Persichetti, "Symphony No. 6 for Band," *Journal of Band Research* 1 (Fall 1964): 17.

16 "The Best in Band Music," *The Instrumentalist* 13 (August 1958): 74–76.

17 Gabriel Kosakoff, "Letters from Readers: Band Transcriptions," *The Instrumentalist* 13 (October 1958): 4.

CHAPTER 6

Growth (Late 1950s to Early 1970s)

| Standardizing Wind Band Instrumentation •
Literature Expansion • Commissioning |

By 1960, there was an ever-increasing number of original works published and available for wind band/ensemble performance. However, only a few were being included on band concert programs. Those shown below, which were performed in 1954 and 1959, reinforce this observation. Two-thirds of the literature on these programs consist of transcriptions and light music. They are typical of the kinds of concerts performed by school, college, university, and military bands during this time.

University of Michigan Symphony Band
William D. Revelli, Conductor
March 28, 1954

Bilik	"M" Signature
Bach	Prelude and Fugue in d minor
Cherubini	Overture to "Anacreon"
Barat	Andante et Scherzo (cornet solo)
Wagner	Siegfried's Rhine Journey from *Götterdämmerung*
Hindemith	Symphony in B-flat
Varman	Cambodian Suite
Sousa	Tribute to Sousa

Ithaca College Band
Walter Beeler, Conductor
March 7, 1954

Rossini	Overture, *The Italian in Algiers*
Donato	The Hidden Fortress
Offenbach	Ballet Parisien
Simeone	Flute Cocktail
Rodgers & Hammerstein	Selections from *The King and I*
Porter	Quadrille from *Can Can*
Benson	Transylvania Fanfare

United States Air Force Concert Band
Holy Cross College
June 20, 1954

Wagner	Introduction to the Third Act of *Lohengrin*
Sousa	Semper Fidelis March
Rossini	La Calumnia é un Venticello from *The Barber of Seville* (Vocal Baritone Solo)
Perkins/Werle	Fandango
Anderson	Chicken Reel

The Singing Sergeants
    Ezekiel Saw the Wheel (arr. Genuchi)
    Tenebrae Facta Sunt (Palestrina)
    Whiffenpoof Song (arr. Werle)
    With a Song in My Heart (arr. Werle)

Falla/Kepner	Fire Dance
Deiro/Lesser	Fantastic Rhapsody (Accordion Solo)
Curzon	In Malaga (Third Movement)
Puccini/Werle	"E lucevan le stelle" from *Tosca* (Vocal Tenor Solo)
Sousa	The Stars and Stripes Forever
Cray (arr.)	Armed Forces Medley

University of Michigan Symphony Band
William D. Revelli, Conductor
January 8, 1959

Verdi	Manzoni Requiem (Excerpts)
Tomasi	Concerto for Clarinet (Finale)
Bloch	Denneriana (Clarinet Solo)
Ward	Jubilation
Bennett	Symphonic Songs for Band
Berlioz	March Hongroise from *The Damnation of Faust*
Work	Portraits from the Bible

Williams	Dramatic Essay for Trumpet and Band
Kalinnikov	Symphony No. 1 (Finale)
Yoder	Silver Anniversary March

In 1958, the following transcriptions were included in *The Instrumentalist* magazine's "The Best in Band Music":

Bach/Leidzén	Jesu, Joy of Man's Desiring
	Komm Süsser Tod
Bach/Moehlmann	Prelude & Fugue in g minor
Bach/Leidzén	Toccata and Fugue in d minor
Berlioz/Henning	Overture to *Beatrice and Benedict*
Couperin/Milhaud	Overture and Allegro from *La Sultane*
Rimsky-Korsakov/Leidzén	Procession of the Nobles from *Mlada*
Shostakovich/Righter	Finale to Symphony No. 5
Wagner/Cailliet	Elsa's Procession to the Cathedral from *Lohengrin*
	Siegfried's Rhine Journey from *Götterdämmerung*
Weinberger/Bainum	Polka and Fugue from *Schwanda* [1]

Formulation of a "standard band instrumentation" became a high priority subject among band associations between 1952 and 1966. Numerous meetings were convened at national and international levels to discuss this subject. Raymond F. Dvorak, Band Director at the University of Wisconsin, in an article published in *The Instrumentalist* in 1952, reported on two meetings of the International Committee for the Standardization of Instrumental Music (CIMI), which were held in Europe in 1948–49. He stated that the CIMI recommended that a concerted effort be made "... to move toward standardization of instrumental music in all forms and principally to music destined for bands (military, concert) and brass bands."[2] He concluded, "Since the time of Haydn the instrumentation of the symphony orchestra has rested on a fixed basis; thus, the great composers of the world have found ready acceptance of their works on all continents. The case of the wind band is considerably different. Instrumentation and scores vary, making performance of band music on an international basis very impractical. . . . As a result of this state of confusion, the repertoire of bands is limited to the country in which the music is written."[3]

William D. Revelli, in a speech at the 1958 CBDNA National Conference, told band directors that "the time is long overdue for reforms in band scoring, particularly for our American bands. Every conductor, teacher, composer, school of music, publisher, and standardizing agency of this country should promote the development of a specific international band instrumentation that would include the best aspects of each nation's instrumentation and scoring. When this is accomplished, the band as a serious medium of musical expression will make its finest cultural contribution."[4]

Bernard Fitzgerald, in an address at the CBDNA National Conference three years later (1961), argued that "... it is imperative that the instrumentation of the band be stabilized with respect to the basic ratios, weights, and balances of the various sections as related to the total instrumental sonority. Composers are handicapped by the absence of a standard instrumentation and balance and must continue to compromise until these factors are definitely established." He invited composers to "... explore further the tonal resources of the band to avoid limiting the band to a relatively small number of scoring effects and devices. New concepts in sonority and scoring are necessary for an emerging musical medium, although many composers appear content to follow the general pattern of a few original band compositions resulting in the overuse of some scoring techniques."[5]

Yale Band Director Keith Wilson did not believe the band's instrumentation should be standardized. "Instrumentation is the composer's prerogative ... [it] should not be absolutely defined but must be as flexible as that for orchestra or any other ensemble.... We conductors must realize that the time has come for the composer, and not us, to determine just how the basic and auxiliary instruments in each of these sections are to be employed.... When the composer can feel free to write for band as he would like—without being restricted and inhibited by all the confusing, pre-cautionary advice usually offered him by conductors and publishers—and when he can be assured of a financial return equal to that provided by other media, then, and only then, can the problems of band instrumentation and worthwhile literature be resolved."[6] Composer Donald O. Johnson added the following, "As long as the composer is expected to work with a standard instrumentation it can be expected that all his works, and those of any other composer working with the same instrumentation, will tend to have a certain color similarity. If a composer is free to choose the specific instruments he desires there is greater chance of variety between works in regard to color. It also can be a boon to the composer if he realizes that he doesn't have to employ instruments which do not seem to have any purpose in the work he is creating."[7]

The debate on band instrumentation reached an apex in 1960 at a special CBDNA Conference called by President James Neilson to discuss and reach a consensus regarding an ideal wind band instrumentation. Attending the conference were two past presidents of CBDNA: William D. Revelli, R. Bernard Fitzgerald; five distinguished composers: Paul Creston, Vincent Persichetti, Morton Gould, Philip Lang, Vittorio Giannini; and three leading publishers: Benjamin Grasso, Ralph Satz, Alfred Reed. The outcome of their deliberations resulted in an announcement declaring the following to be the "ideal" band instrumentation:

1 piccolo (C)	One part for piccolo
6 flute	Two or three parts
2 oboe	First and second parts
1 English horn	Possibly an oboe player doubling
2 bassoon	First and second parts
1 E-flat clarinet	
18 B-flat clarinet	First and second parts
6 E-flat alto clarinet	
3 B-flat bass clarinet	
2 E-flat contrabass clarinet	
1 B-flat soprano saxophone	Straight soprano
1 E-flat alto saxophone	
1 B-flat tenor saxophone	
1 E-flat baritone saxophone	
1 B-flat bass saxophone	
1 E-flat cornet	
3 B-flat cornet	Two parts, three voices
3 B-flat trumpet	Two parts, three voices
4 horn	Four parts
3 trombone	Two parts, three voices
1 bass trombone	
3 euphonium	One or more voices
3 BB-flat tuba	One part
5 percussion	Two parts

Total: 73 players

Source: Charles Minelli, "Conference on the Band's Repertoire, Instrumentation, and Nomenclature," in *The College and University Band*, David Whitwell and Acton Ostling Jr., eds. (MENC Publications, 1977), 103.

Some publishers immediately recommended that their composers/arrangers use this "ideal instrumentation" in writing their pieces. A few publishers even insisted that composers/arrangers adhere to this "ideal instrumentation." Although much time and effort had been spent in trying to formulate standardized band instrumentation it was not successful. Another attempt was made in the late 1960s to establish such an instrumentation, but it was met with no enthusiasm.

In 1959, an important professional wind ensemble appeared on the world band scene—the Netherlands Wind Ensemble (NWE). Thom de Klerk, principal bassoonist of the Concertgebouw Orchestra and teacher at the Amsterdam Conservatory, founded the ensemble which was made up of the best wind players from the Netherlands' finest orchestras. Most of the time the ensemble performed without a conductor but when one was needed, Edo de Waart, the ensemble's principal oboe, led the group. The NWE garnered international recognition through a series of outstanding recordings. It also made several very successful tours in the United States, performing at CBDNA conferences, colleges, and universities throughout the country.

In the 1950s, there were organizations/associations for college/university wind band/ensemble directors and school band directors. However, there was not one for band directors at all levels. In 1960 one was formed—the National Band Association. Its objective was to promote the musical and educational significance of bands and excellence in bands and band music. It soon became the largest band association in the United States.

In 1967, MCA Music Publishers began publication of a series of pieces under the title of "MCA Symphonic Wind Ensemble Editions." Included in the series were works by Warren Benson, Henry Brant, Ingolf Dahl, Walter Hartley, Oskar Morowitz, Bernard Rogers, Robert Starer, John Weinzweig, and John T. Williams. MCA, in conjunction with the inauguration of the series, also began publishing a newsletter, *The Wind Ensemble*, which contained articles written by composers and conductors about newly published wind ensemble works. In its first issue, editor Donald Hunsberger defined the symphonic wind ensemble and the responsibilities of the composer, conductor, performer, and audience:

The symphonic wind ensemble is a concert organization, devoted to granting the composer and his audience the most faithful performances of his music. It is an ensemble which calls upon the strictest disciplines possible, for the composer—in establishing his wants and needs; for the conductor—in placing the composer and his music above personal promotion and peripheral activity interference; for the performer—to assume his rightful position as a legitimate symphonic musician dedicated to the furtherance of wind performance; and, for the audience—to discard past prejudices regarding wind music and wind performance as second class musical citizens.[8]

Carl Fischer Music Publishers initiated a school band works project in the 1970s by commissioning well-known composers to write music appropriate for young players. Composers were given very specific guidelines regarding range of instruments, technical complexity, and doublings they had to use in composing their pieces. The project generated the following works:

Prologue and Parade by Ulysses Kay
Ginger Marmalade by Warren Benson
Front Porch Saturday Night by Elie Siegmeister
American Debate by Henry Brant
Banners and Pennants by Leo Smit
Country Auction by Marga Richter
A Little Night and Day Music by Samuel Adler
Variations on an Ancient Hymn by Howard Hanson
Zanduna Serenade by Carlos Chávez

During this same time period (1970s), Thomas Everett and the Harvard University Band also began a commissioning works project. (Everett had previously commissioned works as the Band Director at Batavia, New York, High School.) The first work commissioned by the Harvard Band was *Streams* by David Cope, a piece for "solo" string septet and wind ensemble. This was followed by Daniel Pinkham's *Serenades* for solo trumpet and wind ensemble, which was commissioned for the 60th anniversary of the Harvard University Band and dedicated to Walter Piston. In 1975 and 1983, the Band commissioned two works from Peter Schickele (P. D. Q. Bach)— *Grand Serenade for an Awful Lot of Winds and Percussion* and *March of the Cute Little Wood Sprites*. Included among the other composers commissioned by the Harvard University Band were Leon Kirchner,

Vivian Fine, Henry Brant, Ivan Tcherepnin, Gordon Jacob, Lukas Foss, and J. J. Johnson.

Interest in new music continued to grow as more and more organizations and foundations began commissioning works for the medium. CBDNA, after lengthy discussions and debate, decided to commission a major composer to write a work for them. Their first commission went to Aaron Copland who proceeded to write an eleven-minute, one movement work entitled *Emblems*, which was premiered at the 1964 CBDNA National Conference in Tempe, Arizona, by the University of Southern California Band, William Schaefer, conductor. "The work is "a sampler" of the composer's varied output: simple triadic passages, polytonality, folk melodies, dissonance, waltzes, polymeters, and elements of jazz. It is certainly not one of Copland's most accessible pieces.[9] "The harmonies that accompany 'Amazing Grace' are unabashedly dissonant major/minor chords [and] at times the texture is so [thin] that only a triangle is playing. Yet the outer sections possess Copland's signature grandiosity [and] energy...."[10] The composer penned the following note about the piece:

> ... I wanted to write a work that was challenging to young players without overstraining their technical abilities. The work is tripartite in form: slow-fast-slow, with the return of the first part varied. Embedded in the quiet, slow music the listener may hear a brief quotation of a well-known hymn tune, "Amazing Grace," published by William Walker in *The Southern Harmony* in 1835. Curiously enough, the accompanying harmonies had been conceived first, without reference to any tune. It was only a chance of perusal of a recent anthology of old 'Music in America' that made me realize a connection existed between my harmonies and the old hymn tune.
>
> An emblem stands for something—it is a symbol. I called the work *Emblems* because it seemed to me to suggest musical states of being: noble or aspirational feelings, playful or spirited feelings. The exact nature of these emblematic sounds must be determined for himself by each listener.[11]

The premiere performance of *Emblems* was not greeted with much enthusiasm by the membership. Nevertheless, five years later at the 1969 National Conference, Keith Wilson, past president of CBDNA and one of the strongest supporters of the Association's commissioning initiative, stated, "I trust that most of the CBDNA membership shares my view that [our] first commission was highly successful, and that in Aaron Copland's *Emblems* we have a genuinely significant new work in our repertory."[12] Wilson's prophesy, over time, has proved true.

Paul Bryan, conductor of the Duke University Wind Symphony, presented a report on the commissioning of wind band/ensemble pieces in the United States at the 1967 CBDNA National Conference.

> The complete list includes more than 40 commissioning agencies. The champion at this date seems to be the Ithaca High School Band, whose Director, Mr. Frank Battisti has placed 22 commissions at last count. I should add that I am not pointing the quantity-only finger in their direction. Theirs has been an incredibly high-quality achievement. Due to the limitation of time, I will not enumerate all the commissioning groups. Several of the band associations, notably the CBDNA and ABA, have been very influential. The band fraternities, especially Kappa Kappa Psi, have provided several commissions. The efforts of the Ithaca High School Band have been abetted by several other localized secondary school groups. The conclusion about the emerging repertoire is, therefore, that there is a tradition whereby composers are actively encouraged to write for band and that it is in a healthy and advancing stage of development.
>
> The results of our efforts will determine whether the great composers will take us seriously or not. Not our technical proficiency but the make-up of our serious programs will persuade our colleagues in the musical world to recognize us as peers ... Only by considering ourselves primarily as artists rather than showmen, as musicians rather than band directors, can we properly fulfill our mission.[13]

In another address at the same CBDNA National Conference (1967), William Schaefer, Director of Bands at the University of Southern California, urged band directors to look beyond the commercially published music available to them and examine the rental works found in publisher's catalogs.

> Orchestra conductors never have restricted themselves to music that is commercially profitable to publish. They always have been accustomed to renting music for performance to augment the published literature they hold in their own libraries. Publishers are in the business to make money and thus must print what they feel to be marketable. Alas, the large quantity of poor published band material reflects the tastes of those who purchase and use it. The overhead on short, easy music is low and the returns great. Thus we find publishers reluctant to publish major

works that are long and difficult and thus performed by fewer groups. Ingolf Dahl's magnificent *Sinfonietta*, conducted by the composer at the CBDNA's national convention in Tempe [1961], is an example of a work that has yet to be published for these reasons. Yet there still have been many performances, each involving a personal arrangement between the composer and the performer.... So [in order] to upgrade our literature, we must use unpublished editions. We must understand that costs of rental [music] exceed costs of purchased materials of comparable length. We must continue to assist composers and performers by compiling lists, by encouraging publishers to publish more difficult works, by performing works that are inconvenient to obtain—perhaps even by going into the rental or publishing business ourselves.[14]

Ingolf Dahl, Norman Dello Joio, Warren Benson, Karel Husa, Vincent Persichetti, and Vaclav Nelhybel were among the composers who wrote significant works for the wind band/ensemble in the 1960s. In 1961, the Western and Northwestern Divisions of CBDNA commissioned Ingolf Dahl (1912–1970) to compose a work for them. Dahl responded by composing *Sinfonietta for Concert Band* (1961), a work of symphonic proportions (referred to by William Schaefer, above). The work's first movement contains references to traditional band sounds. It begins quietly with the ensemble sounding "B-flat," the band's traditional tuning note and ends with a marching band "roll-off." The second movement is a quiet and polyphonic nocturne containing many melodic passages for solo instruments. The finale employs a tone-row melody that is developed into a set of dance variations. The piece ends like it began, quietly and introspectively.

Norman Dello Joio (1913–2008) composed *Variants on a Mediaeval Tune* (1963), in response to a commission from the Mary Duke Biddle Foundation. It was premiered in April 1963 by the Duke University Wind Symphony, Paul Bryan conducting. The piece starts with a brief introduction in which solo woodwind instruments introduce the theme ("In dulci jubilo"). This is followed by five "variants," strongly contrasting in character, that exploit the sonorous resources of the wind band. The original manuscript version of *Variants on a Mediaeval Tune* was longer than the published version. I speculate it was shorted by the publishers to make it more marketable.

In 1963, I asked Kappa Gamma Psi, a national music fraternity, to consider commissioning Warren Benson (1924–2005) to write a wind band/ensemble piece. They followed through on my suggestion and Benson composed *The Leaves Are Falling* (1963–64) which was premiered by the Eastman Wind Ensemble, Clyde Roller conducting, on April 30, 1964, as part of the Eastman School of Music's annual Festival of American Music. The title of this work comes from the poem, "Herbst" (Autumn) by Rainer Maria Rilke. Rilke uses the notion of "falling" throughout the poem to mirror the falling of leaves and the dying of the year. There is a feeling of melancholy that reminds us that our lives are also winding/falling down.

The Leaves Are Falling is an exceptionally intense twelve-minute long work which Benson began composing on November 22, 1963, the date of the assassination of John F. Kennedy. The well-known chorale "Ein' feste Burg" (A Mighty Fortress) is used in the second half of the piece, but never exactly, nor does Benson use its traditional harmonization. "With the half note marked at 32–34 bpm [beats per minute] ♩ = 32–34 [a performance of *The Leaves Are Falling*] demands intense concentration [on the part] of the ensemble and masterly pacing by the conductor. The amount of exposed playing by every section and the level of musicianship demanded of each player also contribute to its difficulty. [However,] a thoughtfully-paced performance ... can be a transcendent experience."[15] Donald Hunsberger wrote the following about the piece: "*The Leaves Are Falling* is undoubtedly one of the most difficult works in the wind repertoire to perform due to the musical and emotional demands imposed upon the conductor and the ensemble ... the first half [of the piece] is original material which is repeated almost exactly in the second section, this time with various statements of "Ein' feste Burg" superimposed on the material previously heard. The infinite control required of each performer produces situations seldom heard in traditional large scale band writing and focuses attention on basic performance techniques such as tone control, extremely quiet entrances and exits, gradual crescendi, intensity and projection of individual and section lines and, at all times, rhythmic control. All these combine to create one of the wind band's most contemplative, yet elegant, statements."[16]

John Paynter, in his review of the piece for *The Instrumentalist* (January 1972) called it "one of the most significant band compositions in the last ten years."

Two years after writing *The Leaves Are Falling*, Benson composed *The Solitary Dancer* (1966) for the Clarence (New York) High School Band. This is a mono-thematic work that undergoes continuous subtle development during its 6 minute and 40 second duration. It is the composer's most-performed work. In the Preface of the score, Benson states that *The Solitary Dancer* deals with the "quiet, poised energy that one may observe in a dancer in repose, alone with her inner music." It was one of the first works for band in which players sing as well as perform on their instruments.

In 1968, Ithaca College commissioned Karel Husa (1921–2016) to compose a work for its Concert Band. Husa responded by writing *Music for Prague 1968*. This work embodies the composer's reaction to the Soviet Union's 1968 invasion of Prague, the capital city of his native Czechoslovakia. It is a work of great intensity and drama. In the program note for the piece Husa wrote about the symbolism in the work: "[I]n addition to the distress calls in the first movement (Fanfares), the unbroken hope of the Hussite song, sound of bells, or the tragedy (Aria), there is also the bird call at the beginning (piccolo solo), symbol of the liberty which the City of Prague has seen for only moments during its thousand years of existence."[17]

John von Rhein added the following about Husa's piece in the *Chicago Tribune*:

> There is an important body of 20th-century works that arose out of their composers' need to express intensely personal reactions to tragic or cataclysmic events in recent history.... Husa ... sets out to evoke the brutality with which the invading Soviet military quashed the libertarian uprising that was centered in his home city of Prague.... Dissonant trumpet fanfares roar through the orchestra like tanks across a public square; muffled snare drums suggest an implacable enemy on the march; massed bells portray the terror and confusion of scattered civilians vainly trying to resist a juggernaut. But the invaders cannot crush the spirit of humanity, and the final brass chorale signals a message of hope—the Czech people will prevail, just as they have throughout their oppressed history.[18]

It is impossible to remain unaffected by Husa's composition. *Music for Prague 1968* is a powerful, dramatic and disturbing work that has received thousands of performances throughout the world. It is a masterpiece of music literature.

The compositional techniques and orchestration used by composers such as Karel Husa or Warren Benson were radically different than those used in traditional band pieces. Composers of this new music employed the instrumentation they needed to realize what they wanted to express. As a result, their pieces included fresh sounds, textures, and colors.

Vincent Persichetti continued to compose pieces for the wind band/ensemble—*Bagatelles for Band* in 1962, *Masquerade* in 1965, and *Parable IX* in 1972. *Masquerade* was commissioned by the Baldwin-Wallace College Conservatory of Music and premiered in 1966 by its Symphonic Wind Ensemble with the composer conducting. It is a tonal work—a theme with ten variations. However, the independent contrapuntal movement within the piece often creates polytonal combinations. Persichetti's unique and imaginative use of percussion color and texture enlarge the overall fabric of the composition.

Vaclav Nelhybel (1919–1996) arrived in the United States in the 1960s. Born in Czechoslovakia, his dramatic compositions instantly captured the attention of school and college band directors and were soon being performed by hundreds of bands throughout the country. He composed *Trittico*, an intense, energetic, passionate work, in 1964 for William D. Revelli and the University of Michigan Symphony Band. Its first and third movements are brilliant and vigorous; the second, turbulent and expressive—its orchestration, bold and striking.

Other composers writing works for the wind band in the 1960s and '70s were Samuel Adler, Donald Erb, Ross Lee Finney, Morton Gould, George Rochberg, William Albright, Martin Mailman, Walter Hartley, Howard Hanson, Roger Nixon, Alfred Reed, Vaclav Nelhybel, Ron Nelson, Ron Lo Presti, Robert Jager, Francis McBeth, John Barnes Chance, and Fisher Tull.

The Ithaca (New York) High School Band began commissioning works in 1958. Its first commission went to Warren Benson who composed *Night Song*, which was premiered by the Band in 1959. During the next thirteen years, under the leadership of Frank L. Battisti and Ron Socciarelli, the Ithaca High School Band commissioned twenty-nine works. The objective of these commissions was to improve the quality of literature available for performance by American high school bands. Other major composers who were commissioned by the Band included Vincent Persichetti, Gunther Schuller, Karel Husa, Warren Benson, John Huggler, Alec Wilder, Leslie Bassett, Alan Hovhaness, Carlos Chávez, Alvin Etler, and Samuel Adler. Seven of these composers were writing their first works for band and all were composing their first pieces for high school band.

Pulitzer Prize winner Leslie Bassett (1923–2016) was one of the composers writing their first piece for band. His *Designs, Images and Textures* (1965) is, in one respect, similar to "Moussorgsky's *Pictures at an Exhibition* in that they both invite the listener to associate music with visual art."[19] Each movement of Bassett's work is a sound image of a different kind of visual art: "Oil Painting," "Water Color," "Pen and Ink," "Mobile," and "Bronze Sculpture." Bassett recalled a remark made by University of Michigan band director William D. Revelli about the piece, "This is the only piece written for band in which all of the movements end quietly."

Barney Child's *Six Events for 58 Players* was premiered by the IHS Band on the same concert that included the premiere of Bassett's piece (April 28, 1965). Child's work is a "chance piece" and, like Bassett's, his first piece for band. It is also the first aleatoric piece ever written for high school band. The work is structured in six sections or events. Players play at timed intervals throughout each event. The conductor provides the "time line" by rotating his/her arms in a clock-like manner.

The program, below, was performed by the Ithaca High School Band on February 12, 1967, at the MENC Eastern Division Conference in Boston, Massachusetts. Five of the six pieces on the program were IHS Band commissions, two of which were receiving their premiere performance at this concert.

Ithaca High School Band
February 12, 1967
Frank L. Battisti, Conductor

Prisms	Herbert Bielawa
Star Edge *	Warren Benson
Donald Sinta, Alto Saxophone	
Serenade for Band *	Vincent Persichetti
Celebration *	John Huggler #

Premiere Performance

Theme and Fantasia *   Armand Russell
Helix *   Warren Benson

Harvey Phillips, Tuba
Premiere Performance

Note: * indicates Ithaca High School Band commissioned work.
# indicates Composer-in-Residence with Boston Symphony Orchestra

The Greensboro (North Carolina) High School Band did not have a formal commissioning works project. However, band director Herb Hazelman was able to persuade Edward Benjamin, a Southern industrialist who spent part of each year in Greensboro, to contribute the money needed to commission three works for his high school band. He commissioned Gunther Schuller, who composed *Meditation* in 1963, Lukas Foss, who wrote *Stillscape* in 1965, and M. Thomas Cousins (composer-in-residence for the city of Greensboro) who composed four works for the Greensboro High School Band between 1960 and 1964.

During the mid-1960s Hazelman also led the American Bandmasters Association's Ostwald Composition Competition Committee. As such, he offered composers, who did not win the competition but received "honorable mention," an invitation and monetary award to come to Greensboro and conduct the premiere of their work with his high school band. As a result, Donald White's *Dichotomy* and Ulysses Kay's *Concert Sketches for Band* were given their world premieres by the Greensboro High School Band in 1965 and 1966, respectively.

From 1960 to 1962, John Barnes Chance was the MENC/Ford Foundation Composer-in-Residence in the Greensboro Public Schools. His first work for the high school band was premiered as *Nocturne and Dance* on November 6, 1960. Later he revised the work and gave it a new name, *Incantation and Dance*. This version of the piece was premiered on March 23, 1961. Band directors responded enthusiastically to the piece and it was soon being performed by hundreds of wind bands/ensembles throughout the country. Between 1960 and 1963, the Greensboro High School Band premiered six works by John Barnes Chance. Hazelman's "informal" commissioning works project produced twenty-two new works for high school band between 1960 and 1968.

In 1965, the North Hills High School Symphony Band of Pittsburgh, Pennsylvania, directed by Warren Mercer, began commissioning works. It has since commissioned at least one work every year. It is now the longest-running high school band commissioning works project in the United States.

ENDNOTES

1 "The Best in Band Music," *The Instrumentalist* 13 (August 1958): 74–76.

2 Raymond Dvorak, "International Band Score," *The Instrumentalist* 7 (October 1952): 12.

3 Ibid.

4 William D. Revelli, "Report on International Instrumentation," in *The College and University Band*, Whitwell and Ostling, eds., 87.

5 Bernard Fitzgerald, "Trends in Contemporary Band Music," *The Instrumentalist* 15 (September 1960): 53.

6 Keith Wilson, "Instrumentation is the Composer's Prerogative," *The Instrumentalist* 18 (October 1963): 85.

7 Donald O. Johnson, "Composing for the Wind Band," *The Instrumentalist* 20 (May 1966): 57.

8 Hunsberger, "The Wind Ensemble Concept."

9 Jennifer DeLapp, "Copland for Winds," National Public Radio NPR Online, 2000, accessed May 15, 2018, https://www.npr.org/programs/specials/copland/notes.html.

10 Andy Pease, "Emblems by Aaron Copland," Wind Band Literature: A Conductor's Perspective, 2012, accessed May 15, 2018, http://windliterature.org/2012/09/05/emblems-by-aaron-copland.

11 Aaron Copland, *Emblems* (Boosey & Hawkes, 1965), Foreword to the full score.

12 Keith Wilson, "A Brief Glance Backward in CBDNA's 25th Anniversary Year," in *The College and University Band*, Whitwell and Ostling, eds., 34.

13 College Band Directors National Association (CBDNA) National Conference Book of Proceedings (1967), 145–146.

14 William A. Schaefer, "The Emerging Band Repertoire," in *The College and University Band*, Whitwell and Ostling, eds., 64–65.

15 Andy Pease, "The Leaves Are Falling by Warren Benson," Wind Band Literature: A Conductor's Perspective, 2012, accessed May 15, 2018, http://windliterature.org/2013/10/18/the-leaves-are-falling-by-warren-benson.

16 Donald Hunsberger, "A Discussion with Warren Benson—*The Leaves are Falling*," *CBDNA Journal* 1 (Spring 1984): 7.

17 Karel Husa, *Music for Prague 1968* (Associated Music Publishers, 1969), Foreword to the full score.

18 John von Rhein, "Leinsdorf rekindles the political drama within "Prague 1968," *The Chicago Tribune* (December 13, 1986), 16.

19 Leslie Bassett, *Designs, Images and Textures: Five Pieces for Concert Band* (C. F. Peters., 1966).

CHAPTER 7

A Broader Vision (Early 1970s)

| *Avant-garde Music for Bands and Wind Ensembles* • *National Wind Ensemble Conferences* |

The avant-garde movement in music began around 1950 and reached the wind band/ensemble world in the mid-1960s. Morton Gould entered the wind bands' avant-garde arena in 1963, composing *Prisms*. In 1965, the University of Houston Band premiered Arthur Jordan's *Interpolations* and in 1967 the American Wind Symphony Orchestra commissioned and premiered Krzysztof Penderecki's *Pittsburgh Overture*. In Penderecki's work the conductor and players take responsibility for determining the actual shape of the composition. Penderecki provides only the basic formal and tonal structures without precise time values or durations. Lukas Foss, William Albright, Donald Erb, George Rochberg, Herbert Bielawa, David Borden, and John Pennington also composed avant-garde pieces for the wind band/ensemble during this period. The works composed by Bielawa, Borden, and Pennington were written for high school band musicians when they were composers-in-residence in the MENC Young Composers-in-Residence project. For most wind band/ensemble conductors, undertaking the performance of avant-garde works was a challenging and new experience.

Herbert Bielawa's piece, *Spectrum* (originally titled *Prisms*), was premiered by the Ithaca (New York) High School Concert Band at the 1967 MENC Eastern Division Conference in Boston, Massachusetts. The work combines prerecorded electronic sounds with music performed by the ensemble. Following its premiere performance it quickly garnered the attention of band directors and received many performances throughout the country. Below is a review of the piece which appeared in the September 1968 issue of *The Instrumentalist*:

> A work must be heard to be controversial, and on that basis alone this work has created as much interest with band conductors and their audiences as any piece in recent years. Although designed to be performed in conjunction with a prerecorded tape, and not-withstanding some sound in both the band and the tape that a layman audience might describe as "weird," the composition continues to be played as often and as regularly as any new composition of the past several years. The answer would seem to lie in the fact that it is somehow "fulfilling," even to the uninitiated, and that young performers enjoy playing it and working with it. Audiences, though sometimes amused by it, are rarely offended, and more often intrigued. A near perfect blending of the two elements of sound, plus a careful plan and skillful execution ... make this both a valid and interesting work for band.[1]

Conductors had to acquire additional knowledge and new musical skills that were needed to comprehend and conduct avant-garde pieces—among them the following:

Ability to read new notation systems (graphic, etc.)
Ability to conduct to "clock time"
Ability to coordinate live musical performance with pre-recorded tape
    sounds
Ability to handle fast changing meters
Knowledge about the production of new sounds: ex. multiphonics, micro-
    tones, glissandi (sometimes on instruments not designed to do so)
Use of "body sounds"
New kinds of conducting techniques for conducting improvisational style
    music
Skills needed to deal with new elements in music performance (ex. the-
    atre presentation, etc.)

Larry Livingston, who in 1974 was Conductor of the Wind Ensemble and Symphony Orchestra at Northern Illinois University, commented on this new development in band music:

> It seems clear that there is now emerging a body of new music for wind band that contradicts, or at least goes far beyond, the formularized compositional perspective long associated with traditional band music. In this new music, unfamiliar notation symbols abound. Time, freed of metric constraints, is measured by the clock or left to the discretion of the conductor. Individual instrumental parts are uncharacteristic and often appear to be unrelated to each other. The resulting textures are frequently either impenetrably thick or sparse bordering on empty. In short, a new sound vocabulary seems to have replaced the old one.
>
> The dilemma surrounding avant-garde band music may be viewed as healthy if it leads to both a careful analysis of its causes and a search for better solutions. Although the issues surrounding this dilemma are somewhat complicated, the following points should be made:
>
> 1. While concert band music in the 20th century has changed slowly, Western art music in general has changed enormously. Pedagogical myopia, an emphasis on developing instrumental skills rather than nurturing musical understanding, and the scarcity of professional wind groups are just a few factors which have contributed to this situation. As a result, the new band music, which represents an abrupt and dramatic change from the usual band fare, is often baffling to conductors accustomed to more predictable performance routines.
>
> 2. In order for band directors to be able to deal with contemporary band music, they should be familiar with recent developments in all areas of new music. A failure on the part of band directors to pay attention to music outside of the band world has resulted in a repertorial/conceptual/stylistic apartheid between band music and music in general.
>
> 3. Band music used to be written by band composers. These composers wrote comfortable derivative music for immediate nationwide consumption. Today much band music is being written by composers who are frequently oblivious to the prescriptive band music mentality. Unaware of the implicit rules for band composition, such a composer often asks for unusual, even exotic, effects, and surprisingly enough, may write a piece for band which does not sound like a band piece.[2]

The chart that follows illustrates the differences in the kinds and styles of music composed for wind bands and other Western Music mediums (i.e., orchestra, chamber music, opera) between 1909 and 1958.

Wind Band Music	Western Art Music
1909 Holst—First Suite in E-flat	Schoenberg—Five Pieces for Orchestra
	Webern—Six Pieces for Orchestra
	Strauss—Elektra
1911 Holst—Second Suite in F	Stravinsky—Petrouchka
	Schoenberg—Gurre-Lieder
	Sibelius—Symphony No. 4
1923 R.V. Williams—Folk Song Suite	Stravinsky—Octet
Jacob—William Byrd Suite	Hindemith—Das Marienleben
	Schoenberg—Five Piano Pieces
1924 R.V. Williams—Toccata Marziale	Sibelius—Symphony No. 7
	Stravinsky—Sonata for Piano
	Varèse—Hyperprism
1937 Grainger—Lincolnshire Posy	Bartók—Music for Strings, Percussion and Celesta
Walton—Crown Imperial March	Shostakovich—Symphony No. 5
	Berg—Lulu
1944 Milhaud—Suite Française	Stravinsky—Sonata for Two Pianos
	Copland—Appalachian Spring
1951 Mennin—Canzona	Carter—String Quartet No. 1
Persichetti—Psalm for Band	Stravinsky—The Rake's Progress
Hindemith—Symphony for Band	Stockhausen—Kreuzspiel
1954 Hanson—Chorale and Alleluia	Varèse—Déserts
H. O. Reed—La Fiesta Mexicana	Boulez—Le Marteau sans Maître
	Leunning & Ussachevsky—A Poem in Cycles and Bells for Tape Recorder and Orchestra
1958 Hovhaness—Symphony No. 4	Nono—Coro di Didone
Persichetti—Symphony for Band	Stravinsky—Threni
	Varèse—Poème électronique

As Livingston pointed out, the band world has always lagged far behind what was happening in the other spheres of Western art music. However, by the 1970s composers were writing wind band/ensemble pieces in truly contemporary and avant-garde styles and wind band/ensemble conductors were performing it. "A corner had been turned" and conductors and ensembles were now participants in the development and evolution of music in the larger musical world.

In 1970, Karel Husa composed another powerful and expressive work, *Apotheosis of this Earth*. It was commissioned by the Michigan School Band and Orchestra Association and is dedicated to Dr. William Revelli, Conductor of Bands at the University of Michigan, upon his retirement, in recognition of his devoted service to music, to education, and to his colleagues. In a "note" included in the score Husa wrote:

> The composition of the *Apotheosis of this Earth* was motivated by the present desperate stage of mankind and its immense problems with everyday killings, war, hunger, extermination of fauna, huge forest fires, and critical contamination of the whole environment. Man's brutal possession and misuse of nature's beauty—if continued at today's reckless speed—can only lead to catastrophy [*sic*]. The composer hopes that the destruction of this beautiful earth can be stopped ....[3]

Apotheosis of this Earth is massive in structure and direct in impact—a challenge for conductors, performers, and audiences. As is customary in Husa's works, he employs many avant-garde compositional techniques—indefinite high and low pitches, quarter tones, etc., and voice parts spoken by the instrumentalists (later scored for chorus). Surprisingly, the work received few performances in the years immediately following its publication but increased in later years. In an interview appearing in *The Instrumentalist*, Husa recalled a disappointing experience he once had when guest conducting the *Apotheosis of this Earth*.

> I remember rehearsing my *Apotheosis of this Earth* at some school, but I noticed that it was the piece the students least liked. When conducting, you can see the interest or lack of interest, and in despair I told the performers that if they did not want to play it, we would replace it with something they liked. When they voted, only three students raised their hands, so I changed the piece. I think that later the students regretted their decision, but it was too late then. I made this decision because it was my own music; I [would] never [do this regarding another] composer's [work].[4]

In 1966, Betsy Jolas (b. 1926) composed *Lassus Ricercare*, a very unique and innovative piece for 2 trumpets, 2 trombones, 2 percussion, harp, 2 pianos, and celesta. There is not a single note in this piece that is not taken from Lassus's music. However, the composer emphasizes that the piece was not a simple transcription of any of his music. She provided the following information about the work.

[That] would only have given a fragmentary picture of this great musician—but rather [the piece is] an 'aerial' view of his whole output, one that allows us to perceive his basic drives and constants. These are expressed by means of a few characteristic elements which may be identified in the course of flight: melodic patterns, rhythmic patterns, rhythmic figures, harmonic progressions. Removed from their original context and in a way, therefore, 'de-composed,' these characteristic materials are 're-composed,' and set in a completely different context to which however, stylistically, they could quite well have belonged from the outset.[5]

A small number of transcriptions were created between 1960–74. Those below are among the best.

Arnold/Paynter	Four Scottish Dances
Bernstein/Beeler	Overture to *Candide*
Copland/Copland	The Red Pony
Grainger/Goldman	Handel in the Strand
Grainger/Goldman	The Sussex Mummers' Christmas Carol
Ives/Elkus	Old Home Days (Suite for Band)
Ives/Schuman/Rhoads	Variations on "America"
Kennan/Kennan	Night Soliloquy

Paul Bryan, addressing college and university band and wind ensemble conductors at the 1967 CBDNA National Conference, urged them to accept the challenges and responsibilities necessary to improve the wind band/wind ensemble position within the musical culture of the country.

Because of our position as leaders of college bands, we must be willing to extend ourselves beyond the seeming demands of our jobs. Although few of us are forced by our superiors to do more than tread musical water, we must get into the pounding surf! Whether we are protecting the future of the band, developing artists and appreciators of the future, or fulfilling and satisfying our own artistic potentialities, we must realize that it all depends on us as individuals. For better or worse, we are the professionals and developers of our highest standards. There are no giants to guide us—there are mostly scoffers, or worse yet, those who would ignore us. Our efforts will determine whether great composers will take us seriously or not. Not our technical proficiency but the makeup of our serious programs will persuade our colleagues in the music world to recognize us as peers. The real challenge is music—not the band in the neighboring school. We must challenge ourselves and our students to the utmost of our ability. Only by considering ourselves primarily as artists rather than showmen, as musicians rather than band directors, can we properly fulfill our mission.[6]

Robert Boudreau and the American Wind Symphony Orchestra continued to commission and premiere pieces during this time, including works by David Amram, Georges Auric, Henk Badings, Warren Benson, Elmer Bernstein, Eugène Bozza, Henry Brant, Chou Wen-Chung, Luboš Fišer, Alan Hovhaness, George Kleinsinger, Ton de Leeuw, Krzysztof Penderecki, Nicolai Lopatnikoff, Ivana Loudová, Toshiro Mayuzumi, Colin McPhee, Quincy Porter, Joaquín Rodrigo, Bernard Rogers, Ned Rorem, Carlos Surinach, and Heitor Villa-Lobos. Probably the most performed work written by the composers above, is the *Adagio for Wind Orchestra (Adagio para Orquesta de Instrumentos de Viento)* by Spanish composer Joaquín Rodrigo (1901–1999), which the AWSO premiered in 1966. The piece is a reflection of Rodrigo's desire to bring the sounds of his native Spain to life in his music. His melodic material is modal in flavor and harkens back in Spanish history not only in the Catholic chant but also its Moorish counterpart. Rodrigo was a representative of the romantic and impressionistic traditions of twentieth-century Spanish music—"an impressionistic painter of the Iberian landscape."

Of the over 400 works commissioned by the AWSO, 150 of them have been published by the C. F. Peters Publishing Company (American Wind Symphony Editions). They vary in musical styles and instrumentation; the majority of them have to be rented. Since rental of scores and parts is not a standard practice in the band world, most of these works receive few performances.

Other composers writing pieces in the 1960s and 1970s that added to the ever-growing body of wind band/ensemble literature included:

Gordon Binkerd	Noble Numbers (1973)
Eugène Bozza	Children's Overture (1964)
Alan Bush	Scherzo, Op. 68 (1969)
Alvin Etler	Concerto for Clarinet with Chamber Ensemble (1962)

Lukas Foss	For 24 Winds (1966)
Alexander Goehr	Bach Variations (1972)
Rudolf Kelterborn	Miroirs (1966)
Oliver Knussen	Chorale (1972)
Elizabeth Maconchy	Music for Woodwind and Brass (1966)
Olivier Messiaen	Colors of the Celestial City (1963)
	Et exspecto resurrectionem mortuorum (1964)
Verne Reynolds	Scenes (1977)
Robert Selig	Pometacomet, 1676 (1974)
Eric Stokes	Continental Harp and Band Report (1974)
Boris Tishchenko	Music for Cello and Wind Orchestra (1963)
Iannis Xenakis	Akrata (1965)

The above listed works by Bozza, Bush, Goehr, Kelterborn, Knussen, Maconchy, Messiaen, Tischecko, Stokes, and Xenakis are all unique. Olivier Messiaen's *Et exspecto resurrectionem mortuorum* (And I Await the Resurrection of the Dead) was composed in 1964 as a result of a commission received from André Malraux, the French Minister of Cultural Affairs. The composer wanted the piece performed in environments having vast spaces: churches, cathedrals, even in the open air, as on mountain heights. Messiaen surrounded himself with pictures of the stepped pyramids of Mexico, the temples and statues of Ancient Egypt, and Romanesque and Gothic churches when composing the piece in the high Alps. He also re-read Saint Thomas Aquinas's *The Resurrection* and *The World of the Resuscitated*. The instrumentation used in the piece consists of three ensembles: woodwinds, brass, and metallic percussion, which includes multiple gongs, tam-tams, and chromatic cowbells. For Messiaen, music was "an act of faith." In *Et exspecto resurrectionem mortuorum* he strives to express his Roman Catholic belief in the Resurrection of the Dead and the second coming of Jesus Christ.

"It was a feast—an orgy. Four whole days of perpetual singing and playing, either properly arranged in the church or impromptu in various houses or still more impromptu in ploughed fields during thunderstorms, or in the train going home."[7] Gustav Holst organized the first Thaxted Festival in 1916, which was held in the town's parish church. Fifty years later (1966) Elizabeth Maconchy (1907–1994) wrote a piece, *Music for Woodwind and Brass*, which was designed to be performed in this church. The piece begins with the trombones playing and processing up the aisle and the horns entering from the church's Lady Chapel. The opening section of the piece is liturgical in character and punctured with trumpet fanfares. Following an energetic *scherzando* middle section, the opening theme is restated and the piece ends quietly. *Music for Woodwind and Brass* lay neglected for almost two decades until it was revived through a performance by the Royal Northern College of Music Wind Orchestra in 1984.

The Continental Harp and Band Report (1974–75) by Eric Stokes (1930–1999) is a unique work! It was commissioned by the Minnesota Symphony Orchestra for the American Bicentennial Celebration in 1976. Its title is a broad play on words. "The artist uses a harp and 'band' (orchestra without strings) to 'harp' on various aspects of American life and culture (movement titles include "No Deposit— No Return;" "Watergate Galop;" "Revolution, An American Birth-Wright, A Bicentennial Meditation"). The piece is a musical 'report' that is as sharp and stinging as the 'report' of a Continental musket. To express his message with such immediacy, the composer [used] a wide variety of extra-musical devices. The score is punctuated with poetry and philosophy; the musicians beat upon their instruments and hold them aloft; there is even a moment of pantomime."[8]

When Stokes was trying to decide what kind of piece to write for the Minnesota Symphony Orchestra commission, the idea of composing a piece for winds, brass, and percussion intrigued him. He wrote:

> It offered an opportunity to turn the manner and skills of the symphonic wind ensemble (essentially European in their traditions and basic repertoire) to the service of a thoroughly American impulse. With that in mind, I determined to write in the spirit of those early American "Miscellanies," "Songsters," "minstrels," "Harmonys," and "Tunebooks" that constitute such an important part of our musical tradition.[9]

Musical America described Stokes's piece as "one of the damnedest conglomerations of things and stuff ever assembled . . . a work of live fantasy and humor, poetic evocation, rich imagery, and freewheeling exuberance."[10] The work is challenging, satirical and provocative.

The programs, below, contain both selectively orchestrated and fully orchestrated wind band/ensemble works. Most are quite long. Programs containing many short pieces (see those at the beginning of Chapter 6) were being replaced by ones with fewer, but longer works.

Hartt Symphonic Wind Ensemble
Donald Mattran, Conductor
March 18, 1969

Strauss—Suite for 13 Wind Instruments, Op. 4
Franchetti—Chimaera for Cello and Wind Ensemble
Lanza—Interferences II
Husa—Music for Prague 1968

San Fernando Valley State College Symphonic Wind Ensemble
David Whitwell, Conductor
November 20 & 21, 1970

Triebensee—"Echo" Partita, for two wind ensembles
Mailman—Alarums
Grainger—Lincolnshire Posy
Salieri—Music for a Temple of the Night
Orrego-Salas—Concerto for Wind Orchestra, Op. 53
Hindemith—Symphony in B-flat

New England Conservatory Wind Ensemble
Frank L. Battisti, Conductor
November 18, 1971

Stölzel/Rogers—Concerto Grosso a Quattro Chori
Dvořák—Serenade in d minor, Op. 44
Gabrieli—Sonata XIX à 15
Stravinsky—Octet for Wind Instruments
Husa—Music for Prague 1968

A "List of Recommended Published Band Music" was included in the 1971 CBDNA National Conference Book of Proceedings. Of the 318 original works of various kinds and styles included on this list, all but four were for the full wind band instrumentation. It is surprising that a recommended list of works, compiled by such a prestigious college band association, would not include more of the many excellent selectively instrumented wind works, available at the time.[11] However, these works were not omitted by conductor Kenneth Moore on the programs he conducted with the Oberlin Wind Ensemble during the 1971–72 season. The eighteen works on these programs were of varying size and instrumentation and composed by some of the world's great composers. The make-up of the ensemble performing them consisted of thirty woodwind, brass, and percussion players, plus individual string players, and two pianists (programs on next page).

Oberlin Wind Ensemble
Kenneth Moore, conductor
1970-71 Season

October 14, 1971

Music for the Royal Fireworks	G. F. Handel
Elegy for J.F.K.	I. Stravinsky
Berseuses du Chat	
Pastorale	
La Création du monde	D. Milhaud
Concert Music for Wind Orchestra, Op. 41	P. Hindemith

December 6, 1971

Octet in F for Wind Instruments	F. J. Haydn
Octandre	E. Varèse
Concert Music for Piano, Brass, and Two Harps, Op. 49	P. Hindemith
Symphonies of Wind Instruments	I. Stravinsky

Tour (January 14–20, 1972)

Serenade in d minor, Op. 44	A. Dvořák
Concert Music for Piano, Brass, and Two Harps, Op. 49	P. Hindemith
Déserts	E. Varèse
La Création du monde	D. Milhaud

February 25, 1972

Octet in C minor, K. 388	W. A. Mozart
Sonata for Two Pianos and Percussion	B. Bartók
Déserts	E. Varèse

April 13, 1972

Septet for Wind Instruments	P. Hindemith
Chamber Concerto for Piano, Violin, and Thirteen Wind Instruments	A. Berg
Musen Sicilien: for Chorus, Two Pianos and Wind Instruments	H. W. Henze[12]

In contrast to the programs performed by the Oberlin Wind Ensemble, as well as by other ensembles such as the Hartt Symphonic Wind Ensemble, San Fernando State College Symphonic Wind Ensemble, and New England Conservatory Wind Ensemble, there were many ensembles performing programs that were "mixed bags" of different kinds and styles of music. A symphony by Persichetti or

Hindemith might be followed by a Leroy Anderson piece and/or a medley of tunes from a Broadway musical. The format of these concerts often resembled that of a variety show. Whereas orchestra concertgoers expected to be intellectually and emotionally stimulated by the music they heard, band concertgoers seemed to be content to just "listen to the band" and be entertained.

By the early 1970s, there were an increasing number of college and university wind band/ensemble conductors who were committed to advancing the medium into the mainstream of American musical art. In a letter to the editor in the October 1970 issue of *The Instrumentalist*, H. Robert Reynolds, then Director of Bands at the University of Wisconsin, stated, "... many of us ... are working (and I believe succeeding) to ... shift the role of the university band from a provider of 'situational' music to a medium for the performance of music of aesthetic worth."[13]

Frank L. Battisti organized and hosted the first National Wind Ensemble Conference at the New England Conservatory in Boston, Massachusetts, on February 12–14, 1970. The conference provided conductors, composers, and publishers with an opportunity to meet and discuss issues of mutual concern and listen to performances of new works for wind ensemble. During the three-day event Frederick Fennell, Robert Boudreau, Donald Hunsberger, Gunther Schuller, James Neilson, Frank Battisti, and Willis Traphagen conducted reading sessions of new works; composers Leslie Bassett, Warren Benson, and Karel Husa talked about their newest works, and inventor Robert Moog demonstrated his new instrument—the Moog Synthesizer. Looking back on the inaugural National Wind Ensemble Conference, Frederick Fennell wrote,

> As the Eastman group was actually born, some who had read my initial letter to composers were urging me to establish a formal association, in the image, I presume, of those alphabetically lettered organizations that so dominate all educational musical life in this country. But this was never my need in what I grew to know at Rochester. In 1954 we had a one-day gathering like this and in the Hanson tradition of that school, it was called a symposium. But I resisted all moves at organizing.
>
> I like the loose, unstructured, non-political format established at the start by Frank Battisti in the first of these [conferences] at the New England Conservatory, and which all who have hosted [one] since have continued. I like it because it is simply and purely dedicated to the

re-creation of musical ideas and the unfettered performance for the scrutiny of musicians and listeners.[14]

The works read and rehearsed at the first National Wind Ensemble Conference included:

Leslie Bassett	Designs, Images and Textures
	Nonet for Winds, Brass and Piano
Karel Husa	Music for Prague 1968
	Music for Brass Quintet and Strings
Alan Hovhaness	Symphony No. 4
Krzysztof Penderecki	Pittsburgh Overture
J. S. Bach/Hunsberger	Passacaglia and Fugue in c minor
Dmitri Shostakovich/ Hunsberger	Festive Overture, Op. 96
Warren Benson	The Leaves Are Falling
	The Mask of Night
	The Solitary Dancer
Gunther Schuller	Meditation
	Diptych for Brass Quintet and Band
Toshiro Mayuzumi	Concerto for Percussion and Wind Orchestra
Willis Traphagen	Patterns for Wind Orchestra
Charles Gross	Alle Psallite
Armand Russell	Symphony in Three Images

At conference reading sessions composers interjected comments about their works and scholars and artists presented informative sessions on topics ranging from "Mozart's *Serenade in E-flat, K. 375*" (Raphael Druian) to "Contemporary Techniques and Performance Practices" (Arthur Weisberg). Composers and conductors also met with representatives of publishing companies, including Kurt Michaelis representing C. F. Peters, Inc. and the American Wind Symphony Editions; Lewis Roth, representing MCA and the MCA Symphonic Wind Ensemble Editions; Earl Wilhoite of Shawnee Press; Stewart Pope of Boosey & Hawkes; and Arnold Broido of the Theodore Presser Company to discuss issues concerning the publication of new contemporary wind ensemble works.

A special award was presented to Frederick Fennell by the New England Conservatory. The inscription on the award read in part:

The New England Conservatory, Gunther Schuller, President … is pleased to honor Frederick Fennell for his service to American music … for his initiative in founding and development of a uniquely American orchestra instrument, the wind ensemble ... this citation is awarded to Frederick Fennell for his sustained excellence as conductor, teacher and pioneer in American music.

Fennell also received awards from Boosey & Hawkes, the Ludwig Drum Company, C. G. Conn Corporation, the Avedis Zildjian Company, and Crest and Mercury Records.

National Wind Ensemble Conferences continued to be held every year from 1970 through 1977—in 1970 and 1971 at the New England Conservatory; in 1972 at the Eastman School of Music; in 1973 at the University of Wisconsin; in 1974 at the University of Illinois; in 1975 at University of California at Northridge; in 1976 at Yale University; and in 1977 at Northern Illinois University.

The following musicians (composers, conductors, performers, and scholars) participated in these conferences:

Composers

Robert Ceely	Les Thimmig
Norman Dinerstein	Gordon Binkerd
Donald Martino	Paul Zoom
Daniel Pinkham	William Hill
Gunther Schuller	Robert Morris
Alec Wilder	Krzysztof Penderecki
Sydney Hodkinson	Donald Erb
Alan Stout	Frank McCarty
Russell Peck	

Conductors

Frank L. Battisti	Robert Gray
Frederick Fennell	Jack Williamson
Donald Hunsberger	Larry Curtis
H. Robert Reynolds	Ronald Johnson
David Whitwell	Robert Wojciak
John Paynter	James Sinclair
Henry Romersa	Eugene Corporon
Norbert Buskey	Larry Livingston
Keith Brion	

Performers/Scholars

John Heiss	Keith Wilson
Harvey Phillips	Keith Brion
Soulima Stravinsky	Raphael Druian

Robert Bloom
John Kirkpatrick
Arthur Weisberg

Ron Grun
Peter Middleton
Elwood Smith

**Ensembles that performed at
National Wind Ensemble Conferences**

New England Conservatory Wind Ensemble
Greater Boston Youth Wind Ensemble
Eastman Wind Ensemble
Eastman Symphony Band
Greater Rochester Youth Wind Ensemble
Northwestern University Wind Ensemble
University of Wisconsin Chamber Singers
University of Wisconsin Wind Ensemble
University of Illinois Wind Ensemble
California State University, Northridge, Singers
California State University, Northridge, Wind Ensemble
California State University, Northridge, Orchestra
California State University, Long Beach, Symphonic Wind Ensemble
California State University, Los Angeles, Wind Ensemble
Modesto College Wind Symphony
University of Southern California Wind Symphony
Villa Park (CA) High School Wind Ensemble
Western States Junior College Honor Wind Ensemble
New England Chamber Orchestra
Yale University Ensembles and Concert Band
Netherlands Wind Ensemble
Blackearth Percussion Group
Illinois Chamber Orchestra
Northwestern University Wind Octet
Northern Illinois University Concert Choir
Northern Illinois University Symphony Orchestra
Northern Illinois University Wind Ensemble
Wheeling (IL) High School Wind Symphony

One of the important offshoots of the National Wind Ensemble Conference was the establishment of the National Center for the Symphonic Wind Ensemble at the Eastman School of Music in Rochester, New York, which was started in 1973. Its mission was/is to establish a comprehensive collection of scores, recordings, and reference materials and to document and disseminate all matters pertaining to the repertoire, history, and concepts of performance of the symphonic wind ensemble and the wind band at large. Donald Hunsberger was designated to be the Executive Secretary of the Center. The members of its Advisory Council were Frank Battisti (New England Conservatory), Warren Benson (Eastman School of Music), Richard Franko Goldman (Goldman Band and Peabody Conservatory of Music), Vincent Persichetti (Juilliard School of Music and Elkan-Vogel music publishers), Ruth Watanabe (Librarian, Sibley Music Library, Eastman School of Music), and Edward Waters (Chief, Music Division, Library of Congress).

In 1973, a group of high school band directors expressed a desire to organize a conference to investigate how the wind ensemble concept regarding literature and performance might be incorporated into a traditional high school band program. A year later, in 1974, the First National High School Wind Ensemble Conference was held at Hewlett High School on Long Island. Stephen Work, Hewlett Wind Ensemble director, hosted the conference and David Amram, Frank Battisti, Warren Benson, Mario Di Bonaventura, Frederick Fennell, Donald Hunsberger, Martin Mailman, and James Petercsak were the guest conductors and composers. Clinic sessions focused on score study, rehearsal/coaching procedures, and contemporary/avant-garde compositions for young instrumentalists.

Two years later (1976) a second National High School Wind Ensemble Conference was held at East Williamsville (New York) High School. Fennell, Hunsberger, and Battisti once again served as guest conductors/clinicians and Sydney Hodkinson was the featured composer.

The expanding number of wind ensembles on college/university campuses prompted CBDNA to add a Wind Ensemble Committee to its standing committees structure in 1974. Most of the conductors appointed to this committee were also active participants in National Wind Ensemble Conferences. By the time Frank Battisti became president of CBDNA in 1979, the objectives of CBDNA and the National Wind Ensemble Conference were very similar—in a sense, they became "two sides of the same coin." As a result, National Wind Ensemble Conferences were ended.

Frank Battisti founded the first Metro/Regional Youth Wind Ensemble in the United States at the New England Conservatory in 1970—the Massachusetts Youth Wind Ensemble (MYWE). For the past 48 years this ensemble has provided opportunities for outstanding New England area high school woodwind, brass, and percussion players to perform music of exceptional quality for small and large wind ensembles. Similar ensembles were soon formed in towns and cities throughout the United States including Rochester, New York, Milwaukee, Wisconsin, Ann Arbor, Michigan, and Atlanta, Georgia.

* * * * * * * * * *

In the 1950s, there was a body of works that both college/university and high school bands could and did perform. Through the "sharing of a common repertoire" a strong and important relationship developed between these two levels of bands. However, in the late 1960s, the attention of college wind band/ensemble conductors turned to elevating the quality of wind band/ensemble music. They commissioned and performed works that were more sophisticated, complex, and technically challenging—too difficult for many high school bands to play. Gradually band literature developed at two different levels—one for college and university bands and one for school bands. The loss of a "shared common repertoire" diminished the strong relationship that had existed between these two constituencies and weakened the influence exerted by college/university wind band/ensemble directors on school band development.

ENDNOTES

1   [John Paynter], "New Music Reviews," *The Instrumentalist* 23 (September 1968): 102.

2   Larry Livingston, "Band Music: A New Horizon," *The Instrumentalist* 28 (May 1974): 82.

3   Karel Husa, *Apotheosis of This Earth* (Associated Music Publishers, 1971), Note in full score.

4   Harvey Phillips, "Karel Husa: Musician from Prague," *The Instrumentalist* 47 (September 1992): 29.

5   Betsy Jolas, *Lassus Ricercare* (Heugel & Co., 1972), Foreword.

6   Paul R. Bryan, "Band Literature Developed by Band Associations," in *The College and University Band*, Whitwell and Ostling, eds., 49–50.

7   Gustav Holst in a letter to W. G. Whittaker, quoted in *Gustav Holst*, by Imogen Holst (Oxford University Press, 1938), 47.

8   Eric Stokes, *The Continental Harp and Band Report*, Louisville Orchestra, First Edition Records LS760, Liner notes by Marshall A. Portnay.

9 Ibid.

10 Ibid.

11 College Band Directors National Association (CBDNA) National Conference Book of Proceedings (1971), 33–52.

12 Kenneth Moore, "The Oberlin Wind Ensemble," *The Instrumentalist* 26 (February 1972): 27.

13 H. Robert Reynolds, "Letters from Readers: Re: CBDNA (Bowles) Position," *The Instrumentalist* 32 (September 1977): 44.

14 Hunsberger, "The Wind Ensemble Concept," 29.

CHAPTER 8

Continued Expansion and New Connections (1975–1989)

> *Works by Pulitzer Prize and Grawemeyer Award Composers • Defining the Repertoire • Important Commissions and Premieres • Transcriptions • Founding of World Association of Symphonic Bands and Ensembles • Wind Works of "Artistic Merit" • "Windworks" Broadcasts*

Four Pulitzer Prize winning composers were commissioned to write wind ensemble pieces between 1977 and 1985: Joseph Schwantner, Mario Davidovsky, Gunther Schuller, and Michael Colgrass.

Joseph Schwantner (b. 1943) composed his piece *...and the mountains rising nowhere...* in 1977 for the Eastman Wind Ensemble. The musical ideas for the piece were based on images generated by a poem of the same name by Carol Adler.

Arioso

Arioso bells
sepia
moonbeams
an afternoon sun blanked by rain
and the mountains rising nowhere

and sound returns
and the sound and the silence chimes

...and the mountains rising nowhere... is a "tour de force" that exploits the tonal possibilities of wind instruments (savage rhythmic drive, dramatic sustained arpeggios, abrupt soft and gentle chords, a majestic melody). It is scored for a wind orchestra of woodwind and brass instruments in fours, amplified piano, and a large complement of percussion instruments, including two gongs struck and immersed in water and vibraphones played with string bass bows, as well as seven crystal glasses (played by the oboists). The work includes sounds that had never been heard before in wind band/ensemble pieces (ex. woodwind and brass players sing like a "celestial choir" and whistle).

Schwantner composed another work for wind ensemble in 1980, *From a Dark Millennium*. The inspiration for this piece was one of his own poems.

Sanctuary . . .

Deep forests
A play of shadows
Most ancient murmurings
From a dark millennium,
The trembling fragrance
Of the music of amber.

From a Dark Millennium and *...and the mountains rising nowhere...* are both single movement pieces in which the amplified piano, supported by a huge percussion section, presents the primary melodic, gestural, harmonic, and sonoric elements and functions as the unifying element in interactions between woodwinds, brass, and percussion instruments.

Consorts by Mario Davidovsky (b. 1934) is the composer's only work for wind band/ensemble. It was commissioned by CBDNA and premiered at its 1981 National Conference in Ann Arbor, Michigan. The piece is a long, expressive adagio which is periodically interrupted by angular episodes. Instruments are used in groups to produce coloristic combinations which exploit the textual contrast potential of wind and percussion instruments.

Gunther Schuller (1925–2015) composed his *Symphony No. 3 (In Praise of Winds)* for the 100th anniversary of the School of Music at the University of Michigan. Like Mario Davidovsky's work, this piece was also premiered at the 1981 CBDNA National Conference by the University of Michigan Symphony Band, H. Robert Reynolds, conductor. It is a four-movement work scored for an enormous wind ensemble that includes 4 alto clarinets, 2 contra-alto clarinets, and 2 contrabass clarinets!! Tightly-crafted, atonal, and partially serial, it is a superbly orchestrated piece. Schuller describes the first movement's opening as "... somewhat somber and portentous ... [which develops] ... into a bright Allegro.... The second movement as ... mostly slow and serene, exploiting quartal harmonies and the more pastel colors of the ensemble.... A virtuoso Scherzo follows, in which three shiny-bright high register chords unleash—three times—the breathless running Scherzo proper.... Movement four is cast in a Rondo form in which both the main thematic material (fanfare in character) and the interspersed 'episodes' are constantly varied, either in orchestration or in substance." In conclusion Schuller stated, "My fondest wish ... is that my symphony, despite its gigantic demands, will show others what a remarkable vehicle of musical/artistic expression the modern band is and can be."

The *Winds of Nagual* (subtitled "A Musical Fable for Wind Ensemble on the Writings of Carlos Castaneda") was composed by Michael Colgrass (b. 1932) in 1984–85. It was commissioned by the New England Conservatory and premiered by the NEC Wind Ensemble, Frank L. Battisti, conductor, on February 14, 1985. Colgrass was inspired by the writings of Carlos Castaneda and his fourteen-year apprenticeship with Juan Matisse, a Yaqui Indian sorcerer from northwestern Mexico. Juan becomes Castaneda's mentor and trains him in Pre-Columbian techniques of sorcery, the overall purpose of which is to find the creative self—what Juan calls the Nagual. (Note: The listener doesn't have to read Castaneda's books to enjoy this piece.) Harold C. Schoenberg, in an article in *The New York Times* (October 18, 1969), describes Colgrass as "... something of a maverick. He will use serial textures, but will mix them with jazz, or outright romanticism, or dissonance à la Ives." The *Winds of Nagual* is a programmatic piece written in a combination of diverse styles ranging from atonal chromaticism to romantic lyricism. Colgrass states that the frequent, abrupt changes in "... styles and feelings and moods and tempos ... are indigenous to the book, where a humorous situation will be followed instantly by a terrifying one. I tried to capture these changes and moods in the music."[1] The *Winds of Nagual* has received both critical and popular acclaim, been performed hundreds of times, and is now a standard work in the wind ensemble's literature.

It received the 1985 Sudler International Wind Band Composition Prize (208 entries from twenty-three countries). The second and third prizes in this Competition went to Gunther Schuller for his *Symphony No. 3* and Leslie Bassett for his *Concerto Grosso for Brass Quintet*, respectively. The superior quality of these three award winning compositions is evidence that music of excellent artistic merit was being composed for wind bands/ensembles in the 1980s. The *Winds of Nagual* also received the National Band Association Composition Award and the prestigious Barlow Composition Prize.

Pulitzer Prize winner Leslie Bassett (1923–2016) composed a second work for wind band/ensemble, *Sounds, Shapes and Symbols*, in 1977. Its title does not reflect the "meaning" of the piece but rather suggests how to listen to it. The work is a panorama of musical "sounds, shapes, and symbols" in which instrumental colors are uniquely highlighted and carefully orchestrated. Bassett composed two additional works for wind ensemble in the 1980s: *Concerto Grosso for Brass Quintet, Wind and Percussion Ensemble* (1983) and *Colors and Contours* (1984).

Sir Michael Tippett (1905–1998), one of the twentieth century's greatest composers, composed his *Concerto for Orchestra* in 1962–63 and dedicated it to Benjamin Britten "with affection and admiration in the year of his fiftieth birthday." The composer described the piece as a "concerto for various instrumental ensembles." Its first movement is written for woodwind, brass, percussion, harp, and piano. Ian Kemp likens it to a series of "nine recitals in a row.... [Tippett sought] to write a movement in which dramatic conflict is replaced by its opposite, a kind of relaxed enchantment where events seem to mark time and yet where everything is still rich and weighty enough to warrant single-minded attention."[2] In 1983, Tippett approved the performance of the first movement as a separate stand-alone piece under the title, *Mosaic*.

Other composers who wrote their first piece for the wind band/ensemble between 1975 and 1989 included:

Loris Chobanian	The Id (1975)
Nicholas Thorne	Adagio Music (1981)
David Maslanka	A Child's Garden of Dreams (1981)
Ronald Perera	Chamber Concerto for Brass Quintet, Nine Winds, Piano and Percussion (1984)

Robert Rodríguez	The Seven Deadly Sins (1984)
Dana Wilson	Piece of Mind (1987) — *First Prize Winner of the 1987 Sudler International Wind Band Composition Competition*
Michael Ball	Omaggio (1987)
Rodney Rogers	Prevailing Winds (1983)
Guy Woolfenden	Gallimaufry (1983)
Philip Wilby	Firestar (1983)
Jochem Slothouwer	Concert Variations for Piano and Band (1987)
Tristan Keuris	Catena (1989) *Commissioned by the Royal Concertgebouw Orchestra*
Ellen Taaffe Zwilich	Symphony for Winds (1989) (later renamed Ceremonies for Band)

In 1981, John and Marietta Paynter commissioned David Maslanka (1943–2017) to write a piece for the Northwestern University Symphonic Wind Ensemble. Maslanka responded by writing *A Child's Garden of Dreams* which was premiered by the Northwestern University Wind Ensemble, John Paynter conducting, on February 26, 1982. The inspiration for the piece came from the dreams of a young girl as recorded by psychologist C. G. Jung in *Man and His Symbols*. Maslanka selected five of the twelve dreams as inspirational motifs for each movement of the work. The work is a study of balances and contrasts in which the composer exploits the color palette of the wind ensemble. In program notes for the piece, Maslanka wrote that his goal in writing this piece was "to pull the player and listener forcefully through a musical space. If it works right, all elements of the conscious and unconscious are engaged."

In the 1970s and 1980s, works by Warren Benson (1924–2005) were among the most performed by wind bands/ensembles. In 1982, the Gamma Epsilon chapter of Phi Mu Alpha Sinfonia at Michigan State University commissioned Benson to write a piece for the Michigan State Symphony Band. *Symphony II—Lost Songs* was premiered by the Band, Stanley E. DeRusha conducting, on May 26, 1983, at the newly constructed Clifton and Dolores Wharton Center for the Performing Arts. The following is included in the preface of the score:

Dedicated to those wonderful bands of my youth:

The Fisher Y. M. C. A. Boys Band, Joseph Osley, conductor. Detroit: 1935–38.

The Cass Technical High School Band, Francis Hellstein, conductor. Detroit: 1939–1943.

The Leonard Smith Band, Leonard Smith, conductor. Detroit: 1940–42.

Benson stated that the title of the piece itself has no programmatic meaning. However, the work exemplifies Benson's dedication to the simplicity of melodic and harmonic elements and his interest in resetting rather than developing material. Indeed, he said that "formally ... my music is not very tidy in an 'old style' sense, [but] rather more complicated and multilayered as real-life experiences seem to be." Benson composed two other works for wind band/ ensemble in the 1980s: *Wings* (1984) for the University of Rochester and *Dawn's Early Light* (1987) for the U. S. Air Force Band.

In 1975, Karel Husa, in response to an Ithaca College Walter Beeler Series commission, composed a work for high school band, *Al Fresco*. This was the first in the series of Walter Beeler Memorial Commissioned Pieces. Walter Beeler was the legendary conductor of the Ithaca College Concert Band from 1935 until 1973. Under his leadership the band became recognized as one of the country's leading collegiate music ensembles. Joel E. Pugh, in his Master of Music dissertation, "The Legacy of Walter Beeler," describes Beeler's contribution to music education and band development:

> Walter Beeler made a marked impact on instrumental music education. In addition to the many ways he positively influenced his students and prepared them as educators, he contributed to their music education in still other ways. He frequently appeared as a guest lecturer at national music clinics and conferences. Of the many records he made with the Ithaca College Concert Band, several were designed solely as instructional tools. Of particular importance was Beeler's six-record set on Golden Crest Records entitled, *Band Development Series*. It featured Beeler discussing many of the problems of bands and utilized the Ithaca Band as a demonstrating model for ways to solve problems. This was one of the first instructional series of record sets designed specifically for music educators. Once it was made available to the public, it became a popular instructional tool for many band directors around the country.[3]

Ten Walter Beeler Memorial Commission Series pieces were composed between 1975 and 1984.

| 1975 | Karel Husa | Al Fresco |
| 1976 | Paul Creston | Liberty Song '76 |

1977	Armand Russell	Myth for Winds and Percussion
1978	Alfred Reed	Othello
1979	Anthony Milner	Concerto for Symphonic Wind Band
1980	Fisher Tull	Concerto Grosso for Brass Quintet and Band
1981	Robert Jager	Concerto for Band
1982	Philip Lang	Tribute
1983	Roger Nixon	San Joaquin Sketches
1984	David Amram	Andante and Variations on a Theme for Macbeth

Starting in 1987, Ithaca College instituted a biannual Walter Beeler Memorial Composition Prize. The winning composers and their compositions are listed below.

1987	Paul Reale	Moonrise, A Polonaise, Early Light
1988	Frank Ticheli	Music for Winds and Percussion
1992	Warren Benson	Adagietto (commissioned in honor of the Ithaca College centennial)
1994	Adam Gorb	Metropolis
1996	Jeffrey Hass	Lost in the Funhouse
1998	Evan Chambers	Polka Nation

Cornell University's inaugural commission went to Karel Husa, who composed the *Concerto for Alto Saxophone and Band*. The piece was premiered by the Band in 1968, with Sigurd Rascher as soloist. The Cornell Band/Wind Ensemble also premiered numerous compositions written by graduate composition students at Cornell who studied with Karel Husa, Robert Palmer, and Steven Stucky. Performing works composed by young composers is an important responsibility of wind band/ensemble conductors since it provides opportunities for young composers to hear their works (and learn) as well as to cultivate and strengthen the relationships between wind band/ensemble conductors and composers. The following are among the works premiered by the Cornell University Band/Wind Ensemble under Maurice Stith and William Campbell:

Gunther Schuller	Diptych for Brass Quintet and Concert Band (1964)
Karel Husa	Concerto for Alto Saxophone and Band (1968)
Robert Palmer	Choric Song and Toccata (1969)
Frank Erickson	Chroma (1970)
Richard Toensing	Doxologies I (1971)
Christopher Rouse	Vulcan (1975)
David Cope	Re-birth (1975)
Daniel Dorff	Concertino Molto Grosso (1977)

Alfred Reed   The Garden of Prosperine (1982)
Anthony Iannaccone   Images of Song and Dance No. 1: Orpheus (1983)
Thomas Duffy   Rage Against the Dying of the Light (1979)
Steve Stucky   Threnos (in memoriam Brian M. Israel) (1988)
Jack Gallagher   The Persistence of Memory (1988)

Stith, in the late 1960s, tried very hard to get Benjamin Britten to compose a work for band. Stith recalled: "I saved money from my Cornell Band budget for three years in order to offer Benjamin Britten a $5,000 commission, plus another $5,000 to come to Cornell to conduct the premiere of his piece. He promised he would have a piece for me by January 1, 1970. When I didn't receive a piece by February (1970), I called him and he told me it would have to be the following January (1971). The same thing happened the following year (1972). When I went to England later that year I called him. His friend, Peter Pears, answered the phone and told me that Britten was writing an opera and would probably never get around to writing a piece for concert band or wind ensemble. I was crushed!"[4]

Karel Husa composed one of his most brilliant pieces, the *Concerto for Wind Ensemble*, for the Michigan State University Wind Ensemble in 1982. It was awarded the Sudler International Wind Band Composition Prize in 1983. Cast in the traditional three movement concerto form, the two outside movements are energetic and powerful, teeming with virtuoso passages for solo woodwind, brass, and percussion instruments, as well as instrumental groupings. Its middle movement is intense and expressive. A unique aspect of the piece is the seating arrangement which is specified in the preface of the score. Donald McLaurin commented on this unusual seating arrangement:

> Instead of the traditional homogeneous seating, the seating plan calls for the brass section to be grouped into four quintets. The row of brass quintets is designated to be on risers in one arched row behind the other winds. The composer also provides the remaining winds with exact locations, which closely resemble standard orchestra wind seating.
>
> Another feature of this seating plan is the location of the percussion instruments. The five timpani are located on the conductor's left, beside the woodwinds, with the other percussion instruments on the opposite side of the ensemble.
>
> The unique seating arrangement provides [opportunities] for interesting spatial effects.... [The] layered entrances create interesting colors of sound-masses.[5]

Derrick Henry in his *Boston Globe* review of a 1984 performance of Husa's *Concerto for Wind Ensemble* by the New England Conservatory Wind Ensemble, Frank L. Battisti, conductor, wrote,

> For many of us, the very thought of a wind ensemble concert sends us scurrying to the film listings. Last Thursday the New England Conservatory Wind Ensemble presented a program so challenging and well played as to obliterate any doubts as to the musical viability of this medium.... The evening's concluding piece, Karel Husa's *Concerto for Wind Ensemble* (1982), was conducted by the composer. Husa speaks with an arresting individual voice, that of a master of sonority and structure. [The] music seethes with repressed emotions that ever so often explode with tremendous force. The cathartic resolution left me shaking.[6]

In 1984 Husa composed two additional wind ensemble pieces— the *Concertino for Piano and Winds*, a "petite" piece for piano and winds, and the *Smetana Fanfare* that includes two excerpts from Smetana's symphonic poem, *Wallenstein's Camp*.

The United States Air Force Band commissioned Gunther Schuller to write a piece for them in 1989. The piece he wrote, *On Winged Flight: A Divertimento for Band*, is very different than the massive *Symphony No. 3* (*In Praise of Winds*) he composed earlier for the University of Michigan Symphony Band. As the title implies, it is a lighthearted work although there are moments—even movements—that are "serious. "Its opening movement is ... relatively short ... an explosion of color and sound.... [In] The second movement, Pastorale ... a solo alto saxophone [reiterates] lyric phrases against a delicate pointillistic [background].... The mood of the third movement, Nocturne, [is rather] somber and thick.... The fourth movement, Scherzo, exploits the virtuosic capacities of the wind ensemble [and] the last movement, Parody, is a ... wild melange of ... early band manifestations ... treated in an Ivesian 'take-off' fashion ... [that brings] the whole work to an engaging, dazzlingly conventional 'fun' climax." The last movement carries the following legend, 'With a respectful bow to Mssrs. Charles Ives, James Reese Europe, and Henry Fillmore.'"[7]

The following composers in the United States, United Kingdom, and Europe wrote works for wind band/ensemble between 1975 and 1989:

Howard Hanson	Laude (1975)
Sydney Hodkinson	Stone Images (1975)

Edward Gregson	Metamorphoses (1975)
Verne Reynolds	Scenes Revisited (1976)
Henry Brant	American Debate (1977)
John Corigliano	Gazebo Dances (1978)
Ross Lee Finney	Skating on the Sheyene (1978)
Alec Wilder	Serenade for Winds (1979)
Daniel Pinkhm	Serenades for Trumpet and Wind Ensemble (1979)
William Kraft	Dialogues and Entertainments (1980)
Ernst Krenek	Dream Sequence, op. 224 (1981)
John Adams	Grand Pianola Music (1982)
David Bedford	Sun Paints Rainbows on the Vast Waves (1982)
Karlheinz Stockhausen	Luzifer's Tanz (1984)
Joseph Horovitz	Bacchus on Blue Ridge (1985)
Vincent Persichetti	Chorale Prelude: O God Unseen (1985)
Jacob Druckman	Paean (1986)
John Harbison	Music for Eighteen Winds (1986)
Ivan Tcherepnin	Statue (1986)
Jacob Druckman	In Memoriam Vincent Persichetti (1987)
Richard Rodney Bennett	Morning Music (1987)
Mark Camphouse	Elegy (1987)
Johan de Meij	Lord of the Rings (1987)
Leo Brouwer	Canción de Gesta (1988)
William Thomas McKinley	Symphony of Winds (1988)
James Syler	The Hound of Heaven (1988)
Ivan Tcherepnin	Concerto for Two Continents (1989)
David Gillingham	Heroes Lost and Fallen (1989)
Daron Aric Hagen	Sennets, Cortege and Tuckets (1989)

In 1980, William Kraft (b. 1923) received a commission from the University of Michigan Wind Ensemble. At the time, Kraft was Composer-in-Residence with the Los Angeles Philharmonic (he had been the Philharmonic's principal timpanist for seventeen years, and its assistant conductor under Zubin Mehta for three seasons). The piece he wrote, *Dialogues and Entertainments*, was premiered by the University of Michigan Wind Ensemble, H. Robert Reynolds conducting, at the 1981 CBDNA Conference. Instrumental color is very important in this piece and various sections of the work are performed from different positions in the concert hall. The first movement, "Prelude," is constructed around the names (in Morse code) of Kraft's faculty friends at the University of Michigan. The second movement is scored only for percussion and the third movement, which is performed "in the round," includes numerous bell sounds and quotes from three Renaissance composers (Lappi, Gabrieli, and Hassler). A soprano soloist joins the ensemble for the finale of the piece in which the following poems serve as the text.

> Let not the black sun deceive you
> Let not the son of the black knight deceive you
> Let not the sun of the black knight deceive you
> —*William Kraft*

> The leaves, tree at my window, window tree,
> My sash is lowered when night comes on;
> But let there never be curtain drawn between you and me.
> The leaves shall bear their truths …
> —*Robert Frost*

Between 1977 and 1997 the University of Michigan Band commissioned and premiered seven works, all by important composers. Listed below are the composers and their works.

1977   Leslie Bassett—Sounds, Shapes and Symbols
1980   William Kraft—Dialogues and Entertainments
1981   Gunther Schuller—Symphony No. 3, "In Praise of Winds"
1984   Karlheinz Stockhausen—Luzifer's Tanz
1992   Bernard Rands—Ceremonial
1997   William Albright—Flights of Fancy
1997   Michael Daugherty—Niagara Falls

Conductor Robert Boudreau and the American Wind Symphony Orchestra (AWSO) toured the Caribbean islands in 1981 playing concerts and conducting educational clinics and programs for young players. Leo Brouwer (b. 1939), Cuba's leading contemporary composer, was so impressed by their concerts and educational efforts that he composed a work for them—*Canción de Gesta* (subtitled "For the Boat Loaded with the Future"). Brouwer's piece is dramatic and exciting—a "tour de force" for wind orchestra. Its principal thematic material is a hornpipe tune from Handel's *Water Music*.

On July 14, 1986, the AWSO participated in festivities that celebrated the rededication of the Statue of Liberty. Grawemeyer Award winning composer Ivan Tcherepnin (1943–1998) was commissioned to compose a work for this special occasion. The premiere of the piece, *Statue*, took place on the Orchestra's concert barge, "Point

Counterpoint," which was docked underneath the Brooklyn Bridge. The first movement of the piece, "Fanfare," is based on a rising fanfare-like arpeggiated figure that is developed and combined with "The Star Spangled Banner" and the "Marseillaise." The harmonies in the second movement, "Canzona: Beethoven-Gagaku-America," at first suggest "America, the Beautiful," and then are gradually brought more directly to the forefront. A slow-moving melody, rhythmically impelled by a solemnly rising drum figure, evokes "Gagaku" (an ancient music of the Japanese Imperial Court), and is intermingled with "America, the Beautiful." The music reaches its climax with "three swells of cheers for the Freedom Lady."

Three years after the premiere of *Statue* (1989), Tcherepnin was again commissioned by the AWSO to compose a work for the Orchestra's forthcoming European tour. *Concerto for Two Continents*, is a one-movement piece for synthesizer soloist and wind orchestra. In the piece, Tcherepnin exploits the variety of "sounds" that can be produced on the synthesizer, using it at times to sound like "a vocal choir, a clarinet trio, horn quartet, celesta, electric bass, or a mistuned balalaika-like piano." He mixes melodic material drawn from North American and Russian folk music—for example, the blending of "Turkey in The Straw" with "My Green Fields," or Black American with Central Asian (Tartar) folk tunes. The composer described the piece as being "... a joyful celebration of the power of music to cross borders and bring peoples together through a commonly shared world of tones and rhythms." It was premiered by the AWSO in Vaasa, Finland, with the composer as soloist.

A year after John Harbison (b. 1938) won the 1987 Pulitzer Prize in Music for his cantata, *The Flight into Egypt*, he composed his first work for wind instruments, *Music for Eighteen Winds* (1986). The piece was commissioned by the Massachusetts Institute of Technology (MIT) Arts Council and was very unique. It granted Harbison the freedom to compose a work "of any length and intent" for any MIT performance organization. Commissions seldom allowed composers to choose both the ensemble and the length of the piece they will write. Harbison's decision was to write a piece for winds, something he had thought about for a long time. *Music for Eighteen Winds* is scored for 2 flutes, 2 oboes, 2 clarinets, 2 bassoons, alto saxophone, 4 French horns, 2 trumpets, 2 trombones, and tuba and consists of two large sections, both based on the same musical material. The first section is very fast and urban; the second, more rural and metaphysical in character. An ensemble of MIT students, faculty, and guests premiered the piece in the University's Kresge Auditorium on April 18, 1986.

Richard Rodney Bennett (1936–2012) was a very versatile English musician. As a solo pianist, accompanist, and composer he contributed much to international musical life. In 1986, the British Association of Symphonic Bands and Wind Ensembles (BASBWE) commissioned him to write a piece for wind band. His *Morning Music* (1986) is a seven-movement work, played without breaks. It is scored for the instruments found in the woodwind, brass, and percussion sections of a symphony orchestra plus four saxophones, piano, harp, and string bass. Bennett drew his inspiration for the piece from William Wordworth's sonnet "Composed upon Westminister Bridge."

> This city now doth a garment wear
> The beauty of the morning, silent, bare.
> Ships, towers, domes, theatres and temples lie
> Open unto the fields and to the sky,
> All bright and glitt'ring in the smokeless air ...

As is the case in all of Bennett's music (and music-making), *Morning Music* is elegant and filled with rich colors, energy, and lyricism.

Mark Camphouse (b. 1954) composed his beautifully crafted *Elegy*, a fifteen-minute, single movement work, for the United States Marine Band. It was premiered on July 11, 1988, at a concert celebrating the Band's 190th anniversary at the John F. Kennedy Center for the Performing Arts in Washington, DC. The composer provided the following information about the piece:

> The inspiration and origins of this work are many and varied. Some of the principal thematic material originated from an earlier *a cappella* choral work based on the poem "Morning" by the Scottish writer and poet John Henry Mackay. The only non-originally composed thematic material is borrowed from the hymn "The Church in the Wildwood" by Dr. William S. Petts. Among the composer's earliest memories is his father singing him to sleep with this wonderfully simple tune.[8]

The Hound of Heaven, composed by James Syler (b. 1961) in 1988, is an evocative, programmatic work in six sections, scored for large wind ensemble. It was inspired by a poem of the same name by British poet Francis Thompson. Syler uses a variety of musical styles to create a piece that is beautifully orchestrated and dramatic. *The Hound of Heaven* received both the Colonel Arnald D. Gabriel Composition and National Band Association Composition awards in 1993.

David Gillingham (b. 1947) composed *Heroes Lost and Fallen*, a memorial tone poem, for the Ann Arbor Symphony Band in 1989. The work is based on events in the Vietnam War and underscores the strife of conflict, its potential for peaceful resolution and the sense of alarm that conflicts can stimulate. *Heroes Lost and Fallen* was awarded the prestigious Barlow Foundation Prize for Band Competition ($10,000) in 1990.

Michael H. Weinstein (b. 1960) composed and dedicated his *Concerto for Wind Ensemble* (1989) to the New England Conservatory Wind Ensemble and conductor Frank L. Battisti. Composed in a Bartókian manner, it is a three-movement work of approximately twenty-five minute duration. The first movement begins with an adagio introduction that leads into a fast-paced sonata form. Its second movement is an introspective adagio which unfolds into a large scherzo trio. The last movement is in an energetic sonata-rondo with a double coda. The *Concerto* received the 1994 Arnald D. Gabriel Composition Award.

When pursuing a DMA degree in Wind Conducting at the University of Cincinnati College-Conservatory of Music in 1985, Patrick Brooks undertook a study of Frank Zappa's music and discovered that two of his works, *Dog Breath Variations* and *Envelopes*, existed in versions for winds and percussion that were orchestrated by Zappa himself. The wind version of *Dog Breath Variations* (1978) was commissioned by the Netherlands Wind Ensemble and is essentially a lively tonal piece. *Envelopes* (1978), in contrast, is a dark, brooding work, full of thickly-voiced dissonances and chromatic melodies. These two Zappa pieces expanded the kinds and styles of music available for performance by wind bands/ensembles.

Although many new original works for wind band/ensemble were composed between 1975 and 1989, a number of excellent transcriptions/arrangements were also added to the literature for the medium, including the following:

William Schuman	Be Glad Then, America (1975) *
Michael Colgrass	Déjà Vu (1987)
David Amram	Ode to Lord Buckley (1981)
Jan Sweelinck/Ramon Ricker	Mein Junges Leben hat ein End (1975)
Jan Sweelinck/David Noon	Variations (1981)
Jan Sweelinck/Michael Walters	Ballo del granduca (1983)
Charles Ives/Jonathan Elkus	Decoration Day (1978)
John Adams/Laurence Odom	Short Ride in a Fast Machine (1988)
Jules Massenet/Verne Reynolds	Le Cid (Ballet Music) (1984)

* This version of the first movement of Schuman's *New England Triptych* made it possible for wind bands//ensembles to perform the entire work.

All excellent transcriptions or arrangements retain the integrity of the original work and display the same qualities of craftsmanship and composition embodied in the original version of the piece. Some transcriptions are made contemporaneously to their originals—those of the Viennese Octet School quickly comes to mind. Other are created in a stylistic environment completely different from that in which the original piece was composed. Sometimes this happens because the original music was composed for instruments very different from those that we have in good supply today, or sometimes simply because the work may be interesting or rewarding in another setting. A transcription can be a great piece of music if the transcriber becomes a composer of sorts and succeeds in "recomposing" a work with everything as clear and comfortable to him/herself as it was to the composer. There is a difference between inventiveness and creative genius. The latter is the stock of the composer, and the best transcriptions will be marked by its presence. Every good transcription must at least show the utmost respect for it and never degenerate into a mere vehicle for displaying inventiveness without understanding.

A *Short Ride in a Fast Machine* by John Adams (b. 1947) is an energetic and exciting minimalistic work. Subtitled *Great Woods Fanfare*, it was originally written for the Great Woods Music Festival (Massachusetts) and premiered by the Pittsburgh Symphony Orchestra, Michael Tilson Thomas conducting, on June 13, 1986. The transcription for wind band was created by Laurence Odom in 1988 for the United States Air Force Band. The work begins with steady quarter notes (woodblock, soon joined by four trumpets) and eighth-notes (clarinets and synthesizers). The woodblock is played at a "fortissimo" dynamic while the other instruments play only "forte." Adams describes the woodblock's persistence as "almost sadistic" and thinks of the rest of the ensemble as running the gauntlet through that rhythmic tunnel. The piece embodies all the usual minimalistic features: repetition, a steady beat, and harmonic language that relies on consonant harmony. Commenting on the work's title, Michael Tilson Thomas says, "You know how it is when someone asks you to ride in a terrific sports car, and then you wish you hadn't?"[9]

The Yale University Band, under the direction of Keith L. Wilson, began commissioning works in 1950. His successor Keith Brion continued and expanded the band's commissioning activity. In 1973, the Band commissioned Alec Wilder's *Entertainment No. 5*; in 1974, Henry Brant's *Sixty* and Barney Childs's *The Golden Shore*; in 1975, Jonathan Elkus's *The Apocalypse—A Rag* and Peter Schickele's *The Tribe of the Ahasueras*; in 1976, Robert Morris's *In Different Voices* and Robert Dick's *Concerto for Electric Flute and Winds*; in 1977, Cindy McTee's *Sonic Shades*; in 1978, David Mott's *Earthbound/Skywide*; and in 1979 David Snow's *Guernica*. Under band director-composer Thomas Duffy, who succeeded Brion as director of the Yale University Band, an additional fourteen works were commissioned and premiered between 1984 and the mid-1990s including Steven Stucky's *Voyages for Cello and Wind Ensemble* (1984), Jonathan Berger's *A Soweto Lullaby* (1986), and Augusta Read Thomas's *Wheatfield and Lark* (1988). In the early 1990s, the Yale University Band initiated a commissioning works project entitled "Pictures at an Exhibition," designed to produce musical works based on paintings and artifacts in the Yale Art Gallery.

The United States Air Force Band and the United States Marine Band were both very involved in commissioning works in the 1980s. The Air Force Band was particularly busy between 1987 and 1991. During this five-year period the band commissioned and premiered nineteen new works composed by William Kraft, Warren Benson, Libby Larsen, Ron Nelson, Alfred Reed, Gunther Schuller, James Barnes, Walter Hartley, David Maslanka, Georgy Salnikov, Fisher Tull, Jerzy Sapieyevski, Daniel Pinkham, Norman Dello Joio, Malcolm Arnold, John Harbison, James Syler, Robert Jager, Francis McBeth, and Johan de Meij. In 1993 the Air Force Band inaugurated a competition designed to identify and encourage promising young composers to write for the wind band. The competition was named after Colonel Arnald Gabriel, former long-time conductor of the Air Force Band. Its first winner was Michael Weinstein (b. 1960) for his *Concerto for Wind Ensemble* (1994). The award also included a commission to write another work. In 1997, the Air Force Band premiered Weinstein's *Two Elegies for Wind Ensemble*.

The Marine Band's first commission went to Thomas Knox, who composed *Sea Songs* (1980) for the 350th anniversary of the city of Boston. The Band's next commission went to Robert Jager who composed two works for the band, *Tableau* in 1982 and *Esprit de Corps* in 1984. Three works were commissioned in 1987: *The Deathtree* by David Holsinger, *Concord* by Clare Grundman, and *Elegy* by Mark Camphouse. From 1988 to 1990, the Band premiered one commissioned work each year: James Barnes's *Fantasy Variations on a Theme by Niccolo Paganini, Op. 71* in 1988, Martin Mailman's *Concertino for Clarinet and Winds, Op. 83* in 1989, and Warren Benson's *Meditation on "I Am for Peace"* in 1990. The Benson work was composed for the raising and setting of the final stone in the ceremony dedicating the National Cathedral in Washington, D. C. on September 29, 1990.

* * * * * * * * * * * *

When I became president of CBDNA in 1979, I decided to undertake a project that I had been considering for a long time—the establishment of a worldwide organization for wind band/ensemble conductors, composers, publishers, and performers. I believed that an international association of this kind could help develop and advance the wind band/ensemble as a viable musical medium on a global scale. With "seed" money from CBDNA and much assistance from both William Johnson, then Director of Bands at California Polytechnic State University, and Timothy Reynish, then Head of Winds and Percussion at the Royal Northern College of Music, an "International Conference for Composers, Conductors and Publishers" was organized and held at the Royal Northern College of Music in Manchester, UK in July 1981. Delegates, meeting daily, decided that a world association should be formed. A board of directors was elected and the World Association of Symphonic Bands and Ensembles (WASBE) was founded.

The inaugural WASBE Conference took place in Skien, Norway, in 1983. Since then, the organization has held week-long conferences every two years in various parts of the world including Belgium, United States, Netherlands, England, Spain, Japan, Austria, Taiwan, Switzerland, Singapore, and Ireland. These conferences feature numerous performances by bands and wind ensembles from different countries that perform works written by composers from around the world. Additionally, the conferences also include lectures, panel discussions and clinics presented by distinguished composers, conductors, and performers. WASBE has served as an important agent for increasing the communication and contact among wind band/ensemble conductors throughout the world. It has also helped conductors discover music written by composers beyond their national borders which has sometimes led to the commissioning of composers from another country. In 1986, I organized a consortium of United States colleges and universities to commission a piece from UK composer Robin Holloway (b. 1943). His piece, *Entrance: Carousing: Embarkation, Op. 70*, is a large-scale work for full wind ensemble which was premiered in 1991 by the Florida State University Wind Orchestra, conducted by James Croft.

* * * * * * * * * *

From 1973 to 1978, Acton Ostling Jr. undertook a doctoral research project at the University of Iowa in which he attempted to define a repertoire of "serious and artistic merit" for the college and university wind band/ensemble. The works selected by Ostling for evaluation were scored for at least ten wind instruments (excluding percussion), called for mixed instrumentation, and required a conductor for performance.

Ostling selected evaluators for his study by surveying 312 conductors throughout the country. Those surveyed were asked to nominate ten wind band/ensemble conductors who sought out and consistently programmed music of "artistic merit" and whose evaluation of the literature would be most respected. The twenty evaluators selected were:

Frank Battisti, New England Conservatory
Harry Begian, University of Illinois
Frank Bencriscutto, University of Minnesota

Paul Bryan, Duke University
Frederick Ebbs, Indiana University
Frederick Fennell, University of Miami
Charles Gallagher, University of Maryland
Robert Gray, University of Illinois
Donald Hunsberger, Eastman School of Music
Donald McGinnis, Ohio State University
James Matthews, University of Houston
Kenneth Moore, Oberlin Conservatory of Music
James Neilson, G. Leblanc Corporation, Educational Department
John Paynter, Northwestern University
H. Robert Reynolds, University of Michigan
William D. Revelli, University of Michigan (Emeritus)
Richard Strange, Arizona State University
Robert Wagner, University of Oregon
David Whitwell, California State University—Northridge
Keith Wilson, Yale University[10]

Next, he sent each of the evaluators a list of the 1,481 compositions and asked them to judge the "serious artistic merit" of each
work. The criteria used in evaluating the works were:

1. The composition has form—not "a form," but form—and reflects a
proper balance between repetition and contrast.

2. The composition reflects shape and design, and creates the impression of conscious choice and judicious arrangement on the part of the
composer.

3. The composition reflects craftsmanship in orchestration, demon-
strating a proper balance between transparent and tutti scoring, and
also between solo and group colors.

4. The composition is sufficiently unpredictable to preclude an immediate grasp of its musical meaning.

5. The route through which the composition travels in initiating its
musical tendencies and probable musical goals is not completely direct
and obvious.

6. The composition is consistent in its quality throughout its length and
in its various sections.

7. The composition is consistent in its style, reflecting a complete grasp
of technical details, clearly conceived ideas, and avoids lapses into triv-
ial, futile, or unsuitable passages.

8. The composition reflects ingenuity in its development, given the stylistic context in which it exists.

9. The composition is genuine in idiom, and is not pretentious.

10. The composition reflects a musical validity which transcends factors of historical importance, or factors of pedagogical usefulness. [11]

Of the 314 compositions selected, 158 were compositions for the standard wind band instrumentation and 156 for selectively orchestrated wind ensemble. The works receiving the highest evaluation were all original works.

Berg, Alban	Chamber Concerto, Op. 8
Grainger, Percy	Lincolnshire Posy
Mozart, W. A.	Serenade No. 10, K. 370a
Hindemith, Paul	Symphony in B-flat
Stravinsky, Igor	Octet
	Symphonies of Wind Instruments
	Concerto for Piano and Wind Instruments
Holst, Gustav	Suite No. 1 in E-flat
Schoenberg, Arnold	Theme and Variations, Op. 43a
Husa , Karel	Music for Prague 1968
Holst, Gustav	Suite No. 2 in F
Vaughan Williams, Ralph	Toccata Marziale
Schuman, William	New England Triptych
Copland, Aaron	Fanfare for the Common Man
Dukas, Paul	La Peri: Fanfare
Dahl, Ingolf	Sinfonietta for Band
Holst, Gustav	Hammersmith
Schuller, Gunther	Symphony for Brass and Percussion, Op. 16
Dvořák, Antonín	Serenade in d, Op. 44
Milhaud, Darius	Suite Française
Persichetti, Vincent	Symphony No. 6
Handel/Baines/Mackerras	Music for The Royal Fireworks
Husa, Karel	Apotheosis of this Earth[12]

Robert Hornyak of the Cincinnati Conservatory of Music conducted another research project dealing with wind band/ensemble repertoire in 1983. He studied hundreds of wind band/ensemble programs performed at (1) four-year colleges and universities offering only the baccalaureate degree and (2) colleges and universities offering baccalaureate, masters, and doctoral degrees in music. In his report, "The Repertoire of the College and University Band: 1975–1982," Hornyak identified the twenty-four most-performed works by wind bands/ensembles in both categories. They consisted of twenty original works and four transcriptions.

Shostakovich/Hunsberger	Festive Overture, Op. 96
Grainger, Percy	Lincolnshire Posy
Holst, Gustav	Suite No. 1 in E-flat
Sousa, John Philip	The Stars and Stripes Forever
Grainger, Percy	Irish Tune from Country Derry
Holst, Gustav	Suite No. 2 in F
Reed, H. Owen	La Fiesta Mexicana
Vaughan Williams, Ralph	English Folk Song Suite
Bennett, Robert Russell	Suite of Old American Dances
Milhaud, Darius	Suite Française
Vaughan Williams, Ralph	Toccata Marziale
Jenkins, Joseph Wilcox	American Overture for Band
Hindemith, Paul	Symphony in B-flat
Wagner/Cailliet	Elsa's Procession to the Cathedral
Persichetti, Vincent	Symphony No. 6
Jacob, Gordon	William Byrd Suite
Chance, John Barnes	Incantation and Dance
	Variations on a Korean Folk Song
Bernstein/Beeler	Overture to Candide
Sousa, John Philip	The Fairest of the Fair
Grainger, Percy	Shepherd's Hey
Ives/Schuman/Rhoads	Variations on "America"
Arnold/Paynter	Four Scottish Dances
Jacob, Gordon	An Original Suite[13]

In the process of tabulating data, Hornyak noticed correlations between the nature of the institution and the tendency to program music of certain composers. The works of John Philip Sousa were the most performed by ensembles in colleges and universities offering only the baccalaureate degree, and those of Percy Grainger by ensembles in colleges and universities offering baccalaureate, masters, and doctoral degrees. Hornyak also observed that ensembles from colleges and universities offering baccalaureate, masters, and doctoral degrees more frequently performed extended works and thus tended to have fewer compositions on each concert. Works by the following composers were performed predominantly by ensembles in colleges and universities offering only the baccalaureate degree:

Claude Smith
Francis McBeth
George Gershwin
Leroy Anderson
John Zdechlik
Clare Grundman
Samuel Ward
Richard Rodgers
Peter Schickele (P. D. Q. Bach)
Elliot Del Borgo
Kenneth Alford
Piotr Tchaikovsky
Camille Saint-Saëns[14]

Works written by the composers below were performed predominantly by ensembles in colleges and universities offering baccalaureate, masters and doctoral degrees:

Igor Stravinsky
Karel Husa
Warren Benson
H. Owen Reed
Roger Nixon
Walter Hartley
Ingolf Dahl
Ludwig van Beethoven [15]

Hornyak stated that the evidence gathered in his study suggests that there was not a basic repertoire of any substance common to all college and university band programs. He observed patterns of repertoire development that differed significantly between colleges and universities with only baccalaureate degree programs and those which offered baccalaureate, masters, and doctoral degree programs.

Many pieces on Ostling's repertoire of works of "serious artistic merit" do not appear on Hornyak's 1975–82 performance repertoire list. Pieces on Hornyak's list are generally for standard wind band instrumentation, technically less demanding, and shorter and/or lighter in character. Absent from Hornyak's "performance repertoire" were the Berg—*Chamber Concerto, Op. 8*; Mozart—*Serenade No. 10*;

Stravinsky—*Octet, Symphonies of Wind Instruments,* and *Concerto for Piano and Wind Instruments;* Husa—*Music for Prague 1968* and *Apotheosis of this Earth;* Dahl—*Sinfonietta;* Holst—*Hammersmith;* Schuller—*Symphony for Brass and Percussion, Op. 16;* Strauss—*Serenade, Op. 7;* Dvořák—*Serenade, Op. 44;* and Handel—*Music for the Royal Fireworks*—all masterpieces of wind literature.

A few years later, Richard K. Fiese conducted another research project to determine what pieces college and university bands performed between 1980 and 1985. Fiese sent his "Frequency of Performance Report Form (FPRF)," to 930 college and university band directors in the United States and Canada. From a list of 260 works composed by 103 composers, he asked them to identify those pieces performed by their ensemble(s) during the six-year period. Another form, the "Additional Response Form," allowed the respondents to list compositions not included on the FPRF.

The band directors' responses identified 546 composers and 1,389 works performed between 1980 and 1985, with a total number of 23,615 performances. Listed below, in rank order, are the most-performed composers and their most frequently performed composition:

Sousa, John Philip *	The Fairest of the Fair
Grainger, Percy *	Irish Tune from County Derry
Holst, Gustav *	First Suite in E-flat
Reed, Alfred *	Russian Christmas Music
Vaughan Williams, Ralph *	English Folk Song Suite
Fillmore, Henry *	Americans We
Chance, John Barnes *	Incantation and Dance
Bach, Johann Sebastian *	Jesu, Joy of Man's Desiring
Copland, Aaron *	Fanfare for the Common Man
Dello Joio, Norman *	Scenes from *The Louvre*
Williams, Clifton *	The Sinfonians
Bernstein, Leonard *	Overture to *Candide*
Persichetti, Vincent *	Divertimento for Band
Smith, Claude *	God of Our Fathers
Jacob, Gordon *	William Byrd Suite
Shostakovich, Dmitri *	Festive Overture, Op. 96
Wagner, Richard *	Elsa's Procession to the Cathedral
Arnold, Malcolm *	Four Scottish Dances
Nelhybel, Vaclav *	Praise to the Lord
Bennett, Robert Russell *	Suite of Old American Dances

McBeth, Francis *	Masque
Ives, Charles *	Variations on "America"
Gershwin, George	Selections from Porgy and Bess
Hanson, Howard	Chorale and Alleluia
Gould, Morton	American Salute
Hindemith, Paul	Symphony in B-flat
Alford, Kenneth	Colonel Bogey
Zdechlik, John	Chorale and Shaker Dance
Rimsky-Korsakov, Nicolai	Procession of the Nobles
King, Karl L.	Barnum and Bailey's Favorite
Fučik, Julius	Florentiner
Jenkins, Joseph Wilcox	American Overture for Band
Stravinsky, Igor	Octet for Wind Instruments
Jager, Robert	Third Suite
Hanssen, Johannes	Valdres
Walton, William	Crown Imperial
Rossini, Gioachino	Overture to *The Barber of Seville*
Strauss, Richard	Allerseelen
Handel, George Frideric	Water Music
Nelson, Ron	Rocky Point Holiday
Saint-Saëns, Camille	Pas Redouble
Texidor, Jaime	Amparito Roca
Benson, Warren	The Solitary Dancer
Mendelssohn, Felix	Overture for Band, Op. 24
Tull, Fisher	Sketches on a Tudor Psalm
Milhaud, Darius	Suite Française
Reed, H. Owen	La Fiesta Mexicana
Husa, Karel	Music for Prague 1968
Del Borgo, Elliot	Music for Winds and Percussion
Barber, Samuel	Commando March
Wood, Haydn	Mannin Veen
Mozart, Wolfang Amadeus	Serenade No. 10 in B-flat, K. 370a
Mennin, Peter	Canzona
Dvořák, Antonín	Finale from "New World Symphony"
Creston, Paul	Celebration Overture
Nixon, Roger	Fiesta del Pacifico
Prokofiev, Serge	March, Op. 99[16]

The twenty-two composers, marked with asterisks, above, represent only 4% of all the composers identified in the survey. However, works by these composers accounted for 57% of all reported performances.[17] It is surprising to see respected and important contemporary composers, such as Richard, Strauss, Igor Stravinsky, Warren Benson, and Karel Husa ranked so low and composers such as Leslie Bassett, Ingolf Dahl, Olivier Messiaen, Gunther Schuller, and William Schuman completely absent. Again, as with Hornyak's list of top-rated works, many of the pieces in Ostling's repertoire of works of "serious artistic worth" are absent from Fiese's list of most-frequently performed compositions.

The College Band Directors National Association published the first issue of the *CBDNA Journal* in 1984. The fourteen issues of the *Journal* (publication was terminated in 2000) contain articles and transcripts of lectures presented at CBDNA Conferences by composers, conductors, historians, and theorists. Included among them were "Leslie Bassett—*Colors and Contours*" by Larry Rachleff, "Gustav Holst: The *Hammersmith* Sketches" by Jon C. Mitchell, "Karel Husa's Contribution to the Wind Band" by Donald McLaurin, "The Wind Ensemble and Band Compositions of Darius Milhaud" by Stephen Miller, "Wind Music and the 1926 Donaueschingen Music Festival" by John C. Carmichael, "Musings for Prague—1990: Reflections on February 13, 1990" by Thomas C. Duffy, "Concert Band Music of African-American Composers" by Myron D. Moss, and "Thematic Borrowing and Musical Influence in Mozart's *Serenade, K. 361/370a*" by Bradley P. Ethington.

In 1981, National Public Radio (NPR) produced and broadcast a series of thirteen one-hour concert programs featuring wind band/ensemble music. The series, entitled "Windworks," was hosted by NPR's Fred Calland, with commentary by Frederick Fennell. It was produced by Evelyn Grimes and featured outstanding performances by some of the finest wind ensembles and concert bands in the country. The pieces included in this series represented a cross-section of wind works composed from the sixteenth to the twentieth century. It was broadcast over eighty stations. When asked what he thought about "Windworks," Frederick Fennell replied, "I hope it will encourage people to listen to music for winds in a different way than they had before. For some people, 'Windworks' [has] opened a window on a new music world."[18]

Wind bands/ensembles performing pieces on "Windworks":

Baldwin–Wallace College/Conservatory of Music Symphonic Wind Ensemble
Dwight Oltman, conductor

Brooklyn College Symphonic Band
    Dorothy Klotzman, conductor
University of Cincinnati College–Conservatory of Music Symphonic Band
    Terry G. Milligan, conductor
Eastman Wind Ensemble
    Donald Hunsberger, conductor
Hartt Symphonic Wind Ensemble
    Donald Mattran, conductor
University of Illinois Symphonic Band
    Dr. Harry Begian, conductor
University of Illinois Wind Ensemble
    Robert Gray, conductor
Interlochen Arts Academy Band
    Dennis L. Johnson, conductor
University of Michigan Wind Ensemble
    H. Robert Reynolds, conductor
Michigan State University Wind Symphony
    Stanley E. DeRusha, conductor
New England Conservatory Wind Ensemble
    Frank L. Battisti, conductor
North Texas State University Chamber Wind Ensemble
    John C. Stansberry, conductor
North Texas State University Symphonic Wind Ensemble
    Robert A. Winslow, conductor
University of Northern Colorado Wind Ensemble
    Eugene Corporon, conductor
Northwestern University Wind Ensemble
    John Paynter, conductor
Oberlin Wind Ensemble
    Gene Young, conductor
Ohio State University Wind Ensemble
    Craig Kirchhoff, conductor
University of Southern California Wind Ensemble
    Robert Wojciak, conductor
Yale University Band
    Keith Brion, conductor

"Windworks" was selected as the U.S. entry for the 1981 Prix Italia, which commended it for presenting serious music in a manner accessible to a large audience. Radio, TV, and other electronic devices should be used to introduce and promote wind bands/ensembles and their music to the general public. There should to be more programs like "Windworks."

* * * * * * * * * * * *

A comparison of the four mid-1940s wind band concert programs found in Chapter 4, pages 58–60, and the four shown below performed in 1977–1987, reveal the marked changes in wind band/ensemble literature and programing that occurred between the mid-1940s and 1987. All but one of the pieces included on the 1977–87 programs are original works for large and small wind band/ensemble. In contrast, the mid-1940s programs contain many transcriptions/arrangements and are all for full wind band instrumentation. The average number of works on the 1977–1987 programs is just over 5; the mid-1940s programs contain 11.5.

WIND BAND/ ENSEMBLE PROGRAMS—1977 TO 1987

Eastman Wind Ensemble
Donald Hunsberger, Conductor
February 28, 1977

Hill Song No. 2	Percy Grainger
Music With Sculpture	Toshiro Mayuzumi
Evosträta	Keith Foley
...and the mountains rising nowhere...	Joseph Schwantner
La Fiesta Mexicana	H. Owen Reed

University of Northern Colorado Wind Ensemble
Eugene Corporon, Conductor
April 11, 1980

Hammersmith, Op. 52	Gustav Holst
Trauersinfonie	Richard Wagner
Colloquy	William Goldstein
Kleine Blasmusik, Op. 70a	Ernst Krenek
Three Japanese Dances	Bernard Rogers

University of Michigan Wind Ensemble
H. Robert Reynolds, Conductor
November 1, 1981

A Flourish for a Festive Occasion	Daniel Pinkham
Divertissement, Op. 36	Émile Bernard
The Bear and the Nightingale	Umberto Bertoni
Partita for Brass	Usko Meriläinen
Concerto for Wind Orchestra, Op. 41	Nicolai Lopatnikoff

New England Conservatory Wind Ensemble
Frank L. Battisti, Conductor
November 13, 1985

Octet for Wind Instruments	Igor Stravinsky
Music for Woodwind and Brass	Elizabeth Maconchy
Serenade in d, Op. 44	Antonín Dvořák
Slavonic Dances, Op. 27, Nos. 1 & 7	Antonín Dvořák
Chamber Concerto for Brass Quintet, 9 Winds, Piano and Percussion	Ronald Perera
Sounds, Shapes and Symbols	Leslie Bassett

ENDNOTES

1   James Mathes, "Analysis: *Winds of Nagual* by Michael Colgrass," *Journal of Band Research* 23 (Fall 1987): 4–5.

2   Ian Kemp, *Tippett, The Composer and His Music* (Oxford University Press, 1987), 381.

3   Joel E. Pugh, "The Legacy of Walter Beeler: His Contributions to the Concert Band and its Literature in the College and Secondary Curricula" (M. M. thesis, Bowling Green State University, 1988), 25.

4   Maurice Stith, letter to the author.

5   Donald McLaurin, "Karel Husa's Contribution to the Wind Band," *CBDNA Journal* 4 (Summer 1987): 28–29.

6   Derrick Henry, "NEC Wind Ensemble Creates New Believers," *The Boston Globe*, February 18, 1984.

7   New England Conservatory, Concert of October 26, 1989, Program notes.

8   Mark Camphouse, letter to the author, October 1999.

9   Michael Steinberg, Program notes for the premiere performance of *Short Ride in a Fast Machine*, Great Woods Festival (Mansfield, MA), June 13, 1986.

10 Acton Ostling Jr., "An Evaluation of Compositions for Wind Band According to Specific Criteria of Serious Artistic Merit" (Ph.D. diss., University of Iowa, 1978), 1.

11 Ibid., 237.

12 Ibid., 155, 158, 163.

13 Robert Hornyak, "The Repertoire of the College and University Band, 1975–82 (A Preliminary Report)," Paper presented at the College Band Directors National Association Conference, Atlanta, GA (March 18, 1983), Appendix 1, pp. 1–9.

14 Ibid., 4, 8, 9.

15 Ibid., 10.

16 Richard K. Fiese, "College and University Wind Band Repertoire 1980–85," *Journal of Band Research* 23 (Fall 1987): 20–35.

17 Ibid., 37.

18 Frederick Fennell, National Public Radio News Release for "Windworks" (Washington, D.C., 1981), 4.

CHAPTER 9

An Expanding World (1990–1994)

> *Schuller Sounds the "Battle Cry" • Major Composers Compose Works for Wind Band/Ensemble • 40th Anniversary of Founding of Eastman Wind Ensemble • Identifying Works of "Artistic Merit"*

In his keynote address to the 1991 WASBE Conference at the Royal Northern College of Music in Manchester, England, Gunther Schuller sounded the battle cry for wind bands/ensembles—"Storm the Establishment!" Schuller was echoing the message he delivered to U. S. band and wind ensemble conductors at the 1981 CBDNA National Conference at the University of Michigan. Noting that the wind band/ensemble world is often isolated from the rest of the musical community, Schuller pleaded that a great effort be made to . . .

> . . . get the rest of the music world to hear [you] perform, to participate in [your] conferences and conventions, to understand what an important part of the developing musical tradition [you] are. I'm afraid this lamentable situation, that is to say this lamentable view of [you], will not change much until [you] in the wind ensemble and symphonic band world fight back. Nothing much will change until (a) [you] are able to professionalize [your] ensembles with full-time professional status (and not just in the army, navy and air force bands), (b) [you] get symphony

orchestras to play [your] best literature, and (c) [you] go even further in [your] commissioning of major works by the major composers of our time.[1]

After acknowledging the excellent work being done by many individuals, ensembles, and associations to elicit music from contemporary composers, Schuller re-emphasized the importance of asking the great composers to write music for the wind band/ensemble.

> This will take some enterprise and some money! But it will be money well spent and will eliminate the misbegotten notion by some that wind band music is music of a lesser stripe, composed by lesser composers, and thus performed by lesser musicians.[2]

Conceding that it would be a tough chore to get orchestras to play the best of the wind literature, Schuller urged that "energy and resources be committed to making myopic *maestri* of symphony orchestras aware of the richness of the existing literature for winds beyond Mozart's *Serenade No. 10, K. 370a.*"

* * * * * * * * * * *

Numerous premiere performances of new works by world class composers took place between 1990 and 1994. In 1990, *Sowetan Spring* by James MacMillan (b. 1959) was premiered at the British Association of Symphonic Bands and Wind Ensembles (BASBWE) Conference in Glasgow, Scotland. In 1991, Richard Rodney Bennett's *The Four Seasons* and Nicholas Maw's *American Games* were premiered by the Royal Northern College of Music Wind Orchestra (Manchester, England). The premiere of the latter work was at a "Proms" concert at the Royal Albert Hall in London. *American Games* by Nicholas Maw (1935–2009) received the 1991 Sudler International Wind Band Composition Prize. Even though this work was commissioned by the British Broadcasting Corporation (BBC) and written by an English composer, it has a decidedly American feel about it. For the composer, the idea of writing a wind band/ensemble piece conjured up associations with characteristics connected with life in the United States, such as energy and youth, unlimited space and outdoor activity, small-town and city life. Maw used an original hymn-tune ("my version of a Baptist hymn"), a "whiff of marching bands," and traces of jazz. The single-movement work consists of an introduction, seven connected sections, and a coda. Its melodies are unashamedly singable and its harmonies largely triadic. It is scored for the woodwind, brass, and percussion instrumentation of the large symphony orchestra, plus an E-flat and additional B-flat clarinet, alto saxophone, euphonium, and second tuba. Edward Greenfield, in *The Guardian* newspaper (July 25, 1991), described the piece as "… a sequence of dances which make up a vigorous rhythmic romp, brilliantly written for the instruments."

During the same year in the United States, Michael Colgrass's *Arctic Dreams*, a tone poem for symphonic wind ensemble, was premiered by the University of Illinois Band which commissioned the piece. It was inspired by the Arctic and by the lives and legends of the Inuit ("Eskimos") who live there. Prior to composing the piece, Colgrass lived for a short time with an Inuit family in Pangnirtung, Baffin Island, just north of the Arctic Circle. He writes of his experience, "I was fascinated by their way of life, their humor, and their sense of mystery and wonder at the awesome nature around them. To me the Arctic is like a great unconscious; therefore the title of Barry Lopez's wonderful book *Arctic Dreams* seemed also an apt description of this music." The six sections of the piece bear the titles, "Inuit Landscape," "Throat Singing with Laughter," "The Whispering Voices of the Spirits Who Ride with the Lights in the Sky," "Polar Night," "Spring Light: Ice Floating in the Sun," "The Hunt," and "Drum Dancer." Like Colgrass's *Winds of Nagual*, this work is rich in imagery, color, and drama. Music commentator Leonard Burkat wrote this about Michael Colgrass and his music, "Colgrass has created a number of fancifully titled works that defy classification and that are much less difficult to listen to than to describe. In his work, the differences that conventionally distinguish 'program music,' which is related in some way to extra-music subject matter, from 'absolute music,' in which the music itself is the subject, blend and disappear. It is sometimes tempting to apply to his music the concepts of 'concrete' and 'abstract' or 'fiction' and 'non-fiction,' or even to call them history, biography or poetry."[3]

Richard Strange, conductor of the Arizona State University Symphonic Band, persuaded the Barlow Foundation to commission 1989 Grawemeyer Award winning composer, Chinary Ung (b. 1942), to write a piece for the American Bandmasters Association. Ung's piece, *Grand Spiral* (1991), was premiered at the 57th ABA National Convention in Tempe, Arizona by the Arizona State University Symphonic Band on March 7, 1991. In the program note prepared for the performance by conductor Richard Strange, he wrote, "Dr. Ung has spent approximately one-half of his life in Cambodia and one-half … of it in America. He knows Cambodian music, the Gamelan orchestra, and all types of percussion. He is also a devotee of American jazz. I might liken some small parts of this composition to a gigantic jam session on a 'blues in B-flat' (except it's not in B-flat). There are short tunes built on pentatonic scales that flash in and out from time to time (with those little hints of jazz to intrigue the ear), many, many densely scored sections with textures and melodic ideas that are totally different, and some extremely difficult writing for the saxophones."

In 1992, the New England Conservatory Wind Ensemble premiered Gunther Schuller's *Festive Music*, and the University of Michigan Band commissioned Bernard Rands (b. 1935) to write a piece for them. Rands is one of the major composers of his generation. His piece, *Ceremonial*, was premiered at the 1993 CBDNA National Conference in Columbus, Ohio, by the University of Michigan Symphonic Band. *Ceremonial* is a monothematic composition in which an extended, doleful, sinuous melody is repeated ten times. First heard in the solo bassoon, it is subsequently played by various combinations of instruments, always with an increase in density and complexity of timbre. This latter quality is central to the design of the work, which employs unusual and unconventional mixtures of instrumental groups—sometimes in extreme registers—so that the melody is continuously transformed. Each statement of the melodic theme is separated from the next by a dense harmonic passage which serves to interrupt the forward motion of the melodic and rhythmic flow. The mood and pace of this "Ravel Boléro-like" piece gradually but deliberately moves through its rituals to an inevitably brilliant climax.

John Cage (1912–1992) composed *Fifty-eight* "for a concert band," specifically the Pannonic Wind Orchestra of Obershützen, Austria, just before his death in 1992. The instrumentation of the piece is for 3 piccolos, 4 flutes, and 3 alto flutes, 4 oboes, 3 English horns, 4 B-flat clarinets, 3 bass clarinets, 4 bassoons, 3 contrabassoons, 12 saxophones (3 sopranos, 3 altos, 3 tenors, and 3 baritones), 4 French horns, 4 trumpets, 4 tenor trombones, and 3 tubas. Hartmut Lück authored the program note which is included in the CD recording of the premiere performance of the piece.

> It was Solf Schaefer, head of music at Austrian radio's provincial studio in Graz, who commissioned John Cage. Cage, who had never been to Graz, had construction plans and photos of the "Landhaushof" sent to him and then composed spatial music for 58 wind players to be positioned in the 58 arches of the "Landhaushof." Cage wanted to conduct the rehearsals and supervise the positioning of the individual musicians himself on the spot but sadly his death on August 12, 1992 prevented him from doing this. Andrew Culver, a long-standing colleague of John Cage, and Wim van Zutphen, a pianist and conductor working in Graz, then arranged a version of the piece for performance, which was oriented according to the spatial conditions of the "Landhaushof" as well as to the experience of the "other pieces" for large bands written by Cage during his last years.
>
> In the piece every musician receives his/her part consisting of five double sheets as well as a stopwatch. Every part, which is different from instrument to instrument, contains between 64 to 71 individual notes (pitch levels), the length of which is left up to the interpreter. Cage did, however, specify duration limits, defined according to random procedures taken from the old Chinese book, *I Ching*, which he had used for decades.
>
> The outcome of the actual world premiere ... was ... more than can be described in ... technical explanation; it was fascinating spatial music of solemn, almost ceremonial severity, but also of that cheerful composure associated with all that is casually significant.[4]

In 1993–94, two of the world's best composers, Sir Michael Tippett (1905–1988) and John Harbison (b. 1938), were commissioned to write wind band/ensemble pieces by the same consortium of ensembles: the New England Conservatory Wind Ensemble, University of Michigan Symphony Band, Florida State University Band, University of Southern California Wind Ensemble, Cincinnati College-Conservatory Wind Symphony, Ohio State University Wind Ensemble, United States Air Force Band, and Baylor University Wind Ensemble.

Triumph by Michael Tippett is a paraphrase on *The Mask of Time,* which was commissioned by the Boston Symphony Orchestra (BSO) and premiered by the Orchestra in Symphony Hall, Boston, Massachusetts, on April 5, 1984. Tippett's "paraphrase" could be compared to a nineteenth-century operatic overture, in that while it incorporates some of the complete work's most important musical motifs and episodes, it is a piece in its own right. Tippett's score for *The Mask of Time* features a sizeable contingent of brass, woodwind, and percussion instruments. In his "paraphrase," Tippett's original "blocks" of solo and choral sonorities are freely transferred to wind sonorities fresh to the work—four saxophones, cornets, and tenor tubas (euphoniums)—resulting in a dazzling display of the composer's kaleidoscopic vision. This is an extremely challenging work to perform, demanding professional-level players and meticulous and thorough rehearsing in order to clarify and expose the work's complex details in performance.

Three City Blocks, John Harbison's second work for wind ensemble, is a rambunctious, powerful urban tone poem whose musical language consists of everything from Gershwin to rock music and dissonant crunching sounds. Movement headings such as "Fervent and resolute," "Tough driving," and "With relentless energy" provide clues to the intensity level of this piece. Harbison provided three slightly different "comments" about this piece between 1992 and 1995. The following is the note that was attached to the score used for a performance of *Three City Blocks* at the New England Conservatory on October 7, 1993.

> There are three blocks, each at a faster speed, each at a hotter temperature. The language is urban, the architecture is blunt and sharp. For many years the romanticism of the rural ideal dominated American arts, even as fewer and fewer people actually experienced the countryside, or pursued its labors or its pleasures.
>
> But what still exists out there somewhere as a source of renewal or regeneration, or sheer escape, the rural vision, has been replaced by the reality. We are ruled politically by the suburbs, which are neither here nor there, but we are haunted, challenged, terrorized, and energized by the city. So the composer who wants to deal with live material opens his ears to the sounds of downtown. These sounds cannot simply be transcribed. They must be somehow essentialized—made to stand for more.

The grand expanses of the American wind orchestra, one of our most abundant and flexible resources, seems a good place to explore both the jangle and the clarity of this powerful urban experience. *Three City Blocks* should suggest places we have been, places we would like to be, places we might be afraid to be.[5]

Below is the composer's final program note which is included in the 1995 published score of the work:

Over the radio, in the early fifties, came sounds played by bands in hotels and ballrooms; now distant memories that seemed to a seventh-grade, small-town, late-night, listener like the true pulse of giant imagined cities.

Years later, these sounds—layered with real experience of some of their places of origin; magnified, distorted, idealized and destabilized—came into contact with other sounds, some of recent origin, and resulted in these celebratory, menacing, *Three City Blocks*, completed in the fall of 1991 at Nervi, near Genoa, on the Mediterranean coast of Italy.[6]

Composer Thea Musgrave (b. 1928) was born in Scotland. Her works, in various styles, have been performed many times and have earned her praise and appreciation from both critics and audiences. In 1993, she received a commission from the British Association of Symphonic Bands and Wind Ensembles to compose a concerto for marimba and wind orchestra. The result was *Journey Through a Japanese Landscape* (1993–94) which was premiered at the 1994 BAS-BWE Conference with Evelyn Glennie as the marimba soloist.

Journey Through a Japanese Landscape is a four-movement work (based on a series of haiku) which represents an emotional journey through the four seasons. In the first movement, Musgrave creates a gently undulating spring sea which serves as a background for the free, improvisatory character of the skylark (solo marimba). The second movement (summer) recalls glorious dreams of ancient warriors (march for brass instruments) which, after a violent "musical" storm, is echoed on the solo marimba. In the third movement, an autumnal fog envelopes a colossal Buddha, a lonely watcher sounds "one gong after another," and a cricket (woodblocks, temple blocks, slap strokes on the marimba) is asked to "act as a grave keeper." In the final movement, glass wind chimes introduce the frozen winter landscape, sleet and snow builds to a big storm—then silence, followed by echoes of the first movement suggesting the return of spring and thus rebirth. Anthony Burton, critic of *The Musical Times* (London) wrote, "… there is an eastern meditative quality in much of the music, often expressed in floating free-time textures, which should make it an especially useful addition to two predominantly hard-edged repertoires, those of solo percussionists and of symphonic wind ensembles."

Nikos Skalkottas (1904–1949) is best known for his numerous twelve-tone orchestral works and concerti. However, he was also an avid collector of Greek folk and dance music—the Bartók of Greece. According to his countryman, conductor Dimitri Mitropoulos, Schoenberg considered Skalkottas as second only to Berg among the musicians with whom he had worked. In 1933–36 Skalkottas composed a series of thirty-six dances for symphony orchestra. Four years later (1940–42) he arranged nine of them for a Greek military band. It appears that they were never performed since the Skalkottas Archives in Greece contains only the manuscript scores (no parts) for these works. In 1989, Gunther Schuller, working from the composer's manuscript scores, transcribed nine of these dances for modern wind band/ensemble which were published under the title *Greek Dances*. This nine-movement suite is approximately twenty minutes in length and each movement has a unique character. The score contains suggestions for dividing the nine dances into two separate suites, each of about ten minutes in length. Schuller's edition of Skalkottas's *Greek Dances* was premiered by the New England Conservatory Wind Ensemble on October 25, 1990, with Schuller conducting.

In 1991, Esa-Pekka Salonen, conductor of the Los Angeles Philharmonic, suggested to Steven Stucky (1949–2016), who at the time was the Philharmonic's composer-in-residence, that he transcribe Henry Purcell's *Funeral Music for Queen Mary* for orchestra. Stucky welcomed Salonen's suggestion because he had always had a great love of Purcell's music. From Purcell's music he selected a solemn march, the anthem "In the Midst of Life We Are In Death," and a canzona in imitative polyphonic style. Stucky did not create a pure, musicological reconstruction of Purcell's music but, on the contrary, he recreated it through the lens of the three hundred intervening years. Even though most of Stucky's version is a straightforward, modern orchestration of Purcell's originals, there are moments when Purcell's music drifts "out of focus." Stucky's "additions" to the piece provides new and expanded images of this moving and expressive music. The work is scored for the wind section of a symphony orchestra plus 3 percussion, harp, piano, and celesta. It was premiered by Esa-Pekka Salonen and the Los Angeles Philharmonic on February 6, 1992.

Two years after he completed his Purcell piece (1994), Stucky was commissioned by the Big Eight Band Directors Association to write another wind work, this time for the fully instrumentated wind ensemble. His piece, *Fanfares and Arias,* was premiered by the University of Colorado Wind Ensemble, Allan McMurray, conductor, at the CBDNA National Conference on February 22,1995. The composer stated that "*Fanfares and Arias* [is] an alternating series of fast sections (the 'fanfares') and slow sections (the 'arias'), in which all the business of making a musical work coherent—beginning and ending clearly, for example, or signaling where we are in the 'story'— is carried out by the fanfares, while all the expressive, emotional freight is borne by the arias."[7]

Francis McBeth (1933–2012) composed over fifty works for wind band/ensemble which were played by bands throughout the world. He was also a much sought-after guest conductor. McBeth stated that he wanted to "compose twentieth-century music with twentieth-century harmonic and melodic techniques, no matter what the performance level, [is] my goal. In my writings I have purposely avoided marches, arrangements, folk songs, and other usual band fare to prevent myself from slipping back into the nineteenth century, which is such a powerful magnet to most ears."[8]

McBeth composed *Of Sailors and Whales, Five Scenes from Melville, Op. 78* (1990) for the California Band Directors Association. The piece was premiered by the California All-State Band under the composer's direction in February 1990. It is a seventeen-minute, five-movement work with narrator that is based on the five major characters in Herman Melville's *Moby Dick.* The work begins with music that depicts the expansive sound of the sea ("Ishmael"), followed by musical episodes sketching "Queequeg," "Father Mapple," and "Ahab" before ending with the climatic "White Whale" movement.

Anthony Iannaccone (b. 1943) was commissioned by the Delta Iota Chapter of Phi Mu Alpha Sinfonia and the Sinfonia Foundation to write a piece in celebration of the 25th Annual Spring Conference of Wind and Percussion Music at Western Michigan University. The piece he wrote, *Sea Drift* (1992), was inspired by three poems from Walt Whitman's collection entitled *Sea Drift* ("Out of the Cradle, Endlessly Rocking," "On the Beach at Night," and "Song for All Seas"). "Out of the Cradle, Endlessly Rocking" is set as a childhood reminiscence, told by the poet, about an experience involving a mockingbird that loses his mate, the sea, and the poet's self-discovery of his poetic voice. The second movement, "On the Beach at Night," is a reflective scene in which a father and child are contemplating a sky of shimmering stars, some of which appear to be devoured by ravenous dark cloud masses. The final movement, "Song for All Seas," is marked "like wind over waves" and suggests the mercurial energy of the sea. This programmatic piece is beautifully orchestrated, resulting in sonorities ranging from transparent, gentle chamber music-like sounds to resonant, rich and massive full ensemble textures and colors. *Sea Drift* was chosen to receive the ABA Ostwald Composition Competition Prize in 1995.[9]

Passacaglia (Homage to B-A-C-H) was composed by Ron Nelson (b. 1929) in 1992. It received all three of the major wind band/ensemble composition awards in 1993: the National Band Association Prize, the American Bandmasters Association Ostwald Prize, and the Sudler International Prize. The piece is a series of continuous variations in moderately slow triple meter, constructed on an eight-measure melody that is repeated twenty-seven times in various registers of the ensemble. The composer has described the work as a "seamless series of tableux that move from darkness to light."

Zion (1994) by composer Dan Welcher (b. 1948), is one of a collection of four pieces that were inspired by national parks in the western part of the United States. Collectively these pieces are titled, *Four Places in the West*. (Originally *Zion* was the terminal composition in a work entitled *Three Places in the West*.) Welcher's intention in composing *Zion* was to convey the feelings he experienced during his visits to Zion National Park in Utah. *Zion* is dedicated to the memory of Aaron Copland.

David Maslanka (1943–2017) wrote nearly 130 pieces, including nine symphonies (seven of which are for concert band), fifteen concerti, and a full Mass. His *Symphony No. 3* (1991) was commissioned by the University of Connecticut and premiered by its Symphonic Wind Ensemble, Gary Green, conductor, in November 1991. The composer stated that "I was asked to write a 'major' piece, yet not necessarily one as big as this [the piece is 50 minutes long].... The impetus for this piece was in part my leaving university life [Kingsborough Community College of the City University of New York] ... and moving from New York City to the Rocky Mountains of western Montana. The mountains and the sky are a living presence. Animal and Indian spirits still echo strongly in this land, and these elements have found their way into my music."[10] The *Symphony* is in five movements—the first, forceful; the second, serene; the third, fierce and bristling; the fourth a series of song-like episodes, and the fifth a lamentation called "Song for a Summer Day." Maslanka's style has been characterized as a contemporary blend of heart-felt lyricism and rhythmic drive coupled with a sensitive ear for musical sonorities. Many of his works for winds and percussion have become standard compositions in wind band/ensemble literature.

A *Movement for Rosa* by Mark Camphouse was commissioned by the Florida Bandmasters Association in 1992. The piece honors civil rights heroine Rosa Parks who was arrested on December 1, 1955, for refusing to give up her seat to a white man on a segregated city bus in Montgomery, Alabama. This courageous act sparked the Civil Rights movement of the 1950s and earned her the title, "Mother to a Movement." *A Movement for Rosa* is a "quasi-tone poem" with three contrasting sections. Section 1 evokes her early years. Section 2 portrays the years of racial strife in Montgomery, and the third section is one of quiet strength and serenity in which the hymn, *We Shall Overcome*, is heard in its entirety (fragments appear earlier in Sections 1 and 2). *A Movement for Rosa* has received many performances by both high school and college/university bands.

Other works performed numerous times between 1990–1994 were *Crystals* (1985) and *Snakes* (1990) by Thomas Duffy (b. 1955), *Gloriosa* (1990) by Japanese composer Yasuhide Ito (b. 1960), *Dance of the New World* (1993) by Dana Wilson (b. 1946), *Desi* (1991), *Bizarro*, (1993) and *Motown Metal* (1994) by Michael Daugherty (b. 1954), *Circuits* (1990) and *California Counterpoint "The Twittering Machine"* (1993) by Cindy McTee (b. 1953), *Bum's Rush* (1993) by Donald Grantham (b. 1947), and *Ghost Train Triptych* (1994) by

Eric Whitacre (b. 1970). Composers who wrote their first piece for wind band/ensemble during this period are Irwin Bazelon (*Midnight Music*—1992), Adam Gorb (*Metropolis*—1992), John McCabe (*Canyons*—1991), and Augusta Read Thomas (*Danse*—1994).

In 1991, the Glyndebourne Opera (UK) commissioned five composers to write wind serenades (Harmoniemusik) for their Mozart Bicentenary Celebration. The composers were Jonathan Dove (*Figures in the Garden*), Nigel Osborne (*Albanian Nights*), Jonathan Harvey (*Serenade in Homage to Mozart*), Stephen Oliver (*Character Pieces for Wind Octet derived from Metastasio's 'La Clemenza di Tito'*), and Robert Saxton (*Paraphrase on Mozart's 'Idomeneo'*). Each serenade was musically connected in some way with one of Mozart's operas.

* * * * * * * * * *

The Eastman School of Music hosted a conference from February 7–9, 1992, to mark the fortieth anniversary of the founding of the Eastman Wind Ensemble. The highlight of the conference was a gala concert by the Eastman Wind Ensemble conducted by founder Frederick Fennell, A. Clyde Roller, and Donald Hunsberger, the second and third conductors of the Ensemble. Those attending the conference had an opportunity to reflect on the growth and development of the wind ensemble since its founding forty years earlier. In the 1950s the wind band was considered to be a functional, entertainment medium. By the 1990s it had become a viable artistic medium.

In 1993, composer/conductor Morton Gould, President of the American Society of Composers, Authors and Publishers (ASCAP), presented CBDNA with a special award in recognition of the support college/university wind bands/ensembles were giving to American composers and their music. The Massachusetts Institute of Technology Concert Band and conductor John Corley is an excellent example of this support. For the past five decades they have commissioned and premiered over fifty pieces, all by American composers.

WASBE began publishing its Journal of the World Association for Symphonic Bands and Ensembles in December 1994. Jon C. Mitchell was the Journal's Principal Editor and Vondis Miller its Assistant Editor. The inaugural issue contained articles on a broad range of subjects, including "Wind Instruments and Wind Sonorities in the

Music of Zoltán Kodály" by Wolfgang Suppan, "The Evolution of Wind Music in Germany" by Mark Reimer, and "Bands and the Visit of the Japanese Embassy" by Clyde S. Shive.

Listed below are six concert programs performed by two bands and four wind ensembles between 1991 and 1994. They contain thirty different works, including four world premieres. Thirteen are wind band works, thirteen are wind ensemble works, and four are transcriptions. Eleven (36.6%) were composed before 1950 and fifteen (50%) after 1980.

The University of Illinois Symphonic Band
James F. Keene, Conductor
February 20, 1991

D. Gillingham	Heroes Lost and Fallen
Y. Ito	Concerto Fantastique for Saxophone and Wind Orchestra
E. Goossens/Grainger	Folk Song—Sheep Shearing Song from Somerset, England
P. Grainger	Shepherd's Hey
M. Colgrass	Arctic Dreams (World Premiere)
P. Hindemith/Wilson	Symphonic Metamorphoses on Themes of Carl Maria von Weber

Central Michigan University Symphonic Wind Ensemble
John E. Williamson, Conductor
February 21, 1991

D. Gillingham	Serenade for 10 Winds and Percussion (Songs of the Night)
F. Ticheli	Music for Winds and Percussion
D. Wilson	Calling, Ever Calling—Concerto for Oboe and Wind Ensemble (World Premiere)
P. Grainger	Country Gardens

Baylor University Wind Ensemble
Michael Haithcock, Conductor
November 10, 1992

F. Mendelssohn/Boyd	Overture for Winds, Op. 24
D. Shostakovich	Two Scarlatti Pieces, Op. 16
I. Stravinsky	Ebony Concerto
D. Maslanka	A Child's Garden of Dreams
P. Grainger	Children's March

New England Conservatory Wind Ensemble
Frank L. Battisti, Conductor
November 17, 1993

G. Binkerd	Noble Numbers
P. Hindemith	Konzertmusik für Klavier, Blechbläser und Harfen, Op. 49
M. Tippett	Triumph (World Premiere)
R. Strauss	Einleitung und Allegro (Symphonie für Bläser in E-flat)
B. Rands	Ceremonial

Lamar University Symphonic Band
Barry W. Johnson, Conductor
February 26, 1994

J. Stamp	Gavorkna Fanfare
K. Gates	Icarus and Daedalus: The Fantasy of Flight
E. Goossens/Grainger	Folk Tune, Op. 38, No. 1
M. Satterwhite	Llanto por Cristina Gomez
W. Benson	The Leaves Are Falling
M. Gould	Symphony for Band, "West Point"

The University of Texas Wind Ensemble
Jerry Junkin, Conductor
February 26, 1994

M. Daugherty	Bizarro (World Premiere)
L. Gannon	Symphony No. 1 (In One Movement)
D. Grantham	Bum's Rush
D. Maslanka	Symphony No. 4 (In One Movement)

Composers who continued to compose music for wind band/ ensemble during the first part of the 1990s included:

Richard Rodney Bennett	Concerto for Trumpet and Wind Orchestra (1993)
Warren Benson	Meditation on "I Am for Peace" (1990)
	Danzon (1991)
	Adagietto (1992)
Edward Gregson	Celebration (1991)
Robert Jager	The Wall (1993)
Libby Larsen	Sun Song (1990)
Tim Mahr	The Soaring Hawk (1991)
David Maslanka	Symphony No. 3 (1991)
	Symphony No. 4 (1993)
Dana Wilson	Calling, Ever Calling (1991)

On July 16, 1994, the band world was diminished by the death of William D. Revelli ("the Chief") at the age of 92. This legendary band-master and teacher was one of the major figures in the development of bands in the United States during the twentieth-century. Revelli began his career as a high school band director in Hobart, Indiana, where he won five consecutive national championships before becoming Director of Bands at the University of Michigan. There he directed both the Michigan Symphony and Marching Bands for thirty-six years (1935 to 1971) and became the most influential band director in the nation. He championed excellence and perfection in band performance and was a mentor to numerous individuals who became future school and university band/wind ensemble leaders.

Revelli strove to make his band sound like a symphony orchestra in its sonority and technical execution. As a violin player he was familiar with orchestra literature, its practices and traditions. This was a huge asset in the performance and interpretation of band transcriptions of orchestral music, which was the mainstay of the repertoire he conducted.

Revelli took the University of Michigan Symphonic Band on annual tours across the United States, performing in hundreds of small towns and cities, as well as major concert venues such as Carnegie Hall in New York City and Orchestra Hall in Chicago. In 1961, the University of Michigan Symphony Band traveled to the Soviet Union and the Middle East on a fifteen-week U. S. State Department concert tour which drew much national and international attention and critical acclaim.

William D. Revelli was an energetic, ambitious, dominant, dedicated, dogmatic, and tyrannical conductor, but also honest and sincere. When the history of twentieth century instrumental music education is written, William Revelli will be included among its most influential and important teachers, band directors, and leaders.

In 1992, Jay W. Gilbert replicated Acton Ostling Jr.'s 1973–78 research project (see Chapter 8, pages 134–136) in the continuing effort to identify the repertoire of "serious artistic merit" for the contemporary wind band/ensemble. As previously done by Ostling, Gilbert surveyed 356 college and university wind band/ensemble conductors to select the group of twenty conductors who were to evaluate the literature. The evaluators selected were:

Frank Battisti	Craig Kirchhoff
Eugene Corporon	Allan McMurray
Ray Cramer	John Paynter
James Croft	Larry Rachleff
Stanley DeRusha	H. Robert Reynolds
Howard Dunn	James Smith
Richard Floyd	Richard Strange
Donald Hunsberger	Myron Welch
Jerry Junkin	David Whitwell
Mark Kelly	Frank Wickes[11]

Six of these, Battisti, Hunsberger, Paynter, Reynolds, Strange, and Whitwell, were repeat evaluators, having been participants in Ostling's original research project in 1978.

Each of the twenty conductors evaluated 1,261 compositions, including the 285 works rated as being of "serious artistic merit" in Ostling's 1978 study. In Gilbert's project, 171 of these works "of serious artistic merit" were not re-selected. However, twenty-three compositions not evaluated as works of "serious artistic merit" in Ostling's study were elevated to the list of "meritorious" works in the 1992 re-evaluation. These works are listed below and consist of seventeen original pieces for winds and six transcriptions:

J. S. Bach/Leidzén	Toccata and Fugue in d minor
Alfred von Beckerath	Sinfonie für Blasorchester
Jacques Castérède/Cramer	Concertino for Trumpet and Trombone
Aaron Copland/Hindsley	El Salón Mexico
Norman Dello Joio	Fantasies on a Theme by Haydn
Vittorio Giannini	Symphony No. 3
Morton Gould	Symphony for Band, "West Point"
Percy Grainger	Molly on the Shore
Reynaldo Hahn	Le Bal de Béatrice d'Este
Paul Hindemith/Wilson	Symphonic Metamorphosis on Themes by Carl Maria von Weber
Gordon Jacob	Old Wine in New Bottles
Nikolai Lopatnikoff	Concerto for Wind Orchestra, Op. 41
Oskar Morawitz	Memorial to Martin Luther King Jr.
Carl Orff/Krance	Carmina Burana: Suite
Bernhard Rovenstrunck	Kammersinfonie für 15 Bläser und Kontrabass
Florent Schmitt	Lied et Scherzo, Op. 54

Arthur Shepherd	Hilaritas
Gottfried Stoeltzel/Rogers	Concerto Grosso a Quatro Cori
Igor Stravinsky	Ebony Concerto (1945)
Michael Tippett	Concerto for Orchestra: First Movement (Mosaic)
Kurt Weill	Concerto for Violin and Wind Orchestra, Op. 12 (1924)
Kurt Weill	Das Berliner Requiem (1928)
Kurt Weill	Vom Tod in Wald, Op. 16 (1927)[12]

Fifty-two compositions, (forty of which were composed or transcribed after the Ostling study—from 1978–1992) were evaluated for the first time and met the criteria used by Ostling.

John Adams/Odom	Short Ride in a Fast Machine
J. S. Bach/Stokowski	Chorale Prelude, "Wir glauben all'an einen gott"
Samuel Barber	Mutations from Bach (brass choir and timpani)
Leslie Bassett	Concerto Grosso for Brass Quintet, Winds and Percussion
	Fantasy for Clarinet
	Sounds, Shapes and Symbols
Warren Benson	Dawn's Early Light
	Symphony II, "Lost Songs"
	Wings
Luciano Berio	Magnificat
	Points on a Curve to Find
Émile Bernard	Divertissement pour Instruments à vent, Op. 36
Leonard Bernstein/ Bencriscutto	"Profanation" from Jeremiah Symphony
Michael Colgrass	Winds of Nagual
	Déjà Vu
John Corigliano	Gazebo Dances
Jacob Druckman	"Engram" from Prism
Paul Epstein	Matinee Concerto
Alvin Etler	Concerto for Clarinet and Chamber Ensemble
Ross Lee Finney	Skating on the Sheyenne
Frederick Fox	Polarities
Percy Grainger/Stout	Hill Song No. 1
John Harbison	Music for 18 Winds

Walter Hartley	In Memoriam
Karel Husa	An American Te Deum
	Concerto for Wind Ensemble
	Smetana Fanfare
Brian Israel	Concerto for Clarinet
Jeffrey King	Dénouement Symphonic Variations
István Láng	Concerto for Violin and Wind Ensemble
David Liptak	Soundings
Witold Lutosławski	Trois poèmes d'Henri Michaux
Martin Mailman	For Precious Friends Hid in Death's Dateless Night
David Maslanka	A Child's Garden of Dreams
	Concerto for Piano
Felix Mendelssohn/Boyd	Overture for Winds, Op. 24
David Noon	Sweelinck Variations (I, II, III)
George Perle	Concertino for Piano, Timpani and Winds
Paul Reale	Concerto "Dies Irae"
	Moonrise, A Polonaise, Early Light
Verne Reynolds	Scenes Revisited
Rudolf Schmidt-Wunstorf	Ardennen Symphony
Gunther Schuller	On Winged Flight: A Divertimento for Band
	Symphony No. 3: In Praise of Winds
William Schuman	A Free Song
Joseph Schwantner	...and the mountains rising nowhere...
	From a Dark Millennium
Richard Strauss	Festmusik der Stadt Wien, AV 133
Igor Stravinsky	Symphonies of Wind Instruments
Steven Stucky	Voyages (for cello and wind orchestra)
Tielman Susato/Walters	Suite from the "Danserye"
Kurt Weill	Mahagonny: Songspiel[13]

Listed below are the compositions rated "meritorious" and familiar to all twenty evaluators. They are listed in rank order based upon the percentage of maximum possible points each work received.

Antonín Dvořák	Serenade in d minor, Op. 44
Percy Grainger	Lincolnshire Posy
Karel Husa	Music for Prague 1968
W. A. Mozart	Serenade No. 10 in B-flat, K. 370a
Ingolf Dahl	Sinfonietta
Paul Hindemith	Symphony in B-flat
Gustav Holst	Hammersmith (Prelude and Scherzo), Op. 52

Igor Stravinsky	Concerto for Piano and Wind Instruments
Igor Stravinsky	Symphonies of Wind Instruments (1947)
Florent Schmitt	Dionysiaques, Op. 62
Arnold Schoenberg	Theme and Variations, Op. 43a
Joseph Schwantner	...and the mountains rising nowhere...
Gustav Holst	Suite No. 1 in E-flat
Warren Benson	The Leaves Are Falling
Warren Benson	The Passing Bell
Aaron Copland	Emblems
Richard Strauss	Serenade in E-flat, Op. 7
Michael Colgrass	Winds of Nagual
Ingolf Dahl	Concerto for Alto Saxophone and Wind Orchestra
Charles Gounod	Petite Symphonie
Gunther Schuller	Symphony for Brass and Percussion
Vincent Persichetti	Symphony No. 6, Op. 69
Richard Wagner	Trauersinfonie (revised by Erik Leidzén)
Anton Bruckner	Mass No. 2 in e minor
Karel Husa	Apotheosis of this Earth
Karel Husa	Concerto for Wind Ensemble
Karel Husa	Concerto for Alto Saxophone and Concert Band
Gordon Jacob	William Byrd Suite
Percy Grainger	Colonial Song
Gustav Holst	Suite No. 2 in F
Vincent Persichetti	Masquerade for Band, Op. 102
Verne Reynolds	Scenes
William Schuman	New England Triptych: Be Glad Then, America; When Jesus Wept; Chester
David Maslanka	A Child's Garden of Dreams
Darius Milhaud	Suite Française
Ralph Vaughan Williams	Toccata Marziale
Norman Dello Joio	Variants on a Medieval Tune
Robert Kurka	The Good Soldier Schweik: Suite, Op. 22
H. Owen Reed	La Fiesta Mexicana
Ralph Vaughan Williams	English Folk Song Suite
J. S. Bach	Fantasia in G major (transcribed by R. F. Goldman and R. L. Leist)
Robert Russell Bennett	Suite of Old American Dances
Warren Benson	The Solitary Dancer
John Corigliano	Gazebo Dances
William Schuman	George Washington Bridge: An Impression for Band

Leslie Bassett	Designs, Images and Textures
Morton Gould	Symphony for Band (West Point Symphony)
Vincent Persichetti	Divertimento for Band, Op. 42
Paul Hindemith	Symphonic Metamorphosis on Themes by Weber (transcribed by Keith Wilson)
Karel Husa	Concerto for Percussion and Wind Ensemble
Ralph Vaughan Williams	"Scherzo alla Marcia" from Symphony No. 8
Leonard Bernstein	"Profanation" from Jeremiah Symphony (transcribed by Frank Bencriscutto)
Percy Grainger	Molly on the Shore
Walter Hartley	Concerto for 23 Winds
Krzysztof Penderecki	Pittsburgh Overture
J. S. Bach	Passacaglia and Fugue in C minor (transcribed by Donald Hunsberger)
Paul Hindemith	"Geschwindmarsch" from Symphony Serena
Ernst Toch	Spiel für Blasorchester, Op. 39
Robert Russell Bennett	Symphonic Songs for Band
Hector Berlioz	Symphonie Funèbre et Triomphale, Op. 15
Aaron Copland	An Outdoor Overture
Aaron Copland	Lincoln Portrait (transcribed by W. Beeler)
Charles Ives	Variations on "America" (from the William Schuman orchestration, transcribed by William Rhodes)
Vincent Persichetti	Celebrations (Cantata No. 3), Op. 103
Aaron Copland	El Salón Mexico (transcribed by Mark Hindsley)
Norman Dello Joio	Fantasies on a Theme by Haydn
Vittorio Giannini	Symphony No. 3
Howard Hanson	Chorale and Alleluia, Op. 42
Karel Husa	Smetana Fanfare
Carl Orff	Carmina Burana: Suite (transcribed by John Krance)
Vincent Persichetti	Psalm for Band, Op. 53
Bernard Rogers	Three Japanese Dances
Joseph Schwantner	From a Dark Millennium[14]

Of the seventy-three works on this list, only nine were composed before 1900, twenty-seven between 1900 and 1950, and thirty-seven between 1950 and 1985. Gilbert concludes, "the 191 compositions identified [as works of serious artistic merit] in this study provide the basis for a wind-band repertoire of high quality. [They]... represent a quality of literature at least as strong as that of any other music performance medium."[15]

ENDNOTES

1   Gunther Schuller, "Storm the Establishment," *WINDS* 6 (Winter 1991): 9.

2   Ibid.

3   Leonard Burkat, Program notes for the Atlanta Symphony; Shared in a letter by Michael Colgrass to the author, January 1992.

4   John Cage, *Fifty-Eight*, Pannonisches Blasorchester, Wim van Zutphen, conductor, HatHut Records hat ART CD 6135, 1992, Liner notes by Hartmut Lück.

5   John Harbison, *Three City Blocks*, note attached to the manuscript score used in performance at the New England Conservatory (Boston, MA), October 7, 1993.

6   John Harbison, *Three City Blocks for Wind Ensemble* (Associated Music Publishers, 1993), Program Note in full score.

7   Steven Stucky, letter to the author, October 1, 1998.

8   W. Francis McBeth, *Heritage IV: The Music of W. Francis McBeth*, United States Air Force Band of the West (Lackland Air Force Base, San Antonio, TX), 1997, Liner notes by W. Francis McBeth.

9   Anthony Iannaccone, letter to the author, November 1999.

10 David Maslanka, *Symphony No. 3*, (Carl Fischer, 1991), Program note by the composer.

11 Jay W. Gilbert, "An Evaluation of Compositions for Wind Band According to Specific Criteria of Serious Artistic Merit: A Republication and Update" (D.M.A. diss., Northwestern University, 1993), 148.

12 Ibid., 177–178.

13 Ibid., 179–182.

14 Ibid., 151–154.

15 Ibid., 182.

CHAPTER **10**

The Final Five Years of the Twentieth Century (1995–1999)

New Compositions in a Diversity of Styles •
"Bandanna," an Opera for Voices and Wind Ensemble
• More Performances of Wind Chamber Works • Wind
Band/Ensemble Recordings

The number of established as well as young composers writing music for wind bands/ensembles in the 1980s and 1990s increased dramatically. Composer Francis McBeth speculated that this occurred because of "better university pedagogy, natural odds from the increased population, and finally acceptance at the university level that the band is a viable artistic medium, the latter being the most important. No longer did teachers of composition turn up their noses at the winds, but they actually encouraged students to study the repertoire."[1] Among the most prolific composers of wind band/ ensemble works at this time were Frank Ticheli, David Gillingham, Donald Grantham, Michael Daugherty, Dan Welcher, Thomas Duffy, Mark Camphouse, James Barnes, Cindy McTee, and Jack Stamp.

Below is a select list of works that are representative of the various kinds/styles of music composed for the wind band/ensemble in 1995–1996.

John Adams	Scratchband (1996)
James Barnes	Symphony No. 3, Op. 89 (1995)
Ken Benshoof	Out and Back Again (1995)
Carolyn Bremer	Early Light (1996)
Michael Colgrass	Urban Requiem (1996)
Norman Dello Joio	Fantasies on an Original Theme (1995)
Andrew Downes	Symphony No. 4, Op. 59 (1996)
Thomas Duffy	Gnomon (1995)
Nancy Galbraith	Danza de los Duendes (1996)
Adam Gorb	Awayday (1996)
Morton Gould	Remembrance Day (Soliloquy for a Passing Century) (1995)
John Harbison	Olympic Dances (1996)
Karel Husa	Divertimento for Symphonic Winds (arranged by John Boyd) (1995)
Karel Husa	Les Couleurs Fauves (1995)
Anthony Iannaccone	Psalm for a Great Country (1996)
William Kraft	Concerto for Four Solo Percussion and Wind Ensemble (revised 1995)
William Kraft	Quintessence Revisited (revised 1996)
Libby Larsen	Concert Dances (1996)
David Maslanka	Mass (1996)
Walter Mays	Dreamcatcher (1996)
Cindy McTee	Soundings (1996)
John Moody	Sinfonia for Winds and Percussion (1995)
Joseph Schwantner	In Evening's Stillness (1996)
Gunther Schuller	Blue Dawn into White Heat (1996)
Philip Sparke	Dance Movements (1996)
David Stanhope	Folk Songs for Band, Suite No. 1 (1995)
Steven Stucky	Fanfares and Arias (1995)
Augusta Read Thomas	Vivace (1995)
Frank Ticheli	Blue Shades (1997)
Michael Weinstein	Two Elegies for Wind Ensemble (1995)
Dana Wilson	The Shifting Bands of Time (1995)
Guy Woolfenden	Suite Français for Woodwind Octet (1995)

John Harbison's *Olympic Dances* (1996), his third work for wind ensemble, was commissioned by a consortium of twelve university wind bands/ensembles. The composer provided the following comments about his piece:

> When the College Band Directors asked me to do a piece for dancers and winds, it immediately suggested something classical, not our musical eighteenth century, but an imaginative vision of ancient worlds. The clear, un-upholstered timbres of the winds—not colored by the throbbing emotive vibratos of our modern string players—playing in small, unconventional chamber subgroups, constituted my first musical images. Along with these, I thought of an imagined harmony between dance, sport and sound that we can intuit from serene oranges and blacks on Greek vases, the celebration of bodies in motion that we see in the matchless sculpture of ancient times, and perhaps most important to this piece, the celebration of the ideal tableau, the movement frozen in time, that is present still in the friezes that adorn the temples, and in the architecture of the temples themselves.[2]

Olympic Dances was premiered at the 1997 CBDNA Conference (University of Georgia) by the Pilobolus Dance Theatre and the University of North Texas Wind Symphony, Eugene Corporon, conducting. Critic Robert Carl, commenting on Harbison's piece wrote, "As it comes from the master of contemporary American Neoclassicism, it is not surprising that this music would evoke associations to Stravinsky and Hindemith, but there is also a harmonic freshness and general athleticism about the piece that reminds one of Tippett as well."[3] Karen Campbell, *Boston Herald* dance critic, wrote that Harbison's score "... is a colorful, meticulously crafted multipart suite that evokes another time and place while remaining contemporary."[4]

Out and Back Again (1995) for violin, cello, and twelve winds was composed by Ken Benshoof (b. 1933) in 1993 as the result of a commission from the Rainier Chamber Winds. The first of its three movements is very "Americana" in character; the second, lyrical and pensive, and the third, dramatic with an ending that recalls fragments from the first and second movements. One critic describes *Out and Back Again* as "... eighteen minutes of delightful Americana, a tone painting with thoughts of Charles Ives in the number of ideas he [Benshoof] weaves in, but with more a feeling of Copland in its harmonies and a definite, flavor of the American West."[5]

James Barnes (b. 1949) won the American Bandmasters Association's Ostwald Award twice, the first time in 1978 for his *Symphony, No. 1, Op. 35*, and three years later, in 1981, for his *Visions Macabre*. In 1991 he received a commission from the United States Army Field Band to write "a major work." His *Lonely Beach (Normandy, 1944)* was premiered by the Band in 1992. The piece is a tone poem that depicts the isolated beaches of the northern coast of France, the location of the Allied Forces D-Day invasion of Fortress Europe on June 6, 1944. Its instrumentation is extensive and includes eight trumpets (which perform from positions located throughout the concert hall), four offstage percussion, a harp, and an optional women's chorus.

Three years later (1995) Barnes received another commission to compose a "major work for wind band," this time from the United States Air Force Band. The work he composed, *Symphony No. 3, Op. 89*, is a forty-minute long piece in four movements, scored for expanded full wind band instrumentation (alto flutes, soprano saxophone, flugelhorns, harp, string bass, and a large percussion section). Barnes employs all the harmonies and textures appropriate for use by composers at the end of the twentieth century, but contains them within the traditional symphonic movement forms. This is a deeply personal work, born out of the emotional trauma that Barnes experienced at the loss of his daughter, Natalie. There are passages that recall both despair and joy, and contain some of the composer's most sensitive writing. The work ends with a feeling of reconciliation and spiritual renewal. Three days following the completion of *Symphony No. 3*, Barnes's son Billy was born.

Philip Sparke (b. 1951) is an English composer who has received numerous commissions from brass, symphonic, and military bands in the UK, Europe, United States, and New Zealand. His *Dance Movements* (1996), composed for the United States Air Force Band, won the Sudler International Wind Band Composition Prize in 1997. The piece is a four-movement instrumental showcase which features the virtuoso possibilities of the woodwind and brass sections. All movements are dance inspired. The first has a Latin American feel. The second "woodwind" movement features a tune in the style of an English country dance. The "brass" third movement does not have a specific dance analogy, however the composer suggests that it might be viewed as a love duet in classical ballet. The music in the final movement is reminiscent of the dance music found in Leonard Bernstein's *West Side Story*.

Morton Gould (1913–1996) wrote music for orchestra, band, ballet, musical comedy, television, and motion pictures. He also conducted many of the major orchestras in the United States and Europe and was a dedicated supporter of young American composers and their music. His *Ballad for Band* (1946), *American Salute* (1943), and *Symphony for Band, "West Point"* (1952) have become standard works in wind band/ensemble literature.

His final wind band/ensemble work, *Remembrance Day: (Soliloquy for a Passing Century)*, was premiered on February 21, 1996, by the University of Connecticut Wind Ensemble, Jeffrey Renshaw conducting, as part of the ceremonial opening of the University's year-long retrospective, "Fifty Years After Nuremberg: Human Rights and the Rule of Law." Gould provided the following program note about his piece which he described "as a guide to the musical gestures and terrain that make up the work."

> *Remembrance Day* opens softly with a prologue evoking a distant nostalgic lullaby. As it fades, a sudden loud chime combines with high clarinets in an anguished sequence that cries out a musical pattern establishing and shaping the body of the work. The music alternates between elegiac thematic references and the pulsings and accents of chimes and tolling bells. A slight pause—then ... a sudden explosive interruption, brutal and violent.... This leads to a full blown and affirmative chorale. Following this climax the work winds down, diminishing in intensity.... Now comes a last variation on the chant, and a "pianissimo" echo variant ... of the hymns and chorales. As this recedes come the plaintive "cry of anguish" again—unresolved. Once again, quiet pulsations, short silence—and the epilogue—a few fragments of the opening lullaby— some final pulsings—a few timpani beats—silence.[6]

Thomas Duffy (b. 1955) visited Frankfort, Kentucky, in 1995 to attend the premiere of his piece, *The Miracle Mile*. While there he was taken to see the Kentucky Veterans Vietnam Memorial—the "Gnomon" (Greek word for the pointer of a sundial). This is how he described what he saw and felt:

> What I saw was absolutely overwhelming—physically, spiritually and emotionally. I was moved to silence. In the quiet of the moment— a quiet accompanied by the sound of birds, in that sacrosanct place

surrounded by distant trees, I conjured up the sounds of distant bugles, martial drumming, marching, funeral hymns and the popular folk songs that represented the anguish of America in the 1960s.[7]

A month after returning home, Duffy received a telephone call inviting him to compose a piece for the Capital City Community Band. This stimulated a remembrance of the sounds and feelings he had experienced when he stood in front of the Gnomon the previous month and inspired him to write *Gnomon* (1995). His work deals with the passing of time, the presence of death, loss, and sadness. It is a mixture of "civilian and military sounds" associated with the Vietnam War years in the United States, plus a sixteenth-century death-chant, marching music, and the constant ostinato of a military drum.

In 1996, Gunther Schuller was invited by Frederick Harris to compose a piece for his Belmont (Massachusetts) High School Symphonic Band. Schuller responded by writing *Blue Dawn into White Heat* which the Band premiered, with the composer conducting, on March 20, 1996. *Blue Dawn into White Heat* is a one movement piece that is divided into three sections, each of which is delineated by clearly discernible ever faster tempos as well as changing meters (3/4, 5/4, 7/4). Although the work is mostly written-out (through-composed), it does have some brief improvisational episodes for trombone, tenor saxophone, and piano. *Blue Dawn into White Heat* is one of the earliest jazz compositions written for the concert band. In addition to its intrinsic musical merit, the piece can also be used for an educational, didactic purpose, i.e., teaching "classically oriented players" something about jazz—specifically, *modern* jazz.

Michael Manning, writing in the *Boston Globe,* said this about Schuller's piece:

> "In it, you hear the influence of Ellington more than anyone. It's clearly a didactic (though not in the least pedantic) work, one that provides selective opportunities for improvisation and serves as a primer in big band sound—from the muted wah-wah trumpets of Harlem's Cotton Club to the harder edges of Basie.[8]

Cindy McTee (b. 1953) composed *Soundings* in 1995 for the Big Eight Band Directors Association. The composer explains that each of the work's four movements "explores different musical territory.

'Fanfare' employs familiar material ... but departs from traditional fanfares in its use of woodwind as well as brass instruments ... 'Gizmo' reflects my fascination with gadgets ... 'Waves' was born out of my ... preference [for] sounds whose shapes slowly expand and contract ... 'Transmission' ... [interest in the transference of] musical information using 'metric and temporal modulation,' a process analogous to that executed by the drives of a BMW 328, smoothly, shifting gears to change engine speed."[9]

Karel Husa received a commission from alumni and friends of the Northwestern University School of Music to compose a piece for the 40th anniversary of John Paynter's appointment to the faculty. Sadly, John passed away before Husa's new piece was completed and premiered. Paynter was a beloved teacher, valued colleague, and friend of hundreds of band directors throughout the world. During his career he was president of every U. S. band association, as well as president of the Midwest International Band and Orchestra Clinic and the World Association of Symphonic Bands and Ensembles. His founding of the Northshore Concert Band in 1956 stimulated the rebirth of American community bands. In addition to his conducting activities, Paynter was also a composer/arranger of over 400 works for wind band

The piece Husa wrote to honor Paynter, *Les Couleurs Fauves,* was premiered by the Northwestern University Symphonic Wind Ensemble, with the composer conducting, on November 16, 1996. Husa provided the following words about the piece:

> I have always been fascinated by colors, not only in music but also in nature and art. The paintings of the Impressionists and Fauvists have been particularly attractive to me, and their French origin accounts for the French title of my piece. The two movements ("Persisting Bells" and "Ritual Dance Masks") gave me the chance to play with colors—sometimes gentle, sometimes raw—of the wind ensemble, something John [Paynter] also liked to do in his conducting.
>
> I was reminded of those French painters, whom I admired as a young student in Paris. They called themselves fauvist (vivid, wild), for they used bold, often powerful strokes of brushes with unmixed colors. Their paintings, though, breathe with sensitivity, serenity and gentleness.[10]

Robert Carl, in a review of the New England Conservatory Wind Ensemble recording of *Les Couleurs Fauves,* wrote, "Karel Husa is one of the masters of this medium, and his *Les Couleurs Fauves* is a feast of lush colors and harmonies in its opening movement, followed by new primitivist dances in its following two."[11]

Michael Colgrass's *Urban Requiem* (1996) was commissioned by the University of Miami School of Music. The instrumentation of this "after-hours requiem" for four saxophones and wind orchestra is for the non-string instrumentation of a symphony orchestra (triple winds and brasses, four horns, tuba, harp, synthesizer, timpani, and four percussion). The saxophone soloists, in the composer's designed seating plan, are encircled by the players in the ensemble which Colgrass divides into four groups. The composer explains, "... each sax has its own little neighborhood. The soloists interact with virtuoso displays and play duets and trios with principal players in their bands. The sax players are occasionally called upon to improvise over basic material in sometimes jazz, sometimes ethnic music styles." He concludes, "... *Urban Requiem* might be described as an urban tale ... I was inspired by the energy and power of our cities and the humor inherent in their conflicts. I feel that the saxophone is particularly well suited to express the variety of emotions required for this idea.... It can howl like a banshee or purr like a kitten.... It is written for all urban souls, living and dead, who like myself, love our cities and continue to be inspired by them."[12]

In 1996, Joseph Schwantner used a commission he received from the Illinois College Band Directors Association to compose *In Evenings' Stillness*. The piece is the last of Schwantner's three works for woodwinds, brass, percussion, and piano and serves as the middle movement in his trilogy which includes *...and the mountains rising nowhere* and *From a Dark Millennium*. Even though each of these works are independent and self-contained, Schwantner stated that he " ... always envisioned the possibility that they could be combined to form a larger and more expansive three-movement formal scheme." *In Evening's Stillness* is a dramatic work in quasi-minimalist style with interesting sonorities, "... clever writing for high winds [and] a nicely contrasting lyrical section."[13]

Composer William Kraft's *Concerto for Four Solo Percussion and Wind Ensemble* (1966/1995) is a "re-composing" of a piece originally written for orchestra. Wind instruments play a very prominent role in the original version of the piece, so much so that when Erich

Leinsdorf performed the work with the Boston Symphony Orchestra, he rearranged the orchestra seating so that the winds were brought forward and the strings moved back. Kraft's *Concerto* is structured in the conventional three-movement form. Its first movement is in a slow tempo and features expressive solos for the glockenspiel, vibraphone, graduated drums, and timpani, against a light accompaniment in the ensemble. This is Kraft's way of saying "percussion can be beautiful." The second movement is fast and rides "on a jazz-like ostinato" stemming from the way Count Basie's drummer Jo Jones would reverse the hi-hat rhythm. The third movement consists of a cadenza and variations in which the timpani plays the cadenza that sets off the twelve variations that follow. Kraft's *Concerto for Four Solo Percussion and Wind Ensemble* is an important addition to the concerto literature for percussion and wind ensemble.

Russell Platt, a music and book critic for the *Saint Paul Pioneer Press, The New Yorker*, and other publications, presented an address at the 1999 World Association of Symphonic Bands and Ensembles conference in San Luis Obispo, California, in which he questioned whether band music was "... truly part of what we would call 'classical music,' or is it a cousin whose life parallels that of its high-born relation?

> ... in America the division between orchestral music and wind ensemble music has been not one of the head and heart so much as it is been a division of social function: mainstream classical music has inhabited the professional world of the concert hall and opera house, while wind ensembles, with some exceptions, are usually linked (at least indirectly) to collegiate athletic programs or to the ceremonial tasks of our nation's military. The great accuracy, polish, and enthusiasm of many fine wind ensembles (many of which are performing here) has greatly impressed me. But like a lot of classical types I'm sometimes impatient with band music—it's great for what it says, but I want it to say more—and I think some of you want it to say more too."[14]

The avalanche of new works written for the wind band/ensemble continued from 1997 to 1999. Below is a select group of works composed during those years.

Warren Benson	The Drums of Summer (1997)
	Daughter of the Stars
	(A Reminiscence of Shenandoah) (1998)

Judith Bingham	Three American Icons (1997)
Henry Brant	On the Nature of Things (1997)
John Casken	Distant Variations (1997)
Michael Daugherty	Desi (1991)
	Bizarro (1993)
	Niagara Falls (1997)
	Red Cape Tango (arr. Mark Spede) (1999)
Martin Ellerby	Venetian Spells (1997)
Alan Fletcher	An American Song (1999)
David Gillingham	Waking Angels (1997)
	Concertino for Four Percussion (1997)
Peter Gramm	Montage: A Symphony for Winds (1998)
Donald Grantham	Fantasy Variations on Gershwin's Prelude II for Piano (1997)
	Southern Harmony (1998)
	J'ai été au bal (1999)
Adam Gorb	Yiddish Dances (1998)
Daron Hagen	Bandanna (Opera) (1999)
Jere Hutcheson	Caricatures (1997)
Charles Ives	"The Alcotts" (1911–15, transcribed 1999 by Jonathan Elkus)
David Maslanka	Mass (for winds and voices) (1994-95)
Francis McBeth	When Honor Whispers and Shouts (1998)
Daniel Pinkham	Music for an Indian Summer (1998)
Aulis Sallinen	The Palace Rhapsody (1997)
Jack Stamp	Pastime (1999)
Augusta Read Thomas	Danse (1994)
	Cathedral Summer (1999)
Frank Ticheli	Blue Shades (1997)
Joseph Turrin	Chronicles (1998)
Dan Welcher	Symphony No. 3, "Shaker Life" (1997)
Charles Rochester Young	Tempered Steel (1997)

In 1997–98, Warren Benson composed both *The Drums of Summer* (1997) and *Daughter of the Stars (A Reminiscence of "Shenandoah")* (1998). The Southern Methodist University Meadows School of Music Wind Ensemble commissioned *The Drums of Summer* for a performance at the World Association of Symphonic Bands and Ensembles Conference in Schladming, Austria, in 1997. "[The work's] first movement, 'The Walden Pond Parade,' offers a glimpse into Thoreau's expression that our great variety and unity in the United States exists because we march to the beat of different drummers.... The second movement, 'Hermanitos,' was inspired by the first line of a poem by Angel Torres, a New York City elementary school student, that Benson remembers as going something like '. . . a little brother is like a room full of drummers.' 'Dark Girl' is a moving elegy for a beautiful young dancer and is based on a text by Arna Bontemps. The final movement, 'River-bed,' speaks to the primeval ferment of a riverbed and the natural sounds that emanate from that place. 'River-bed' makes use of a text by Mexican poet Octavio Paz, which is recited by the chorus in the language of the composer."[15]

Daughter of the Stars was commissioned and premiered by the Bishop Ireton Symphonic Wind Ensemble (Alexandria, VA), Dr. Garwood Whaley, conductor, on April 4, 1998, at a gala concert inaugurating a new concert hall at Bishop Ireton High School. The work, subtitled "A reminiscence on 'Shenandoah,'" is an eleven and a half minute piece which is transparent in texture and gentle and reflective in expressive character.

Augusta Read Thomas (b. 1964) is the recipient of many awards and fellowships. She is currently a University Professor at The University of Chicago. When she was at the University of Kansas School of Music in 1993, she was invited (commissioned) to write a work for the Symphonic Band. On March 11, 1995, the Kansas University Symphonic Band, James Barnes, conductor, premiered *Danse* at the American Bandmasters Association Convention. *Danse* is a short, extremely abrupt work that is based on several short motives (tone cells). "The emphasis in the music is on flashes of pure color and complex, jutty rhythms . . . that continually flash by in different instrumental textures."[16]

American popular culture inspired many of Michael Daugherty's compositions. *Desi* (1991) for symphonic winds is a tribute to Desi Arnaz, who played Ricky Ricardo in the 1950s *I Love Lucy* television series. Arnaz had made the *Conga Dance* famous in the 1940s through his singing and playing of bongo and conga drums in Hollywood film musicals. In *Desi*, the bongo soloist and percussionists provide an energetic counterpoint to intricately structured canons and four-note clusters that create a polyrhythmic layering that intensifies to a sizzling conclusion.

Two years later Daugherty composed *Bizarro* (1993) for the Detroit Chamber Winds and a year later, in 1994, *Motown Metal* for the Summit Brass. *Motown Metal* is a seven-minute long piece for four horns, four trumpets, three trombones, tuba, and percussion (vibraphone, glockenspiel, cymbals, and brake drum). The inspiration for the piece came from the rhythms, automobile clamor, 60s Motown sound, and the 90s techno-beat of the industrial city of Detroit.

Daugherty received another commission in 1997, this time from the University of Michigan Band to write a work for its 100th Anniversary. The work he wrote, *Niagara Falls,* has been described as "...a ten-minute musical ride down the Niagara River, with an occasional stop at a haunted house or wax museum along the way."[17]

In 1999, Mark Spede created a band version of the finale from Daugherty's 42-minute orchestral work *Metropolis Symphony* (1993) and titled it *Red Cape Tango.* The inspiration for the piece came from Superman comic book characters. Its principal melody is based on the medieval Latin death chant *Dies irae.* Daugherty depicts Superman and Doomsday's fight/dance of death as a tango which gradually undergoes a timbral transformation, concluding dramatically with crash cymbals, brake drum, and timpani. The alternating legato and staccato sections suggest a musical bullfight.

Dan Welcher's *Symphony No. 3, "Shaker Life"* (1997) came about as the result of two commissions. Welcher wrote the work's first movement, "Laboring Songs," for a consortium of three Texas high school bands: The Colony High School Band, L. D. Bell High School Band, and Duncanville High School Band. Its second movement, "Circular Marches," was commissioned by the American Bandmasters Association. The composer provided the following information about the *Symphony*:

> For the *Symphony No. 3,* I have mined the deep spiritual and musical lode of the Shakers ... "Laboring Songs" begins with a wordless melody attributed to Mother Anne Lee, founder of the "Shaking Quakers." A second melody, "Sad Days," contains words about the sorrow and anguish which are surely to come. The melody which follows, "Turn to the Right," refers both to the turning movement of the march-step and to the "getting right with God" message. The melody is interrupted twice by the shuffle tune "Followers of the Lamb."
>
> "Circular Marches" is named for a certain kind of worship practiced by the Shakers. A "circular march" was a kind of elaborately choreographed patterned march, almost like a square dance.... The vocal band

would remain stationary while the other worshipers executed wheels-within-wheels, counter-marches, and other elaborate patterns.... There are several places where two or three different marches appear at once, loosely descriptive of the worship activity itself. The work concludes with antiphonal "Shaker Shouts" and with a spirit of unbounded joy.[18]

Blue Shades by Frank Ticheli was commissioned by thirty university, community, and high school bands under the auspices of the Worldwide Concurrent Premieres and Commissioning Fund. In 1992, Ticheli wrote a concerto for traditional jazz band and orchestra, *Playing With Fire*, which was dominated by traditional jazz influences and left little room for his own musical ideas. Five years later, in 1997, Ticheli decided to write a piece that combined his love of early jazz with his own stylist ideas. *Blue Shades*, the title of the piece, alludes to the blues, however the work is not literally a blues piece.

There is not a single 12-bar blues progression in the piece, and, except for a few isolated sections indicated in the score, the eighth note is not swung. The work is, however, heavily influenced by the blues ... blues harmonies, rhythms, and melodic idioms pervade the work, and many "shades of blue" are depicted, from bright blue, to dark, to dirty, to hot blue. At times, the work parodies some of the clichés from the Big Band era, not as a mockery of those conventions, but as a playful tribute to them.[19]

The original version of Donald Grantham's *Fantasy Variations* was composed for two pianos. In 1996, Grantham was commissioned and composed a second version of the piece for the University of Texas Wind Ensemble's 1997 Carnegie Hall concert. The primary material in the work is derived from George Gershwin's *Second Prelude* (*Piano Preludes, Book 1*). Obscure fragments drawn from the introduction, accompaniment figures, transitions and cadences of Gershwin's work opens the piece. These fragments eventually give way to more familiar motives from the *Prelude*'s two "big themes." During the last half of the piece the "big themes" appear in more or less their original form. *Fantasy Variations* (1997) won both the NBA Revelli Composition and ABA Ostwald Composition Awards in 1988.

A year following the premiere of *Fantasy Variations* (1998), Grantham received another commission, this time from the Southeastern Band Directors Conference and composed *Southern Harmony* which was premiered by the Louisiana University Wind Ensemble,

Frank Wickes, conductor, at the 1999 College Band Directors Association National Conference. The primary material in the work is derived from "Singin' Billy" Walker's 1835 songbook, "Southern Harmony," which is a collection of tunes, hymns, psalms, odes, and anthems "selected from the most eminent authors in the United States."

In 1999, Jerry Junkin and the University of Texas Wind Ensemble once again commissioned Granthan to write a piece for them. This time he responded by writing a piece that celebrates Cajun music and the brass band tradition of New Orleans—*J'ai été au bal*.

David Gillingham (b. 1947) composed five wind band/ensemble works between 1997 and 1999: *Waking Angels* and *Concertino for Four Percussion and Wind Ensemble* in 1997; *A Crescent Still Abides* and *Galactic Empires* in 1998; and *When Speaks the Signal-Trumpet Tone* in 1999. The inspiration for *Waking Angels* was a poem on the subject of AIDS, "Mercy" by Olga Broumas. The composer wrote, "Through the imagery of music, *Waking Angels* emanates the mysteriousness, the pain and the ruthlessness of the disease ... [and] ... also ... the warmth and comfort of hope and the peace of eternity." The old hymn, "Softly and Tenderly, Jesus is Calling," provides a source of reflection and unifies the work. The hymn motive, through a degenerative process, parallels the nature of the disease.

The Palace is an opera by Finnish composer Aulis Sallinen (b. 1935). It was premiered at the Savonlinna Festival in Finland in 1995. An English version of the opera was premiered in 1998 by the New York City Opera. The work is a satire with dark undertones on the subject of authoritarian power. The libretto comes from two different sources—characters from Mozart's opera, *Die Entführung aus dem Serail*, and ideas from Ryszard Kapuściński's novel, *The Emperor*, which deals with the fall of Haile Selassie, last Emperor of Ethiopia. The Royal Northern College of Music (Manchester, UK) and the College Band Directors National Association commissioned Sallinen to compose a wind band/ensemble work based on music from the opera. His piece, *The Palace Rhapsody,* is rhapsodic in form and character. It was premiered by the Royal Northern College of Music Wind Orchestra, Timothy Reynish, conductor, at the Cheltenham International Festival of Music on July 6, 1997.

Charles Rochester Young (b. 1965) has received many honors and prizes as a saxophonist and composer. In 1997, he was commissioned by the Big 12 Band Directors Association and composed *Tempered Steel*. Young, in his comments about the piece, stated, "As we grow stronger and more resilient through hardship, we become 'tempered.' [My piece] is a celebration of our triumph over these unavoidable hardships and obstacles that we regularly face." As the title implies, the metallic sonorities of the wind band are explored and developed throughout the work, while the "tempest" is a symmetric hexachord that is exposed and developed through a variety of juxtaposed gestures and themes.

In an effort to elevate the profile of the band and band music in American musical life, the College Band Directors National Association and a consortium of seventy-eight college/university wind bands/ensembles commissioned Daron Hagen (b. 1961) to compose an opera. The commission stipulated that the instrumentation of the opera's orchestra would consist of woodwind, brass, and percussion instruments. Hagen, working with librettist Paul Muldoon, composed *Bandanna*, a two-act opera that retells the story of Shakespeare's *Othello*, with a contemporary twist. The composer perceived *Bandanna* to be "both an opera and a musical." One critic described it as *"Touch of Evil* meets *Othello." Bandanna* was premiered at the 1999 CBDNA National Conference by the University of Texas Opera Theatre, Robert Simone, director, and Michael Haithcock, conductor. It received a second performance in March 2000 by the University of Nevada Las Vegas Opera Chorus and Wind Orchestra. A review of the performance, published in the *Las Vegas Review-Journal*, proclaimed, "... Hagen's work is glorious.... The sweep of the music is compelling."

In 1995, Gregg Hanson, Director of Bands at the University of Arizona, organized a consortium of ten university and college bands to commission a *Mass* for winds and voices from David Maslanka. Maslanka's work, one hour and forty-six minutes in length, is a setting of the Latin Ordinary, including the "Hymn to Sophia, Holy Wisdom" by poet Richard Beale. The forces used in this work consist of wind orchestra, organ, SATB choir (minimum of 100), boys choir, and soprano and baritone soloists. Conductor Hanson wrote the following about the work,

> "The inspiration for him [Maslanka] stemmed from his ongoing spiritual quests as well as his evolving spiritual beliefs. He was fascinated by

the text of the Ordinary and its continuing reference to God as a male energy. Further, he wished to explore the female implications of the Holy Mother and, hence, determined to write a piece which would literally express the Ordinary and rather figuratively explore the figure of Sophia … The result of all of the above became a gigantic and billowing work which is at once profound and simplistic and pure and dark and full of joy and meaning." Hanson concluded, "… the music is extraordinarily difficult on technical and spiritual levels. The choral writing is 'instrumentally' conceived to be sure. It requires … amazing extremes in tessitura, rhythmic accuracy and sheer endurance."[20]

In 1999, the U. S. Marine Band commissioned Jonathan Elkus (b. 1931) to transcribe "The Alcotts," the third movement of Ives's *Second Piano Sonata ("Concord, Mass., 1840–1860")*, for wind band. Elkus offered the following background on the work:

"The Alcotts" is the subject of one of Ives *Essays Before a Sonata*, which he published concurrently with the *Concord Sonata* in 1920. In the essay, Ives takes us inside the elm-shaded Orchard House where "sits the old spinet piano Sophia Thoreau gave to the Alcott children, on which Beth played the old Scottish airs, and played at Beethoven's Fifth Symphony." Warming as always to such a scene at home music-making, he continued: "All around you, under the Concord sky there still floats … that human faith melody reflecting an innate hope, a common interest in common men, a tune that the Concord bands are every playing while they pound away at the immensities with a Beethoven-like sublimity, and with vengeance and perseverance."[21]

In 1999, Alan Fletcher (b. 1956) composed *An American Song* for the retirement of Frank L. Battisti as conductor of the New England Conservatory Wind Ensemble. Battisti founded and conducted the NEC Wind Ensemble for thirty years from 1969 to 1999. *An American Song* is a meditation on the patriotic song *America, the Beautiful* and a commentary on American life. Included in the work are quotations from twelve American songs that range in style from *Swing Low, Sweet Chariot* and *Deep River* to *Body and Soul* and *I'll Get By*. In a program note attached to the piece, Fletcher wrote,

"… one might say that while collage is an expected procedure in late twentieth-century composition, this piece represents a sort of ultra-collage. The music is painted in the simple glowing colors of American singing, finding the even simpler elements that make up our songs—a falling third, a rising fourth, a returning neighbor pattern—and laying them onto the score in a series of thin translucent glazes. The rhythms and meters float subtly free, placed so that coincidence makes for happy accidents."

An American Song won the United States Military Academy Band Composition Competition in 2000.

The compositions of Jack Stamp (b. 1954) are performed by college/university, school, and military bands around the world. In 1999, he was commissioned and wrote *Pastime*, a uniquely American piece, for the Band Directors Association of Santa Clara County, California. The piece is a salute to "America's pastime—baseball," especially the 1962 Giants and the 1998 baseball season (the McGuire-Sosa homerun derby year!). *Pastime* includes numerous meter changes; polytonality, and a double fugue based on the "anthem of the seventh-inning stretch," *Take Me Out to the Ball Game*. Knowing of my passionate love of baseball, Stamp dedicated the piece to me.

* * * * * * * * * *

The seven wind band/ensemble concerts, below, were performed between 1995 and 1999. By comparing them to the 1954 and 1959 concerts listed in Chapter 6, pages 83–85, one can observe the distinct differences in the kinds of literature and number of pieces included on these concerts. The average number of pieces on the 1954/1959 programs is 10, on the 1995–1999 programs only 5.6. Half (50%) of the pieces on the 1954/1959 programs are transcriptions of light music, only three such pieces are included on 1995–1999 programs. 83% of the works on the 1995–1999 programs are original wind band/ensemble compositions, only 40% of those on the 1954/1959 programs are original works.

Baldwin–Wallace Symphonic Wind Ensemble
Dwight Oltman, Conductor
February 17, 1995

Loris O. Chobanian	Fanfare and Songs of Ararat
Dana Wilson	Piece of Mind
Tarachow	Ether (World Premiere)
Malcolm Arnold/Paynter	Tam O'Shanter Overture, Op. 51

Ithaca College Wind Ensemble
Rodney Winther, Conductor
March 5, 1995

Karel Husa	Smetana Fanfare
Jeffrey Hass	Lost in the Funhouse
Carlos Surinach	Paeans and Dances of Heathen Iberia
Aaron Copland/Hunsberger	Quiet City
Ron Nelson	Passacaglia (Homage on B-A-C-H)

Baylor University Wind Ensemble
Michael Haithcock, Conductor
Gary Hardie, Cello Soloist
November 19, 1996

Steven Stucky (after Purcell)	Funeral Music for Queen Mary
J. S. Bach/Holst	Fugue à la Gigue
Percy Aldridge Grainger	Blithe Bells
Norman Dello Joio	Variants on a Medieval Tune
Steven Stucky	Voyages for Cello and Wind Orchestra

Gary Hardie, Cello

Richard Wagner/Cailliet	Elsa's Procession to the Cathedral (from *Lohengrin*)

New England Conservatory Wind Ensemble
Frank L. Battisti, Conductor
Ruth Birnberg Dance Ensemble
October 23, 1997

Leon Kirchner	Illuminations
Walter Piston	Divertimento for Nine Instruments
Ivan Tcherepnin	Statue
John Harbison	Olympic Dances

Ruth Birnberg Dance Ensemble

Bernard Rands	Ceremonial

University of Texas at Austin
Jerry F. Junkin, Conductor
Mark J. Spede, Guest Conductor
Kraig A. Williams, Guest Conductor
Frank Ticheli, Visiting Composer
May 2, 1997

Frank Ticheli	Blue Shades

Mark J. Spede, Conductor

Joseph Schwantner   From a dark millennium

Kraig A. Williams, Conductor

Percy Aldridge Grainger	Irish Tune from County Derry
	Shepherd's Hey
Gunther Schuller	Symphony No. 3, "In Praise of Winds"

United States Marine Band
Colonel Timothy W. Foley, Conductor
February 21, 1999

Daniel S. Godfrey	Jig
Thea Musgrave	Journey through a Japanese Landscape
Charles Ives/Elkus	"Decoration Day" from *Four New England Holidays*
Tristan Keuris	Catena: Refrains and Variations for
	31 Wind Instruments and Percussion
Percy Grainger	Lincolnshire Posy
Adam Gorb	Awayday
John Philip Sousa/Byrne	March, Comrades of the Legion

Louisiana State University Wind Ensemble
Frank B. Wickes, Conductor
H. Robert Reynolds, Guest Conductor

Donald Grantham	Southern Harmony
Nicholas Maw	American Games
Stephen David Beck	The Wild Rumpus
Percy Aldridge Grainger	Colonial Song

H. Robert Reynolds, Conductor

Michael Daugherty	Niagara Falls
Jack Stamp	Pastime

Jack Stamp, Conductor

Adam Gorb	Yiddish Dances
Frank Ticheli	Vesuvius

* * * * * * * * * * * * *

During the last two decades of the twentieth century there was a growing interest in the performance of wind chamber music. Chamber music is considered by musicians to be the highest form of musical participation. This type of musical experience offers the player a closer and more intimate glimpse into the music he/she is performing. It also provides opportunities for woodwind, brass, and percussion players to perform quality literature from periods and in styles not found in wind band literature. Composers responded to this growing interest in chamber wind ensemble music and began to write works for smaller groups of woodwind, brass, and percussion instruments. Some colleges and universities created separate ensembles (generally called "Chamber Winds" or "Chamber Wind Ensemble"), while others incorporated the performance of chamber wind works into regular large ensemble concerts.

In 1996, Kenneth G. Honas, as part of his work towards a D.M.A. in conducting at the University of Missouri–Kansas City, undertook a research project entitled "An Evaluation of Compositions for Mixed-Chamber Winds Utilizing Six to Nine Players: Based on Acton Ostling's Study, 'An Evaluation of Compositions for Wind Band According to Specific Criteria of Serious Artistic Merit.'" As Ostling and Jay W. Gilbert had done in 1973–78 and 1992 respectively, Honas surveyed 341 college music faculty to solicit the names of the wind-band conductors considered to be the most diligent, consistent searchers for and programmers of wind band music of serious artistic merit. The eighteen conductors receiving the highest ratings served as the evaluators in Honas's project. They were:

Frank L. Battisti	Jerry Junkin
Carl Bjerregaard	Craig Kirchhoff
Jim Cochran	Daniel Leeson
Eugene Corporon	Charles Neidich
James Croft	H. Robert Reynolds
Randall Faust	Ronald Roseman
Frederick Fennell	Wolfgang Suppan
Robert Grechesky	Christopher Weait
Donald Hunsberger	David Whitwell

Fennell had served as an evaluator in Ostling's study; Corporon, Croft, and Kirchhoff in Gilbert's study; and Battisti, Hunsberger, Reynolds, and Whitwell in both Ostling's and Gilbert's studies.

Honas asked each conductor to judge 1,683 compositions using the criteria formulated by Ostling for works of "serious artistic merit." (see Chapter 8, pages 135–136) The evaluators selected 288 works, of which only twenty were compositions written in the twentieth century. Listed below are the top twenty rated compositions in rank order.

Wolfang A. Mozart	Serenade No. 11, K. 375 (octet version)
	Serenade No. 11, K. 375 (sextet version)
	Serenade No. 12, K. 384a (K. 388)
Igor Stravinsky	Histoire du Soldat
	Histoire du Soldat Suite
	Octet for Wind Instruments
Wolfgang A. Mozart	Serenade No. 10 in B-flat, K. 361 (370a)
Paul Hindemith	Septet for Wind Instruments
William Walton	Façade, An Entertainment
Ludwig van Beethoven	Octet in E-flat Major
Leoš Janáček	Mládí (Youth Suite)
Giovanni Gabrieli	Symphoniae Sacre No. 6: Sonata Pian e Forte
Edgard Varèse	Octandre
Ludwig van Beethoven	Rondino in E-flat Major, WoO 25
Ingolf Dahl	Music for Brass Instruments
Giovanni Gabrieli	Symphoniae Sacre No. 1: Canzon Primi Toni
	Symphoniae Sacre No. 2: Canzon Septimi Toni
	Symphoniae Sacre No. 4: Canzon Noni Toni
	Symphoniae Sacre No. 5: Canzon Duo Decimi Toni
Charles Gounod	Petite Symphonie

In 1996, John L. Baker undertook another research project dealing with the literature for chamber wind ensembles. Baker sought to identify the core repertoire for mixed-wind chamber ensembles.[22] In his study, Baker examined compositions for mixed ensembles of seven to sixteen instrumentalists, having one player to a part, and in which wind instruments function in a primary role. Strings, keyboards, and percussion could be included if they comprised less than half of the ensemble. The use of a conductor is implied but is not required. Although Baker's study was modeled after the research of Honas (1996), Gilbert (1993), and Ostling (1973–78), it differed in the simplification of criteria used to define "artistic merit." Ostling created comprehensive criteria for judging musical quality, which were used in the Gilbert and Honas studies. Baker gave his evaluators more latitude in the rating process, placing emphasis on the musical awareness and professional experience of the evaluator.

The evaluators for Baker's study were selected through a three-step process: (1) identification of wind-band conductors in each college or university with fifteen or more full-time faculty members, as listed by the College Music Society; (2) from these conductors, the solicitation of nominations of the wind-band conductors whom they considered to be the most diligent and consistent programmers of music of serious artistic merit; and (3) the selection of the twenty conductors receiving the highest number of nominations. For various reasons six of the twenty selected evaluators declined to participate. The evaluation committee for Baker's study consisted of:

Frank Battisti	Craig Kirchhoff
Eugene Corporon	H. Robert Reynolds
Ray Cramer	James Smith
James Croft	Richard Strange
Donald Hunsberger	Myron Welch
Jerry Junkin	David Whitwell
Mark Kelly	Frank Wickes

These fourteen conductors evaluated approximately 400 compositions and selected eighty-nine compositions as being works of "serious artistic merit." Of these, forty-six (over half of them) were pieces composed in the twentieth century. The twenty top-rated compositions selected by Baker for his Mixed-Wind Chamber Ensembles Core Repertoire are, in rank order:

Wolfgang A. Mozart	Serenade No. 10 in B-flat, K. 361 (370a)
Igor Stravinsky	Octet for Wind Instruments
	Histoire du Soldat
Alban Berg	Chamber Concerto for Piano and Thirteen Winds
Wolfgang A. Mozart	Serenade No. 12 in c minor, K. 388
Richard Strauss	Serenade in E-flat, Op. 7
Edgard Varèse	Intégrales
Ludwig van Beethoven	Rondino in E-flat Major, WoO 25
Paul Hindemith	Septet for Wind Instruments
Robert Kurka	The Good Soldier Schweik Suite
Wolfgang A. Mozart	Serenade No. 11 in E-flat Major, K. 375
Charles Gounod	Petite Symphonie in B-flat, Op. 90
Felix Mendelssohn	Notturno, Op. 24
Ludwig van Beethoven	Octet in E-flat Major, Op. 103
Edgard Varèse	Octandre
Francis Poulenc	Suite française
Richard Strauss	Suite in B-flat, Op. 4
Paul Hindemith	Concerto for Organ & Wind Instruments (Kammermusik No. 7)
Jacques Ibert	Concerto for Cello and Winds
Jacques Ibert	Concertino da Camera

In the course of his study Baker collected data that supported the collegiate wind band community's strong belief in the importance of performing mixed-wind chamber music. In the "Summary and Conclusions" section of his dissertation, Baker poses the following questions: If chamber wind ensembles are truly important, why is so little emphasis placed on the idiom? Does the conductor feel uncomfortable with the idiom or is this music reserved for the intellectually "elite" of the profession? To what extent do collegiate wind conductors specialize in chamber performance? Are the majority of collegiate wind band conductors sufficiently familiar with this repertoire or do they only know the most frequently performed works in this repertoire? Are the nation's college and universities including chamber wind experiences in their curriculum: are there benefits that result from the study and the performance of this literature that are not obtainable in larger ensembles? 64% of those questioned by Baker rated chamber wind music activity "important" or "very important" but only 34% reported that their institutions placed enough emphasis on "Chamber Wind Ensemble" participation. Baker concluded that a dichotomy existed within the collegiate wind band community between philosophical beliefs and practice regarding wind chamber music activity.

Below are four chamber wind ensemble concert programs presented between 1995 and 1999. These programs contain fourteen different works, one in classical style, five in romantic/late romantic style, and eight twentieth-century works in various styles.

New England Conservatory Wind Ensemble
Frank L. Battisti, Conductor
Tamara Brooks, Conductor NEC Chamber Singers
October 21, 1995

Francis Poulenc	Suite Française (1935)
	(d'apres Claude Gervaise ...)
Libby Larsen	The Settling Years (1988)

NEC Chamber Singers

Kurt Weill	Little Threepenny Music (1929)

Catholic University of America Chamber Winds
Robert Garofalo, Music Director
Eric Culver, Guest Conductor
Thomas Mastroianni, Soloist
April 4, 1997

Reynaldo Hahn	Le Bal de Béatrice d'Este
Kamilló Lendvay	Concertino for Piano, Percussion & Harp

Thomas Mastroianni, Soloist

Leland Cossart	Suite für Zehn Blasinstrument und Harfe, Op. 19

Florida State Winds
James Croft, Conductor
J. Jossim, Conducting Associate
Leonard and Norma Mastrogiacomo, Duo Pianists
April 13, 1997

Thomas Schudel	Triptych
Paul Bowles	Concerto for Two Pianos, Winds and Percussion

Leonard and Norma Mastrogiacomo, Duo Pianists

Max Reger	Serenade
Alfred Uhl	Drei Tänzstücke für Blaserokett
Émile Bernard	Divertissement, Op. 36

University of Massachusetts (Amherst) Chamber Winds
Malcolm W. Rowell, Jr., Conductor
January 31, 1999

Wolfgang Amadeus Mozart	Serenade in c minor, K. 388
Igor Stravinsky	Octet for Wind Instruments
Antonín Dvořák	Serenade in d minor, Op. 44

* * * * * * * * * * *

No work for wind band/ensemble has won either the Pulitzer Prize or the Grawemeyer Award for Music Composition. However, eight of the composers who have received one or both of them composed ten wind band/ensemble pieces in the 1990s—Gunther Schuller composed *Song and Dance* (1990) and *Festive Music* (1992); Michael Colgrass, *Arctic Dreams* (1991) and *Urban* Requiem (1996); John

Harbison, *Three City Blocks* (1992) and *Olympic Dances* (1996); Bernard Rands, *Ceremonial* (1992); Karel Husa, *Les Couleurs Fauves* (1995); Morton Gould, *Remembrance Day (Soliloquy for a Passing Century)* (1995), and Joseph Schwantner, *In Evenings' Stillness* (1996). In the previous decade (1980–1989), nine Pulitzer Prize winning composers wrote seventeen wind band/ensemble pieces. Since 1943, when the prize was first given, thirty-nine of the fifty-three winning composers wrote at least one piece for wind band/ensemble.

* * * * * * * * * * * *

By the end of the twentieth century, recordings of wind bands/ensembles, which were once very hard to come by, were plentiful and easily available. Wind symphonies led by Eugene Corporon at the Cincinnati College–Conservatory and the University of North Texas had recorded twenty-three CDs for the Klavier Wind Recording Project. The Tokyo Kosei Wind Orchestra, Dallas Wind Symphony, Keystone Wind Ensemble, DePaul University Wind Ensemble, New England Conservatory Wind Ensemble, Washington D. C. military bands, and many other ensembles, had also produced numerous CD recordings of contemporary and standard wind band/ensemble works. These recordings were played on many FM radio classical music stations throughout the country. The easy availability of wind band/ensemble recordings, as well as the exposure they were receiving through radio broadcasts, stimulated a rethinking of the position of wind bands/ensembles within the larger musical community.

ENDNOTES

1   McBeth, "The Evolving Band Repertoire," 22.
2   Scott Judson, "John Harbison," in *A Composer's Insight, Volume 1*, ed. Timothy Salzman (Meredith Music Publications, 2003), 60.
3   Robert Carl, "Review: New England Conservatory Wind Ensemble (TROY 340)," *Fanfare* 23 (January-February 2000): 409–410.
4   Karen Campbell, "Dance Underscores Composer's Vision," *Boston Herald* (October 19, 1997): 48.
5   *Soundscapes*, North Texas Wind Symphony, Eugene Migliaro Corporon, conductor, Klavier Records KCD-11098, 1999, Liner notes by Glen Hemberger.
6   Morton Gould, *Remembrance Day: Soliloquy for a Passing Century* (G. Schirmer, 2004), Programme Note.
7   Thomas Duffy, *Gnomon* (Ludwig Music, 1995).

8   Michael Manning, "Mr. Schuller's Opus: Belmont's 'Blue dawn,'" *The Boston Globe* (March 22, 1996): 63.

9   Cindy McTee, "Soundings for wind symphony: Program Notes," *Cindy McTee, Composer*, accessed June 21, 2018, http://www.cindymctee.com/soundings .html.

10   David Fullmer, "Karel Husa," in *A Composer's Insight, Volume 1*, ed. Timothy Salzman (Meredith Music Publications, 2003), 74.

11   Robert Carl, *"Les Couleurs Fauves,"* *Fanfare* (January–February 2000).

12   Stephen Clickhard, "Michael Colgrass," in *A Composer's Insight, Volume 1*, ed. Timothy Salzman (Meredith Music Publications, 2003), 24.

13   Lawrence Johnson, "Review: *Wind Dances*, North Texas Wind Symphony (Klavier KCD-11084)," *Fanfare* (March-April 1998): 294.

14   Russell Platt, "The Quest for Good Music and the Role of the Symphonic Band," *Journal of the World Association for Symphonic Bands and Ensembles* 6 (1999): 58.

15   *The Drums of Summer*, Meadows Wind Ensemble , Jack Delaney, conductor, Gasparo Gallante GG-1017, 1999, Liner notes.

16   "Program note," University of Kansas Symphonic Band, concert of March 9, 1995.

17   "Program notes," Baylor University Wind Ensemble, concert of May 1, 1999.

18   *Sojourns*, North Texas Wind Symphony, Eugene Migliaro Corporon, conductor, Klavier Records KCD-11099, 1999, Liner notes by Glen Hemberger.

19   Frank Ticheli, *Blue Shades: The Music of Frank Ticheli*, Michigan State University Wind Symphony, John L. Whitwell, conductor, Mark Custom Recording Service 2744-MCD, 1998, Liner notes.

20   Gregg I. Hanson, letter to the author, November 1, 2000.

21   Charles Ives, *Charles Ives's America*, United States Marine Band, Timothy W. Foley, conductor, USMC CD19, 2003, Liner notes by Jonathan Elkus.

22   John L. Baker, "Mixed-Wind Chamber Ensembles and Repertoire: A Status Study of Selected Institutions of Higher Learning" (Ph.D. diss., Florida State University, 1997).

CHAPTER 11

Into the New Millennium (2000–2001)

Composers' Growing Interest In the Wind Band/ Ensemble • "Wind Music Across the Century" • "Ten of a Kind" finalist for Pulitzer Prize • Wind Chamber Music • American Bandmasters Association's Statement on School Band Programs • Re-creation of First Eastman Wind Ensemble Concert

By the beginning of the twenty-first century many major composers had become enthusiastic supporters of the medium. Included among them was Pulitzer Prize winning composer John Corigliano who had composed three works for wind band/ensemble including his colossal *Circus Maximus*. He stated:

> Most composers I know, you mention bands and their eyes light up. Bands have got fabulous instruments that aren't in orchestras, and actually you don't miss the fact that the strings aren't there because there's so many other timbral resources. I might add that bands commission works ... It's a much healthier atmosphere for the composer because not only is music learned well and played better than an orchestra can play it, but there's an eager, willing audience to listen to it.[1]

Corigliano's statement reflected the sentiments of many other composers who had also discovered the rewards of working with and writing music for wind bands/ensembles. No longer were composers reluctant to accept a commission to compose a piece for wind band/ensemble.

* * * * * * * * * * * * *

The University of North Texas hosted the 31st CBDNA National Conference from February 19–24, 2001. Fourteen new works received their premiere performances at the conference.

Timothy Broege	Sinfonia XXI
David Gillingham	*Cantus Laetus*
Adam Gorb	*Downtown Diversions for Trombone*
Erich Korngold	*Marietta's Lied* from *Die tote Stadt*, Op. 12 (trans. Larry Odom)
David Maslanka	*Symphony No. 5*
Cindy McTee	*Timepiece*
Richard Peaslee	*Arrows of Time* (trans. Joshua Hauser)
Richard Prior	*earthrise*
Jack Stamp	*Escapade*
Joan Tower	*Fascinating Ribbons*
George Walker	*Canvas*
Dan Welcher	*Songs Without Words*
George Wramage	*The Last Days of Summer*
Bruce Yurko	*Concerto for Bassoon*

The Keystone Wind Ensemble, conducted by Jack Stamp, premiered *Sinfonia XXI* by Timothy Broege (b. 1947). (Broege wrote his first *Sinfonia* in 1971.) The composer stated that he tried to write a piece that mediated "... between the forms, gestures, and language of Baroque music and those of the present day." He rejected using "... a completely non-tonal/non-metrical language [and] ... chose to let the musical materials range far and wide while at the same time maintaining fairly traditional structural processes in each movement."[2]

Downtown Diversions for trombone and wind ensemble was written by UK composer Adam Gorb (b. 1958) and premiered by the Texas Tech University Symphonic Wind Ensemble, John Cody Birdwell, conductor. Timothy Reynish, conductor and wind-music critic, wrote the following about the piece:

The first movement begins with a cadenza for trombone, accompanied by percussion and clapping, before opening out into a brilliant up-tempo allegro reminiscent of *Awayday* and its homage to the American musical. The last continues this restless energy, with mixed meters and an un-academic jazz fugue. The ballad which these two sections enclose could have become sentimental, but for me is lyrical without being hackneyed.[3]

David Maslanka's 35-minute *Symphony No. 5* was commissioned by a consortium of wind bands/ensembles organized by Stephen K. Steele, who also conducted the premiere of the piece with the Illinois State University Wind Symphony. The work is composed around three well-known Chorale melodies: *Durch Adams Fall* (Through Adam's Fall) in the first movement, *O Lamm Gottes, Unschuldig'* (O Lamb of God Without Blame) in the second, and *Christ Lag in Todesbanden* (Christ Lay in the Bonds of Death) in the third and fourth. In his program note about the piece, Maslanka wrote,

> I have used the words "aggravated," "angry," and "overwhelming" by way of description. But for all its blunt and assertive force, the *Symphony* is not tragic. It is filled with a bright and hopeful energy. The music does not try to illustrate the story of the Mass, but rather continually speaks to the theme of transformation—the transformation of tears into power, and the victory of life over death.[4]

In 2000, Cindy McTee (b. 1953) composed a wind version of *Timepiece*, a work she wrote for the 100th Anniversary Season of the Dallas Symphony Orchestra. It is a bold and elegantly crafted piece which she dedicated to the memory of Martin Mailman, a friend and colleague for many years at the University of North Texas. McTee titled the piece *Timepiece*, "not only for its connection to the celebration of special events marking the Dallas Symphony Orchestra's one hundredth anniversary and the beginning of a new millennium, but also for the manner in which musical time shapes the work."[5]

Probably the most anticipated premiere performance at the CBDNA Conference was Joan Tower's new piece, *Fascinating Ribbons*. Tower (b. 1938) has received many awards including the prestigious Grawemeyer Composition Prize as well as a Grammy Award. *Fascinating Ribbons*, her only piece for wind band, is a sophisticated, colorful and rhythmically energetic work. Tower stated this about "entering the band world":

I am happy to finally be entering the band world—a generous and hard-working one, that has generated so many excellent wind, brass and percussion players. It seems also to be a place of people that actually love living composers! In naming the piece, I noticed that there were many contours of motives that are shaped in curved "ribbon" patterns. I immediately thought of the word "fascinating," and the dotted-rhythm reminded me of Gershwin's *Fascinating Rhythm*—hence the title. I hope that my piece will live long enough for me to get to know this world a lot better.[6]

George Walker (b. 1922) was awarded the Pulitzer Prize in Music in 1996 for *Lilacs*, a work for voice and orchestra he wrote for the Boston Symphony Orchestra. He was the first African-American composer to receive a Pulitzer Prize in Music. In 2000, Walker composed *Canvas*, a large work in three movements (called "Extracts") for five narrators, wind ensemble, and chorus, and dedicated it to his parents. The piece was premiered by the University of North Texas Wind Symphony, Eugene Migliaro Corporon, conductor; the North Texas A Cappella Choir, Jerry McCoy, conductor; and narrators Lynn Eustis, Jeffrey Snider, Aaron Logan, Richard Novak, and Gregory Wascoe. Walker wrote the following about his piece:

The first Extract, subtitled "Landscape," is a purely instrumental movement that is arch-like in its formal construction.... The second Extract, "Commentary," introduces a conversational element that ranges from the philosophical, through points of whimsy, to a declaration of social awareness from the five speaking voices employed. It concludes with a musical quote from the popular standard, *I'm Confessing That I Love You.* The third Extract, "Psalm 121," utilizes a chorus with two brief tenor solos in a setting of the King James Version of this text.[7]

Dan Welcher's *Songs without Words*, subtitled "Five Mood Pieces for Wind Ensemble," was commissioned by a consortium of twenty-two colleges and universities and premiered at the CBDNA Conference by the National Small College Intercollegiate Band conducted by Allan McMurray. The piece consists of five short, mood-oriented "impressions and feelings"—"Manic," "Reflective," "Giddy," "Stunned," and "Confident." Welcher (b. 1948) describes each movement in his program note.

I began by imagining five moods that could be portrayed by wind, brass and percussion colors—then expanded on the idea by linking

the separate motives together in the fifth "song." ... "Manic" was originally entitled *Almost Too Happy* ... It is very short and over the top in
terms of energy. "Reflective" was inspired by a series of days in which
it never stopped raining ... [it] is introspective [in] mood. The effect is
somewhat like sitting in a Zen garden listening to the tiny waterfall.
"Giddy" is pure silliness and good humor.... "Stunned" is what happens in life when we aren't looking ... almost like running into a wall....
"Confident" ... [emerges] from the unsettled final chord of "Stunned," a
repeated chord begins tapping at our consciousness as if trying to pull
us out of our despair ... the music becomes faster and more assured....
The piece ends in a buoyant cloud of optimism.[8]

The Conference also included numerous presentations and panel
discussions, including the following:

"The Wind Music of Kurt Weill," presented by Jeff Gershman.
"Hindemith's *Symphony in B-flat*—a Four Movement Work?" presented by
Matthew Mailman.
"The Wind Ensemble Music of Frank Zappa: *Envelopes* and *Dog Breath
Variations*," presented by Patrick Brooks.
"The Musician's Soul," presented by James Jordan.
"Grainger Perspectives," presented by John Bird.
"Composer Confluence" (Panel Discussion): Jack Stamp, Moderator;
Composers Cindy McTee, Joan Tower, Dan Welcher, and George
Walker.
"Looking Forward, Looking Back" (Panel Discussion): Michael Haithcock,
Moderator; conductors Frank Battisti, Donald Hunsberger, H. Robert
Reynolds, and David Whitwell, past-presidents of CBDNA.

* * * * * * * * * * * *

A special symposium, "Wind Music Across the Century," took
place at the New England Conservatory in Boston, Massachusetts,
on April 26–28, 2001, to honor Frank L. Battisti, who had recently
retired as conductor of the NEC Wind Ensemble. The opening statement in the symposium program booklet defined the purpose of the
symposium:

A meeting to reflect on past accomplishments
while focusing on the possibilities,
and defining the challenges, of the future.

A forum for ideas, freely expressed.
Ideas concerning new music,

ideas reflecting on familiar music,
ideas that arise outside of the music itself.
All ideas necessary for the healthy growth of the art.

A place to define the common missions
to be taken up as wind music proceeds
into the new century.

Numerous composers attended and participated in symposium events, among them Warren Benson, Michael Colgrass, John Harbison, John Heiss, Karel Husa, Malcolm Peyton, Daniel Pinkham, Bernard Rands, Gunther Schuller, and Guy Woolfenden. Joining them were conductors Frank L. Battisti, Robert Boudreau, Frederick Fennell, Donald Hunsberger, Timothy Reynish, Michael Haithcock, Tim Foley, Craig Kirchhoff, Jerry Junkin, and John Whitwell.

The symposium opened with a concert performed by the New England Conservatory Wind Ensemble and Jordan Winds (program, below).

Richard Rodney Bennett *Reflections on a Sixteenth Century Tune* (1999)

Timothy Reynish, guest conductor

Colin McPhee *Concerto for Piano and Winds* (1931)

Stephen Drury, piano soloist
William Drury, conductor

Michael Weinstein *Concerto for Wind Ensemble* (1989)

Carl Atkins, guest conductor

Harry von Bulow *Textures* (1978)

Donald Hunsberger, guest conductor

Michael Colgrass *Dream Dancer* (2001)

Kenneth Radnofsky, saxophone soloist
Charles Peltz, conductor

The symposium program also included panel discussions and the presentations of scholarly papers. The subjects discussed by the panels included: "A Global Perspective—Wind Music Without Borders," "New Advocacy—Wind Music in the Professional Paradigm," and "The Ensemble or the Music—Setting Priority of Message over Medium." Scholarly papers were presented by Mark Hopkins ("Alan

Fletcher's *An American Song: A Performer's Analysis*"), D. Antoinette Handy ("African-Americans in Wind Music"), and Greg Smith ("Tuba mirum spargen sonum: The French Revolution and the Liberation of the Winds"). The performance of a solo wind or percussion piece preceded the start of all discussions and presentations. Included among these solo pieces were: *Inventions for a Young Percussionist* by John Harbison, *Memo 6 for Solo Alto Saxophone* by Bernard Rands, *Largo Tah for Bass Trombone and Marimba* by Warren Benson, and Malcom Peyton's *Suite for Clarinet*.

Charles Peltz, New England Conservatory Wind Ensemble conductor and organizer of the symposium, described the "extraordinary transformation" that took place among those who attended the symposium:

> Presenters, performers and audience ... evolved into a forum in which all became participants. Beginning as informed glances or comments between strangers, evolving next to questions and observations offered from all assembled and concluding with sustained applause at each event for the contributions of all, this forum generated new ideas and challenged old ones, drew from experienced hands and solicited newer ones.[9]

At the luncheon which concluded the symposium, Frederick Harris, Massachusetts Institute of Technology Wind Ensemble conductor, announced that a consortium of twenty university/college wind bands/ensembles had commissioned four composers to write pieces in celebration of Frank Battisti's 70th birthday. All commissioned composers were closely associated with Battisti during his years at the New England Conservatory. Michael Gandolfi, chair of the Composition Faculty at the New England Conservatory and the Tanglewood Music Center, was asked to write a tango for wind ensemble (*Vientos y Tangos*)—Battisti specifically requested that he write such a piece. Michael Weinstein, NEC graduate and a member of faculty in of New England Conservatory's Extension Division, was commissioned to write a serenade that employed the same instrumentation as Dvořák's *Serenade in d, Op. 44* (*Serenade for Twelve Instruments*). Kenneth Amis, another NEC graduate and tuba player for the Empire Brass Quintet, was asked to write an 8 to 10 minute overture-type work that used the same instrumentation as Stravinsky's *Symphonies of Wind Instruments* (*Driven!*). Lior Navok, a doctoral student at NEC studying composition with John Harbison, was asked to compose a 25-minute piece for chorus and wind ensemble (*Gleams from the Bosom of Darkness*).

* * * * * * * * * * *

The American Bandmasters Association's 66th Annual Convention, held in Austin, Texas, from February 29–March 4, 2000, celebrated the 70th anniversary of the first formal meeting of the ABA and the Centennial of Bands at the University of Texas. In observance of the ABA anniversary, all delegates were presented with a packet containing a "Collection of ABA Historic Documents" that included a copy of the 1936 "Examination for Membership." This was a rigorous exam that all candidates had to pass in order to become members of the Association.

An ABA Position Statement entitled "The American School Band Program: Focus on the Future" was also distributed to the membership. It contained three guidelines for school band programs:

1. The school band curriculum should be one that "... develops comprehensive musicianship with appropriate tests for accountability."

2. School band students should study and perform "... great artistic literature from all periods of western history as well as a variety of contemporary American styles from 'pop' to 'classical.'"

3. School bands should focus "... on the value of artistic musical expression."

* * * * * * * * * * *

U. S. wind band/ensemble conductors were gradually becoming more aware of works written by non-American composers through attendance at WASBE Conferences, reading of *WASBE WORLD* (which replaced the WASBE *Newsletter*), and the information posted on Timothy Reynish's website (www.timreynish.com). The works of UK composers, especially those of Adam Gorb, Philip Sparke, Kenneth Hesketh, Martin Ellerby, and Guy Woolfenden, received the most attention. Adam Gorb's *Yiddish Dances* and Kenneth Hesketh's "dancing and dicing" *Masque* were performed numerous times by American bands. In 2001, Philip Sparke was commissioned by Colonel Finley Hamilton to write a work for the United States Army Field Band. The inspiration for Sparke's piece, *Sunrise at Angel's Gate* came from a visit he made to the Grand Canyon in 1999. What he saw overwhelmed him.

> It's really not possible to describe this amazing natural phenomenon—it's just too big. You can't even photograph it effectively but it undoubtedly leaves a lasting impression on anyone who visits it ... Angel's Gate is one of the many named rock formations on the northern side of the Canyon and in this piece, I have tried to depict [its] sights and sounds [at] dawn.[10]

The Finnish composer Magnus Lindberg (b. 1958) composed *Grand Duo* for the City of Birmingham Symphony Orchestra and Royal Festival Hall Millennium Celebration. It was premiered on March 8, 2000, by the Birmingham Symphony Orchestra, conducted by Sir Simon Rattle. The work's instrumentation is virtually the same as that used by Stravinsky in his *Symphonies of Wind Instruments*.

Lindberg's compositional style is often referred to as "modernist classicism," an idiosyncratic style that combines techniques from different periods and schools of composition from J. S. Bach to Schoenberg. In *Gran Duo*, Lindberg makes conscious links to two wind ensemble masterpieces: Stravinsky's *Symphonies of Wind Instruments* and Mozart's *Serenade No. 10, K. 361 (Gran Partita)*. The *Gran* in the work's title alludes to the expanded scale of Mozart's work; the *Duo* "... to the dichotomy inherent in the instrumentation of thirteen woodwinds and eleven brass instruments. Much of the work is characterized by dialogue and discourse between the two families."[11] The texture of the work ranges from large sound masses ("sound pyramids") to chamber music-style sub groupings and instrumental solos. Music critic Fiona Maddox, writing in the December 3, 2000, issue of *The Observer*, stated,

> ... [Lindberg spins] his textures and timbres with clean precision. The cycle of different harmonic and rhythmic moods flickers from skittering to sombre, airy to dense. He teases the instrumental lines apart then presses them back together as if opening and closing a beautiful agile squeeze-box. It is no sin for the listener, freed from an obligation to unearth hidden meaning, to relish Lindberg's power to charm.[12]

The works below are representative of the kinds/styles of music composed for wind band/ensemble in 2000-2001.

Henk Alkema	*Sunset Jericho*
Bedson Beltrami	*Concerto for Band*
William Bolcom	*Song*
Steven Bryant	*Alchemy in Silent Spaces* (wind version)
Roger Cichy	*First Flights*
Michael Colgrass	*Dream Dancer*
Michael Daugherty	*Rosa Parks Boulevard*
Michael Daugherty	*UFO*
Thomas Duffy	*Corpus Callosum*
Eric Ewazen	*From a River Valley*
David Gillingham	*Be Thou My Vision*
Daniel Godfrey	*Shindig*
Adam Gorb	*Symphony No. 1 in C*
Donald Grantham	*Kentucky Harmony*
Donald Grantham	*Variations on an American Cavalry Song*
Jeffrey Hass	*Concerto for Amplified Piano and Wind Ensemble*
Kenneth Hesketh	*Masque*
Wataru Hokoyama	*Beyond*
David Kechley	*Restless Birds Before a Dark Moon*
Timothy Mahr	*Mourning Dances*
Toshio Mashima	*Three Notes of Japan*
Daniel McCarthy	*Chamber Symphony No. 2*
Jonathan Newman	*Moon by Night* (wind version)
Robert Patterson	*Symphonic Excursions*
David Rakowski	*Ten of a Kind*
Jan van der Roost	*Sinfonia Hungarica*
Edwin Roxburgh	*Time Harvest*
Felicia Sandler	*Rosie the Riveter*
Charles Shadle	*Coyote's Dinner* (one-act comic opera)
Joseph Spaniola	*Escapade*
David Stanhope	*Symphony No. 1*
Augusta Read Thomas	*Magneticfireflies*
Frank Ticheli	*An American Elegy*
Michael Torke	*Grand Central Station*
Eric Whitacre	*October*
Dana Wilson	*Vortex*
Dana Wilson	*Leader, Lieder*

In March 2000, Timothy Foley, conductor of the U. S. Marine Band, attended a concert and heard a performance of David Rakowski's *Sesso e Violenza* for two flutes and chamber ensemble. He was so impressed he decided to commission Rakowski to write a piece for the Marine Band. David Rakowski (b. 1958) is a teacher of composition at Brandeis University and a winner of numerous awards. The Marine Band's commission was Rakowski's first for a wind band work. He recalled that when he accepted it, he had no idea of how to write a band piece.

> ... I approached [it by listening] to a whole bunch of recent band music that the Marine Band sent me. The piece that had the most to do with the way I eventually came to think about the band was *American Games*, the Nicholas Maw piece, which treated everyone very soloistically and which had some virtuosic woodwind writing. I found it very attractive because it was a piece that was quite different from all the others in the way that it treated this big "bunch o' winds." ... I didn't know how to write a band piece, and I still don't know how to write a band piece. I've written a band piece that isn't really a band piece. It's my music that happens to be written for band.[13]

Rakowski provided the following program note for *Ten of a Kind*:

> *Ten of a Kind* is structured like a four-movement symphony and acts like a concerto with a section of ten variously sized clarinets acting as the concerto soloist. The first movement, "Labyrinth," travels through various musics and tempi as if the listener is moving from room to room; all the musics in all of the rooms unfold bits of the work's thematic material, not heard in full until the second movement. The entry of the "soloist" in this movement is like someone at a party who does not know anyone there and blurts out, "Hey, I'm here!" The second movement is the slow movement, which introduces and passes the thematic materials through the various sections. "Yoikes and Away" is a scherzo with several overstated climaxes, taking the Warner Brothers cartoon "Robin Hood Daffy" as its inspiration. The finale, "Martian Counterpoint," is built around several canonic treatments of a new theme which dissolve into various syncopated patterns to end the movement.[14]

Ten of a Kind was premiered on May 20, 2001, by the U. S. Marine Band, Timothy W. Foley conducting, at the Center for the Arts at George Mason University. It was given its European premiere at the WASBE Conference in Lucerne, Switzerland, in July 2001. The piece was a finalist for the 2001 Pulitzer Prize in Music. It was the first time a wind band/ensemble work had been included among the three finalists for the Prize. In 2006 it won the Barlow Music Composition Award.

Michael Colgrass's *Dream Dancer* is a fantasy for alto saxophone and wind ensemble. It was commissioned by World-Wide Concurrent Premieres and Commissioning Fund, Inc. and premiered on April 6, 2001, in Manchester, England, by Kenneth Radnofsky and the Royal Northern College of Music Wind Orchestra, Clark Rundell conducting. The U. S. premiere took place in Boston, Massachusetts, three weeks later on April 26, 2001. Radnofsky was once again the soloist with the New England Conservatory Wind Ensemble, Charles Peltz, conductor. Colgrass has described *Dream Dancer* as a . . .

> . . . fantasy about a musical instrument that feels attracted to various styles of music [Mideast, Asian and American (especially jazz) and is] trying to decide which one to play. . . . The concept of mixing cultures in music is natural to me living in Toronto, perhaps the world's most cosmopolitan city, which offers a rich palette of authentic folk music from around the world.[15]

In his review of the Boston premiere of *Dream Dancer*, *Boston Globe* music critic Richard Dyer wrote, ". . . the music felt—and you do feel Colgrass's music—gorgeous, dramatic, compelling. *Dream Dancer* issues a promissory note for an even more exciting century for this exciting medium. Colgrass uses tradition as a basis for creating a future."[16]

In 2000, Gary Stith, Supervisor of Music in the Williamsville, New York, Public Schools, organized a consortium of twenty-five high school bands to commission a piece from Augusta Read Thomas (b. 1964). The piece, *Magneticfireflies*, was premiered on December 2001 by the Lakota West High School Band of West Chester, Ohio, Gregory I. Snyder conductor. The work features cross fades and lightening-fast contrasts in colors, rhythms, and dynamics—there is constant movement. Thomas says she was inspired by the imagery of . . .

> . . . a magnetic fire like the sun, or stars, or a pulsar, of some beautiful cosmic object in the sky. The work is, in some ways, an etude in fluttertongue and grace notes. . . . One of the main intentions of this music is the juxtaposition of stark, bold, individual colors, such as a loud solo trumpet (Mahler style) with a completely blended timbre (Debussy style).[17]

Dana Wilson (b. 1946) composed *Leader, Lieder,* a work for solo trumpet and wind ensemble, in 2001. It was premiered at the International Trumpet Guild Conference in Manchester, UK, by the Royal

Northern College of Music Wind Orchestra, James Gourlay, conductor, with James Thompson as trumpet soloist. Thompson is Professor of Trumpet at the Eastman School of Music and former principal trumpet of the Atlanta Symphony Orchestra. The title of the work, *Leader, Lieder*, conveys the essence of the piece. Its first movement is energetic and jazz influenced; the second, lyrical and meditative; the third, intense and fiery. Wilson comments, "... in times of crisis, we turn to our leaders to inspire us to act nobly and firmly, to direct our grieving, and respond to our needs. This concerto is an exploration of those relationships, with the trumpet soloist in the role of the leader."[18]

Steve Bryant's *Alchemy in Silent Spaces* is a three-movement work. Its first movement ("the logic of my dreams") was premiered on October 31, 2000, by the Indiana University Wind Ensemble, Ray Cramer, conductor. Four months later, on March 4, 2001, its final two movements, "points of attraction" and "the still point of destruction," were premiered by the Indiana University Wind Ensemble, again with Ray Cramer conducting. Bryant (b. 1959) offered the following description of his work.

> ... The [first movement] is for the most part delicate and quiet, relying on silence and space to create drama.... The second movement ... opens slowly, gradually ... spirals upward and outward... [winding] itself out and comes to a grinding halt in the upper range of the ensemble. Five brief, solemn chords conclude the movement, which immediately erupts into "the still point of destruction." The third movement... is of unceasing, but also unsettling, motion, propelled by a driving ostinato which is repeatedly interrupted by bittersweet moments of lyricism, all the while pushing toward an unforgiving climax.[19]

The stimulus for Bryant's piece was a chance meeting he had with Maestro James DePreist at The Juilliard School of Music. When DePreist discovered that Bryant was a composer, he asked if he could see some of his scores. He found *Alchemy in Silent Spaces* to be particularly attractive and suggested that Bryant make a version for orchestra. In May 2006, DePreist conducted the Julliard Symphony Orchestra in the premiere performance of the orchestra version of the piece at the school's annual Commencement Concert. (Note: Not many wind band/ensemble pieces at this time were being transcribed for orchestra by their composer.)

On June 17, 2001, the Goldman Memorial Band premiered *Grand Central Station*, a new work for winds by Michael Torke (b. 1961). Although the huge station in Midtown Manhattan (it covers 48 acres and has 44 platforms) is usually called "Grand Central Station," its official name is "Grand Central Terminal." Built during the heyday of American long-distance passenger train service, it underwent a major renovation in the 1990s. The dazzle of the old station's new look inspired Torke to write his piece.

> As I wrote this piece, I thought of the tremendous energy of arrivals and departures, the swirling shapes and patterns of people with optimistic expectations. Newly renovated, Grand Central Station has that wonderful mix of the classically old, along with its shiny, new, welcoming appearance. Like the Goldman Band itself, it has decades of rich, New York history, but it is very much alive today.[20]

Although Grand Central Terminal continues to be one of New York City's most famous attractions this is no longer true for the Goldman Band, which was disbanded and went out of existence in 2005.

Compositions by Eric Whitacre (b. 1970) are played by bands throughout the United States and world. Probably his most performed piece, *October*, was commissioned by a consortium of thirty Nebraska high school bands organized by band director Brian Anderson and premiered on May 14, 2000. The composer penned the following words about the piece:

> Something about the crisp autumn air and the subtle change in light always makes me a little sentimental, and as I started to sketch I felt that same quiet beauty in the writing. The simple, pastoral melodies and subsequent harmonies are inspired by the great English Romantics (Vaughan Williams, Elgar) as I felt that this style was also perfectly suited to capture the natural and pastoral soul of the season. I'm quite happy with the end result, especially because I feel there just isn't enough lush, beautiful music written for winds.[21]

Williams College professor David Kechley's *Restless Birds Before a Dark Moon* for alto saxophone and wind ensemble was commissioned by the United States Military Academy Band. It was premiered at the 12th World Saxophone Congress in Montreal on July 7, 2000, by the Academy Band, David Deitrick, conductor, with SSG Wayne

Tice, saxophone soloist. As the title suggests, the mood of the piece ranges between the frenzied to the foreboding. Kechley employs both modal and chromatic materials and often presents the same idea transformed from one to the other of these poles. *Restless Birds Before a Dark Moon* won the 2000 National Band Association William D. Revelli Memorial Composition Contest.

* * * * * * * * * * *

In 1999, James Croft and Robert Garofalo conducted a survey of CBDNA and WASBE members concerning performances of chamber wind music. The results revealed that 18% of the CBDNA respondents (32 of 169 respondents) and 56% of WASBE respondents (21 of 38) performed one to three concerts of chamber wind music each year with separate small wind groups. Over 50% of the surveyed conductors indicated they "occasionally" performed chamber works on their regular full wind band/ensemble concerts.[22]

* * * * * * * * * * *

The American Bandmasters Association Committee on School Bands issued a report at its 67th Annual Convention (Las Vegas, Nevada, from March 6–10, 2001) that focused on two topics: teacher attrition and music mentoring for young music educators. In his report, "Teacher Shortages ... An Old Issue, A New Face," David Gregory stated,

> Today there are thousands of classrooms in public [schools] across America that do not have professionally certified teachers in them. Instead, they are being filled by "extended substitute teachers," persons who possess college degrees but have not been trained in educational and pedagogical techniques ... The ease with which local school systems can place non-certified personnel into teaching situations might entice some administrators to experiment with the idea in the area of music, provided that they do not make the decision to eliminate existing programs entirely.[23]

Another member of the committee, Gil Lettow, cited the Iowa music teacher-mentoring program which is an alliance of the Iowa Bandmasters Association, Iowa Choral Directors Association, Iowa

String Teachers Association, and the Iowa Music Educator National Conference. This program provides mentoring assistance to all beginning music teachers, teachers who have recently moved to Iowa, and music teachers who have moved within the state to a new district. Lettow's concluding statement focused on teacher recruitment and retention.

> Though we must continue to deal with the issues of inadequate budgets and block scheduling, they no longer [are] our major concerns ... rather, it's getting and holding quality teachers in music education. How can we make the teaching profession more attractive? How might we improve strategies for recruitment and retention of quality music educators?[24]

* * * * * * * * * * *

As noted in Chapter 5, Frederick Fennell conducted a "Concert of Music for Wind Instruments" at the Eastman School of Music in Rochester, New York, on February 4, 1951, which led to the formation of the Eastman Wind Ensemble. It was an "unusual" band concert at the time since it consisted entirely of original works for wind instruments (program, below).

Concert Music for Wind Instruments
(Orchestra Department)
Frederick Fennell, Conductor
Kilbourn Hall, February 5, 1951

Willaert	*Ricercare for Wind Instruments* (1559)
Scheidt	*Canzon XXVI* (Bergamasca) for Five Instruments
DiLasso	*Motet: Tui Sunt Coeli* for Eight-voice Double Brass Choir
G. Gabrieli	*Sonata pian e forte*
G. Gabrieli	*Noni Toni a 12* from *Sacrae Symphonie* (1597)
Pezel	*Suite No. 2 for Brass Instruments* (*Turmmusik*) (1685)
Beethoven	*Three Equali* for Four Trombones (1812)

Intermission

Mozart	*Serenade No. 10 in B-flat major for Wind* Instruments (1781)

Intermission

Strauss	*Serenade in E-flat major, Op. 7*, for Thirteen Wind Instruments
Ruggles	*"Angels" from Men and Angels* (1921)
Stravinsky	*Symphonies for Wind Instruments* (1920)

(In Memory of Claude Debussy)

Fifty years later, on February 5, 2001, Fennell guest conducted the Arizona State University Chamber Winds and Wind Symphony in a repeat performance of this historic concert. Gary Hill, conductor of the Arizona State University Wind Symphony, recalled that everyone at the concert was aware of its significance: "... we were all thrilled! Several in attendance were former students of Fred's, some from the 1940s! All in all, [it was] an exhilarating near-three hour spectacle!"[25]

A few months later, on April 21, 2001, Frederick Fennell was inducted into the American Classical Music Hall of Fame. His co-inductees included Antonín Dvořák, Sergei Rachmaninov, Paul Hindemith, Itzhak Perlman, Juilliard String Quartet, and the New York Philharmonic.

* * * * * * * * * * * *

In 1966, Boston Symphony Orchestra Conductor/Music Director Erich Leinsdorf invited Boston University's School of the Arts to develop a summer institute that would offer musical training and education to outstanding high school orchestral and vocal students at the Berkshire Music Center in Lenox, Massachusetts (summer home of the Boston Symphony Orchestra). In 2000, under the leadership of Frank L. Battisti, a wind ensemble—the Young Artists Wind Ensemble (YAWE)—was added to the Institute's curriculum. Every year the 45–50 talented high school woodwind, brass, and percussion students rehearse and perform two wind ensemble concerts and four chamber music programs during a four-week residency at Tanglewood. Below is the program performed by the YAWE on August 2, 2001.

Boston University Tanglewood Institute
Young Artists Wind Ensemble
Frank L. Battisti, Conductor
Frederick Harris, Jr., Assistant Conductor
Ozawa Hall
Thursday, August 2, 2001
7:30 PM

Richard Strauss (1864–1949)   *Wiener Philharmoniker Fanfare* (1934)
Vincent Persichetti (1915–1987)   *Divertimento for Band* (1951)

Frederick Harris, Jr., Conductor

Rafael A. Hernandez (b. 1975)   *Inconnurvana* (2001)

World Premiere

Gunther Schuller (b. 1925)   *Blue Dawn into White Heat* (1996)

Frederick Harris, Jr., Conductor

Intermission

Joaquín Rodrigo (1902–1999)   *Adagio* (1965)

Karel Husa (b. 1921)   *Music for Prague* 1968

* * * * * * * * * * * * *

The 10th WASBE International Conference was held in Lucerne, Switzerland, from July 8–14, 2001. Nine new works were premiered at the conference: *Prospero* by Thüring Bräm (b. 1944), *Conatus* by Thomas Doss (b. 1966), *Divertimento* by Erland Freudenthaler (b. 1963), *... bis ins Unendliche...* by Rolf Rudin (b. 1961), *... und wo sich Wort und Ton gesellt ...* by Gunter Waldek (b. 1953), *Pictures of Imaginary Windscapes* by Frank Zabel (b. 1968), and *Ten of a Kind* by David Rakowski (b. 1958). The Chor des Collegium Musicum Luzern and the Bläser der Jungen Philharmonie Zentralschweiz, Alois Koch, conductor, performed Arthur Honegger's little known *Nicolas de Flüe*, a 1939 dramatic legend in three acts for solo voice, children's choir, chorus, and wind orchestra. Reports posted on the WASBE website by attendees during the Conference focused on the artistic merit of the music being performed.

ENDNOTES

1   Chris Pasles, "Look Who's Marching In," *Los Angeles Times* (March 29, 2008): E14–15.

2   "Sinfonia XXI by Timothy Broege performed by the Keystone Winds, Jack Stamp, conductor," *CBDNA Report* (Spring 2001): [4].

3   Tim Reynish, "CBDNA 2001 Conference," Tim Reynish, accessed June 1, 2018, http://www.timreynish.com/conferences/cbdna-2001.php.

4   David Maslanka, *Symphony No. 5*, Illinois State University Wind Symphony, Stephen K. Steele, conductor, Albany Records TROY 500, 2002, Liner notes by David Maslanka.

5   Cindy McTee, "Timepiece for Wind Symphony," Cindy McTee, Composer, accessed June 1, 2018, http://cindymctee.com/timepiece_band.html.

6   "Fascinating Ribbons by Joan Tower performed by the Keystone Winds, Jack Stamp, conductor," *CBDNA Report* (Spring 2001): [4].

7 "Canvas by George Walker performed by the North Texas Wind Symphony, Eugene Migliaro Corporon, conductor", *CBDNA Report* (Spring 2001): [5].

8 Scott Carter, "Dan Welcher: *Songs Without Words*," in *Teaching Music Through Performance in Band*, Volume 4, ed. Richard Mills (GIA Publications, 2002), 556–557.

9 Charles Peltz, "Introductory Comments," *Journal of the World Association for Symphonic Bands and Ensembles* 8 (2001): 62.

10 Philip Sparke, "Sunrise at Angel's Gate," *The Music of Philip Sparke*, accessed June 1, 2018, http://www.philipsparke.com/sunrise.htm.

11 *Originals: Unique Works for Winds*, United States Marine Band, Timothy Foley, conductor, USMB-CD-22, [2006], Liner notes.

12 Fiona Maddocks, "The Holy Grail is in Scotland (not for long)," *The Observer* (London) (March 11, 2000).

13 Michael Colburn, "Special Feature," *CBDNA Report* (Fall 2001): 6.

14 David Rakowski, "Program Note," United States Marine Band, concert of May 20, 2001.

15 Michael Colgrass, "Composer's Program Note," New England Conservatory Wind Ensemble, concert of April 26, 2001.

16 Richard Dyer, *Boston Globe* (April 27, 2001).

17 *Toccata Festiva*, Depauw University Band, Craig Paré, conductor, Mark MCD-5438, 2004, Liner notes.

18 Timothy Reynish, "The Wind Music of Dana Wilson," *WASBE Newsletter* (December 2006): 7.

19 "Alchemy in Silent Spaces (wind ensemble)," Steven Bryant: Composer/Conductor, accessed June 1, 2018, https://www.stevenbryant.com/music/catalog/alchemy-in-silent-spaces-wind-ensemble.

20 "Torke's 'Grand Central Station,'" *Composer's Datebook*, American Public Media (June 16, 2011), accessed June 1, 2018, https://www.iheart.com/podcast/3-composers-datebook-27977125/episode/torkes-grand-central-station-28234453/.

21 "October," Eric Whitacre: Composer, Conductor, Speaker, accessed June 1, 2018, https://ericwhitacre.com/music-catalog/wind-symphony/october.

22 "Chamber Winds Survey (1998–1999)," *CBDNA Report* (Spring 2000), 21.

23 David Gregory, "Teacher Shortages … An Old Issue, A New Face." *Book of Proceedings*, 67th American Bandmasters Association Convention (March 6–11, 2001), 54–55.

24 Gil Lettow, "Music Mentors of Iowa." *Book of Proceedings*, 67th American Bandmasters Association Convention (March 6–11, 2001), 56.

25 Gary Hill, letter to the author, September 9, 2009.

CHAPTER 12

Moving Forward and Looking Back (2002–2003)

"Focusing on the Future, Discovering our Heritage" •
Gotham Wind Symphony • *School Band Programs and*
Activities

A conference, "Focusing on the Future, Discovering our Heritage," was held at the Eastman School of Music in Rochester, New York, on February 6–9, 2002 to celebrate the 50th Anniversary of the founding of the Eastman Wind Ensemble. Over 200 delegates attended concerts performed by the Eastman Wind Ensemble, Ithaca College Wind Ensemble, Cincinnati Conservatory of Music Chamber Winds, and the United States Military Academy (West Point) Band. Among the conference's many highlights were premiere performances of two new works: Bernard Rands's *Unending Lightning* and Steven Stucky's *Concerto for Percussion and Wind Orchestra*. Rands's piece was performed by the Eastman Wind Ensemble, Donald Hunsberger, conductor and Stucky's piece by the Ithaca College Wind Ensemble, Stephen Peterson, conductor, with Gordon Stout as percussion soloist.

In his program note about *Unending Lightning*, Rands (b. 1934) wrote:

[The work was] completed in June 2001 [and] takes its title from a poem by Dylan Thomas. Its formal structure ... juxtaposes two markedly different, seemingly irreconcilable musical ideas and alternates them throughout the duration of the work—both elements undergoing transformation on each of their subsequent appearances.... *Unending Lightning* engages the wind ensemble in a virtuosic display of rhythmic agility, timbre, and dynamic range and, though challenging in these respects, it does so without placing taxing demands on individual players. In short, it aims at a collective, ensemble virtuosity rather than a soloistic one.[1]

Stucky also attached a program note to his *Concerto*.

There are a number of timbre groupings: wood and drum sounds in the first movement, set against boisterous, big-band-like riffs from the ensemble, for example; or marimba paired with steel drum as the lyrical voices in the slow second movement. The third movement, a scherzo, uses only keyboards ... and ... winks broadly at Strauss's *Till Eulenspiegel*. The fourth movement turns to solemn, metallic resonances—gongs, Japanese temple bells, Almglocken (tuned European cowbells)—and it sets these against the ominous heartbeat pattern of the bass drum. This movement reflects the somber atmosphere of the fall of 2001.... Ordinarily I am skeptical of musical responses to outside events, and I never planned to write a piece "about" the attacks of September 11; yet, as I was writing this movement I asked myself why the music seemed so dark, so serious, and only then I realized that the world had thrust itself into my music whether I wanted it or not. Hence the dedication "To the victims of September 11, 2001," added after the fourth movement was finished.[2]

Interspersed between concerts were numerous presentations and panel discussions covering a wide range of subjects including "Richard Strauss' Final Works," "Charles Ives' Musical World," "Orchestrating for Winds," and "The West Point Commissions, 1952 & 2002." A panel consisting of international wind band/ensemble conductors—Timothy Reynish (England), Felix Hauswirth (Switzerland), Toshio Akiyama (Japan), and Dennis Johnson (USA)—discussed the emerging international repertoire. Another panel made up of composers—Richard Rodney Bennett, Karel Husa, Verne Reynolds, Steven Stucky, Bernard Rands, and Dana Wilson—discussed composing for wind bands/ensembles. Warner Brothers issued a multi-CD set of never-before-released Eastman Wind Ensemble recordings to commemorate the Ensemble's golden anniversary.

* * * * * * * * * * * *

The American Bandmasters Association's 68th Convention was held on March 5–10, 2002, in Wichita, Kansas. Two new works were also premiered at this Convention. The first, *Illuminations* by Dean Roush (b. 1952), was commissioned for the Centennial Celebration of the Wichita State University Bands and premiered by the University's Wind Ensemble, Victor Markovich, conductor. The second was a wind band version of *Harrison's Dream* by Peter Graham (b. 1958), which was commissioned and performed by the United States Air Force Band, conducted by Commander Colonel Lowell E. Graham.

There is a very interesting story behind the commissioning of Graham's piece. The commission from the Air Force Band came immediately after Graham had just received one from Boosey & Hawkes to compose a brass band work for the UK National Brass Band Contest. Graham wanted to accept both commissions. He hoped an agreement could be worked out between the two commissioning parties that would allow him to compose two versions of his piece at the same time—one for wind band and one for brass band. An agreement was made and Graham proceeded to compose. He stated that because both versions were composed simultaneously, "... neither [was] an arrangement of the other—brass ideas fed the wind and wind ideas fed the brass."[3]

The inspiration for Graham's piece was a massive wreck of four Royal Navy ships off the Scilly Isles in 1707, which was caused primarily by the lack of highly accurate clocks which are needed to calculate position of ships at sea. In an attempt to solve this problem, Parliament funded a prize for the development of clocks that would remedy this situation. Clockmaker John Harrison (1693–1776) worked more than 40 years to create highly-accurate clocks that could provide the longitude information needed for safe navigation of ships.

The composer added the following about his piece:

> Much of the music is mechanistic in tone and is constructed along precise mathematical and metrical lines. Aural echoes of the clockmaker's workshop alternate with nightmare dream pictures—Harrison was haunted by the realization that countless lives depended on a solution to the longitude problem. The emotional core of the work reflects on the

evening of 22nd October 1707 [the date of the massive wrecking of the four Royal Navy ships].[4]

* * * * * * * * * * * *

In 2002, the American Bandmasters Association awarded its prestigious Edwin Franko Goldman Memorial Citation to Jonathan Elkus, former Band Director at Lehigh University and the University of California, Davis. The citation honored Elkus for his "significant contributions to bands and band music in America," specifically for his research on Charles Ives and the American Band, as well as his transcriptions of Ives works for band.

* * * * * * * * * * * *

The National Band Association and the Texas Bandmasters Association held a joint conference in San Antonio, Texas, on July 28–31, 2002, which attracted 6,500 people and over 1,000 exhibitors. One of the convention sessions focused on the NBA Young Composer Mentor Project. Convention attendees were given an opportunity to witness the "creative compositional process" through the teaching of master composers Mark Camphouse, David Gillingham, and Frank Ticheli as they worked with three Young Composers in rehearsals of their pieces with the 323rd U. S. Army Band.

The works below are among the many that were commissioned by university wind groups and professional symphony and wind orchestras in 2002. They are examples of the varied styles of music included in the works written for wind bands/ensembles at the time.

Laurence Bitensky	Awake, You Sleepers!
Peter Child	Concertino for Violin & Chamber Winds
Donald Grantham	J. S. Dances
Christian Lindberg	Concerto for Winds and Percussion
Carter Pann	Slalom (wind version)
Joseph Turrin	Hemispheres
Eric Whitacre	Sleep (wind version)
Dana Wilson	Concerto for French Horn and Wind Ensemble
Evan Ziporyn	Drill

Much of the music of *Awake, You Sleepers!* By Laurence Bitensky (b. 1966) is based on Rosh Hashanah motives and melodies that occur in the German/East-European musical tradition. The blowing of the shofar in the Rosh Hashanah service is a call for repentance, symbolically awakening the sleeper from moral and spiritual slumber. Commenting on his work, Bitensky stated,

> *Awake, You Sleepers!* is based on the free and supple improvisation of traditional Jewish chant and some of its spirit of metrically-free improvisation should be maintained. The soloist and conductor should strive for a very fluid and flexible sense of tempo throughout, using much rubato.[5]

Awake, You Sleepers! was premiered at the International Trumpet Guild Conference in Manchester, England, on July 2, 2002. John Hagstrom was the trumpet soloist with the Royal Northern College of Music Wind Orchestra conducted by Timothy Reynish.

Peter Child (b. 1953) is a British-born composer and professor at MIT. He wrote his *Concertino for Violin and Chamber Winds* in 2002 for violinist Young-Nam Kim and the MIT Wind Ensemble. The work is in three short sections, fast-slow-fast, compressed into one movement, for violin and ten wind players. The string soloist's music is etched in sharp relief of the wind ensemble. The individual wind players step forward frequently to collaborate with the violin in the unfolding of the piece.

Donald Grantham (b. 1947) composed *J. S. Dances* in 2002. It was commissioned by the University of Akron Symphonic Band, Robert Jorgensen, conductor, and is based on two dances (*Minuet II* and *Gigue*) from Johann Sebastian Bach's *Partita I* (*Clavierübung, Part I*). The composer describes the eight-minute "free fantasy" piece as "[relentless] and reckless ... with the gigue character predominating." Grantham often employs quotations from other composers' music in his pieces—"[I] hope [to] ... put my own stamp on the material and show it ... in a fresh light."[6] Both Bach dances used in this piece appear in more or less their original forms, complemented by other material that develop and elaborate some of the many interesting aspects of the music.

Christian Lindberg (b. 1958), in addition to being one of the world's great trombone artists, is also a composer and conductor. His seventeen-minute *Concerto for Winds and Percussion* is a fresh, bold, and exciting piece. It was commissioned in 2002 by Timothy Reynish, President of WASBE, and premiered at the 2003 WASBE International Conference in Jönköping, Sweden, by the Swedish

Wind Ensemble, conducted by the composer. Lindberg tailored each solo passage in the work specifically for the Swedish Wind Ensemble player who would be performing it. Timothy Reynish provided the following description of the piece:

> The striking opening fanfare for brass plays an integral part in the piece, here ushering in the first section, a funky post-Zappa *allegro* in which every section is highlighted against jagged ostinato on trumpets and timpani.... The fanfare motto moves us forward into an extended passage for solo percussion, which in turn gives way to a reflective Schoenbergian few bars for woodwind soloists with a brief energetic coda. The fanfare slows the pace again, this time to a series of cadenzas for euphonium, baritone saxophone, two horns, two clarinets, and two trumpets, in turn. The final section gives differing rhythmic and harmonic twists to the opening material, and as the pace quickens, the writing becomes even more virtuosic, and the work erupts into a final triple forte climax.[7]

Carter Pann (b. 1972) created the wind version of *Slalom* in 2002. The original piece was composed for and premiered by the Haddonfield (New Jersey) Symphony Orchestra in March 2000. John P. Lynch, Director of Bands at the University of Kansas, heard a recording of the piece, liked what he heard, and decided to commission Pann to write a piece for wind ensemble. "We met to discuss whether it should be a completely new piece or a wind version of *Slalom*— we decided on *Slalom*." The wind version of the piece was premiered by John Lynch and the University of Kansas Wind Ensemble in fall 2002. The composer stated that the piece has the "taste of the thrill of downhill skiing."

> ... it's a collection of scenes and events one might come by on the slopes. The score is peppered with phrase-headings for the different sections such as "First Run," "Open Meadow, Champagne Powder," "Straight Down, Tuck," and "On One Ski, Gyrating," among others. In this way *Slalom* shares its programmatic feature with that of Richard Strauss's *Alpine Symphony*. The similarities end there, however, for *Slalom* lasts ten minutes ... precisely the amount of time I need to get from Storm Peak (the peak of Mt. Werner, Steamboat Springs) to the mountain base, skiing full throttle.[8]

The New York Philharmonic commissioned Joseph Turrin (b. 1947) to write a piece for the retirement of Music Director/Conductor, Kurt Masur. The piece he wrote for the occasion, *Hemispheres*, is a twenty-minute work in three movements for orchestra winds, harp, percussion, and piano/celesta. In the program note for the piece, Turin wrote,

> While composing [the piece], I began to explore the concept of the hemisphere and how individual parts come together forming a larger more perfect whole. The idea of a sphere, a circle, the earth, evolution, the cycle, the journey, and returning to the origin seem to take hold. I thought how every culture has beliefs about creation and that somehow they are all based on a similar idea—that of returning to the origin, the full circle.[9]

Prior to conducting the premiere of *Hemispheres* on May 30, 2002, Mazur observed a moment of silence for the victims of the 9/11/01 tragedy. Bernard Holland, *New York Times* music critic, wrote this about the piece:

> *"Hemispheres"* is everything the other two items [Bartók's *Divertimento for String Orchestra* and Beethoven's *Violin Concerto*] at this concert were not. Stripped of strings and fully loaded with winds, brass and percussion, Mr. Turrin's music is nervous, loud, swift and aggressive to the point of violence. It is also beautifully made, negotiating its constant changes of speed and pulse with grace.[10]

Eric Whitacre's wind version of *Sleep* was commissioned by the Big East Band Director's Association. Discussions between the composer and the Association led to a decision that Whitacre (b. 1970) would create a wind version of one of his choral pieces, *Sleep*. This new version was premiered on April 26, 2002, by the Rutgers Wind Ensemble, William Berz, conductor. Commenting about his piece Whitacre stated,

> *Sleep* began its life as an a cappella choral setting, with a magnificent original poem by Charles Anthony Silvestri. The chorale-like nature and warm harmonies seemed to call out for the simple and plaintive sound of winds, and I thought that it might make a gorgeous addition to the wind symphony repertoire.[11]

Dana Wilson's *Concerto for French Horn and Orchestra* was commissioned by horn virtuoso Gail Williams, who premiered the work with the Syracuse Symphony Orchestra in 1997. Five years later (2002), Williams premiered the composer's wind ensemble version of the *Concerto* with the Ithaca College Wind Ensemble, Stephen

Peterson, conductor, at the Eastman Wind Ensemble's 50th Anniversary celebration in Rochester, NY. The piece is structured in the traditional three-movement concerto form and begins with a cadenza that evolves into a very rhythmic and dramatic first movement. The middle movement (marked "plaintively") is lyrical and expressive; the final movement, dramatic, and "molto" energetic. It is a "tour de force" for both soloist and ensemble players.

Composer/clarinetist Evan Ziporyn (b. 1959) is a member of the "Bang On A Can All-Stars" and founder-director of Gamelan Galak Tika, a Balinese music and dance company located in Boston, Massachusetts. His music is drawn from world and classical music, the avant-garde, and jazz. *Drill,* Ziporyn's concerto for bass clarinet and wind ensemble, was commissioned and premiered by Frederick Harris and the MIT Wind Ensemble in 2002, with the composer as soloist. Composer Peter Child wrote this about *Drill,*

> Clarinets, other woodwinds, and eventually the entire ensemble periodically shadow the brisk, athletic lines of the soloist in unison, octaves or strictly parallel intervals. The texture is fresh, dense and transparent.... The influence of Balinese music ... is never far off [and] is reflected in the cycling modal figures ... and in the percussion writing. Loud, autonomous, scintillating percussion provides the rhythmic foundation, at once metrical and mercurial, to this bracing, exuberant work.[12]

* * * * * * * * * * * *

The American Bandmasters Association held its 69th convention in Baltimore/College Park, Maryland, on March 4–9, 2003. A concert by the Allentown (Pennsylvania) Band featured the premiere performance of Francis McBeth's *Three Scenes for Bret Harte's The Outcasts of Poker Flat.* The piece was commissioned by the Band for its 175th Anniversary Celebration. Founded in 1828, the Allentown Band is the nation's oldest non-military wind group.

The Educational Projects Committee of the American Bandmasters Association announced that it would initiate and support a project to create new urtext editions of selected band masterpieces, including full scores and corrected parts. The first three works selected for this project were *American Overture for Band* by Joseph Wilcox Jenkins (1928–2014), *An Original Suite for Band* by Gordon

Jacob (1895–1984), and Robert Leist and Richard Franko Goldman's arrangement of *Fantasia in G* by J. S. Bach (1685–1750).

CBDNA's 32nd National Conference, held at the University of Minnesota on March 26–29, 2003, featured the premiere performances of five new works for wind band/ensemble:

"Tattoo" from *Symphony for Wind Orchestra* by Judith Lang Zaimont
Fanfare Canzonique by Brian Balmages
Jubilare! by John Stevens
Ra! by David Dzubay
Bliss, *Variations on an Unchanging Rhythm* by Michael Torke

Tattoo by Judith Zaimont (b. 1945), is the final "scene" in her *Symphony for Wind Orchestra*. The work was commissioned by the University of Minnesota to celebrate the Centennial of the School of Music and was premiered by the University of Minnesota Wind Ensemble, Craig Kirchhoff, conductor.

> [It is] ... a seven-minute wild ride in galloping compound meters. Rapid, rollicking beats and pinpoint tonguing send a "call" to all to gather and make a big sound together. In addition to an overall sound calibrated for brilliance, many solo moments are embedded—particularly the English horn and bass clarinet—the winds, brass and saxophone sections are spotlighted repeatedly throughout the piece.[13]

Fanfare Canzonique by Brian Balmages (b. 1975) was the opening piece on the program performed by the University of Miami Wind Ensemble, Gary Green, conductor, at the Conference. It was written in memory of Gilbert Johnson, principal trumpet of the Philadelphia Orchestra and professor of trumpet at the University of Miami. The composer tried to embody some of Johnson's strongest qualities in the piece. Since *The Antiphonal Music of Gabrieli* and Respighi's *Pines of Rome* were two of Johnson's most famous recordings, Balmages included musical quotations from each of these in his piece. The composer explained,

The opening fanfare becomes the structural canvas on which Gabrieli's *Canzona per sonare no. 2* is painted. This explains the beginning and the ending of the work. The middle section is a little more elusive.... It was only [after] I heard the eulogy at Mr. Johnson's funeral (which made a significant reference to his off-stage solo in *Pines of Rome*) that I was able to understand the need [to place it in] this section. There is a strong spiritual climax in the piece as the antiphonal trumpet solo fades, only to be "caught" by the on-stage trumpet soloist who [completes] the phrase.[14]

The original version of *Jubilare!* by John Stevens (b. 1951) was commissioned by the Madison Symphony Orchestra for its 75th anniversary season in 2000. Later the Ohio State University Wind Symphony commissioned Stevens to create a wind version of the piece. *Jubilare!*—"to shout for joy"—is a joyous and energetic work which celebrates the present and future of music.[15]

Ra! by David Dzubay (b. 1964) was originally composed for orchestra. The Indiana University Wind Ensemble, Ray Cramer, conductor, commissioned Dzubay to create a wind ensemble version of the piece, which won the William D. Revelli Memorial Composition Contest in 2003. The composer wrote the following information about *Ra!*:

> The sun god Ra was the most important god of the ancient Egyptians. Born anew each day ... Ra would do battle with his chief enemy, a serpent named Apep, usually emerging victorious, though on stormy days or during an eclipse, the Egyptians believed that Apep won and swallowed the sun.
>
> *Ra!* is a rather aggressive depiction of an imagined ritual of sun worship, perhaps celebrating the daily battles of Ra and Apep. There are four ideas presented in the [piece]: 1) a "skin dance" featuring the timpani and other percussion, 2) a declarative, unison melodic line, 3) a layered texture of pulses, and 4) sun bursts and shines. The movements alternate abruptly between these ideas, as if following the precise dictates of a grand ceremony.[16]

Michael Torke (b. 1961) is a master orchestrator who creates music that is joyful and uplifting. His *Bliss, Variations on an Unchanging Rhythm* was commissioned by a consortium of thirty CBDNA member institutions and premiered by the Williams College Symphonic Winds, Steven Dennis Bodner, conductor, on May 9, 2003. The composer wrote,

> A simple rhythm (4 eighth notes, rest, 1 eighth note, rest, 2 eighth notes, rest) is the underpinning that [is heard] throughout. What changes is the melodies assigned to these rhythmic values, and the harmonies that support them. With percussionists tapping out the rhythm (including amplified clapping) the accumulation becomes an ever-increasing celebration; a state of Bliss.... [The] music ... expresses an unfettered, joyous state.[17]

Among the other recently composed pieces performed at the 2003 CBDNA National Conference were Michael Daugherty's *Bells for Stokowski* (2002), Robert Xavier Rodriguez's *Decem perfectum, Concertino for Woodwind Quintet, Brass Quintet and Wind Ensemble* (2002), Michael Djupstrom's *Homages* (2002), Scott Lindroth's *Spin Cycle* (2001), and Scott McAllister's *Black Dog* (2002).

* * * * * * * * * * * *

The 11th Conference of the World Association of Symphonic Bands and Ensembles took place in Jönköping, Sweden, from June 29–July 7, 2003. Thirteen concerts were performed during the weeklong event that included seventy-two works written by composers from Austria, Belgium, Brazil, Canada, Croatia, Denmark, New Zealand, Russia, and the United States. One of the Conference highlights was the premiere performance of the first two movements of Frank Ticheli's *Symphony No. 2* by the Florida State University Wind Orchestra conducted by James Croft, the retiring Director of Bands at FSU. Students and friends of Croft commissioned the piece to celebrate his many contributions to music education and bands. Other works receiving premiere performances at the Conference included *Recollection* by Czaba Deák (b. 1932), *Dance Sequence* by Marco Pütz (b. 1958), and *Cyrano* by Piet Swerts (b. 1960).

Gary W. Hill, Director of Bands at Arizona State University and President of the College Band Directors National Association, was the keynote speaker at the Conference. His address focused on "the future of the wind band." It was provocative and challenging.

> Our hope for a better tomorrow lies not in "teaching the way we were taught," in perpetuating worn-out paradigms of performance, or in preserving a second-rate body of literature, but in moving the wind band field from its present place on the cultural fringe, where it is a marginal player, to the cultural edge, where it can become "the next big thing." It is only there that the fervent dream we have, a dream inherited from our ancestors—to see wind bands share center stage in both music education and art music—can someday be realized.[18]

There were a number of very good pieces written for wind band/ensemble during 2003, among them the following:

Chris Brubeck	On the Threshold of Liberty
Steven Bryant	Rise
David Del Tredici	In Wartime
Eric Ewazen	Visions of Light
Michael Gandolfi	Vientos y Tangos
Sydney Hodkinson	Monumentum Pro Umbris
Morten Lauridsen	O Magnum Mysterium (arranged by H. Robert Reynolds)
Christopher Marshall	L'Homme Armé Variations for Wind Ensemble
Jonathan Newman	As the scent of spring rain . . .
Kevin Puts	Millennium Canons

Chris Brubeck (b. 1952) is the son of the legendary pianist Dave Brubeck. He is a talented and versatile musician who plays string bass, trombone, piano, and guitar and also sings. As a composer he writes music in a genre-bending modern classical style. The *Chicago Tribune* describes him as a 21st century Lenny Bernstein with a real flair for lyrical melody. His works have been performed by many orchestras including the Boston Symphony Orchestra, London Symphony Orchestra, and Russian National Orchestra. Two wind works by Brubeck were premiered in 2003—*Vignettes for Nonet* (jazz quartet and woodwind quintet), which was commissioned by the St. Paul Chamber Orchestra and Philadelphia Chamber Society, and *On the Threshold of Liberty*, which was written for and premiered by the U. S. Army Field Band at the 2003 Midwest International Band and Orchestra Clinic.[19]

Rise by Steven Bryant (b. 1972), and *As the scent of Spring Rain...* by Jonathan Newman (b. 1972) were both premiered by the Emory University Wind Ensemble, Scott Stewart, conductor, on October 8, 2002. *Rise* is a wind ensemble arrangement of the first movement of Bryant's saxophone quartet of the same name. Commenting on the piece the composer wrote,

> ... there is no extra-musical imagery or narrative structure associated with the music. It is a lush adagio built upon a repeated cycle of chords ascending in stepwise motion. The music gradually gains upward momentum over this cyclical progression, reaching a powerful dramatic climax. The energy and momentum dissipate, returning the music to its opening contemplative quietness. Though *Rise* is not programmatic, I believe the connotation of the title, and the corresponding nature of the music, implies a clear, unsentimental sense of optimism and hope.[20]

David Del Tredici (b. 1937) is one of the fathers of the Neo-Romantic movement in music (rather amazing considering he was trained as an atonal composer) and one of America's leading composers. He won the Pulitzer Prize in Music in 1980 for *In Memory of a Summer Day*, the first part of his *Child Alice*.

His first, and only wind work, *In Wartime*, was commissioned by the wind bands/ensembles of Florida State University, University of Texas, Baylor University, University of Michigan, and University of Tennessee, and premiered on April 30, 2003, by the University of Texas Wind Ensemble, Jerry Junkin, conductor. Del Tredici composed the piece during the 2003 invasion of Iraq by the United States, United Kingdom, and small contingents of troops from Australia, Denmark, and Poland. The composer commented on the experience of writing the piece:

> *In Wartime* ... was begun on November 16, 2002, and completed on March 16 (my birthday), 2003—as momentous a four-month period in U. S. history as I have experienced. With my TV blaring, I composed throughout this period, feeling both irresistibly drawn to the developing news and more than a little guilty to be unable to turn the tube off. Composing music at such a time may have seemed an irrelevant pursuit, but it nevertheless served to keep me sane, stable and sanguine, despite the world's spiraling maelstrom.[21]
>
> *In Wartime* consists of two connected movements—Hymn and Battle March. The first has the character of a chorale prelude, with fragments of *Abide with Me* embedded beneath a welter of contrasting and contrapuntal musical material.
>
> Heralded by a long, ominous roll on the snare drum and a steady, measured beat, "Battlemarch" announces the start of war ... Like the incoming tide, the "waves" encroach inexorably on new harmonic ground; like a gathering storm, the waveforms grow in enormity and frenzy, until their fateful confrontation with *Salmati, shah!* (the national song of Persia), laced as well with quotes from the opening of Wagner's *Tristan und Isolde*. With East battling West in musical terms, this trio section of the march builds to the movement's climax. As the over whelming wash of sound subsides, the opening march returns, now battle-weary but growing nevertheless to a full-throttled recapitulation and finale—marked inevitably by a wail of pain.[22]

Eric Ewazen (b. 1954) composed *Visons of Light* (Concerto for Trombone and Wind Ensemble) for Joseph Alessi, Principal Trombonist of the New York Philharmonic. Alessi and the Indiana

University Wind Ensemble, conducted by Ray Cramer, premiered the work at the 2003 Midwest International Band and Orchestra Clinic in Chicago. Each of the concerto's three movements was inspired by an Ansel Adams photograph. Wayne Groves, writing in the *International Trombone Association Journal* (January 2008) described each movement.

> The first movement, subtitled "Monolith, The Face of Half Dome" is both rhythmic and lyrical, depicting the contrast between sky and the rock face as well as the shapes and lines of the mountain. The second movement, "Moonrise, Hernandez, New Mexico" makes frequent use of three against two rhythms and minor tonality to reflect the mysterious landscape of buildings, a village cemetery, and rising hills and mountains with the moon rising behind it. The third movement, "Thunderclouds, White Mountain Range" begins ... with rising and falling lines that depict the gathering storm clouds. Driving exchanges between soloist and accompaniment suggest the gathering energy of the approaching storm ... the piece ends in blazing glory.[23]

Michael Gandolfi's *Vientos y Tangos* is an homage to the tango. Frank Battisti requested that Gandolfi write a tango for wind ensemble. It was premiered on March 2, 2003, by the United States Marine Band, Major Michael J. Colburn conducting. Battisti was scheduled to conduct the premiere, but illness prevented him from doing so. In a program note for the piece, Gandolfi (b. 1956) describes how he went about writing the work:

> I decided to write a piece that explores several aspects of tango, from the early style to the "nuevo" style to the current disco-laden style. Of course, I focused on the instrumental tango, but I also listened to a wealth of vocal tangos, which more accurately express the full meaning of this genre. (It's kind of like the blues.) I prepared by studying and transcribing Tangos by D'Arienzo, Pugliese, Piazzolla, and the Bajofondo Tango Club, primarily. I then set out to write a three part piece that explores each of these three styles. A brief introduction gives way to the first tango, which is a homage to D'Arienzo and the older style. An interlude/cadenza follows and leads to a nuevo style tango (somewhat Piazzolla inspired). Finally we veer into a disco-tango, which rocks the house (hopefully).[24]

The Stetson University Wind Ensemble, Bobby Adams, conductor, premiered Sydney Hodkinson's *Monumentum Pro Umbris* (Memorial for the Departed Spirits) on November 3, 2003. The twenty-minute long work, scored for standard wind ensemble, large battery of percussion instruments, piano, and harp, is a meditation on the lives lost to wars, disease, and natural disasters in the past decade. Hodkinson (b. 1934) states that the "... music has a dark, meditative, 'processional' aspect, perhaps evoking a somewhat Byzantine religious ritual.... All of the sonic material... is generated from a brief fragment of Claudio Monteverdi's 1608 *Lamento d'Arianna* ... heard very distantly near the close of the piece."[25] Chris Vancil, writing in the *Society of Composers Newsletter* described the work as, "... dazzling.... Brilliant timbral gems melded one into the next, with orchestration that [resembles] a large symphonic work more than the usual band fare."[26]

Morten Lauridsen's choral work, O *Magnum Mysterium,* was premiered by the Los Angeles Master Chorale, Paul Salamunovich, conductor, in 1994. The genesis of H. Robert Reynolds's wind band/ ensemble arrangement of the piece began when Lauridsen (b. 1943) approach him in 2002 and inquired if he knew the piece. Reynolds assured him that he did—he said he even had a recording of it. Lauridsen mentioned that there was a brass ensemble version of the work and asked Reynolds if he might be interested in performing it with the University of Southern California Wind Ensemble. Reynolds relates the rest of the story.

> Several times over the next few weeks I suggested that he make a wind ensemble version of the piece. Lauridsen said he was uncomfortable writing for the wind ensemble and suggested that perhaps Frank Ticheli (also on the USC faculty) or I could do an arrangement of the piece. I told him I would take it on—which I did. I made two different arrangements of the piece and played both of them through with the USC Wind Ensemble. Afterwards Lauridsen and I discussed both versions and decided on the one we thought was the best. I premiered that version with the USC Wind Ensemble on March 9, 2003, after which I made one change—I rescored the second statement of the melody for solo trumpet instead of solo oboe. Since Kristin, my wife, teaches oboe—I had heard many young oboists. I felt that some of the ensembles that would be performing my arrangement might not have a really good oboist—so I decided to have the part played by a trumpet. To make sure everything was correct I played through the arrangement again with the USC Wind Ensemble and asked the players if their parts had any idiomatic issues.

All responded that their parts were fine except one horn player who said that while his part was well written idiomatically, "It would be nice to have a least one measure rest in the piece" (much laughter ensued). I made an edit to satisfy the horns. [Note: Reynolds was a horn player.][27]

New Zealand-born composer Christopher Marshall's *L'Homme Armé: Variations for Wind Ensemble* was commissioned by Timothy and Hilary Reynish in memory of their third son, William, who died in a mountain climbing accident. The Guildhall Symphonic Wind Ensemble, Peter Gane, conductor, premiered the work on July 3, 2003, at the WASBE Conference in Jönköping, Sweden. Marshall (b. 1956) states that he had to find proper balance between three competing and apparently incompatible intentions when he decided to write a work based on the ancient tune, *L'Homme Armé*.

> Firstly, given the text of the song and the time at which I was writing the music—prior to and during the hostilities in Iraq—I wanted it to express something of my feelings towards the institution of war. Secondly, since the melody of "L'homme armé" had been an inspiration to dozens of composers over more than five centuries since its composition, I intended to honour that tradition.... Thirdly, some evidence points to the origin of this tune as a drinking song, so it was important that the music should have an element of enjoyment and exuberance ... The "homage to musical tradition" is seen in the form of the whole piece—that most ancient of musical structures, variations on a theme.... I quickly came to the conclusion that "L'homme armé" owed much of its popularity with composers to its great contrapuntal potential.... Gradually I came to see that my three intentions for this piece were not entirely incompatible.[28]

Jonathan Newman's short, gentle and expressive work, *As the scent of spring rain ...* was inspired by his "remembrance" of a poem by Leah Goldberg.

> *As the scent of spring rain ...* comes from a translation of the evocative first line of a love poem by Israeli poet, author and playwright Leah Goldberg. The poem itself was introduced to me by a good friend of mine a number of years ago, and I have a strong memory of how much the beauty of the original Hebrew and the imagery in her translation touched me. Because of that I deliberately did not work from the poem itself but only from my memory of it, which was so special to me that I didn't want to disturb it with a re-reading which would create a new and different experience. As a result, the harmonic language, structure, and

orchestration all aim to conjure the intense juxtaposition of sweetness and sadness which I most remember from the poem.[29]

Kevin Puts (b. 1972) has been the recipient of many commissions from leading orchestras in the United States and abroad. He won the Barlow International Composition Competition in 1999, a John Simon Guggenheim Memorial Foundation Fellowship in 2001, American Academy in Rome Prize in 2001–2002, and the Pulitzer Prize in Music in 2012. In 2001 the Boston Pops Orchestra, Keith Lockhart, conductor, premiered his seven-minute long *Millennium Canons*. Two years later (2003) Jerry Junkin and the University of Texas Wind Ensemble premiered Mark Spede's wind version of the work. Puts said he composed the piece "... to usher in a new millennium with fanfare, celebration and lyricism." Later that year the University of Texas Wind Ensemble premiered another piece by Puts, *Chorus of Light*. This piece begins with very high, delicate sounds, which eventually coalesce into a melody. The opening melody assumes many guises throughout the piece—sometimes rich and lush, sometimes brutal and accented and sometimes triumphant and brassy.

* * * * * * * * * * *

Michael Christianson founded the Gotham Wind Symphony (GWS) in 2003. When Broadway musicians went on strike that year and won all their demands, Local 802 decided to celebrate "conspicuously" by playing informal concerts in Duffy Square (a concrete island in the middle of Times Square). When Christianson was asked to organize a brass ensemble for one of these concerts, he instead organized a 45-member wind ensemble and performed a concert in Times Square at the height of rush hour. Included in the music the group played were Bob Brookmeyer's *Celebration Jig*; Gustav Holst's *First Suite in E-flat*; George F. Handel's Overture to the *Royal Fireworks Music*; Sauter-Finegan's *Doodletown Fifers*; J. S. Bach/Holst's *Fugue a la Gigue*; Percy Grainger's *Irish Tune from County Derry*; Thad Jones's *The Great One*; and John Philip Sousa's *The Black Horse Troop*. In spite of the 50-degree temperature, swirling winds, and general commotion, the musicians truly enjoyed playing in a wind band again and issued their highest praise: "When's the next gig?"[30]

The personnel of the GWS consist of New York City musicians who perform in symphony orchestras, ballet orchestras, jazz/popular music groups, and Broadway show pit bands. The music they play ranges from standard wind band/ensemble pieces to modern jazz influenced compositions by Gil Evans, Miles Davis, and others. Christianson has been able to entice some of New York's best jazz musician-composers to compose new works for his ensemble which expand the stylistic dimensions of wind band/ensemble literature.

On July 12, 2003, the United States Marine Band, "The President's Own," performed a concert at the John F. Kennedy Center for the Performing Arts in Washington, D.C., to celebrate its 205th Anniversary. (The Marine Band is America's oldest professional musical organization.) Academy Award-winning composer John Williams guest conducted the Band in a program of music from his award-winning film scores including *The Cowboys Overture*, *Olympic Fanfare and Theme*, *Escapades for Alto Saxophone and Orchestra* from *Catch Me If You Can*, Theme from *Schindler's List*, "Raiders March" from *Raiders of the Lost Ark*, and "Adventures on Earth" from *E. T. the Extra-Terrestrial*. The enthusiastic applause at the end of the concert garnered four encores. Prior to conducting the last one, Williams addressed the audience—"My father, who was a professional musician, always imparted the idea that the maximum quality of wind and brass playing in our country was the U.S. Marine Band—so it was then, and so it is today. This tradition is in the capable hands, the nurturing hands, of each man and woman up here."[31]

* * * * * * * * * *

In January 2001, President George W. Bush revealed his "No Child Left Behind" education reform plan and called for bipartisan solutions to the challenges and problems of accountability, choice, and flexibility in Federal education programs. Within a year, despite the nation's economic problems and the terrorism challenges, Congress passed Bush's "No Child Left Behind Act." The new law's objective was to improve the performance of America's elementary and secondary schools while at the same time ensuring that no child is trapped in a failing school. The consequences of this law created serious problems for music education in public schools. Elevated academic expectations and an increase in time allotted to priority academic subjects diminished the position of music and the arts in the school curriculum. Music teachers faced the challenge of justifying the inclusion of music education for young people. School band directors also faced the criticism of some college/university wind band/ensemble directors and professional music educators regarding how and what was being taught in school band programs.

Two members of the ABA Committee for School Bands presented reports at the Association's 2003 Convention that focused on high school band programs and activities. The first, "What Are We Here For?," was presented by William A. Gora, Chairperson of the Committee and Emeritus Director of Bands at Appalachian State University. Below are excerpts from his report.

> As usual, the wonderful school bands and their directors in our country continue doing a great job. That is, those who continue to balance the weekly traditional responsibilities of leading a school program with teaching kids how to make music and [foster] a lifelong love for [the] art.
>
> While I cannot speak on a nationwide scale, there are a few locales whose state band organizations appear to be heading towards membership in Drum Corps International! A neighboring state organization, in an effort to improve their scheduling pattern (they are presently on a block schedule) is seeking to have marching band replace physical education by referring to marching band as "The Sport of the Arts!" They have authored a position statement that includes the following:
>
>> "Band offers much more that playing music. Students learn leadership, competitive skills, motivation, personal interaction, a team concept, community involvement, and much more. Any interested student is eligible and will be found a place to contribute. No one "sits on the bench."
>
>> I have read and reread this statement and still do not understand the term "competitive skills." And especially how they relate to teaching music!

Gora concluded,

> … the American Bandmasters Association, through each individual member, [should] … lead discussions across the country [on the state of the American high school band]. Perhaps the big question continues to be WHAT ARE WE HERE FOR?[32]

The second report was presented by Otis Kitchen, retired Director of Bands at Elizabethtown (PA) College, who also registered concern over the priorities of many high school band directors and their programs.

> The "school band" is a paradox! ... some of the best composing for winds is happening at the present, yet much of this fine literature is being ignored by a number of school band directors.
>
> Unfortunately, too often the "band" is a victim of tradition; that of being used as a functional and exploited catalyst for entertainment purposes. Examples are, the highly promoted marching competitions, performing at athletic events, and numerous frivolous parades and community/school functions.
>
> Too many school conductors refrain from encountering the mental discipline required in preparing fine band literature because they are often tempted with enthusiastic response by huge crowds at [sporting] events, parades and marching festivals.
>
> In my opinion, the concert [band] is in trouble because of the lack of demand regarding the development of meaningful, long lasting musicianship. Simply compare the energy that is devoted to one marching band competition to that of an entire concert season and it becomes clear where the priorities lie.[33]

CBDNA President Michael Haithcock, writing in his "From the Podium" column in the Summer 2002 issue of *CBDNA Report*, urged college/university wind band/ensemble directors to get more involved in public school music education and bands programs.

> As an educational vehicle our national system for music education is unique. The amount of time, resources, and energy spent is far greater than in any other society ... Yet most of us have the feeling that our system is in trouble, that we are not maximizing the opportunity to make music a meaningful part ... of our students lives, and that somehow, we are not appreciated by the educational community at large. While everyone does certainly not hold these feelings, they represent a consistent theme I hear from our membership and public school band directors across the country. How do we respond? ... school band programs ... desperately need our help?[34]

Cynthia Johnston Turner in an article, "The Wind Band Concert: A Bleak Future? A Qualitative Study," pondered the future of public concerts and specifically the future of wind band concerts. Her article was based on interviews with twenty-five conductors and composers. Three of her respondents commented upon bands in the public schools. Malcolm Rowell, former conductor of the University of Massachusetts Wind Ensemble, said that he was very concerned about the direction high school bands were taking in public education. "It is activity driven and so little music is being taught." Christopher Weait, composer and conductor at The Ohio State University, stated, "Marching band programs in some places dominate the band program to the detriment of valid music education precepts." Mark Camphouse, then composer and conductor of bands at Radford University, added, "high school bands as we know them will gradually diminish in number and importance."[35]

ENDNOTES

1 Bernard Rands, "Composer's Program Note," Eastman Wind Ensemble 50th Anniversary Gala Concert, February 8, 2002.

2 "Program Note: Concerto for Percussion and Wind Orchestra," Composer Steven Stucky, accessed June 1, 2018, http://www.stevenstucky.com/docs/Perc-Cto-note.html.

3 Peter Graham, email to the author, November 16, 2010.

4 Mick Dowrick, "Peter Graham Talks to Mick Dowrick," *Winds Magazine* (Spring 2002): 8.

5 Laurence Bitensky, *Awake You Sleepers! for Trumpet & Wind Ensemble*, "Performance notes" (Silly Black Dog Music, 2002), Full score.

6 Mark Camphouse, "Donald Grantham," in *Composers on Composing for Band, Volume 2* (GIA Publications, 2004), 101.

7 *Timothy Reynish, Live in Concert with the University of Kentucky Wind Ensemble*, University of Kentucky Wind Ensemble, Timothy Reynish, conductor, Mark Custom Recording Service, 4949-MCD, 2003. Liner notes by Timothy Reynish.

8 *Carter Pann: American Composer*, accessed 2002, www.carterpann.com/works_slalom-orchestra.htm.

9 "Hemispheres (2002), Program Notes," Joseph Turrin, Composer," accessed June 1, 2018, www.josephturrin.com/comp.works/hemis.html.

10 Bernard Holland, "Music Review; Cordial Notes Resound, As Tough Downbeats Fade," *The New York Times* (June 1, 2002).

11 Eric Whitacre, Sleep (Eric Whitacre, 2003), Program Note.

12 *Waking Winds*, Massachusetts Institute of Technology Wind Ensemble, Frederick Harris, conductor, Innova Recording 621, 2004, Liner notes by Peter Child.

13 "Premieres: Tattoo from Symphony for Wind Orchestra by Judith Lang Zaimont; University of Minnesota Symphonic Wind Ensemble," *CBDNA Report* (Spring & Summer 2003): 5.

14 "Premieres: Fanfare Canzonique by Brian Balmages; University of Miami Wind Ensemble," *CBDNA Report* (Spring & Summer 2003): 5.

15 "Premieres: Jubilare! by John Stevens; The Ohio State University Wind Symphony," *CBDNA Report* (Spring & Summer 2003): 5.

16 David Dzubay, "Ra! Program Note." Pronova Music: David Dzubay, accessed June 1, 2018, http://pronovamusic.com/notes/Ra.html.

17 "Conference Premieres: Bliss: Variations on an Unchanging Rhythm by Michael Torke; Indiana University Wind Ensemble," *CBDNA Report* (Spring & Summer 2003): 4.

18 Gary W. Hill, "The Future of the Wind Band Field: Promise or Peril?" *Journal of the World Association for Symphonic Bands and Ensembles* 10 (2003): 47.

19 Chris Brubeck, email to the author, March 14, 2011.

20 "Rise (band)," Steven Bryant: Composer/Conductor, accessed June 1, 2018, https://www.stevenbryant.com/music/catalog/rise-band.

21 "In Wartime, for wind ensemble: Program Note," David Del Tredici, accessed June 1, 2018, http://www.daviddeltredici.com/works/in-wartime/.

22 Timothy Reynish, "Repertoire: In Wartime," Timothy Reynish, accessed June 1, 2018, http://www.timreynish.com/repertoire/categories/serious.php.

23 Wayne Groves, "Visions of Light Concerto for Trombone and Wind Ensemble," *International Trombone Association Journal* 36 (January 2008): 75.

24 "News," *CBDNA Report* (Spring & Summer 2003): 6.

25 "Premieres," *CBDNA Report* (Summer 2004): 6.

26 "Reviews: Monumentum pro umbris for wind ensemble," The Official Website of Sydney Hodkinson, accessed June 1, 2018, http://www.sydhodkinson.com/reviews.html.

27 H. Robert Reynolds, email to the author, October 1, 2010.

28 "L'Homme armé: Program Notes," Christopher Marshall: Composer, http://www.vaiaata.com/music/lhomme-arme-variations/.

29 "As the scent of spring rain..., for wind ensemble," Jonathan Newman, Composer, accessed June 1, 2018, https://jonathannewman.com/music/as-the-scent-of-spring-rain.

30 Michael Christianson, email to the author, November 1, 2010.

31 "News," *CBDNA Report* (Fall 2003): 4.

32 William A. Gora, "What Are We Here For?" *Program of the 2003 ABA Convention*, Report of the American Bandmasters Association, Committee for School Bands, 52–53.

33 Otis Kitchen, "A Point of View," Program of the 2003 ABA Convention, Report to the American Bandmasters Association, 55.

34 Michael Haithcock, "From the Podium," *CBDNA Report* (Summer 2002), 1.

35 Cynthia Johnston Turner, "The Wind Band Concert: A Bleak Future? A Qualitative Study," *Journal of the World Association for Symphonic Bands and Ensembles* 10 (2003): 62.

CHAPTER 13

Expanding Horizons (2004–2005)

NBA Young Composer/Conductor Mentor Project • "A Wind Band Celebration" in New York City • "The Kids Play Great. But that Music…"

The wind band/ensemble world lost one of its most distinguished conductors and leaders when Frederick Fennell died on December 7, 2004. The founder of the Eastman Wind Ensemble was born in Cleveland, Ohio, on July 2, 1914. At the age of 7 he was performing in the fife-and-drum corps at Camp Zeke, the family summer encampment. Every Fourth of July "the corps" recreated performances of Revolutionary War music. As a student at John Adams High School, Fennell played the "kettledrum" in the orchestra and was the drum major of the band. He also attended the Interlochen National Music Camp and played bass drum in the National High School Band which was directed by Albert Austin Harding. In fall 1931, Fennell entered the Eastman School of Music as a percussion major. During his undergraduate years he conducted the Eastman Symphonic Band and led the University of Rochester marching band. After earning a Master's Degree in 1939 he joined the Eastman faculty as a percussion instructor and conductor of the Symphony Band.

In summer 1942, Fennell was a conducting fellow at the Tanglewood Berkshire Music Center. His fellowship colleagues were Leonard Bernstein, Lukas Foss, and Walter Hendl. During World War II he served as a National Musical Advisor for the USO (United Service Organizations).

After his discharge from the military, Fennell returned to the Eastman School of Music and conducted the Symphony Band, Eastman Opera Theatre, and Eastman Chamber Orchestra. He returned to Tanglewood in 1948 as an assistant to Maestro Serge Koussevitzky. In 1952, Fennell founded the Eastman Wind Ensemble (EWE). His work and recordings with the Ensemble had a profound effect on the evolution and development of wind bands and established new standards for wind band/ensemble performance. In 1977, *Stereo Review* selected Fennell and the Eastman Wind Ensemble's recording of Percy Grainger's *Lincolnshire Posy* as one of the "Fifty Best Recordings of the Centenary of the Phonograph."

Fennell left the Eastman School of Music in 1962 and became Associate Music Director of the Minneapolis Symphony. Later he became conductor-in-residence at the University of Miami, conductor of the Kosei Wind Orchestra, and principal guest conductor for the Dallas Wind Symphony and Interlochen Arts Academy.

Fennell's short history about the use of wind instruments in orchestra, band, and wind ensemble literature, *Time and the Winds*, was for many years the only publication available on the subject. He also authored an important series of articles, published in *The Instrumentalist*, on the study, interpretation, and conducting of standard wind band works.

During his career Fennell received many honors and awards including induction into the Classical Music Hall of Fame and National Hall of Fame for Distinguished Band Directors, the Alice M. Ditson Conducting Award, a Gold Medal from the Interlochen Arts Academy, and an honorary doctorate from the Eastman School of Music. He was also an Honorary Chief of the Kiowa Indian Nation. In 1992, a concert hall honoring him was opened in Kofu, Japan— the Frederick Fennell Hall.

The death of Warren Benson on October 6, 2005, was another great loss to the wind band/ensemble world. As a composer, writer, and educator, Benson was dedicated to creativity and craft, to a student-centered educational philosophy, and to fostering new methods of teaching. He had a major impact on the artistic growth of wind band/ensemble conductors and the advancement of the medium as a vehicle of artistic expression. Benson began his musical career as a percussionist and French horn player at Cass Technical High School in Detroit, Michigan, and later earned Bachelor and Master degrees in Music at the University of Michigan. At the age of fourteen he began performing professionally in theater orchestras and big bands. In 1946, he became timpanist of the Detroit Symphony Orchestra.

Benson held teaching positions at the Brevard Music Center; Anatolia College in Salonica, Greece; and Mars Hill College in North Carolina. From 1953–1967 he taught percussion, composition, and theory at the Ithaca College School of Music. In 1967, he moved to Rochester, NY, where he became Professor of Composition at the Eastman School of Music, remaining there until his retirement in 1994. During the 1960s Benson participated in the Ford Foundation sponsored Contemporary Music Project. His book, *Creative Projects in Musicianship*, was an outgrowth of his work for the Foundation. During his career, Benson composed over 150 works for wind ensemble, orchestra, choir, chamber ensemble, and soloists. A number of his wind ensemble pieces are considered to be masterpieces for the medium (i.e., *The Leaves are Falling, The Passing Bell, Symphony 2: "Lost Songs," The Solitary Dancer*). He was a recipient of numerous awards including four Fulbright Fellowships, three Consortium Composer Fellowships (from the National Endowment for the Arts), a John Simon Guggenheim Fellowship, three MacDowell Colony Fellowships, the Lillian Fairchild Prize, a Citation of Excellence from the National Band Association, election to the Percussive Arts Society Hall of Fame, and nominations for a Pulitzer Prize for his *Drums of Summer*.

The wind band/ensemble works, below, were composed in 2004. Each is interesting, imaginative, and different—each was inspired by a different subject and/or event, among them a stampede, a Beat counterculture poem, the spoken language of the Hmong people of Laos, a spectacular painting by Diego Rivera, a Tibetan love song, as well as Voodoo lore.

Steven Bryant	Stampede for Calgary
Michael Djupstrom	*Gaeng*
Eric Ewazen	*Danzante* (for Trumpet & Wind Ensemble)
Donald Grantham	*Baron Cimetière's Mambo*
John Mackey	*Redline Tango*
Roberto Sierra	*Fandangos (wind version arranged by Mark Scatterday)*
Joseph Schwantner	*Recoil*
Frank Ticheli	*Symphony No. 2*
Augusta Read Thomas	*Dancing Galaxy*
Augusta Read Thomas	*Silver Chants the Litanies* (for Horn & Wind Ensemble)
Mark-Anthony Turnage	*A Quick Blast*

Stampede by Steve Bryant (b. 1959) is a high-spirited piece. It was premiered on February 18, 2004, by the Calgary Stampede Band, Dan Finley conducting, at the Alberta International Band Festival. The composer described the piece as "Copland's *Billy the Kid* meets John Adams' *Short Ride in a Fast Machine*."

> The music is a ... celebration of the Calgary Stampede's cultural amalgamation (from the cowboys and the agriculture and livestock industries they represent, to the First Nations, to the Young Canadians, and of course, the Stampede Band), and the unified spirit of all these groups in promoting their western values and heritage.[1]

Michael Djupstrom's *Gaeng* was commissioned and premiered on April 4, 2004, by the Bishop Ireton High School Wind Ensemble, Randall Eyles, conductor. It was awarded the William Schuman Prize by the BMI Foundation and the 52nd Annual BMI Student Composers Prize (selected from more than 700 submitted manuscripts). The single movement, twelve-and-a-half minute work is scored for standard wind ensemble instrumentation. The composer clarifies what a *gaeng* is in his program note about the piece.

> The *gaeng* or *qeej* is a traditional wind instrument of the Hmong people of Laos, but it is not an instrument designed solely to produce music. By imitating the tones and vowel sounds of the Hmong spoken language on his instrument, the gaeng performer can speak an extraordinary stylized language intelligible to the inhabitants of the spirit world. The voice of the *gaeng* thus pervades the Hmong funeral ceremony, where it guides the soul of the deceased towards the ancestral home.... As the soul leaves the earth, the *gaeng* player begins to combine his songs

with movement, creating an acrobatic, spinning dance designed to confuse any evil spirits seeking to interfere with the ceremony, even as his
continuous playing ensures the soul's safe passage to the world of the
ancestors.[2]

Eric Ewazen's trumpet concerto, *Danzante*, was commissioned by
a consortium of colleges and universities in the Western and Northwestern Divisions of CBDNA. It was premiered on March 27, 2004,
by the Western/Northwestern CBDNA Honors Wind Ensemble,
Gary Hill, conductor, with Al Vizzutti as the trumpet soloist. The
inspiration for the three-movement work came from Diego Rivera's
spectacular painting, *Danzante*, which hangs in the Indiana University Art Museum. Its first movement, *Colores*, is dynamic and expressive; the second, *Recuerdo*, elegiac and wistful, and the finale, *Azteca*,
joyful and rhythmic.

The inspiration for Donald Grantham's *Baron Cimetière's Mambo*
is Russell Bank's fascinating novel *Continental Drift*, which deals
with the collision between American and Haitian culture during the
"boat people" episodes of the late 1970s and early '80s. Grantham
stated that "Voodoo is a strong element of [the] novel, and when my
mambo began to take on a dark, mordant, sinister quality, I decided
to link it to the Baron."[3] Many of Grantham's compositions have "...
multiple layers of musical meaning: creating motivic, harmonic, stylistic or structural material based upon literary, cultural, or historical inspiration. *Baron Cimetière's Mambo* ... [composed in 2004, is]
no exception."[4] Grantham engages "the listener by juxtaposing styles
of raucous Latin-jazz with an interruption by a sardonic and stately
dance."[5] *Baron Cimetière's Mambo* was commissioned by the J. P. Tara-
vella High School Band, Neil Jenkins and Nikk Pilato, directors.

John Mackey's *Redline Tango* was commissioned and premiered
by the Brooklyn Philharmonic, under the direction of Kristjan Jarvi,
in 2003. Later that year a consortium of college wind ensembles
commissioned him to compose a wind version of the piece which was
premiered by the Emory University Wind Ensemble, Scott Stewart,
conductor, on February 26, 2004.

In a program note for the piece, Mackey (b. 1973) wrote,

> *Redline Tango* takes its title from the idea of "redlining an engine,"
> or pushing it to the limit. The work is in three sections. The first sec-
> tion is the initial virtuosic "redlining" ... the second section—the

"tango"—which is a bit lighter, but demented, and even a bit sleazy . . . with a hint of klezmer thrown in. The material for the tango is derived directly from the first section of the work. A transition leads . . . back to an even "redder" version of the first section, complete with one final bang at the end.[6]

Redline Tango won both the 2004 Walter Beeler Memorial Composition Prize and the 2005 ABA Ostwald Award.

Roberto Sierra (b. 1953) is one of the most frequently performed Latin American composers. He composed his *Fandangos* in 2001 for Leonard Slatkin and the National Symphony Orchestra. In 2004, conductor Mark Scatterday transcribed the piece for the Eastman Wind Ensemble's Asian Tour. The composer wrote the following about the piece,

> Antonio Soler's *Fandango* for keyboard has always fascinated me, for its strange and whimsical twists and turns. My *Fandangos* is a fantasy, or a "super-fandango," that takes as points of departure Soler's work and incorporates elements of Boccherini's *Fandango* and my own Baroque musings. Some of the oddities in the harmonic structure of the Soler piece provided a bridge for the incorporation of contemporary sonorities, opening windows to apparently alien sound worlds. In these parenthetical commentaries, the same materials heard before are transformed, as if one would look at the same objects through different types of lenses or prisms. The continuous variation form over an ostinato bass gave me the chance to use complex orchestration techniques as another element for variation.[7]

Recoil for Wind Ensemble by Joseph Schwantner (b. 1943) is structured in a single continuous movement and exploits the rich timbral resources of an expanded percussion section that includes an amplified piano. It was commissioned by the University of Connecticut and the Raymond and Beverly Sackler New Music Foundation and was premiered on November 5, 2004, in Carnegie Hall by the University of Connecticut Wind Ensemble, Jeffrey Renshaw, conductor. Unlike Schwantner's other wind ensemble pieces, the seventeen-minute long work was not inspired by poetry and includes both saxophones and euphoniums.

Donald Hunsberger conducted the premiere of the first two movements of Frank Ticheli's *Symphony No. 2* with the Florida State Wind Orchestra at a concert honoring James Croft on his retirement as Director of Bands at FSU on April 25, 2003. A year later (February

2004), Ticheli's completed *Symphony* was premiered by the University of Michigan Symphony Band, Steven Davis, conductor. The work's score contains the composer's detailed program note about the piece.

> The symphony's three movements refer to celestial light—Shooting Stars, the Moon, and the Sun.
>
> Although the title for the first movement, "Shooting Stars," came after its completion.... White-note clusters are sprinkled everywhere, like streaks of bright light ...
>
> The second movement, "Dreams Under a New Moon," depicts a kind of journey of the soul as represented by a series of dreams.... Many dream episodes follow, ranging from the mysterious, to the dark, to the peaceful and healing ...
>
> The finale, "Apollo Unleashed," is perhaps the most wide-ranging movement of the symphony.... the image of Apollo, the powerful ancient god of the sun, inspired not only the movement's title, but also its blazing energy. Bright sonorities, fast tempos, and galloping rhythms combine to give a sense of urgency that one often expects from a symphonic finale.[8]

Silver Chants the Litanies, in memoriam Luciano Berio, by Augusta Read Thomas (b. 1964) is a concerto for French horn and chamber ensemble (piccolo, flute, 2 oboes, 2 clarinets, 2 horns, 2 trumpets, 2 percussion, 2 pianos/celesta, harp, and string quartet). It is thirteen minutes in length and was premiered on February 20, 2004, by Gregory Hustis, principal horn of the Dallas Symphony Orchestra, and the Southern Methodist University Meadows Wind Ensemble, Jack Delaney, conductor. The work is based on a poem by e. e. cummings, "Impression V," and is dedicated to Jack Delaney.

A second work by Augusta Read Thomas, *Dancing Galaxy*, was premiered on November 11, 2004, by the New England Conservatory Wind Ensemble, Frank L. Battisti, guest conductor. Thomas dedicated the piece to Battisti "with admiration and gratitude." It is based on a work, *Galaxy Dances*, which she composed for Mstislav Rostropovich and the National Symphony Orchestra. The composer provided the following words about the piece:

Dancing Galaxy opens in the lowest register of the wind ensemble in a timeless, floating, and gradually rising tune, which for a brief moment unfolds an impression of the massive, enduring universe. A timeless galaxy is upon us but steadily this music reaches upward and gains momentum, pushing through majestic, fanfare-like music, until it arrives at a driving, relentless dance.... [At the end, a] coda in the lowest register of the band returns to where the composition began, in an ageless, suspended galaxy.[9]

The New York Philharmonic, conducted by Andrew Davis, presented the American premiere of *A Quick Blast* by Mark-Anthony Turnage (b. 1960) on January 2, 2004, in Avery Fisher Hall in New York City. *A Quick Blast* is the first part of a three-movement orchestral work entitled *Etudes and Elegies*, which was premiered at the Cheltenham Festival in 2001 by the BBC Symphony Orchestra. It is scored for the woodwind, brass, and percussion sections of a symphony orchestra and is dedicated to Jonathan Moore. The opening of the piece is loud and rhythmically intense and based on two figures, a flute motive and a three-note trumpet motif. This is followed by a "keening" and lyrical contrasting theme that leads to a scherzo-and-trio form middle section. After a shortened and varied reprise of the first part of the movement, the piece ends abruptly.

* * * * * * * * * * * *

The National Band Association launched the Young Composer Mentorship Project (YCMP) in 2000. This project was the brainchild of composer and music educator Mark Camphouse. His idea was to have talented young composers work with experienced master composers during a three-day residency. When this proved to be successful, a young conductors component, under the leadership of Paula Crider, was added. Forty young composers and twenty-four young conductors have participated in this project since it was inaugurated in 2000. Working in pairs, under the guidance of a master composer and conductor, a young composer and young conductor interact and collaborate in the study and rehearsal of a composition by the young composer which culminates in a performance of the piece conducted by the young conductor.

The College Band Directors National Association held its 2005 National Conference, "A Wind Band Celebration," in New York City from February 24–27. This was a major departure from the tradition of holding conferences on college/university campuses. During the four-day event, eleven concerts were performed at four different sites: Carnegie Hall, Alice Tully Hall, the Skirball Center for the Performing Arts at New York University, and Assembly Hall at Hunter College. The five ensembles performing concerts at Carnegie Hall were the Eastman Wind Ensemble, New England Conservatory Wind Ensemble, University of Michigan Symphony Band, USC Thornton Wind Ensemble, and the University of Texas Wind Ensemble. There was one American, two New York, and nine world premiere performances on the conference concerts, some by major composers. Everyone was hopeful that this would attract the attention of major New York music critics as well as VIPs from the musical establishment. Unfortunately, no critics or VIPs attended any of the concerts. President Jerry Junkin, wrote this about the New York Conference in his "From the Podium" column in the Spring 2005 *CBDNA Report:*

> Certainly we leave New York ... with mixed feelings—excitement over the splendid performances, thought provoking sessions and wonderful new repertoire, yet at the same time struggling to put into context the apparent snub by a major conductor [Lorin Maazel who failed to show up for a panel discussion when he discovered he would be talking to "band directors"] and the lack of any critical acknowledgement of our presence.[10]

Larry Livingston, Music Director of Orchestras at the University of Southern California Thornton School of Music, (formerly Dean of the School), also commented on the "snub" by New York critics and the exceptional quality of the Carnegie Hall performances (Livingston conducted the Small College Intercollegiate Band concert at the conference):

> In the heat of those five unprecedented days, being party to the latest chapter in the band odyssey, euphoria was easy to come by, not so, perspective. It is abundantly clear that bands can play in Carnegie Hall, can meet the acid competency test, can commission and perform virtuoso pieces which would daunt and, as well, irritate the New York Philharmonics of the world, can manifest the same excellence which marks the best concerts given anywhere. It is also undeniable that virtually every living composer is now willing to accept an invitation to write for band, and not just for the lucre. The volcanic reaction of the audiences was more than home-boy backslapping. It was testimony by the NYC hard hats that we are not delusional when we imagine making some dent in the cultural landscape. As an old band guy, son of an old band guy, it was

warming to sense that we may have successfully crawled up out of the water and can now begin to ambulate.[11]

Anne Midgette, *New York Times* music writer/critic, responding to a letter from Paul Bryan inquiring about the lack of media interest in the 2005 Conference concerts, wrote,

> ... I appreciated hearing your thoughts on the wind band, and it's true that we are far too ignorant about the field. I have a lot more experience in the area of choruses, which suffer from a similar lack of respect from the musical establishment, and where a lot of new music is also written and performed under the critical radar, so to speak. I don't know what the solution is to the ghetto-ization of these areas; I just hope that they gradually continue to intrude on the critical consciousness.[12]

By 2005 wind bands/ensembles had gained the interest and respect of many of the "best composers." However, they still had not garnered the attention of the wider musical world's VIPs and print and broadcast media. Wind band conductors, ensembles, and associations need to develop a strategy to enlighten the musical establishment and media critics about the exceptional music that exists for the medium and the excellent performance standards of its elite wind bands/ensembles.

Certainly the most anticipated performance at the conference was the New York premiere of John Corigliano's *Circus Maximus* by the University of Texas Wind Ensemble, Jerry Junkin, conductor. Corigliano (b. 1938) is one of the world's most celebrated composers and winner of a Grawemeyer Award, Pulitzer Prize, and an Academy Award (music for the film *The Red Violin*). His *Circus Maximus* is a thirty-five minute work structured in eight connected sections: Introitus, Screens/Siren, Channel Surfing, Night Music I, Night Music II, Circus Maximus, Prayer, and Coda: Veritas, all of which are played without pause. This is a huge spatial work with players located throughout the hall and on stage. Specifically, eleven trumpets surround the audience; at the next higher level a saxophone quartet plus string bass are positioned to the right, two horns on the left, and single percussionists at the far left and far right. One clarinet is located at the top right of the hall. A seven-piece marching band, consisting of piccolo, E-flat clarinet, 2 trumpets, 2 trombones, and percussion march down the aisle at the climax of the work. The composer wrote the following program note about *Circus Maximus*:

For the past three decades I have started the compositional process by building a shape, or architecture, before coming up with any musical material, In this case, the shape was influenced by a desire to write a piece in which the entire work is conceived spatially. But I started simply wondering what dramatic premise would justify the encirclement of the audience by musicians, so that they were in the center of an arena. This started my imagination going, and quite suddenly a title appeared in my mind: *Circus Maximus.* ...

The parallels between the high decadence of Rome and our present time are obvious. Entertainment dominates our reality, and ever-more-extreme "reality" shows dominate our entertainment. Many of us have become as bemused by the violence and humiliation that flood the 500-plus channels of our television screens as the mobs of Imperial Rome, who considered the devouring of human beings by starving lions just another Sunday show. The shape of my *Circus Maximus* was built both to embody and to comment on this massive and glamorous barbarity.[13]

In 2008 Corigliano added the following thought about *Circus Maximus*:

There's no question as far as I'm concerned that this is a picture of our time and a very frightening one, and I wanted to make it frightening because it is frightening ... This technology we're experiencing, which is extraordinary, which I love—at the same time we know there are technologies that are making weapons that can kill us with one suitcase. So we're in this kind of schizophrenic world of elation and fear. It really is a scary time.[14]

Another highlight of the conference was the premiere performance of Susan Botti's *Cosmosis for Wind Ensemble, Soprano and Women's Voices* by the University of Michigan Symphony Band and women of the University Chamber Choir, conducted by Michael Haithcock. Susan Botti (b. 1962) is both a composer and a brilliant singer who specializes in the performance of contemporary music (i.e., Cage, Crumb, Gubaidulina, Partch, etc.). She was the spectacular soloist in the performance of her piece. Below is the composer's program note:

Cosmosis was created for the talented and inspirational music students at the University of Michigan to tap their boundless imaginations.

The American poet, May Swenson, wrote "The Cross Spider" in response to the news of a Skylab experiment in which a student project proposed to see whether a spider could spin a web in space. A common cross spider (araneus diadematus), named Arabella, is mythically portrayed by Swenson. Her shape poem, "Overboard" (a play of gravity), serves as a prelude.

In *Cosmosis*, "Overboard" plays with musical equivalents of gravitational force following the shapes laid out in the poem, before entering the gravitation-free sea of space. Here, Arabella succeeds in her quest on "The First Night." A musical interlude follows, reflecting on the vastness of space as well as the heroic undertaking. In "The Second Night," Arabella succeeds again ... but is sacrificed in the process ... experiment frittered. Yet the resonant energy of the mission still spins in the air, like the soundwaves in space that echo throughout the cosmos, becoming a part of it, and inspiring others.[15]

There were nine other premiere performances at the 2005 CBDNA Conference:

The Rivers of Bowery by Jonathan Newman
Hysteria in Salem Village by Felicia Sandler
Festival March by Michael Valenti
Blackbird by John Lennon and Paul McCartney (arr. Shelly Berg)
La'I (Tibetan Love Song) for Orchestra without Strings by Bright Sheng
Voice of the City by Richard Danielpour
Concerto for Trombone and Wind Ensemble by Jeff Tyzik
G-Spot Tornado by Frank Zappa (arr. Jeffrey D. Gershman)
Brooklyn Bridge for Solo Clarinet and Symphony Band by Michael Daugherty

Jonathan Newman's *The Rivers of Bowery* was commissioned by the Rutgers University Wind Ensemble, William Berz, conductor. It is a short overture for winds, brass, and percussion. Newman (b. 1972) wrote the following note about his piece:

The Rivers of Bowery is an overture with a triumphant vision of the City as complex machine, capable of incubating the lowest in human nature as well as harnessing the best of Man's intentions. The title comes directly from Allen Ginsberg's glorious chronicle of Beat counterculture, *Howl*. Written in 1956, in a tenement about 2 blocks from where I live on the Lower East Side of Manhattan, *Howl* celebrates the Beat counterculture by breathlessly rejoicing in the underdog grit of Ginsberg's beloved bohemia.

Ginsberg's river is a rush of people, and not the usual sunny city dwellers of an E. B. White essay or an O'Henry story, but his specific anti-community of the lost, the drugged, and the outcast. Ginsberg presents his city as possessing a triumphant spirit, neighbors piled on top of each other, never letting each other down despite being torn apart by society and by themselves.[16]

Four years later, in 2009, Newman used musical and extra-musical themes from *The Rivers of Bowery* to expand the work into his twenty-seven minute *Symphony No. 1, My Hands Are a City*.

Felicia Sandler (b. 1976) is currently a faculty member at the New England Conservatory of Music. She received a Ph.D. from the University of Michigan where she studied composition with William Bolcom, Michael Daugherty, Bright Sheng, and C. Curtis-Smith. *Hysteria in Salem Village* is an eight-minute composition commissioned by the Big East Band Directors Association. Sandler wrote the following about the work:

> When the Big East Band Directors Association commissioned me to write a new piece for their consortium, I had only recently moved to Boston. Being a fan of Charles Ives's *Three Places in New England* and William Schuman's *New England Triptych*, I decided to write my own tri-partite piece based on this region of the United States, my current home. Salem Village is an ideal "place" for me to begin for many reasons. The witch trials of 1692 continue to captivate my imagination. Many consider the trials to be the logical result of Puritan superstitions run amok. I'm not so sure (though a quotation of Stratfield does make its way into the piece). Questions of terror, authority, control, revenge, civil liberties, righteousness, supernatural powers, fear all come to the surface in consideration of the trial—emotions and positions that are strangely familiar in early 21st century America. I suppose my *Hysteria in Salem Village* then, finds itself in the same lineage as *The Crucible* of Arthur Miller—a work that, while cast in the mold of the trials of 1692 New England, is actually a personal reflection on one's own day.[17]

The concert performed by the Goldman Memorial Band, Chris Wilhjelm, conductor, was a very traditional one. It included works by Offenbach, Sousa, Grainger, Peter Mennin (*Canzona*, which was premiered by the Goldman Band in 1951), and a new piece, *Festival March* by Michael Valenti (b. 1942). Valenti has the distinction of having more works premiered by the Goldman Band than any other composer in the band's long history.

Blackbird, the CD by the Shelly Berg Trio, consists of twelve songs including "Blackbird" by John Lennon and Paul McCartney. Larry Livingston, who was Dean of the University of Southern California

Thornton School of Music at the time, commissioned Berg (b. 1955) to compose an orchestral version of *Blackbird,* which he premiered with the USC Symphony Orchestra in 2004. Messiaen's *Oiseaux exotiques* ("Exotic Birds") was an important influence in Berg's writing of the orchestra version of the piece: "I worked bird sounds into the aleatoric opening, along with representations of wind and a feeling of Mother Earth." After Livingston received an invitation to conduct the CBDNA Small College Intercollegiate Band at the 2005 CBDNA Conference, he asked Berg to make another version of *Blackbird,* this time for wind band. Berg's new version of *Blackbird,* with himself as piano soloist, was premiered by Livingston and the Small College Band on February 25, 2005.

Bright Sheng (b. 1955) was born in Shanghai, China. During the Cultural Revolution he played piano and percussion in a folk music and dance troupe stationed in a provincial town near the Tibetan border. It was here that he heard the Tibetan love song, "La'I," which inspired the writing of his short five-minute piece. *La'I* was commissioned by the Philharmonisches Orchester Dortmund, Arthur Fagen, conductor and the University of Michigan Symphonic Band, Michael Haithcock, conductor. The composer wrote the following words about the piece:

> La'l is a form of Tibetan love song. It is most popular in eastern Tibet where I lived for seven years in my teens. I watched men and women approach each other singing La'I while herding, working in the fields, or especially, in festival settings. If things went well, they would exchange memorabilia and set a new date to meet again. The character of the music is lyrical, slow in a free tempo, and quick, moving throaty grace-notes decorating an overall simple melody. The decoration forms a special notation to the melody, a unique feature of *La'I.*[18]

Richard Danielpour (b. 1956) is one of the most recorded composers of his generation and only the third composer—after Stravinsky and Copland—to be signed to an exclusive recording contract by Sony Classical. Besides being a composer, Danielpour is also an active educator. He teaches at the Curtis Institute of Music and the Manhattan School of Music and spends a great deal of time giving master classes throughout the country. *Voice of the City,* his first work for wind band/ensemble, was commissioned by CBDNA and a consortium of thirty-one high school, college, university, and military wind bands/ensembles. Unlike his *Toward the Splendid City,* which was written for the New York Philharmonic in 1991, *Voice of the City* is a portrait of New York in the post-9/11 twenty-first century. The composer felt that the expressive message of the piece should be gleaned from listening to the work itself. The first movement of the piece was premiered by the Ithaca College Wind Ensemble, conducted by Stephen Peterson, at the 2005 CBDNA Conference. Timothy Reynish, who later conducted the premiere of the complete work (November 14, 2007) with the SUNY Fredonia Wind Ensemble, described *Voice of the City* as having "... jazz elements, hints of Bernstein in the funky accompaniment, perhaps of Varèse."[19]

Jeff Tyzik (b. 1951) is a composer, arranger, and trumpeter. He has written music for Erich Kunzel and the Cincinnati Pops Orchestra, Doc Severinsen, and the Royal Philharmonic Orchestra as well as for the Rochester Philharmonic and the Vancouver Symphony. He composed his *Concerto for Trombone and Wind Ensemble* for Mark Kellogg, principal trombonist of the Rochester Philharmonic The work's first movement, "*Scherzo*," is very rhythmic and energetic; the second, "*Lament*," is an expression of the composer's feelings about the 9/11 tragedy; the third, "*Dance*," is a quasi bacchanale. The composer provides the following note about the piece.

> The concerto shows many Latin and Afro-Cuban influences. Another important musical ingredient is a device that was used in early music from the days of Gabrieli and is also an integral part of jazz: call and response, where the trombone makes a statement and the orchestra answers it, and vice-versa. In terms of style, I'd call the concerto contemporary tonal music. It's very accessible and challenging... The trombone part ... is written out, although I wrote it to sound like it includes improvisation. The ensemble's role ... is very important ... It is truly a concerto for Trombone AND Ensemble.[20]

Frank Zappa's *G-Spot Tornado* was written in 1986 and originally realized on a Synclavier synthesizer. Zappa (1940–1993) included the piece in his recording, *Jazz from Hell*, which won the 1987 Grammy Award for Best Rock Instrumental Performance. In 1992, the New Music Festival of Frankfurt, Germany, celebrated the compositional careers of Frank Zappa, John Cage, and Karlheinz Stockhausen. As part of the festival, Ensemble Modern, the European contemporary music group, presented several evening-long concerts featuring both existing and newly commissioned orchestral and chamber works by

Zappa, which are included on the album *The Yellow Shark*. Searching for an encore to conclude the series of concerts, Ensemble Modern asked Zappa to make a new arrangement of *G-Spot Tornado*. The composer explained how the wind ensemble version came to be.

> During ... rehearsals ... a few of the musicians were trying to play that tune [*G-Spot Tornado*]. They really liked it for some reason, and asked whether they could have an arrangement of it for the concert ... I printed out the data [from the Synclavier], and turned it over to Ali [N. Askin], and he orchestrated it. The rest is history. This new arrangement for wind ensemble is largely based on ... Askin's chamber orchestra version written for *The Yellow Shark* concerts. In addition, it draws heavily from the original version, attempting to recreate the style and the unique timbres of the Synclavier.[21]

Michael Daugherty's work for solo clarinet and symphony band, *Brooklyn Bridge*, was commissioned by the International Clarinet Association and premiered in 2005 by the University of Michigan Symphony Band, Michael Haithcock, conductor, with Michael Wayne as clarinet soloist. Commenting on the work, the composer stated,

> Designed by John Roebling (1806–1869), the Brooklyn Bridge endures as the most admired and best-loved bridge in New York City.
>
> Like the four cables of webs of wire and steel that hold the Brooklyn Bridge together, my ode to this cultural icon is divided into four movements. Each movement ... is a musical view from the Brooklyn Bridge: I. East (Brooklyn and Brooklyn Heights); II. South (Statue of Liberty); III. West (Wall Street and the lower Manhattan skyline which was once dominated by the World Trade Towers); IV. North (Empire State Building, Chrysler Building, and Rockefeller Center). In the final movement of the concerto, I also imagine Artie Shaw, the great jazz swing clarinetist of the 1940s, performing with his orchestra in the once glorious Rainbow Room on the sixty-fifth floor of the Rockefeller Center.[22]

Numerous panel discussions, lectures, and presentations, were also included on the conference program, among them:

"The Future of Concert Music: a Roundtable of Music Critics"
"James Reese Europe and African-American Bandleaders of the World War I Era"
"Blue and Blue-Eyed English—The Meeting of Percy Grainger and Duke Ellington"
"Latin American Bands, Music and Composers"
"E. F. Goldman and Erik Leidzén: Musical Partnership and Friendship: 1933–1956"

* * * * * * * * * * * *

All the works below were composed in 2005. Each has its own unique, expressive style. Eight were written for standard wind band instrumentation and one for soprano and a nine-member wind ensemble.

Michael Colgrass	Bali
Peter Maxwell Davies	Commemoration Sixty
Stephen McNeff	Concerto for Clarinet
Lior Navok	Gleams from the Bosom of Darkness
Norbert Palej	Canzona III
Joshua Penman	The Pilgrimage of Fire and Earth
Steve Reich	City Life
Matthew Tommasini	Three Spanish Songs
Dan Welcher	Symphony No. 4 "American Visionary"

The Bishop Ireton High School Wind Ensemble, conducted by Randall Eyles, premiered Michael Colgrass's *Bali* on March 19, 2005, at Bishop Ireton High School in Alexandria, Virginia. Colgrass (b. 1932) wrote the piece after spending two summers in Ubud, the arts and crafts center of Bali. Below is the composer's program note about the piece.

> The bright dance rhythms of the gamelan orchestra are the outer sections [of the piece] and the middle section is the slow lament for the dead, introduced by an explosion representing the 2002 terrorist bombing of the nightclub in the island's capital, Denpassar.... Following the requiem-like music, we hear a gradual build-up of bright sounds representing the sun reflecting off the icon built to the memory of the dead, which then leads to a return of the dance.[23]

Commemoration Sixty is a cantata for SATB Chorus, Children's Chorus (unbroken voices), Military Band, Military Trumpets and Trombones, and Orchestra by Peter Maxwell Davies (b. 1934). It was commissioned jointly by Her Majesty Queen Elizabeth II, the Royal Philharmonic Orchestra and the Royal British Legion to commemorate the Sixtieth Anniversary of the ending of World War II. The work is twenty minutes long and was premiered on June 6, 2005, in Central Hall, Westminster, London, by the Royal Philharmonic Orchestra, London Symphony Chorus, boy choirs of Westminster Cathedral, St. Paul's Cathedral, Westminster Abbey, Chapel Royal St. James's Palace, Chapel Royal Hampton Court, St. George's Chapel

Windsor, the Central Band of the Royal British Legion, and trumpets of the Royal Military School (Kneller Hall), with Sir Peter Maxwell Davies conducting.

Stephen McNeff (b. 1930) is a well-known film and theater composer. His *Concerto for Clarinet* was composed for a consortium of UK ensembles. A "preview performance" of the piece took place in March 2005 at the Finnish Wind Music Conference in Pori. Linda Merrick was the soloist with the Satakunta Wind Orchestra, conducted by Mark Heron. The official UK premiere took place two months later, again with Linda Merrick as soloist, but this time with the Southwark Concert Band. *Fanfare* magazine critic Ronald E. Grames described the work as "... both atmospheric and good humored, even whimsically jazzy at times."[24]

Gleams from the Bosom of Darkness by Lior Navok (b. 1971) was premiered on April 29, 2005, by the MIT Wind Ensemble, Frederick Harris, Jr., conductor, and the MIT Chamber Chorus and Concert Choir, William Cutter, director. This was the last of the four works commissioned for Frank Battisti's 70th birthday to receive its premiere performance. *Gleams* is a large composition for three narrators, on-stage chorus (72–96 voices), back stage women's chorus (21 voices), and large wind ensemble. Navok, in his program note for the piece, explains why he chose poems by Henry W. Longfellow (1807–1882) for the text of his work.

> [I choose them because they are] ... full of descriptive images of light and darkness, both in the visual and the symbolic sense. His poems are the closest written descriptions of light and darkness as I imagined while writing the music.... The endless coloristic opportunities that chorus and wind ensemble can give, drove me to create an atmospheric, mysterious and somewhat meditative work rather than a piece that uses the wind ensemble as an accompanist to the chorus. ... The chorus and the wind ensemble are one body; both are instruments as well as voices.[25]

Norbert Palej (b. 1977) is originally from Miechów, Poland. He is the recipient of numerous awards including the ASCAP Young Composers Morton Gould Award (2004), the Toru Takemitsu Award from the Japan Society in Boston (2002), and a Benjamin Britten Memorial Fellowship (2000). His one movement work, *Canzona III*, was commissioned and premiered by the Cornell University Wind

Ensemble on October 14, 2005, Cynthia Johnston Turner conducting. The composer wrote this about the piece:

> The canzona flourished as an instrumental form in the late 16th cen-
> tury. Giovanni Gabrieli composed a number of terrific canzone, which
> exploited the antiphonal possibilities offered by the performance space
> they were written for, the Basilica di San Marco in Venice. Choirs of
> instruments could be positioned in different balconies of the cathe-
> dral to allow a three-dimensional acoustic experience. *Canzona III* uses
> similar antiphonal effects: choirs of instruments drawn from the wind
> ensemble interact in various ways. They respond to each other, echo
> each other, or they mix to form new colors.[26]

Joshua Penman (b. 1979) has received commissions from the
Albany Symphony, Bang on a Can, Prism Quartet, East Coast Chamber Orchestra, New York Youth Orchestra, and Nouvel Ensemble
Moderne as well as awards from ASCAP, BMI, and Columbia and Yale
Universities. *The Pilgrimage of Fire and Earth* is an eleven minute-long
work for large wind ensemble. It was premiered on April 15, 2005,
by the University of Michigan Symphony Band, Michael Haithcock,
conductor. Penman wrote about his approach to writing a wind
ensemble piece.

> I tried to approach the wind ensemble as a blank slate, just as this enor-
> mous, crazy, wonderful collection of instruments that are each capable
> of such an amazingly wide variety of sounds. I've let all kinds of musics
> seep into this piece, some of which are easily identifiable (Tibetan
> monastic music, Balinese gamelan, breakbeat), and some of which are
> not so easily identifiable, even by me. But the piece isn't really about
> looking at those musics in a new light, or even recognizing them as they
> pass. Rather, it is about the different ritualistic qualities inherent in
> each of them, and the way that these qualities can hybridize, feed each
> other, and melt themselves into something actually quite different: a
> pilgrimage music for a journey of consciousness.[27]

Steve Reich (b. 1936) composed *City Life* in 1995 for the Dutch
music ensemble Orkest de Volharding (perseverance orchestra),
which was originally conceived as a street band with a political
agenda but evolved into a contemporary music ensemble. Ten years
later (2005), Anthony Fiumara created a wind ensemble version of
the piece which he scored for the following instruments:

1 Flute
2 B-flat Clarinets
3 Saxophones (all doubling as follows)
    1 soprano, alto
    2 soprano, alto, tenor
    3 tenor, baritone
1 French horn
3 Trumpets in C
3 Trombones
1 Vibraphone
1 Percussion
2 Samplers/keyboards
2 Pianos
1 Contrabass (or bass guitar)

City Life is a twenty-four minute long minimalist composition. Digital samplers trigger a wide variety of sound and speech samples, including car horns, air brakes, car alarms, and many other sounds associated with the city.

Three Spanish Songs by Matthew Tommasini (b. 1978) is scored for soprano, flute, oboe, clarinet, bassoon, French horn, trumpet, trombone, and two percussion. It was commissioned and premiered by the University of Michigan Symphony Band, Michael Haithcock conductor, with Caroline Helton as soprano soloist, on December 12, 2005. This cycle of songs "... is a setting of three contrasting poems by Latin-American poets Leopoldo Lugones, Rubén Darío, and José Martí. *Olas grises* uses evocative rain and sea imagery to meditate on the nature of life and death.... *Nocturno* is a frantic soliloquy set as an extended opera scene.... *Sueño despierto* is a short poem about the contrasting images of a waking dream."[28] In 2006, *Spanish Songs* received the ASCAP/CBDNA Frederick Fennell Young Composers Prize.

Dan Welcher's *Symphony No. 4, "American Visionary"*, was commissioned by the University of Texas College of Fine Arts in memory of George Kozmetsky, who was an important entrepreneur, businessman, and founder of the School of Business at the University. The three movement, twenty minute-long work was premiered on November 10, 2005, by the University of Texas Wind Ensemble, Jerry Junkin, conductor.

> [The work's first movement, *Machines*, is] ... in strict twelve-tone language.... The second movement, *Family*, is a warmhearted, lyrical song

in expanded ABCA form.... a waltz-like middle section ... grows and then bursts its bounds to restate the opening theme in a broad, full voice. At the end, a chorale appears in muted brass and woodwinds.... *Community*, the work's final movement, begins with a re-statement of the chorale that ended the second movement ... [at its end] a little motor is turned on, and begins to chug.... a joyous melody emerges ... [which is] drawn from the series [of] the first movement, but this time accompanied in tonal harmony.[29]

* * * * * * * * * *

The 12th WASBE Conference was held in Singapore from July 10–16, 2005. Of the eighteen wind bands performing at the Conference, four were from the host country Singapore (Singapore Youth Wind Orchestra, Singapore Chinese Orchestra, West Winds Singapore, Singapore Armed Forces Central Band); nine from Southeast Asia and the Pacific Rim area; three from Europe; one from the United States, plus the International Youth Wind Orchestra. Two premiere performances were included among the ninety-four pieces performed at the Conference: *Shining Light* by Kelly Tang (b. 1961), commissioned for the Conference's opening ceremony, and *Il Cantito* by Oliver Waespi (b. 1971), which was commissioned and performed by the Stadtharmonie Zürich Oerlikon-Seebach.

* * * * * * * * * *

The Washington Post, on January 30, 2005, published an article by Stephen Budiansky, "The Kids Play Great. But That Music ...," which stimulated a great deal of controversy. Budiansky is the author of fourteen books and numerous articles published in *The Atlantic Monthly, The New York Times, The Wall Street Journal, The Washington Post, The Economist,* and many other publications. He is also a parent of children who participated in elementary through high school music programs. His article was a scathing indictment of the inferior quality music often used in school music programs. Budiansky's concern was not about *how* students played and/or made music—it was about *what* they played!

What they play is always That Piece, as I've come to think of it. That Piece is not written by any composer you have ever heard of—not classical, not jazz, not pop, not rock, not blues, not folk, not alternative Czech heavy metal fusion, not nothing. You've never heard it on the radio, not even late at night at the bottom of the dial. It in fact exists nowhere in the known music universe—except for the twilight zone of school musical performance.

Later he wrote:

I've pored over publishers' catalogues and lists of recommended pieces from various state music educators' associations, and it's happening all across the country. In place of genuine folk music, there are compositions "inspired" by the folk music of the American South or West, or Korea, or Africa. In place of real rock numbers are "rock originals" by one of those school band directors with a master's degree. The closest thing I've heard to a real Sousa was a creation called "Sousa! Sousa! Sousa!" that (according to the publisher's description) "includes famous themes from 'Manhattan Beach' and 'El Capitan' along with just a hint of 'Semper Fidelis' and other Sousa favorites.

I do understand the pedagogic purpose behind this stuff. Beethoven didn't have to come up with music scored for middle school bands made up of 57 alto saxophones, 40 trumpets, 15 percussionists, and one oboe. Fair enough.

However, music education is supposed to be about more than just learning to make your fingers move the right way. It's also supposed to be about having the chance to experience firsthand the truly great music of all genres—the great music that, after all, is the whole point of learning to play or sing."[30]

Budiansky's article provoked over 150 responses from school band directors, student musicians and parents, professional musicians, composers, and university music educators. Eighty-eight percent of them agreed with the validity of his critique, frequently adding their own examples and personal experiences. In the first decade of the twenty-first century the quality of music being used "to teach music" in schools became a major concern among professional leaders in music education, band associations, as well as individual college/university band directors (it still is in 2018).

ENDNOTES

1   "Stampede (band)," Steven Bryant: Composer/Conductor, accessed June 1, 2018, https://www.stevenbryant.com/music/catalog/stampede-band.

2   "Michael Djupstrom, *Gaeng*, Program Note," in Jason Scott Ladd, "An Annotated Bibliography of Contemporary Works Programmable by Wind Band and Orchestra" (Ph.D. diss., Florida State University, 2009), 176.

3   "Baron Cimetiere's Mambo: Program Notes," The Wind Repertory Project, accessed June 8, 2018, http://windrep.org/Baron_Cimetiere%27s_Mambo.

4   Bonnie Rebecca Jackson, "An Analysis of Donald Grantham's *Baron Cimetière's Mambo* and *Baron Samedi's Sarabande (and Soft Shoe)*." (M.M. thesis, East Carolina University, 2010), 7.

5   Ibid., viii.

6   *Beyond the Red Line*, Ithaca College Wind Ensemble, Stephen Peterson and Rodney Winther, conductors, Mark Custom Recording Service 6537-MCD, 2006, Liner notes.

7   *Fascinating Ribbons*, University of New Mexico Wind Symphony, Eric Rombach-Kendall, conductor, Summitt Education DCD 519, 2009, Liner notes.

8   "Symphony No. 2 for Concert Band," Frank Ticheli, Composer, accessed 10 June 2018, http://www.manhattanbeachmusiconline.com/frank_ticheli/html/symphony_no_2.html.

9   "Dancing Galaxy (2004): Program Note," Augusta Read Thomas: Composer. Accessed June 10, 2018, http://www.augustareadthomas.com/composition/dancinggalaxy.html.

10   Jerry Junkin, "From the Podium," *CBDNA Report* (Spring 2005): 1.

11   Ibid.

12   Jerry Junkin, email to the author, May 15, 2005.

13   "Circus Maximus (2004)," Composer John Corigliano, accessed 10 June 2018, http://johncorigliano.com/index.php?p=item2&sub=cat&item=38.

14   Chris Pasles, "Look Who's Marching In," *Los Angeles Times* (March 29, 2008): E 15.

15   Susan Botti, "Program Note," University of Michigan Symphony Band, concert of February 25, 2005.

16   "The Rivers of Bowery, for wind ensemble," Jonathan Newman, Composer, accessed June 1, 2018, https://jonathannewman.com/music/the-rivers-of-bowery.

17   Felicia Sandler, "Composer's Program Note," Rutgers University Wind Ensemble, concert of February 25, 2005.

18   Bright Sheng, "Composer's Program Note," University of Michigan Symphony Band, concert of February 25, 2005.

19   "Review Of Selected Premieres 2005-2007: Major Composers," Tim Reynish, accessed June 1, 2018, http://www.timreynish.com/repertoire/premieres/premieres2.php.

20   Jeff Tyzik, "Composer's Program Note," Eastman Wind Ensemble, concert of February 26, 2005.

21   Frank Zappa, "Composer's Program Note," Texas A & M University-Commerce Wind Ensemble, concert of February 24, 2005.

22   "Brooklyn Bridge for solo clarinet and symphonic band (2005): Program Note," Michael Daugherty, accessed June 10, 2018, http://www.michaeldaugherty.net/index.cfm?id=95&i=4&pagename=works.

23 "Bali: Program Notes," The Wind Repertory Project, accessed June 8, 2018, http://windrep.org/Bali.

24 Ronald E. Grames, review from *Fanfare* magazine, reprinted by ArchivMusic: The Source for Classical Music: McNeff:Image In Stone, Clarinet Concerto, Wasteland Wind Music: Notes and Editorial Reviews," accessed June 10, 2018, http://www.arkivmusic.com/classical/album.jsp?album_id=210081.

25 "Gleams from the Bosom of Darkness for Symphonic Band and Chorus: Program Notes," Lior Navok: Contemporary Music Composer, accessed June 10, 2018, https://www.liornavok.com/symphonic-band-and-chorus.

26 "Commissions and Premieres: Cornell University," *CBDNA Report* (Fall 2005): 5.

27 Joshua Penman, "Composer's Program Note," University of Michigan Symphony Band, concert of April 15, 2005.

28 Matthew Tommasini, "Composer's Program Note," University of Michigan Symphony Band, concert of December 9, 2005.

29 Dan Welcher, "Composer's Program Note," Ithaca College Wind Ensemble, concert of October 11, 2007.

30 Stephen Budiansky, "The Kids Play Great. But That Music...," *The Washington Post* (January 30, 2005): B03. Available online at http://www.budiansky.com/MUSIC_files/kidsplaygreat.pdf.

CHAPTER 14

Exploring New Opportunities (2006–2007)

> *Naxos Wind Band Classics • Increase in Works for Solo Instruments and Wind Ensemble • Smaller Instrumentated Wind Groups • Operas for Voices and Wind Ensemble • Wind Repertory Project*

Naxos of America, Inc., the world's leading classical music group, launched a new project in 2006, *Wind Band Classics*. The objective of this initiative was to present "... the best in symphonic band music [original works and arrangements of well-known classical works], performed by international wind ensembles ... [including] world première recordings ...."[1] As of 2017, fifty-five CD recordings have been produced and released. Ensembles performing on these recordings include the Budapest Wind Ensemble, Columbus State University Wind Ensemble, Hartt School Wind Ensemble, Lone Star Wind Orchestra, Ohio State University Wind Symphony, Peabody Conservatory Wind Ensemble, Rutgers University Wind Ensemble, Royal Artillery Band, Royal Norwegian Navy Band, Royal Northern College of Music Wind Orchestra, Toronto Wind Orchestra, University of Georgia Wind Ensemble, University of Kansas Wind Ensemble, University of Miami Frost Wind Ensemble, University of Missouri

Symphonic Wind Ensemble, U. S. Air Force Band, and U. S. Marine Band. The first four CDs to be release in this series were *Redline Tango: Music for Wind Band* (University of Kansas Wind Ensemble, John P. Lynch, conductor); *Vincent Persichetti: Music for Wind Ensemble* (London Symphony Orchestra, David Amos, conductor); *Vittorio Giannini* (University of Houston Wind Ensemble, Tom Bennett, conductor); and *Strike Up the Band* (Royal Swedish Air Force Band, Jerker Johansson, conductor).

* * * * * * * * * * * *

The works below, collectively, reflect the diverse body of literature created for the wind band/ensemble in 2006.

John Adams	*Lollapalooza* (wind version, arr. James Spinazzola)
Louis Andriessen	*Hymne to the memory of Darius Milhaud*
Steven Bryant	*Radiant Joy*
Carter Pann	*The Wrangler: Cowboy Dances for Wind Ensemble*
Peter Child	*Triptych*
Michael Colgrass	*Raag-Mala: Music of India through Western Ears*
David Dzubay	*Shadow Dance*
Adam Gorb	*Adrenaline City*
Karel Husa	*Cheetah*
John Mackey	*Strange Humors*
John Mackey	*Turning*
Norbert Palej	*Song and Dance*
Narong Prangcharoen	*Chakra*
Christopher Rouse	*Wolf Rounds*
Christopher Theofanidis	*I wander the world in a dream of my own making*
Dana Wilson	*Day Dreams*

John Adams (b. 1947) composed the original orchestra version of *Lollapalooza* for the fortieth birthday of his friend and collaborator of many years, Sir Simon Rattle. Rattle conducted the premiere of the piece on November 10, 1985, with the City of Birmingham Symphony. In 2005, James Spinazzola, Director of Bands and Instrumental Activities at the University of Indianapolis, created a wind version of the work which he premiered with the Louisiana State

University Wind Ensemble in 2006. *Lollapalooza* is an exuberant, energetic, and exciting work—bursting with rhythmic motives and jazz-inspired tonality.

Louis Andriessen (b. 1939) composed his *Hymne to the memory of Darius Milhaud* in 1974. It was performed for the first time in the United States by the Williams College Symphonic Winds, Steven Dennis Bodner, conductor, on March 23, 2006, at the Eastern Division CBDNA Conference (Montclair State University). Below is an excerpt from the Bodner's program note for that performance:

> As early as 1923, the Andriessen family became closely associated with Milhaud: when a few months after the premiere of *La création du monde*, Milhaud came to Amsterdam to speak about the piece, Andriessen's father performed the piano four-hand version with Milhaud.... In 1947 ... Andriessen's brother Juriaan composed a piece entitled *Hommage á Milhaud*—a piece that both Hendrik and Louis admired very much. When the Orkest de Volharding was created, it needed a repertoire, and so it seemed natural to Andriessen that he would arrange works of Milhaud for the group.... When Milhaud died in 1974, Andriessen thought "there was nothing better than to write a beautiful chorale to the memory of Milhaud, respecting his ideas about harmony," and so he composed his *Hymne to the memory of Darius Milhaud* (1974) for Volharding and later arranged [it] for symphony orchestra. Andriessen describes Milhaud's harmony not as bi-tonal, but as "a sort of reverse Stravinsky," and as "a simple tonality with a lot of wrong notes"; it is this "magical combination of diatonic melodic material and chromatic harmonic material" which Andriessen sees as being the crux of much of Stravinsky's and Milhaud's music, and that Andriessen reflects in his *Hymne*.[2]

Radiant Joy by Steven Bryant (b. 1959) was the winner of the 2007 National Band Association's William D. Revelli Composition Contest. The work was commissioned and premiered on October 15, 2006, by the Indiana University of Pennsylvania Wind Ensemble, Jack Stamp, conductor. Bryant wrote this about the work,

> *Radiant Joy* ... comes after a difficult period in my personal life, and thus its character was something of a surprise to me. This work began life as a strict, 12-tone, serialized creature modeled on Webern—I wanted something sparse and tightly constructed (in harmonic and intervallic terms), while still retaining a vital rhythmic pulse. After several sketches that ended in anger and frustration, I realized I was metaphorically banging my head against the creative wall, and perhaps I should stop

forcing this music into existence with a prescriptive process, and simply listen inwardly to what I actually wanted to hear. The result is simultaneously the opposite of what I was originally trying to create, and also its direct realization—the vital rhythmic pulse is still prominent, but the harmonic materials veered toward the language of 70s/80s funk/jazz/fusion (take your pick). Regardless, the piece is intended to emanate joy and "good vibes" (literally—the vibraphone is critical to the piece!), for the performers, the audience, and the composer![3]

The Wrangler by Carter Pann (b. 1972) was written for the James Logan High School Wind Ensemble, Ramiro Barrera, director. It was premiered by the group at Carnegie Hall in May 2006. The piece is reminiscent of the film scores written for old Western movies and shares syntax with Aaron Copland's ballets *Billy the Kid* and *Rodeo*. The composer relates the story line of the piece in his program note.

> There are no outlaw characters in *The Wrangler* ... instead, the hero is a good man, a free man.... After a serene chorale-like introduction he is set in motion ... across the landscape. On his journey he encounters gorgeous and treacherous terrain, stumbling upon a saloon where the patrons are engaged in a drunken dance. He manages to evade locals looking for a fight while catching the eyes of many a beautiful woman. Our man is the proto-typical cowboy ....[4]

Triptych by MIT composer Peter Child (b. 1953) was commissioned by a consortium of universities that included Emory University, MIT, New England Conservatory of Music, University of Michigan, University of Minnesota, University of Texas, and Yale University to write a piece for Frank L. Battisti's 75th birthday. It is the composer's first piece for wind ensemble and was premiered on October 11, 2007, by the New England Conservatory Wind Ensemble, Charles Peltz, conductor. Mark DeVoto, in a review for *The Boston Musical Intelligencer*, wrote that *Triptych* was an attractive work and a natural for acceptance by other wind groups.

> The first [movement is] hard-edged and even threatening with its recurrent loud tritone-based chords and ponderous bass beat.... The second section is more playful and with a stronger major-key basis, with a good deal of well-highlighted solo writing (including some contrasting snarls in flutter-tongued low trombones—remember no. 1 of Schoenberg's *Five Orchestral Pieces, op. 16*). It merges easily into the final section,

which features a long treble *ostinato* of five descending notes (I was reminded of the end of the "Saturn" movement of *The Planets* by Gustav Holst . . .), with some elegant timbral contrasts in harp and glockenspiel, which are left alone at the end.[5]

Raag-Mala by Michael Colgrass (b. 1932) was commissioned and premiered on April 19, 2006, by the Southern Utah University Wind Ensemble, James Smart, conductor. The objective of the commission was to have Colgrass compose a piece that could be played by small and mid-sized college/university bands as well as advanced high school bands. Smart describes Colgrass's work as exotic yet accessible, tremendously complex yet transparent and cerebral yet visceral. Colgrass stated that *Raag-Mala* was inspired by the classical Indian music he heard at the "Raag-Mala" (means a garland of ragas), a Toronto-based music society that features the best Indian classical musicians and singers.

> I have often left these concerts singing the ragas I had heard and embellishing on them from my own imagination. *Raag Mala* is the result of those musings. I don't attempt to replicate Indian music in this piece . . . Nor do I intend to create a hybrid of East-West musical styles, which I sometimes do in my pieces. Instead, my aim is to filter Indian music through my Western musical experience and cast it in a new way.[6]

David Dzubay (b. 1954) composed two *Shadow Dances*—one for orchestra in 2002 and another for wind ensemble in 2006. The wind ensemble version was commissioned by the University of North Carolina at Greensboro Wind Ensemble which premiered the piece on October 5, 2006, John R. Locke conducting. In a review that appeared in *Fanfare magazine*, Ronald E. Grames writes,

> Dzubay takes the concept of organum to remarkable extremes, creating a frenzied, irreverent modern equivalent of the 13th century composer's primitive polyphony. It has little to do with the medieval—excepting of course, the concluding monk-like chanting of the cantus firmus—but everything to do with joyful celebration of the past.[7]

The composer added:

> Players in the ensemble are asked to sing portions of the original chant, namely the first and last two words–*Viderunt*, and *justitiam suum*. Like the age in which we live, the character of this dance is unstable: by turns ominous, peaceful, celebratory, reflective, frantic, joyful, raucous, anxious, hopeful.[8]

Adam Gorb (b. 1958) has composed music for all levels of wind bands. His *Adrenaline City* was commissioned in 2005 by a consortium of seven military bands. It was premiered on March 3, 2006, at the Clarinet Summit in New York City by the United States Military Academy Band conducted by Timothy Holtan. The composer provided the following comment about his six-and-a-half minute concert overture:

> *Adrenaline City* ... [was] ... inspired by both the stress and vibrancy of twenty-first century city life. It is in sonata form and is notable for a time signature in 10/8. The harsh and dissonant opening passage is contrasted by a mellow second subject theme in the saxophones. The percussion come to the fore in the middle section, and at the close of the work the harmonic tension reaches an exhilarating breaking point before resolving on the tonal centre of A.[9]

Cheetah by Karel Husa (1921–2016) was commissioned by the University of Louisville Wind Symphony, Frederick Speck conductor, and premiered in Carnegie Hall on March 8, 2007. As it is with all his works, Husa employs a variety of compositional techniques, especially dramatic changes of color and texture, to create a fascinating portrait of this powerful and speedy animal.

The wind version of *Strange Humors* by John Mackey (b. 1973) was commissioned by the American Bandmasters Association and is dedicated to Richard Floyd. (Mackey's original version of the piece was for string quartet and djembe.) Floyd conducted the premiere of *Strange Humors* with the Baylor University Wind Ensemble at the ABA Convention in Richardson, Texas, on March 1, 2006. At the heart of the piece is the pulse of the djembe, an hourglass-shaped drum played with bare hands. It is "a major part of the customs of West African countries such as Mali and Guinea, where djembe ensembles accompany many functional celebrations of society".

> ... The piece opens with a sultry English horn solo, a line laced with Phrygian influences representing the "typical" melodies of the most northeastern parts of the African continent ... [and] also parts of the Arabian Peninsula. Later, the saxophones emulate the snaking lines of the English horn. The addition of brass and auxiliary percussion to the original orchestration makes for particular impact during the shout sections of the piece, and the groove of the djembe combined with the quirky rhythms throughout leave an impression that lingers in the listener's mind long after its conclusion.[10]

Turning is another work Mackey composed in 2006. This time the commission came from a consortium of eight high school bands organized by Josh Thompson, a high school friend of Mackey and Band Director at Lake Zurich (Illinois) High School. The composer stated that the original ideas for *Turning* came from two sources:

> ... a new "sample library" I purchased that contained an instrument called a "Waterphone," and ... the beautiful Brass chorale by Bjork that opens the film "Dancer in the Dark". ... So my first thought was, why not combine waterphone and Bjork, resulting in music that sounds almost like the score for a horror film?[11]
>
> I chose the title *Turning* for this piece because the word can mean any number of things, all of which might be heard in the piece itself. It could refer to the turning of a massive, prehistoric planet, as the first signs of life begin to bubble up from cracks in the ground. It could refer to the turning of leaves in the fall, a beautiful—but melancholy—thing to see. Or in the piece's darkest moments, the title could refer to the turning of a knife into one's chest.[12]

Song and Dance by Norbert Palej (b. 1977) was composed for the Cornell University Winds' "outreach project" which involved local middle and high school bands. Conductor Cynthia Johnston Turner asked Palej to write a piece that was "easy enough for a middle school but meaty enough for a university ensemble."[13] Several area school bands participated in the project. The students in the Boynton Middle School Band in Ithaca, New York, Michael Allen, director, were invited to meet and talk with the composer as well as rehearse the piece with the Cornell University Winds. Palej's one-movement, five minute long piece was premiered on March 11, 2006, by the Cornell Winds conducted by Cynthia Johnston Turner. The composer added the following comment about the piece:

> The piece opens with a broad and sad melody, "sung" by the flutes and later by the clarinets. Suddenly, the listener finds him/herself transported into the middle of a lively, joyful dance. A return of the opening melody closes the piece.[14]

Thai composer, Narong Prangcharoen (b. 1973) has received many awards including the Alexander Zemlinsky International Composition Competition Prize and the Toru Takemitsu Composition Award. He founded the Thailand Composition Festival in Bangkok, Thailand, and was on the faculty of the Western Music Department of

Srinakharinwirot University. His works contain idiomatic techniques and sounds of Thai melodies in various guises. Prangcharoen composed *Chakra* in 2007 and has written the following about the piece.

> The word 'chakra' means wheel and refers to the Hindu-Buddhist concept of the 'Wheel of Life.' It is believed that these wheel-like vortices throughout the human body transmit energy to major nerve centers branching off from the spinal column. The chakras help maintain a good balance in the human body and life itself, and the composer embraces the tradition of each body possessing seven chakras. A chaotic beginning is transformed into a melodic source for the entire composition. The linear flow of the melody and slow evolution of timbral change imitates the surge of energy through the chakras. The music is not intended to portray the sound of each chakra and it is not meant for meditation. Rather, the piece reflects the experience of the life force and the energy of music as it resembles positive energy flowing through the body."[15]

Wolf Rounds by Christopher Rouse (b. 1949) was commissioned by the University of Miami Frost School of Music. It is dedicated to Gary Green who conducted the premiere of the piece on March 29, 2007, with the University of Miami Wind Ensemble in Carnegie Hall. The composer described the "circular, loop" process he used in writing the piece.

> My concept of the work was to introduce a series of "circular" musical ideas that would repeat over and over until metamorphosing to a new idea that would then also be repeated in the same fashion until becoming yet another.... Sometimes these ideas would repeat verbatim; at other times there would be gradual but constant development within each repetition. ...
>
> My first impulse was to entitle the work "Loops," as it seemed to me that this was an accurate description of the processes involved in composing the piece. However, this title seemed a bit prosaic. The word "loops," though, led me to think of the Latin word *"lupus,"* which means "wolf." I was put in mind of the way in which wolves circle their prey, and these predatory rounds of course reminded me of the circular nature of my musical presentation. Thus the final title: *Wolf Rounds*.[16]

In 2005, Christopher Theofanidis (b. 1967), Professor of Composition at the Peabody Conservatory of Music in Baltimore, Maryland, was commissioned by a consortium of nine universities to write a wind ensemble piece. The piece he wrote, *I wander the world in a dream of my own making*, was premiered by the Georgia State University Symphonic Wind Ensemble, Robert J. Ambrose, conductor, at the Southern Division CBDNA Conference in Nashville, Tennessee, on February 24, 2006. The composer provided a short comment about the piece.

> The feeling that pervades the work is one of a sense of mystery, and the sentiment is primarily conveyed through the harmonies and orchestration. The work is based on two ideas: the first a short, two-note motive, and the second is a descending melody of five notes, ending in the repetition of the final note several times. The second material could be called the main melody, and it always appears shrouded in a kind of haze, until toward the very end of the work.[17]

On June 23–24, 2006, more than 350 alumni of the 1955–67 Ithaca High School Band gathered in Ithaca, NY, to celebrate the 75th birthday of their band director, Frank Battisti. At the reunion's concluding banquet composer Dana Wilson (b. 1946) presented Battisti with a score to *Day Dreams*, a work the students had commissioned to honor Battisti on his birthday. Battisti conducted dual premiere performances of the sixteen-minute long work in the fall—the first on October 12 with the New England Conservatory Wind Ensemble, the second on October 17 with the Ithaca College Wind Ensemble. The following program note appears in the score.

> *Day Dreams* traces a metaphorical day: The movement titles (1. Sunrise: an infinite expectation; 2. Morning: all intelligence wake; 3. Afternoon: hopes shot upward, ever so bright; 4. Sunset: having lived the life imagined) all come from Thoreau's *Walden*—a place very close to where Frank spent a good part of his life. The work begins with a dramatic sunrise. The second movement represents morning (or youth) and juxtaposes two extremely contrasting and perhaps irreconcilable types of material (an amorphous blurring with a precise, funk groove) typical of that stage of life. The third movement explores the afternoon (adulthood), a period of sophisticated balancing of life's many forces. The final movement allows each player to say goodbye to Frank individually, but—true to his nature—he does not go gently. Nor do we want him to....[18]

* * * * * * * * * * *

The number of commissions for concerto-type works for instrumental and vocal soloist and wind band/ensemble increased significantly in the first decade of the twenty-first century. The six works below are among those composed in 2006–2007.

Stephen Paulus	*Concerto for Piano and Winds*
Zechariah Goh Toh Chai	*Concerto for Marimba and Wind Ensemble*
Andrew Mead	*Concerto for Winds*
Edwin Roxburgh	*An Elegy for Ur*
Dana Wilson	*Liquid Gold*
Dana Wilson	*The Avatar*

Stephen Paulus's *Concerto for Piano and Winds* was commissioned by the Emory University and Southern Methodist University Wind Ensembles. It is a three-movement, twenty-minute long, large-scale romantic piano concerto that received two premiere performances. The first on February 22, 2006, by the Emory University Wind Ensemble, Scott Stewart, conductor, William Ransom, piano soloist, and the second on April 21, 2006, by Jack Delaney and the Southern Methodist University Wind Ensemble, again with William Ransom as the piano soloist. The *Concerto* is very dramatic and expressive in character with a "Fiery" first movement; a "Tranquil: With Mystery" middle movement; and a "Driving" final movement.

Zechariah Goh Toh Chai (b. 1970) was born and received his early musical training in Singapore. Later he immigrated to the United States and continued his musical studies at the University of Kansas, earning a Masters Degree in Piano and a Doctorate in Composition. Chai's music—a mixture of Western and Eastern idioms and styles— reflects the variance of his background. His *Concerto for Marimba and Wind Ensemble* was commissioned by the University of Kansas and Philharmonic Winds of Singapore. It was premiered on March 27, 2007, by the Kansas Wind Ensemble, John P. Lynch, conductor, with Kevin Bobo as marimba soloist. The composer provided the follow-ing information about his work:

> The two contrasting movements of the concerto feature the unique sounds of smaller instrumental combinations within the ensemble, such as double reed quartets, tuba/euphonium consorts, and the clari-net choir. The nuances of instrumental color throughout are designed to accentuate the woody quality of the marimba.[19]

Andrew Mead (b. 1952) is Professor of Music Theory at the University of Michigan. His *Concerto for Winds* is dedicated to Michael Haithcock and the University of Michigan Symphony Band, which premiered the piece on October 23, 2006. The single movement work consists of a large central section framed by two smaller, quicker

ones followed by a coda. The composer offered the following comment about the piece,

> It is a mosaic of different music characters played in pairs and articulated by ever-changing associations amongst the ensemble's twenty-four players. ... The over-arching shape of the piece emerges from the ways the combinations of musical characters are compounded and ordered in the musical surface. The basic design helped serve my desire to present the virtuosity of the players in a multitude of ways; individually, by instrumental family, and in various mixed combinations.[20]

Edwin Roxburgh's oboe concerto, *An Elegy for Ur*, won the 2007 British Composer Award in the wind or brass band category. The piece was commissioned by Timothy and Hilary Reynish as part of a series of works commissioned in memory of their third son, William Patrick Reynish, who died while climbing in the Pyrenees Mountains in 2001. The fourteen-minute long work was premiered on June 27, 2006, by oboist Melinda Maxwell and the Royal Northern College of Music Wind Ensemble, Timothy Reynish, conductor. Roxburgh (b. 1937) wrote the following about the piece:

> *Ur* could be described as the womb of history. It was a civilization which produced "works of art so rich and technically so perfect," as Sir Leonard Woolley described early Mesopotamian art. Modern Iraq inhabits the same soil and for several millennia the country has cared for its invaluable artifacts. As a result of the catastrophic invasion by the USA and the UK this rich heritage was plundered and despoiled in the looting of the Iraq Museum in Baghdad. The earliest surviving musical instrument, the *Royal Lyre of Ur*, was among the treasures that were either destroyed or stolen. This may not seem as barbaric as the invasion itself, in which thousands of innocent women and children were slaughtered, but it is equally tragic. The world of culture cannot influence the decisions of politicians but it can record a protest for history. Hence, the title of this work. ...
>
> The music takes the form of flourishing rhapsodies for the solo oboist, separated by rhythmic interludes which feature the main orchestra in virtuosic gestures.[21]

Dana Wilson (b. 1946) composed two works for solo wind instruments and wind ensemble in 2006. The first, *Liquid Gold*, was originally a piece for clarinet and piano which was commissioned and premiered by Larry Combs, former principal clarinetist of the Chicago Symphony. The West Point Military Academy Band commissioned

Wilson to make a wind version of the work, which it premiered on March 18, 2006, with Combs again as the soloist. Wilson wrote this about his piece:

> On the surface, each movement is rather different in nature, but the tenacious reinterpretation of the same material in each is intended to reinforce the overlaying of contrasting emotions. The first is exuberant, the second introspective yet purposeful, the third a Bulgarian romp amidst an ominous reality.[22]

A second solo instrumental work written by Wilson in 2006 was *The Avatar*, a three-movement, seventeen minute-long piece for bassoon and small wind ensemble. It was premiered on April 27, 2006, by the Michigan State University Wind Symphony, Kevin Sedatole, conductor, and Michael Kroth, bassoon soloist. Although many pieces have been written that stress the ability of the bassoon to be humorous, Wilson decided to write one that focused on its ability to plead, entice, command, and conjure. Hence the title, *The Avatar*.

* * * * * * * * *

Composers also showed an increased interest in writing operas that employed a wind ensemble as an instrumental consort in the first decade of the new millennium. Included among these composers were Daron Hagen (*Bandanna*, 1999), Charles Shadle (*Coyote's Dinner*, 2001), Joseph Turrin (*The Scarecrow*, 2006), and Justin Dello Joio (*Blue Mountain*, 2007). Conductor Odd Terje Lysebo also created a new version of Dmitri Shostakovich's *The Priest and His Servant Balda* which was premiered at the 2007 WASBE Conference in Ireland.

Daron Hagen's opera *Bandanna was* premiered at the 1999 CBDNA National Conference at the University of Texas, Austin. It received its European premiere on April 29, 2006, in a performance by the North Cheshire Concert Band, conducted by Mark Heron, in Warrington, UK. Reporting on this performance, conductor Clark Rundell wrote,

> ... Hagen's vocal writing is masterful. His use of the wind orchestra is ... stunning, to the point where one was never aware of a wind band, but simply of dramatic music.... [Had] the performance [been] given in a theatre with the orchestra in the pit, the balance, which was generally

excellent, would have been perfect throughout.... The chorus writing
is assured and the singing by Manchester Chamber Choir was simply
impeccable. In fact, the only reason they didn't sound like a fully-fledged
opera chorus was that their intonation was so utterly pure. Senior students of the Royal Northern College of Music sang the principal roles
with distinction... [and] must all be commended, for the clarity of their
diction and the confidence of their singing.

The North Cheshire Concert Band, one of the UK's finest community bands, excelled themselves in what must have been the first full
scale operatic experience for most of them. Like the music itself, one
was never aware of a community band but of music superbly performed
which intensified the drama.[23]

Joseph Turrin's opera, *The Scarecrow,* received its premiere performance on February 24, 2006, at the University of Texas' McCullough
Theatre with the composer conducting. The opera was commissioned
by a consortium of twelve university ensembles. A second performance the work took place at Arizona State University's Lyric Opera
Theatre on November 17–18 and December 1–2, 2006. Turrin (b.
1947) started working on the opera in 1976 but did not complete
it until 2006. It is scored for 10 voices and a wind ensemble consisting of 2 flutes (piccolo), oboe, 2 clarinets (bass clarinet), 2 bassoons
(contrabassoon), 2 trumpets, 2 horns, 2 trombones, harp, piano
(harpsichord, celesta), 4 celli, contrabass, and 2 percussion. The plot
of the opera is based on a play by Percy MacKaye who was inspired
by Nathaniel Hawthorne's last short story, "Feathertop," which deals
with a New England witch who brings a scarecrow to life and then
sends it into town, "causing mischief and mayhem."

Justin Dello Joio (b. 1955) wrote his one act opera, *Blue Mountain,* to commemorate the 100th anniversary of the death of Norwegian composer Edvard Grieg. It was commissioned by the Det Nor-
ske Blåseensemble (Norwegian Wind Ensemble) and premiered on
October 8, 9, 10, 2007, in Oslo, Norway, by that ensemble, Kenneth
Jean conducting, with singers from the Oslo State Opera. The opera
is based on the final days of Edvard Grieg's life in September 1907—
his contemplation of death, anguish over the future of his music,
reoccurring visions of his deceased daughter, and meeting with fellow composer Percy Grainger. Dello Joio uses a wind ensemble (plus
harp, solo violin, and string bass) to accompany the voices in the
opera. The music is "craggily" lyrical and includes references to some

of Grieg's works including the *Piano Concerto, Violin Sonata in c, Evening in the Mountains* (from his *Lyric Pieces for Piano*), and *Peer Gynt*.

Conductor Odd Terje Lysebo conducted the Nanset Wind Ensemble in a performance of his new version of Shostakovich's 1936 opera, *The Priest and His Servant Balda*, at the 2007 WASBE Conference in Killarney, Ireland. The work was originally conceived as a full-length animated film opera by Mikhail Tsekhanovsky (1889–1965). It is based on an eponymous fairy tale in verse by Alexander Puskin. In 1933 Director Tsekhanovsky asked Shostakovich (1906–1975) to write the music for the film. Shostakovich wrote some music but never finished it because of the denunciation of his music in 1936 (the infamous *Pravda* article "Muddle Instead of Music"). Shostakovich's score was finished posthumously by his student, Vadim Bibergan (b. 1937). The opera's plot revolves around a priest, his wife and daughter, a servant named Balda, and various devils. The priest hires Balda, who agrees to work for no money—all he wants is to be able to hit the priest over the head three times at the end of the year. When Balda falls in love with the priest's daughter, the priest sends him on an impossible journey—to a lake where a devil lives to collect payment on a debt owed to him. After much manipulation and some humorous physical play, Balda wins back his master's pay. Upon his return, Balda demands his wages—he hits the priest over the head three times driving him insane.

Dwayne Corbin, in his review of the performance for the *Irish Times*, wrote:

> Lysebo commissioned an animation company to create a new film, as only three minutes of the original film was in existence....The video was used in combination with live actors, wind ensemble (with cello and string bass) accompaniment, a small choir, and vocal soloists. The animation purposefully imitated the appearance of shadow-puppet theatre, drawing connections with another classic story-telling tradition. Thus, in order to create a uniform look, the live actors had costumes that seemed animated, with exaggerated features, large hollow eyes, and disproportionate bodies....
>
> The production was unlike any theatre event I have ever seen. The flow between the music, animation, live acting, and singing was flawless and logically connected. The video and acting alternated, with the screen becoming simple backgrounds to the actors. While it was unusual to have one character represented by two people, an actor and

a singer, it provided for much more freedom on stage, and allowed for some interesting moments when the singers moved onto the stage and interacted with their character. Even the band was involved in the action: players held devil puppets in one scene, and in the prior scene Balda actually came over and pushed Lysebo off the podium and conducted a piece himself!

The music was unmistakably Shostakovich, containing scales, modes, melodic constructions, and folk elements that we have all come to associate with him. The folk element became central in several pieces, as some songs were accompanied with just an accordion or a balalaika, the three-stringed triangle-shaped Russian lute. In another piece, the tenor saxophone player walked to the opposite edge of the stage to play a beautiful duet. Overall, the music was most often light-hearted....[24]

* * * * * * * * * *

The 2007 CBDNA National Conference was held at the University of Michigan, "the womb of CBDNA," from March 28–31. This marked a return to the traditional environment for CBDNA national conferences—the university campus (the 2005 Conference was held in New York City). Of the fifty-two works performed on the Conference's nine concerts, almost 75% of them were composed between 2000–2007; fourteen of them (28%) were written by non-American composers.

There was a large group of composers at the Conference, among them Steven Bryant, Michael Colgrass, Michael Daugherty, David Gillingham, Osvaldo Golijov, Douglas Lowry, John Mackey, Jonathan Newman, Joseph Schwantner, Matthew Tommasini, Frank Ticheli, and Dan Welcher. This was clear evidence that composers were interested in the wind/band ensemble and writing music for the medium. Conference "Break-out Sessions" dealt with a broad range of subjects: "The Wind Music of Heitor Villa-Lobos," "The Vernacular Made Artful: An Analysis of Dana Wilson's Works for Wind Ensemble," "The Wind Music of Colin McPhee," "Tracing the Linage of Nadia Boulanger Through American Wind Repertoire," "Secret Sounds: Berg, Mysticism and the Chamber Concerto," "Wind Bands and the Seventh Edition of Grout's *A History of Western Music.*"

Four premiere performances were included on Conference concerts:

Between Blues and Hard Places by Douglas Lowry
Raise the Roof for Timpani and Symphonic Band (band version)
      by Michael Daugherty
Passaggi by Stephen Gryc
Lullaby for Noah by Joe Turrin

Douglas Lowry (b. 1951), Professor of Music at the Cincinnati College-Conservatory of Music, composed *Between Blues and Hard Places*. He was inspired to write the piece by a PBS special hosted by Eric Clapton that featured performances by some of the world's great guitarists including B. B. King and John Mayer. The composer stated that it was a lesson in history.

> ... many of us grew up in an era rich in rock 'n roll [and were] deeply influenced by these artists. Some of us went on to music schools only to get immersion training in Palestrina and Bach, Mozart and Beethoven, Debussy and Mahler, Schoenberg and Webern, along with scores of other born of Occident. As composers ... we try to reconcile these many "musics" because the musical landscape that ... inhabits us is so complex. The tension is inescapable, and the various ways this tension gets resolved is fundamental to the compositional problem of the twenty-first century. So I guess *Between Blues and Hard Places* is really a short simple essay on this dilemma.
>
> [The piece] probably isn't blues at all. It begins with a soft, lyrical, almost melancholic piano solo. This sets up a smoky sultry scene influenced by the blues whose themes accelerate and compress and finally give birth to "hard places," a zone laced with cross rhythms, nine-eights against four-fours, four-against-threes, all colliding against struggling jazzy figures. A reprise of the melancholy piano finally allows one last set of blues-and-hard-places to drift off, its paradox happily unresolved.[25]

Michael Daugherty's *Raise the Roof* for timpani and orchestra was commissioned for the opening of the Max Fisher Music Center in Detroit, Michigan. It was premiered on October 16, 2003, by the Detroit Symphony Orchestra, Neeme Jarvi, conductor, with Brian Jones as timpani soloist. The wind version of the piece was commissioned by the University of Michigan Symphony Band, Michael Haithcock, conductor. Daugherty (b. 1954) wrote the following about the piece:

> *Raise the Roof* is inspired by the construction of grand architectural wonders such as the Notre Dame Cathedral (1345) in Paris and the Empire State Building (1931) in New York City. I create a grand

acoustic construction by bringing the timpani into the foreground and giving the timpanist the rare opportunity to play long expressive melodies, and a tour de force cadenza. I incorporate a wide variety of timpani performance techniques: extensive use of foot pedals for melodic tuning of the drums, placement of a cymbal upside down on the head of the lowest drum to play glissandi rolls, and striking the drums with regular mallets, wire brushes, maraca sticks, and even bare hands. *Raise the Roof* is in the form of a double variation [that] … rises toward a crescendo of urban polyrhythms and dynamic contrasts, allowing the timpani and the symphonic band to create a grand acoustic construction.[26]

Passaggi by Stephen Gryc (b. 1949) was commissioned by Joseph Alessi, principal trombonist of the New York Philharmonic. Originally written for solo trombone and orchestra, the composer created a wind version of the piece for the Hartt School Wind Ensemble, specifically for its 2007 CBDNA Conference performance. The title *Passaggi*, which in Italian means "passages," has both musical and non-musical connotations. The composer explained,

> The piece is somewhat autobiographical; each of the three movements is dedicated to a different trombonist who has been influential in my musical life. The concerto starts with a slow movement, *Preludio*, [which] … represents the dream of becoming a musician and is dedicated to Daniel Livesay, a wonderful trombonist who, at different times, taught both Joseph Alessi and me.
>
> The second movement, *Variazioni*, is a set of variations on an odd little theme of my own composition…. Each successive variation has a strikingly different character and its own designation: *Marziale* (martial music), *Tarantella* (a frenzied Italian dance scored for woodwinds, percussion and trombone), *Recitative* (a short meditation with accompaniment by the percussion section), *Cantilena* (the lyric highpoint of the work), and *Finale piccolo* (a virtuosic "little ending")….*Variazioni* represents a musician's years as a student and is dedicated to my composition teacher (and former trombonist) Leslie Bassett.
>
> The last movement of *Passaggi* bears the unusual title *Scherzi tempestosi* or "tempestuous jokes." A boisterous evocation of the competition among professional musicians, the movement pits the soloist against the entire brass section of the wind ensemble….Amid the frenzy, the original impetus to become a musician is recalled with music from the *Preludio*, and the movement reaches its climax with music from the *Variazioni*. This movement is dedicated to the supreme musician who commissioned the work, Joseph Alessi.[27]

Conductor Glen Adsit and the Hartt School Wind Ensemble commissioned Joseph Turrin (b. 1947) to write a piece for Adsit's two-year son Noah Donald Koffman-Adsit. The composer was completely captivated with the idea of writing such a work.

> I wanted to write a piece that was simple and eloquent. As I composed this piece, I thought of that wonderful main theme of Elmer Bernstein's score for the film: *To Kill a Mockingbird*—how provocative and song-like—beautifully shaped and filled with a quiet melancholy. There is also a touch of melancholy in this lullaby and perhaps a longing for the innocence that once was our basic nature. "When I approach a child, he inspires in me two sentiments; tenderness for what he is, and respect for what he may become"—Louis Pasteur.[28]

* * * * * * * * * * * *

The American Bandmasters Association's 72nd Annual Convention was held in Dallas/Richardson, Texas from March 1–4, 2006. The Board of Directors announced that ABA and the University of Florida had formed a partnership to commission "outstanding composers to write works for the concert band, wind ensemble, chamber winds, or young band idioms."

The American Bandmasters Association 73rd Convention was held in San Luis Obispo, California, from March 7–10, 2007. The St. Cloud State University Wind Ensemble, Richard K. Hansen, conductor, premiered three new works: *Within the Circles of Our Lives* by Libby Larsen (b. 1950), *Liberty Fallen* by Justin Freer (b. 1980), and *On the Beach at Night* by Ian Kouse (b. 1956). Gary Hill conducted a most interesting concert with the Arizona State University Chamber Winds and Wind Symphony entitled "A Concise History of Wind Band." It consisted of three parts: The first, "Evolution" (works by Gabrieli, Lully, and Cartellieri), the second, "Revolution" (works by Ponchielli and Sousa), and third, "Revelation" (works by Grainger, Turina, and Mackey).

WASBE's 13th International Conference was held in Killarney, Ireland, from July 8–14, 2007. Eleven ensembles performed sixty-two pieces written by composers from around the world. The new works premiered at the Conference included: *Big Jig* by Thierry Besançon (b. 1979), *Concertino for Euphonium* by Marco Pütz (b. 1958), *Dance for Wind Band* by Pavol Simai (b. 1930), *Divertimento for Band* by Guy Woolfenden (b. 1937), *Frenergy* by John Estacio (b. 1966) arranged by Fraser Linkleter, *Image in Stone* by Stephen McNeff (b. 1951), *Miranda, Ariel, Umbriel* by Ian Wilson (b. 1964), *Prelude and Toccata* by John Kinsella (b. 1932), and *The Spiralling Night* by Joseph Phibbs (b. 1974). The performance of the University of Louisville Wind Ensemble, Frederick Speck, conductor, included the European premiere of *Cheetah* by Karel Husa (b. 1921) and Odd Terje Lysebo conducted the Nanset Wind Ensemble and singers in a new version of Dmitri Shostakovich's *The Priest and his Servant Balda* (already mentioned, above, in this Chapter). Composers attending the conference included Thierry Besançon, Thomas Duffy, Jacob de Haan, John Kinsella, Stephen McNeff, Joseph Phibbs, Oliver Waespi, Ian Wilson, and Guy Woolfenden.

* * * * * * * * * *

In the fall of 2006, Nikk Pilato began formulating ideas that eventually would lead to the formation of the *Wind Repertory Project (WRP)*. Speaking about its origin he recalled,

> At that time, I was thinking that my Ph.D. dissertation [at Florida State University] would be a wind band version of David Daniel's book, "Orchestra Music: A Handbook." As the immense scope of such a project began to dawn on me, I abandoned it in favor of other ideas, but the concept stayed with me.... One day, as I looked up information on Wikipedia, I wondered to myself if the project could be made viable in an online format. After teaching myself the 'ins and outs' of maintaining a "wiki" database, I began entering music (essentially all the scores I personally owned as a starter), soliciting ideas from close friends, and ensuring that this type of project didn't already exist. The website went live in February 2008.[29]

The Wind Repertory Project (www.windrep.org) is a comprehensive online database of wind literature which is expanded and enriched through user input, much like Wikipedia. The database includes detailed information about wind literature such as instrumentation, program notes, errata, study resources, articles, and commercially available recordings. In the ten years since its inception, the WRP has amassed over 11,000 pages of information (9,000 pages about individual compositions and 2,100 pages about composers). There are 6,000 registered users and the website, on average, receives over 8,000 hits per month. It has been visited by over 16 million people since it began in 2008.

* * * * * * * * * *

The first of the Fennell Memorial Conducting Masterclasses, sponsored by the Conductors Guild and the Eastman School of Music, took place in Rochester, New York, on October 18–20, 2007. These masterclasses are held biannually and honor the legacy of Frederick Fennell as a conductor and founder of the Eastman Wind Ensemble. The objective of the masterclasses is to provide the maximum amount of specific and insightful guidance on both technical and musical matters to each participant in a constructive and non-competitive environment. Eastman Wind Ensemble Conductor Emeritus, Dr. Donald Hunsberger was the first master conductor/teacher. Other masterclass faculty included current Eastman Wind Ensemble conductor Mark Scatterday, alumnus Michael Votta, and Frank Battisti.

ENDNOTES

1 "Sets/Series: Wind Band Classics," Naxos Records, accessed June 10, 2018, https://www.naxos.com/series/wind_band_classics.htm.
2 Steven Dennis Bodner, "Program Note," Williams College Symphonic Winds, concert of March 23, 2006.
3 "Radiant Joy," Steven Bryant: Composer/Conductor, accessed June 1, 2018, https://www.stevenbryant.com/music/catalog/radiant-joy.
4 Timothy Reynish, "CBDNA 2009 Conference: Americana," Tim Reynish, accessed June 1, 2018, http://www.timreynish.com/conferences/cbdna-2009.php.
5 Mark DeVoto, "Celebrating Well: Three Generations of British Composers," *The Boston Musical Intelligencer* (December 6, 2008), accessed June 10, 2018, https://www.classical-scene.com/2008/12/06/celebrating-well-three-generations-of-british-composers/.
6 "Premieres: Raag Mala: Music of India through Western Ears [by] Michael Colgrass," *CBDNA Report* (Fall 2006): 4.
7 Ronald E. Grames, "Wild Nights!," *Fanfare* 33 (November-December 2009): 353.
8 "Shadow Dance (2006) for wind ensemble," Pro Nova Music: Music by David Dzubay, accessed June 10, 2018, http://pronovamusic.com/notes/SDb.html.

9   "Programme Notes—Adrenaline City (2006)," Adam Gorb, Composer, accessed June 10, 2018, http://www.adamgorb.co.uk/programme-notes/programme-notes-adrenaline-city-2006/.

10 Jake Wallace, "Strange Humors (2006) for concert band," Osti Music: The Website of Composer John Mackey, accessed June 10, 2018, http://www.ostimusic.com/HumorsWinds.php.

11 John Mackey, "Turning—revisited," Osti Music: The Website of Composer John Mackey, accessed August 25, 2010, http://ostimusic.com/blog/turning-revisited/.

12 Jake Wallace, "Turning (2007) for wind ensemble," Osti Music: The Website of Composer John Mackey, accessed June 10, 2018, http://www.ostimusic.com/Turning.php.

13 Cynthia Johnston Turner, email to the author, April 27, 2011.

14 "Premieres: Song and Dance [by] Norbert Palej," *CBDNA Report* (Spring 2006): 4.

15 "Program note," University of Michigan Symphony Band, concert of February 2, 2018.

16 "Wolf Rounds: Program Note by the Composer," Christopher Rouse, Composer, accessed June 10, 2018, http://www.christopherrouse.com/wolfpress.html.

17 *Visions*, Columbus State University Wind Ensemble, Robert Rumbelow, conductor, Summit DCD 486, 2007, Liner notes by Christopher Theofanidis.

18 Dana Wilson, "Composer's Program Note," New England Conservatory Wind Ensemble, concert of October 12, 2006.

19 Zechariah Goh Toh Chai, "Composer's Program Note," University of Georgia Wind Ensemble, concert of March 26, 2009.

20 Andrew Mead, "Composer's Program Note," University of Michigan Symphony Band, concert of October 23, 2006.

21 "Edwin Roxburgh, *Elegy for Ur*: Programme Notes," Tim Reynish, accessed June 10, 2018, http://www.timreynish.com/pdf/programme-notes.pdf.

22 Dana Wilson, "Composer's Program Note," West Point Military Academy Band, concert of March 18, 2006.

23 "News: European Premiere of Bandanna, 29th April 2006, by Clark Rundell," *CBDNA Report* (Summer 2006): 2.

24 Dwayne Corbin, "The Priest and His Servant Balda," *Irish Times* (July 25, 2007).

25 Douglas Lowry, "Composer's Program Note," Cincinnati College-Conservatory of Music Chamber Players, concert of March 30, 2007.

26 "*Raise the Roof* for timpani and symphonic band (2007): Program Note," Michael Daugherty, accessed June 20, 2018, http://www.michaeldaugherty.net/index.cfm?id=108&i=4&pagename=works.

27 "Stephen Michael Gryc: Passaggi," Hartt School Wind Ensemble, Glen Adsit, conductor, Naxos 8.52109 2009, Liner notes by Stephen Gryc.

28 "Lullaby for Noah: Program Notes," C. Alan Publications, accessed June 20, 2018, http://c-alanpublications.com/lullaby-for-noah/.

29 Nikk Pilato, email to the author, May 6, 2011.

CHAPTER 15

Awards and Avalanche of Works (2008, 2009, 2010)

Works by Pulitzer and Grawemeyer Prize winners • *Pieces by Young, Emerging, and Established Composers*

Distinguished American composer Charles Wuorinen stressed the importance of creating wind band/ensemble works of substance and adventure in his essay, "An Elevated Wind Music."

> ... there is not much in the history of wind ensemble music that one would rank alongside, say, the great orchestral works of past or present. Just for this reason, there is a rich opportunity—not to say necessity—for the enrichment of this part of the instrumental scene. The multifaceted timbral range, the agility of all registers, the evenness of acoustic response over the whole audible spectrum: all these characteristics of large wind ensembles fit them to carry a literature of "symphonic" character, expressive, dramatic and complexly structured ... we do not need more Potter-book-style compositions, for there will always be plenty of those. We do not need to be entertained in the wind medium; we need substance, elevated discourse, craft, subtlety. Let us have adventuring into more rarer realms, where dense, complex, and profound musical thoughts may be expressed. Especially in a university setting, but certainly by no means limited to it, such a program seems not only reasonable, but also consonant with the very core of our musical purposes. Only a lazy and cynical construction of these purposes would make one think otherwise.[1]

Included among the composers who did write substantial, imaginative, provocative, and challenging wind band/ensemble works during the first decade of the new century were John Corigliano, William Bolcom, Stanislaw Skrowaczewski, Aaron Jay Kernis, Magnus Lindberg, Bernard Rands, Christopher Rouse, and David Del Tredici. The works by Corigliano (*Mr. Tambourine Man*), Bolcom (*First Symphony for Band*), and Skrowaczewski (*Music for Winds*) were premiered in 2009; Kernis's work (*a Voice, a Messenger*) in 2010.

The wind version of John Corigliano's *Mr. Tambourine Man* was created by Verena Mösenbichler-Bryant who is presently Associate Professor of the Practice of Music, Director of the University Wind Symphony, and Director of Undergraduate Studies for the Music Department at Duke University. The work was premiered by the University of Texas Wind Ensemble, Jerry Junkin, conductor, with Hila Plitman as soprano soloist, at the CBDNA National Conference in Austin, Texas, on March 27, 2009. Corigliano's original version of *Mr. Tambourine Man* was composed for soprano and piano. In 2003, he made two new versions of the piece: one for soprano and chamber ensemble, the other for amplified soprano and orchestra. The latter version was premiered on October 23, 2003, by the Minnesota Orchestra, Robert Spano, conductor; Hila Plitmann, soprano soloist. Plitmann later recorded the piece with the Buffalo Philharmonic, conducted by JoAnn Falletta. This recording received two Grammy Awards in 2009 for "Best Contemporary Composition" and "Best Classical Vocal Performance."[2]

Corigliano offered the following information on how he went about selecting Dylan's poems for his work.

> When Sylvia McNair asked me to write her a major song cycle for Carnegie Hall, she had only one request; to choose an American text. I have set only four poets in my adult compositional life: Stephen Spender, Richard Wilbur, Dylan Thomas ... and William H. Hoffman.... Aside from asking Bill to create a new text, I had no ideas. Except that I had always heard, by reputation, of the high regard accorded the folk-ballad singer/songwriter Bob Dylan.... So I bought a collection of his texts, and found many of them to be every bit as beautiful and as immediate as I had heard—and surprisingly well-suited to my own musical language. I then contacted Jeff Rosen, his manager, who approached Bob Dylan with the idea of re-setting his poetry to my music.

I do not know of an instance in which this has been done before (which was part of what appealed to me), so I needed to explain that these would be in no way arrangements, or variations, or in any way derivations of the music of the original songs, which I decided to not hear before the cycle was complete. Just as Schumann or Brahms or Wolf had re-interpreted in their own musical style the same Goethe text, I intended to treat the Dylan lyrics as the poems I found them to be.... Dylan granted his permission, and I set to work.

I chose seven poems for what became a thirty-five minute cycle. A "Prelude: *Mr. Tambourine Man*," fantastic and exuberant in manner, precedes five searching and reflective monologues that form the core of the piece; and "Postlude: *Forever Young*" makes a kind of folk-song benediction after the cycle's close. Dramatically, the inner five songs trace a journey of emotional and civic maturation, from the innocence of "*Clothes Line*" through the beginning of awareness of a wider world ("*Blowin' in the Wind*"), through the political fury of "*Masters of War*," to a premonition of an apocalyptic future ("*All Along the Watchtower*"), culminating in a vision of a victory of ideas ("*Chimes of Freedom*"). Musically, each of the five songs introduces an accompaniment motive that becomes the principal motive in the next.[3]

William Bolcom's *First Symphony for Band* was commissioned by the Big Ten Band Directors Foundation in 2008 and premiered by University of Michigan Symphony Band, Michael Haithcock, conductor, on February 6, 2009. In the July 2010 issue of the *Records International catalog*, the *Symphony* is described as,

... an ambitious, thoroughly worked out musical argument, beginning with a terse and incisive sonata-form movement, followed by a sardonic scherzo, pastoral slow movement and a rondo-finale that suggests the cortège and dancing traditions of the New Orleans funeral. Tonal and endlessly inventive and ingenious, with the engaging incorporation of popular idioms without a trace of condescension that Bolcom has always done so well, this is as thoroughly "symphonic" a work as any in the more established full-orchestra tradition.[4]

Bolcom (b. 1938) originally planned to call his *First Symphony for Band* his Ninth Symphony—which it is. "On reflection, I realized that, since Beethoven and Mahler, ninth symphonies have been thought of as a composer's last will and testament ... and I'm not really ready for that final word yet."[5]

In liner notes prepared for the University of Michigan Symphony Band CD recording of his *Symphony*, Bolcom addressed the difference in orchestra and wind band "culture":

> ... band is different from orchestra in more than just the absence of strings and the greater number of winds. There is a "culture of the orchestra" that goes back several centuries, one that shapes new pieces for it in subtle ways even a composer may not be fully aware of. The band culture is younger and historically more oriented to outdoors events and occasions. Band players seem now to be mostly of college age; there are very few professional non-university bands today, nothing analogous to the Sousa and Goldman outfits of my youth. The resonance of a long history like that of the orchestra is largely lacking. Against this—and I think this is why more and more composers of art music are turning to the band—is the fact that band people work hard and long on a new piece. They will spend weeks in rehearsal perfecting and internalizing it. And there is something infectious about the youthful enthusiasm a good college band will put into a performance.[6]

Stanislaw Skrowaczewski (1923–2017) was both a major international conductor and highly esteemed composer. On February 4, 5, and 6, 2010, he conducted the Minnesota Orchestra in the American premiere of his new work for winds, *Music for Winds*. The composer had already conducted the world premiere of the work two months earlier (December 11, 2009) with the Deutsche Radio Philharmonie in Saarbrücken, Germany. *Music for Winds* was commissioned by an international consortium of nine orchestras and wind ensembles from four countries: Minnesota Orchestra, University of Minnesota Symphonic Wind Ensemble, Deutsche Radio Philharmonie Saarbrücken Kaiserslautern (Germany), Yomiuri Nippon Symphony Orchestra (Japan), Bruckner Orchester Linz (Austria), MIT Wind Ensemble, New England Conservatory Wind Ensemble, University of Southern California Thornton Wind Ensemble, and The Orchestra of Indian Hill (Littleton, MA).

Skrowaczewski wrote the following about his piece:

> For *Music for Winds* I was commissioned by a consortium of nine orchestras in four countries (the United States, Germany, Austria, and Japan). The initiator of this project is Dr. Frederick Harris, director of the wind orchestra at MIT in Boston. He knew that I had long since wanted to write a kind of symphony or concerto for winds, or more precisely for symphonic winds, the wind instruments that appear in the symphonies of the nineteenth to twenty-first centuries, from Beethoven to Shostakovich and beyond. The repertoire for [these] instruments is rather

scarce, compared to the great repertoire for strings. I added three saxophones, of which two are less common and less often played, soprano and baritone saxophone. They enrich the wind section by extending the possibilities of sound quality. And to that I brought in percussion, very gently along with piano, celesta, and harp.[7]

Music for Winds is a four-movement, twenty-minute long work scored for orchestra woodwinds, brass, percussion (including harp, piano, and celeste), and three saxophones (soprano, alto, and baritone). It is a powerful, demanding, and challenging work that features virtuosic writing for all instruments including solo episodes for the saxophones and introspective solos by flute, clarinet, bass clarinet, and French horn.[8]

A Voice, a Messenger by Pulitzer Prize and Grawemeyer Award winning composer Aaron Jay Kernis (b. 1960) is a 25-minute long concerto for trumpet and "orchestra without strings." It was co-commissioned by the New York Philharmonic and the Big Ten Band Association and premiered on December 28, 2010, by the New York Philharmonic with Philip Smith as trumpet soloist. The instrumentation for Kernis's "orchestra without strings" includes four flutes (two doubling piccolo), three oboes (one doubling English horn), five clarinets (one doubling E-flat clarinet, two doubling bass clarinet, and one doubling contrabass clarinet), three bassoons (one doubling contrabassoon), four horns, three trumpets, three trombones, euphonium, two tubas, three double basses, timpani, percussion, harp, and piano. He also included an enormous consort of percussion instruments.

The following description of Kernis's piece was included in the program booklet for the premiere performance of *a Voice, a Messenger*:

> Kernis' music is characterized by poetic imagery, a colorful instrumental palette, and an eagerness to develop a musical vocabulary specific to the project at hand. All three of these characteristics stand at the heart of *a Voice, a Messenger*. It is explicitly poetic to the extent that it draws from the Old Testament poetry of the Psalms. It is rich in variety and specificity of instrumental tone, even requiring the soloist to play not only on a standard concert trumpet but also on a piccolo trumpet and a flugelhorn (a trumpet cousin, but sometimes classified instead as a bugle or a saxhorn). And its language is specific to the piece, being inspired by the sounds of Jewish liturgical music and hewing to an overall emotional climate that the composer has described as "pensive, highly chromatic, and full of conflict."[9]

Kernis added this about composing the piece for Phillip Smith:

Phil, who is a religious man, requested only that I should draw my inspiration from Scriptural passages that refer to music in general and to the trumpet, shofar, cornet, and horn in particular ... adding quickly, that I shouldn't let that impede me![10]

Many more new works were composed between 2000 and 2010. Below is a collection of pieces that are representative of the various kinds/styles of works composed for wind band/ensemble during the first decade of the new millennium.

Brett Abigaña	*Sketches on Paintings no. 2*
Brett Abigaña	*Chorale and Blaspheme*
Steven Bryant	*Ecstatic Waters*
Steven Bryant	*Concerto for Wind Ensemble*
Chen Yi	*Dragon Rhyme*
Eric Ewazen	*The Eternal Dance of Life*
Eric Ewazen	*Concerto for Oboe and Wind Ensemble*
Stephen Feigenbaum	*Rooms by the Sea*
David Gillingham	*Summer of 2008 (Euphonium Concerto)*
Adam Gorb	*Farewell*
Jennifer Higdon	*Oboe Concerto (wind version)*
Jennifer Higdon	*Concerto for Solo Soprano Saxophone (wind version)*
Jennifer Higdon	*Percussion Concerto (wind version)*
Charles Ives/M. Patterson	*The Concord Symphony (1911–1915) (wind version, 2010)*
Tania León	*Cumba Cumbakin*
Scott Lindroth	*Passage*
David Ludwig	*Missa Brevis*
John Mackey	*Aurora Awakes*
David Maslanka	*Symphony No. 8*
Jonathan Newman	*Symphony No. 1 "My Hands Are a City"*
Carter Pann	*Serenade for Winds*
Joel Puckett	*It Perched for Vespers Nine*
David Rakowski	*Cantina*
Kathryn Salfelder	*Cathedrals*
Kathryn Salfelder	*Crossing Parallels*
Frank Ticheli	*Angels in the Architecture*
Matthew Tommasini	*Torn Canvases*
Melinda Wagner	*Scamp*

In 2009, Juilliard and Boston educated composer Brett Abigaña (b. 1980) was commissioned to write two pieces for the United States Naval Academy Band in Annapolis, Maryland. Upon delivery of the works, Abigaña was invited to conduct the premiere performances of both of them, which he did at the Band's annual "Meet the Composer" concert.

Abigaña's *Sketches on Paintings no. 2* was inspired by the paintings of Claude Monet, Edgar Degas, Jackson Pollock, and Joseph Turner. The composer provided the following information about the music he composed for the painting of each artist.

> The first movement, *Claude Monet–Water Lilies*, is an exploration of sonorities through the ensemble reminiscent of the famous triptych first viewed by the composer at the Musée Marmottan Monet in Paris. *Edgar Degas–L'Étoile* is a whimsical, dream-like waltz to which ghostly ballerinas in the painting may be dancing. *Jackson Pollock–Lavender Mist* is a quasi-minimalist piece written specifically to follow the erratic yet graceful movement of the painter as he created his works, as seen in numerous videos of his process. *Joseph Turner–Norham Castle: Sunrise* is a seemingly un-moving contrapuntal fantasy on a simple tapestry of chords meant to evoke the suspension of time and misty lack of clear definition in the painting.[11]

Ecstatic Waters by Steven Bryant (b. 1972) was commissioned by a consortium of fifteen university and high school wind bands/symphonies and ensembles. It was premiered on October 22, 2008, by the Bowling Green State University Wind Ensemble, Bruce Moss, conducting. It won the 2010 National Band Association William D. Revelli Composition Contest. It is Bryant's first large-scale work for wind ensemble and electronics. The composer provided a description of the piece in his program note.

> *Ecstatic Waters* is music of dialectical tension—a juxtaposition of contradictory or opposing musical and extra-musical elements and an attempt to resolve them. The five connected movements hint at a narrative that touches upon naiveté, divination, fanaticism, post-human possibilities, anarchy, order, and the Jungian collective unconscious. Or, as I have described it more colloquially: W.B. Yeats meets Ray Kurzweil in the Matrix." [Note: W. B. Yeats was an Irish poet and playwright; Ray Kurzweil, an American author, inventor and controversial futurist who argues that our future could resemble the movie, *The Matrix*.]

The overall title, as well as "Ceremony of Innocence" and "Spiritus Mundi" are taken from poetry of Yeats ("News for the Delphic Oracle," and "The Second Coming"), and his personal, idiosyncratic mythology and symbolism of spiraling chaos and looming apocalypse figured prominently in the genesis of the work. Yet in a nod to the piece's structural reality—as a hybrid of electronics and living players—*Ecstatic Waters* also references the confrontation of unruly humanity with the order of the machine, as well as the potential of a post-human synthesis, in ways inspired by Kurzweil.[12]

Bryant's *Concerto for Wind Ensemble* was composed in two stages separated by three years (2007–2010). In 2006, Donald Schofield, Commander of the U. S. Air Force Band of Mid-America, asked Bryant to write a piece that would showcase the Band's skills and viscerally demonstrate their commitment to excellence as representatives of the United States Air Force. Early discussions between Schofield and Bryant centered around the possibility of Bryant writing a concerto grosso type work but gradually evolved into one in which three groups of players would surround the audience. The USAF Band of Mid-America premiered Bryant's *Concerto for Wind Ensemble* in February 2007. While working on the piece, Bryant came to realize that what he really wanted to do was compose a work larger than what had been specified in the original commission. He therefore intentionally left the end of the work "open" in hopes that he might someday have an opportunity to expand the piece. Below is Bryant's explanation on how that opportunity came about.

> That chance came in 2009 shortly after [the University of Texas Wind Ensemble's] fantastic performance of *Ecstatic Waters* at the College Band Directors National Association conference in Austin. [Jerry Junkin and I] discussed my desire to write more movements [for the original *Concerto for Wind Ensemble*], and he graciously agreed to lead a consortium to commission the project.
>
> In expanding the work, I planned to reuse the same few musical elements across all five movements.... The original ascending five-note motive from movement I returns often ... The second movement exploits the antiphonal instruments for formal purposes, as the music gradually moves from the stage to the surrounding instruments....Movement III is bright, rhythmically incessant, and veers toward jazz in a manner that surprised me as it unfolded.... Movement IV's weighty character ... [recalls] various fragments from earlier in the

piece. The movement also pays homage to Webern's *Six Pieces for Orchestra* (elements of which appear in other movements), and Corigliano's score to the film *Altered States*. Both of these have been early, powerful, lasting influences on my compositional choices. Movement V returns to the opening motive of the entire work, this time with a simmering vitality that burns inexorably to a no-holds-barred climax.[13]

Bryant's *Concerto for Wind Ensemble* is a true one-on-a-part wind ensemble piece. It was premiered on October 27, 2010, by the University of Texas Wind Ensemble, Jerry Junkin, conducting.

The Hartt Wind Ensemble, conducted by Glen Adsit, performed at Carnegie Hall on May 30, 2010. Included in their program was the premiere performance of *Dragon Rhyme* by celebrated international composer Chen Yi (b. 1953). The piece was commissioned by the National Wind Ensemble Consortium Group. *Dragon Rhyme* is cast in two contrasting movements: "I. Mysteriously-Harmoniously" (lyrical) and "II. Energetically" (powerful). Basic elements associated with the musical traditions common to Peking Opera are used throughout the work. Chen Yi, in a program note about the piece, wrote,

> The instrumental texture is rich in colors, from transparent and delicate to angular and strong. Taking the image of the dragon, which is auspicious, fresh, and vivid, the music is layered and multidimensional. It symbolizes Eastern culture. When it meets the world, it becomes a part of the global family.[14]

Chen Yi is one of an increasing number of non-American born composers who are now composing music for the wind band/ensemble. Like Chen Yi, most of them incorporate idiomatic techniques and sounds unique to their native cultures into their music.

On November 4, 2008, Jack Delaney conducted the percussion ensemble Nexus and the Southern Methodist University/Meadows Wind Ensemble in the premiere performance of Eric Ewazen's *The Eternal Dance of Life*. Prior to composing the work, Ewazen (b. 1954) traveled to Nexus' home base in Toronto, Canada, to observe and learn about their special approach to percussion instrument performance. While in Toronto Ewazen also visited museums and became captivated and inspired by Inuit philosophies and art, especially the animated sculptures of dancing polar bears. This contact with Inuit culture influenced his writing of *The Eternal Dance of Life*. In a program note for the piece Ewazen wrote,

The first movement is dramatic, capturing the moment of the death of a human soul. An end can be awesome, sudden, shocking—the feeling of loss intense. The music is bold, dramatic—almost tragic.... The second movement is all about swirling gestures as the spirit takes flight ... a journey through space and time. The third movement ... [is] slow ... mysterious and enigmatic, as the spirit enters the various creatures of the earth. How will they react as one life force is transferred to another? The fourth movement is a joyful dance as the bears, otters and beavers not only dance, but sing and perform the many rituals of life.[15]

Two years later, on February 16, 2010, Eric Ewazen's *Concerto for Oboe and Wind Ensemble* was premiered by the Indiana University Wind Ensemble, Stephen W. Pratt, conductor, with Linda Strommen as oboe soloist. It was commissioned by Strommen and the ensemble and is dedicated to Strommen's mother, Ellen Strommen. Ewazen commented on the writing of the work:

[I wanted] to write a work that encapsulates her [Ellen Strommen] personality and life story. As in any life, there are the wonderful highs, and sometimes, very sad lows—but through it all, resilience and hope shine on—and that is certainly the way it is with Ms. Strommen.

The first movement is a loving, gentle waltz, describing the tender spirit that is Ms. Strommen.... The second movement is about those moments in life, such as the tragic loss of a loved one, which is filled with shock, surprise, and an almost agonized questioning. The music is fast, in a minor key—but at the very end—hope and resilience win— and the [movement] ends with a joyful Picardy third. The final movement is the summation of a life ... the oboe is the lyricist, the music singing a personal, sometimes introspective, sometimes joyous, song.[16]

Rooms by the Sea by Stephen Feigenbaum (b. 1989) is based on the painting of the same title by Edward Hopper. It was commissioned and premiered by the Yale University Concert Band, Thomas Duffy, conductor, on October 8, 2010, in Woolsey Hall. *Rooms by the Sea* is in four sections—the first three correspond to the composer's impressions of the painting's three segments. The composer writes,

The first section is inspired by the water texture that appears through the portal on the right of the painting. The second section is inspired by the shapes and textures of the front room in the painting, and the third section addresses the hidden room, a sliver of it appears at the left of the painting. The final section ... expresses a sense of longing for the seascape through the opening, which this viewer sees as the main focus of the painting.[17]

Farewell by Adam Gorb (b. 1958) was commissioned for the National Youth Wind Orchestra of Wales by the Welsh Amateur Federation at Ty Cerydd—Music Centre Wales. Conducted by Timothy Reynish, the Orchestra premiered the work on April 5, 2008. It received the British Composers Award for the best wind work of 2009. *Farewell* is a large-scale, twenty minute long symphonic "Adagio." In the piece Gorb divides the wind ensemble into two separate orchestras. The first, which consists of clarinets, saxophones, trumpets, trombones, tubas, and harsh sounding percussion, performs music that is predominantly desperate and anguished. The second comprised of flutes, oboes, bass clarinet, bassoons, horns, and gentle percussion, sounds music that is more calming and introspective. The composer offered the following comment about the work:

> The title refers to Haydn's *Farewell Symphony*, but instead of all the players walking off leaving two instrumentalists to finish, here a solo oboe and clarinet step forward and quietly lament while the rest of the band intone an eternal *modus in diabilis*.[18]

In 2008–2009 Jennifer Higdon (b. 1962) created wind versions of two concertos she had originally written for orchestra—one for oboe, the other for percussion. Perhaps even more noteworthy is that she made two separate adaptations of the concerto for the oboe, one for oboe and winds and the second for soprano saxophone and winds. The wind version of the *Concerto for Oboe* was premiered on March 6, 2009, by the University of Michigan Symphony Band, Michael Haithcock, conductor, and Nancy Ambrose King, oboe soloist. Higdon showcases the lyrical potential of the oboe in her piece.

> I have always thought the sound of the oboe to be one of the most elegant sounds in the palette of the wind family. When the opportunity came to write a concerto for this wonderful instrument, I jumped at it. As the oboe's tone has always enchanted me, I decided that I wanted to veer from the normal style of concerto writing, where virtuosity is the primary element on display, and feature the rich tone of this double-reed instrument.[19]

The Hartt School Wind Ensemble, Glen Adsit conductor and Carrie Koffman, soprano saxophone soloist, premiered Higdon's

Concerto for Solo Soprano Saxophone and Wind Ensemble on April 24, 2009. The composer penned the following words on the power and beauty of saxophones:

> I have always been struck by the range of power and beauty that comes from saxophones.... Many people don't realize just how much power exists in this group of instruments, and often they may not realize the potential for beauty. The soprano sax in particular produces a tone of warmth and a real agility that allows it to sing like none of the other instruments in this group.[20]

The U. S. Marine Band commissioned the wind version of Higdon's *Percussion Concerto* in 2008. It was premiered by the Band, with MSgt Christopher Rose as percussion soloist, on May 10, 2009. The *Concerto* follows the traditional relationship between soloist and ensemble. However, Higdon expands and embellishes this normal dialogue by adding passages in which the soloist interacts with the other members of the percussion section. The original version of the piece was composed for the Philadelphia Orchestra, Indianapolis Symphony Orchestra, and Dallas Symphony Orchestra in 2005. After it was premiered by the Philadelphia Orchestra with Colin Currie as percussion soloist, a review in *The Philadelphia Inquirer* described the *Concerto* as

> ... a machine whose gears and pistons are its most entrancing qualities. But ... Higdon isn't the sort to write a piece that's nothing but pounding. The slow movement had wave after wave of ecstatic, intense color, with sound shapes created by bowing cymbals. Broad, Coplandesque melodies commanded the ear, though everything around them went in unexpected directions.[21]

Merlin Patterson's wind band version of Charles Ives's (1874–1954) monumental *Piano Sonata No, 2, Concord, Mass., 1840–1860*, which he titled *The Concord Symphony (1911–1914)*, was premiered on November 22, 2010, by the University of Texas Wind Ensemble, Jerry Junkin, conductor. Patterson (b. 1955), who has written many other highly praised band transcriptions, spent two and a half years creating this version of the Ives masterpiece. (It took Ives more than 36 years to write the original piano version!) (Note: Henry Brant also created an orchestra version of Ives's *Concord Sonata* and titled it *A Concord Symphony*.)

Cumba Cumbakin by Tania León (b. 1943) was commissioned by the Harvard Band Foundation for the 90th anniversary of the Harvard Band. It was premiered on March 6, 2010, by the Harvard Wind Ensemble, Mark Olsen, conductor. León is a Cuban-born composer, conductor, and educator, and a founding member and first Music Director of the Dance Theatre of Harlem. In 1978, she established the Brooklyn Philharmonic's Community Concert Series and also served as the New Music Advisor for Kurt Masur and the New York Philharmonic from 1993 to 1997. In 2005, she collaborated with Nobel Prize winner Wole Soyinka to create their award-winning opera, *Scourge of Hyacinths*.

Cumba Cumbakin, the work she wrote for the Harvard Band, is a one-movement work in three sections. Each section presents in rhythm, song, and dance, the gesture of the Cuban *son* (a musical blending of ethnic musics that have influenced Cuban history). The composer provided the following information about the piece:

> *Cumba Cumbakin* is a transliteration of the sound of a certain rhythm played by congeros (conga drummers). Inspired by well-known musical gestures and melodies of the music of Cuba of the 1940's (i.e., son, guaracha, danzon, guajira, guaguanco), I grew up dancing to this rhythm.... Another inspiration for this and several other works has been the poetry of Nicolas Guillen, particularly his collection of poems, *Motivos del Son*. The well known writer Helio Orovio explains "The Son cubano is a style of music that originated in Cuba and gained worldwide popularity in the 1930s. Son combines the structure and elements of Spanish canción and the Spanish guitar with African rhythms and percussion instruments of Bantu and Arará origin. In New York City, it mixed with other musical styles to influence the creation of salsa music. The Cuban son is one of the most influential and widespread forms of Latin American music: its derivatives and fusions have spread across the world."[22]

Passage by Scott Lindroth (b. 1958) was commissioned by the American Bandmasters Association and premiered on December 15, 2010, by the United States Marine Band, Captain Michelle A. Rakers conducting. The composer wrote this about the piece:

> The piece has retrospective character for me. There's a wistful if not melancholy quality to the outer sections of the work. A prominent four-note theme ... comes from a piece I wrote 20 years ago called *Duo for Violins* ... the theme is set with rich harmonies that shift with each

repetition of the four-note figure, and the rhythmic character is supple and nuanced. To me, it's like encountering an old friend who has changed with age, hopefully for the better.

The middle section of the piece does not quote earlier pieces, but the speech-rhythm like melodies in the horns and saxes set against a persistently pulsing accompaniment is something I like to do in my music.

A last bit of retrospection arises from composing for wind symphony in the first place. My most formative and inspiring musical ties as a teenager were playing in public school bands and jazz ensembles, instruction, and priceless opportunities to discover myself as a composer and musician. And so it is with gratitude that I dedicate this piece to Robert C. Shirek, Calvin D. Moely and Raymond C. Wifler, three American Bandmasters who revealed to me what it could mean to live a life in music.[23]

Passages won the 2011 NBA William D. Revelli Composition Contest.

The *Missa Brevis (2009)* by David Ludwig (b. 1974) was commissioned by conductor Michael Haithcock and the University of Michigan Symphony Band. Haithcock requested that Ludwig write a work that

> ... replicated the Dvořák *Serenade* instrumentation at its core with the flexibility to add two flutes or a fourth horn if desired. He stuck with the Dvořák. The piece is five brief movements of the mass and quotes Mauchat (the first *Mass*) and is influenced by the Stravinsky *Mass*.[24]

Ludwig added the following about his piece:

> The "Kyrie" introduces the work with a loud declamatory chord that soon dissolves into floating snapshots of music by Guillaume Machaut, a composer from 14th-century France.... The "Gloria" opens with an extended brass fanfare that is followed by a dialogue between the oboe and English horn. The third movement is the "Credo," which is the large middle part of the traditional mass. As it has by far the most text, many composers have opted to set music that rapidly cycles through the words with a rhythmic chanting quality, and this "Credo" does exactly that. The "Sanctus" and "Agnus Dei" are coupled together, and the "Sanctus" begins with the bright chords of the opening, to be answered by a hushed response in the last movement.[25]

John Mackey (b. 1953) won both the 2009 NBA William D. Revelli Composition Contest and the 2009 ABA Ostwald Composition Contest for *Aurora Awakes* (Mackey's second ABA Ostwald Award). The piece was commissioned and premiered by the Stuart High School Wind Ensemble, Douglas Martin, conductor, on May 8, 2009. *Aurora Awakes* is in two sections. It starts in "a place of remarkable stillness" and moves to an "unbridled explosion of energy." Known for his use of stylistic imitation, Mackey uses two outright quotations in this work. The first appears at the start of the second section of the piece, an ostinato based on the guitar introduction found in U2's *Where The Streets Have No Name*. He expanded this small motive to become a significant factor in his piece.

The second quote comes from Gustav Holst's *First Suite in E-flat for Military Band*—specifically, the final chord of the first movement. Jake Wallace, in his program note for *Aurora Awakes*, stated,

> The brilliant E-flat chord that closes the "Chaconne" of that work is orchestrated (nearly) identically as the final sonority of *Aurora Awakes*— producing an unmistakably vibrant timbre that won't be missed by aficionados of the repertoire." [Mackey added,] "In a piece that's about the awaking of the goddess of dawn, you need a damn bright ending—and there was no topping Holst.[26]

David Maslanka's *Symphony No. 8* was commissioned by a consortium of thirty-six college and university wind bands/ensembles. It was premiered by the Illinois State University Wind Orchestra conducted by Stephen K. Steele on November 20, 2008. Even though the *Symphony* is in three distinct movements, the composer has stated that "the musical layout suggests a single large-scale panoramic vista." Maslanka added the following comment about the piece.

> I began the composition process for this symphony with meditation, and was shown scenes of widespread devastation. But this music is not about the surface of our world problems. It is a response to a much deeper vital creative flow which is forcefully at work, and which will carry us through our age of crisis. This music is a celebration of life. It is about new life, continuity from the past to the future, great hope, great faith, joy, ecstatic vision, and fierce determination.[27]

Jonathan Newman (b. 1972) completed *My Hands Are a City* in 2008. It is a fourteen-minute long work that was inspired by the Beat poetry movement of the 1950s and is derived from an overture, *The Rivers of Bowery*, which Newman composed in 2005. In 2009, when Jeffrey D. Gershman, Associate Director of Bands at Indiana University, commissioned Newman to compose a symphony for band, the composer decided he would do so by adding a first and second move-ment (I. *Across the groaning continent*, II. *The Americans*) to his already composed *My Hands Are A City*. His *Symphony No. 1, My Hands Are a City*, was premiered by the Indiana University Symphonic Band, con-ducted by Jeffrey D. Gershman, on April 23, 2009. Newman offered the following comment about the piece.

> In my neighborhood on the Lower East Side of Manhattan, the musi-cians and poets and characters of our mid-Century "Beats" are still very active ghosts [Allen Ginsberg, Charlie Parker, etc.] ... Surrounded by these spirits, I structured the work in three movements, each taking on a different aspect of the sensory experiences I collected from my months of immersion in the novels, poetry, and photographs of these artists.[28]

Serenade for Winds by Carter Pann (b. 1972) was commissioned by a consortium of university wind groups organized by Richard Floyd. The ten-minute long work was premiered by the University of Colo-rado Wind Symphony, Allan McMurray conducting, in spring 2009. Even though the piece can be played by a full wind ensemble, the composer prefers that it be performed with one player on each part. Pann provided the following note about his piece:

> My *Serenade For Winds* (2008) is ... an exploration into the kind of melodic writing usually equated with Schumann or Brahms. Nearly every gesture in the piece was placed with the hope that the performers who play them would attain their highest echelon of musical expres-sion.... this work is a grand expression *(tempo moderato)* of piquant harmonies and soaring melodies for wind symphony.[29]

Joel Puckett's *It Perched for Vespers Nine* is a joint American Band-masters Association/University of Florida commissioned work, It was premiered by the Michigan State Wind Symphony, Matt Smith conducting, on March 13, 2008. Timothy Reynish describes the piece as "... a slow movement of about ten minutes, tone clusters build-ing quietly interrupted by outbursts in the percussion and some-times brass with a strong climax which dies away to a coda of great beauty."[30] Puckett (b. 1977) wrote this about the piece:

> My wife's grandfather was an extraordinary man ... an immigrant who walked around quoting poetry and whistling tunes from his childhood in Scotland.... In the spring of 2007, he fell into a coma following a severe stroke. After weeks of being in this state he awoke and said:

In mist or cloud . . .
. . . On mast or shroud
It perched for Vespers nine.
While all the night . . .
. . . Through fog-smoke white,
Glimmered the white moon-shine.

These were the final words of a man who always chose the right words. Within the hour he was gone. . . . the emotional core of the work is my trying to work out what my wife's Pop Pop might have been trying to tell us about what awaits us "In mist or cloud."[31]

David Rakowski (b. 1958) was awarded the 2006 Barlow Prize for *Ten of a Kind*, which was written for the U. S. Marine Band. In addition to the monetary award, the prize also included a commission to write a new wind band/ensemble piece which would be performed by the University of Michigan Symphony Band, U. S. Marine Band, Brigham Young University Wind Symphony, University of California at Los Angeles Wind Ensemble, and Southern Methodist University Meadows Wind Ensemble.

The practice of matching Barlow Prize winners with performing ensembles began in 1983 when the Foundation's Board of Directors decided to do more than just stimulate the creation of new works—they wanted to ensure that these works would be played by great artists and ensembles in prominent concert venues throughout the country. Rakowski's commissioned work, *Cantina*, was the first Barlow Prize commission to receive five premiere performances by five different ensembles. The first performance of his piece was by the U. S. Marine Band, Colonel Michael J. Colburn conducting. It took place on March 2, 2008, at the Eastern Division CBDNA Conference at Northern Virginia Community College, Alexandria, Virginia.

Rakowski conceived *Cantina* as a concerto for band (like Bartók and Lutosławski's *Concertos for Orchestra*). "March," the opening movement of the work, is the composer's only march. The slow second movement, "Waves," is for woodwinds and features solos that move across the sections, often under undulating accompaniment patterns in "waves." The third movement, "Fanfares," begins with all four horns playing a concert D. They crescendo to other notes which are picked up by the brass and turned into chords and then fanfares.

Following the climax of the fanfares, the woodwinds take over with warbly music that keeps speeding up. After a series of climaxes the horns reenter followed by the other brass instruments for one final fanfare. The work's final movement, "Toucan," is a freewheeling scherzo.

Kathryn Salfelder (b. 1987) was a student at the New England Conservatory of Music in Boston when she composed *Cathedrals* in 2006. The work was premiered on September 18, 2008, by the Arizona State University Wind Symphony, Gary W. Hill, conductor. Salfelder's piece was awarded three prizes: the ASCAP/CBDNA Frederick Fennell Prize and Walter Beeler Memorial Composition Prize in 2008, and the Colonel Arnold D. Gabriel Prize for a New Symphonic Band Composition in 2009. Salfelder wrote the following about the piece:

> *Cathedrals* is a fantasy on Gabrieli's *Canzon Primi Toni* from *Sacrae Symphoniae*, which dates from 1597. Written for St. Mark's Cathedral in Venice, the canzon [is] scored for two brass choirs [which] were stationed in opposite balconies of the church according to the antiphonal principal of *cori spezzati* (It. 'broken choirs'), which forms the basis of much of Gabrieli's writing.
>
> *Cathedrals* is an adventure in 'neo-renaissance' music, in its seating arrangement, antiphonal qualities, 16th century counterpoint, and canonic textures. Its form is structured on the golden ratio (1: .618), which is commonly found not only in nature and art, but also in the motets and masses of Renaissance composers such as Palestrina and Lassus.... The work is a synthesis of the old and the new, evoking the mystery and allure of Gabrieli's spatial music, intertwined with the rich color palette, modal harmonies, and textures of woodwinds and percussion.[32]

Salfelder composed another wind ensemble piece in 2009, *Crossing Parallels*. It is one of the joint commissions of the American Bandmasters Association and University of Florida. The piece was premiered by the Furman University Wind Ensemble, Les Hicken, conductor, on March 4, 2010, at the ABA Convention in Charleston, South Carolina.

Frank Ticheli's *Angels in the Architecture* is a dramatic work that examines the two extremes of human existence—one divine, the other evil. It was commissioned by Kingsway International, and was premiered on July 6, 2008, at the Sydney Opera House by a massed band of young musicians from Australia and the United States, conducted by Matthew George. The halo-shaped acoustical ornaments hanging above the performance stage of the Sydney Opera House inspired the title of the work which also has a connection to a quote by the 20th century Catholic mystic and writer, Thomas Merton: "The peculiar grace of a Shaker chair is due to the fact that it was built by someone capable of believing that an angel might come and sit on it."

Angels in the Architecture begins with a lone voice singing a 19th-century Shaker song—"I am an angel of Light ...." Ticheli uses themes from different religious traditions—a Hebrew song of peace ("Hevenu Shalom Aleichem") and the well-known 16th-century Genevan Psalter, "Old Hundredth," to surround the singer ("angel") and establish "a protective wall of light and the divine." Ticheli (b.1958) wrote,

> Just as Charles Ives did more than a century ago, *Angels in the Architecture* poses the unanswered question of existence. It ends as it began: the angel reappears singing the same comforting words. But deep below, a final shadow reappears—distantly, ominously.[33]

Torn Canvases by Matthew Tommasini (b. 1978) was commissioned by the Big East Band Directors Association and premiered on September 27, 2009, by the University of Louisville Wind Ensemble, Frederick Speck conductor. The ten-minute long work is scored for chamber winds without double reeds (flute, clarinet, bass clarinet, soprano saxophone, alto saxophone, horn, trumpet, trombone, tubas, vibraphone, chimes, piano), a stipulation which was included in the commission. The composer's inspiration for the piece came from the abstract expressionist painting style of Jackson Pollock. Tommasini wrote,

> The piece imagines a video camera panning across a large canvas made up of layers of fragmented paint drippings and splotches. The ensemble is divided into three groups on stage, each representing musical "layers" of chiming chords and fragmented jazz riffs, which are piled on one another, creating rhythmically charged collages of sound. The climax of the work comes when the entire ensemble plays together, evoking the sound of a giant bell, transforming into the sound of a driving jazz ensemble.[34]

Michael J. Colburn commissioned Melinda Wagner (b. 1957) to compose a work for the U.S. Marine Band. Her new piece, *Scamp*, was premiered by Colburn and the Band on April 11, 2008, at the MENC National Conference in Milwaukee, Wisconsin.

According to the composer, the title *Scamp* is a nod to its mischievous character. After the roguish wink of its opening bars, a bright and rollicking scherzo of sorts takes hold. Throughout the piece, the music makes several attempts at a serious turn, morphing into more lyrical passages. A quasi hymn-tune emerges multiple times, trying in vain to calm the skittering arguments between the choirs of winds, but the efforts are repeatedly foiled. The interruptions continue until the "Scamp" at the heart of the piece finally wins the battle once and for all and dashes for the end with one final, incorrigible poke at the ribs.[35]

ENDNOTES

1   Charles Wuorinen, "An Elevated Wind Music," *Journal of the World Association of Symphonic Bands and Ensembles* 7 (2000): 18.

2   John Corigliano, *Mr. Tambourine Man: Seven Poems of Bob Dylan / Three Hallucinations (from* Altered States*)*, Buffalo Philharmonic Orchestra, JoAnn Falletta, conductor; Hila Plitmann, soprano, Naxos 8.559331, 2008.

3   John Corigliano, "Composer's Program Note," University of Texas Wind Ensemble, concert of March 27, 2009.

4   *Classic Structures*, University of Michigan Symphony Band, Michael Haithcock, conductor, Equilibrium EQ 97, 2010, Review by Records International (July 2010), https://www.recordsinternational.com/cd.php?cd=07M095.

5   *Classic Structures*, University of Michigan Symphony Band, Michael Haithcock, conductor, Equilibrium EQ 97, 2010, Liner notes by William Bolcom.

6   Ibid.

7   Stanislaw Skrowaczewski, "Music for Winds by Stanislaw Skrowaczewski," Tim Reynish, accessed June 20, 2018, http://www.timreynish.com/news/article.php?&id=poland&month=December&year=2012.

8   Frederick Edward Harris Jr., *Seeking the Infinite: The Musical Life of Stanislaw Skrowaczewski*, (BookSurge Publishing, 2011).

9   New York Philharmonic, 2010 Dec 28, 29, 30 / Subscription Season / Gilbert (New York: New York Philharmonic Archives, 2010); cited in Pagean Marie DiSalvio, "'A Voice, A Messenger' by Aaron Jay Kernis: A Performer's Guide and Historical Analysis." (D.M.A. diss., Louisiana State University, 2016), 36n.

10 Jason Scott Ladd, "An Annotated Bibliography of Contemporary Works Programmable by Wind Band and Orchestra." (Ph.D. diss., Florida State University, 2009), 276.

11 Tim Reynish, "The Wind Music of Brett Abigaña," Tim Reynish, accessed June 20, 2018, http://www.timreynish.com/repertoire/composers/abigana.php.

12 "Ecstatic Waters (wind ensemble + electronics)," Steven Bryant: Composer/Conductor, accessed June 20, 2018, https://www.stevenbryant.com/music/catalog/ecstatic-waters-wind-ensemble-electronics.

13 "Concerto for Wind Ensemble," Steven Bryant: Composer/Conductor, accessed June 10, 2018, https://www.stevenbryant.com/music/catalog/concerto-for-wind-ensemble.

14 Chen Yi, *Dragon Rhyme for Symphonic Band.* Program Note by the Composer (Theodore Presser, 2010) [1].

15 Eric Ewazen, "Composer's Program Note," Southern Methodist University Meadows Wind Ensemble, concert of November 4, 2008.

16 Eric Ewazen, "Composer's Program Note," Indiana University Wind Ensemble, concert of February 27, 2010.

17 Stephen Feigenbaum, composer, accessed April 2012, http://www.stephenfeigenbaum.com/IndividualWorksPages/Rooms%20by%20the%SeaRooms.htm.

18 "Programme Notes—Farewell," Adam Gorb, Composer, accessed June 10, 2018, http://www.adamgorb.co.uk/programme-notes/programme-notes-farewell/.

19 Jennifer Higdon, "Program Notes: 'Oboe Concerto for Solo Oboe and Wind Ensemble,'" Jennifer Higdon, accessed June 20, 2018, http://www.jenniferhigdon.com/pdf/program-notes/Oboe-Concerto-wind.pdf.

20 Jennifer Higdon, "Program Notes: 'Soprano Sax Concerto for Solo Soprano Sax and Wind Ensemble,'" Jennifer Higdon, accessed June 20, 2018, http://www.jenniferhigdon.com/pdf/program-notes/Soprano-Sax-wind.pdf.

21 David Patrick Stearns, "Percussion the star in Higdon premiere," *The Philadelphia Inquirer* (November 28, 2005): E05; Quoted at "Reviews of Orchestral Works," Jennifer Higdon, accessed June 20, 2018, http://jenniferhigdon.com/orchestralreviews.html#percussionconcerto.

22 Scott, Lozier, "Music is a Language: Tania León," Harvard University: Office for the Arts at Harvard, Harvard Arts Blog, March 4, 2010, https://ofa.fas.harvard.edu/blog/music-language-tania-león.

23 Scott Lindroth, "Composer's Program Note," United States Marine Band, concert of December 15, 2010, The Midwest Clinic International Band and Orchestra Conference.

24 David Ludwig, email to the author, February 10, 2010.

25 *Classic Structures*, University of Michigan Symphony Band, Michael Haithcock, conductor, Equilibrium EQ 97, 2010, Liner notes by David Ludwig.

26 Jake Wallace, "Aurora Awakes (2009) for wind ensemble," Osti Music: The Website of Composer John Mackey, accessed June 10, 2018, http://www.ostimusic.com/Aurora.php.

27 "Symphony No. 8: Program Note," David Maslanka, accessed June 20, 2018, http://davidmaslanka.com/works/symphony-no-8/.

28 Jonathan Newman, "Symphony I: Program Notes," Wind Repertory Project, accessed June 20, 2018, http://windrep.org/Symphony_I_(Newman).

29 Carter Pann: American Composer, accessed April 2012, www.carterpann.com/works_serenade.htm.

30 Timothy Reynish, "CBDNA 2009 Conference: University of North Carolina at Greensboro Wind Ensemble," Tim Reynish, accessed June 1, 2018, http://www.timreynish.com/conferences/cbdna-2009.php.

31 Joel Puckett, "It perched for Vespers nine: Program Note," Joel Puckett, Composer, accessed June 20, 2018, http://joelpuckett.com/music/vespersnine/.

32 Kathryn Salfelder, *Cathedrals* (Boosey & Hawkes, 2008), Full Score, Program Note.
33 Frank Ticheli, *Angels in the Architecture* (Manhattan Beach Music, 2009), Full Score, Program Note.
34 Matthew Tommasini, *Torn Canvases* (Matalex Press, 2009), Program Note.
35 Jason K. Fettig, "Program Note," United States Marine Band, concert of April 11, 2008.

CHAPTER 16

Conferences, Conventions, and Initiatives (2008, 2009, 2010)

ABA, CBDNA and WASBE Conferences • Facsimile Edition of Mozart Gran Partita • Composers Datebook • Second Replication of Ostling's "Evaluation of Compositions"

Unlike other national and international wind band associations that hold conferences every other year, the American Bandmasters Association holds one every year. Its 74th Convention, "The Sounds of Sand and Sea," took place in Miami, Florida, from March 5–8, 2008. All concerts were held in Maurice Gusman Concert Hall at the University of Miami. The Ostwald Composition Competition winning work, Michael Daugherty's *Raise the Roof* for timpani and wind band, was performed by the United States Army Field Band, Jerry F. Junkin, conductor, with Staff Sergeant Robert Marino as timpani soloist. The ABA/University of Florida Commissioning Committee announced that they would award a commission to Ricardo Lorenz, Venezuelan-born composer and Associate Professor of Composition at Michigan State University.

The ABA's 75th Convention was held at College Station, Texas (Texas A & M University) from March 4–7, 2009. The Edwin Franko Goldman Memorial Citation was awarded to Robert Austin Boudreau for his founding of the American Wind Symphony Orchestra and unprecedented series of 400 commissioned wind orchestra works by important composers from around the world.

The ABA's final Convention of the new millennium's first decade was held in Charlestown, South Carolina, on March 3–6, 2010. The first ABA/University of Florida commissioned works, *Crossing Parallels* by Kathryn Salfelder (b. 1987), was premiered by the Furman Wind Ensemble, Ray E. Cramer, conductor. James Barnes conducted the premiere performance of *Tribute*, a piece commissioned by former students and friends of James K. Copenhaver for his retirement after thirty-four years as Director of Bands at the University of South Carolina.

* * * * * * * * * * *

CBDNA held its 2009 National Conference at the University of Texas, Austin from March 25–28. Of the fifty-six works performed at the Conference, forty-one (almost 75%) were composed during the first decade of the twenty-first century including the following eleven which were being given their premiere performance at the Conference:

> *Mr. Tambourine Man: Seven Poems of Bob Dylan* (2003) by John Corigliano
> (wind version by Verena Mösenbichler-Bryant, 2009) (Note: this
> work was commented upon in Chapter 15.)
> *Apollo's Fire* (2008) by Glen Cortese
> *Symphony for Winds and Percussion* (2008) by Donald Grantham
> *Eviler Elves* (2008) by James Kazik
> *The Future of Fire* (2009) (wind version) by Zhou Long
> *Asphalt Cocktail* (2008) by John Mackey
> *La Pequeña Habana* (2008) by Todd Malicoate
> *Popcopy* (2009) by Scott McAllister
> *Toward Ascending* (2009) by Wayne Oquin
> *Southern Comforts* (2008) (wind version) by Joel Puckett
> *UMKC Fanfare* (2009) (wind version) by Chen Yi

Glen Cortese (b. 1960) is both a composer and conductor. His compositions have been performed by major orchestras, ensembles, and soloists including the New Jersey Symphony Orchestra, the

Mexico City Philharmonic, the American String Quartet, soprano Dawn Upshaw, and instrumentalists Ransom Wilson and Carol Wincenc. When he was asked by Donald Lefevre, conductor of the West Texas A & M University Band, to write a work for solo flute and band in 2009, he decided to make a wind version of one of his earlier pieces, *Apollo's Fire*, which was for flute and harp. The piece is a miniature portrait/tone poem based loosely on the legend of the musical contest between Marsyas and Apollo. Using material from his earlier work he did away with the harp (Apollo) and cast Marsyas as the principal character in the piece.

Donald Grantham's three movement, twenty-minute long *Symphony for Winds and Percussion* was premiered by the West Texas A & M University Symphonic Band, Donald J. Lefevre, conductor, on March 26, 2009. (Note: Grantham had three of his pieces performed at the 2009 CBDNA National Conference!) "The work is in three movements with a gradual shift in style from movement to movement. A minimalist style defines the first movement and is "more symphonic and contemporary in structure," according to Grantham. "The overall style and character of the first movement becomes the basis for the jazz-inflected material of the second movement. The third movement progresses to a full out jazz swing style and dance groove completing the shift in style. The thematic evolution takes the listener for a relaxed voyage, crossing effortlessly between two contrasting musical styles ... as the piece progresses."[1]

James Kazik (b. 1974) is a staff arranger for the U. S. Army Band in Washington, D. C. His *Eviler Elves* was originally commissioned by the Oklahoma State University Trombone Choir, Paul Compton, director, for performance at the Emory Remington Trombone Choir Competition at the International Trombone Festival in Salt Lake City, Utah in 2008. Attracted to the piece, Joseph Missal, Director of Bands at Oklahoma State, commissioned Kazik to compose an expanded version of the piece for wind ensemble. In his program note, the composer wrote the following:

> Evil elves served as programmatic inspiration for the piece. The thought of the trombone representing an evil elf opened up wondrous possibilities for experimental tone colors that could not possibly be used in other homogenous ensembles. Considering the fun I had playing with colors in the trombone ensemble, it was a pleasure to expand it

and utilize tone colors present in the modern wind band. The low brass, and the trombones in particular remain the focus of the primary color anchors in this piece.[2]

Zhou Long (b. 1953) is a Chinese-born American composer. In 2003, the American Academy of Arts and Letters presented Zhou with an award recognizing his lifetime achievements. In part, the citation read: "Zhou Long has found a plausible, rigorous, and legitimate way of consolidating compositional methods and techniques that allow him to express brilliantly both his experiences as a composer of Western music and his considerable knowledge of his native China." In 2011, his opera, *Madame White Snake,* won the Pulitzer Prize in Music.

During China's Cultural Revolution, Zhou was deployed to a rural state farm in northeast China. Every spring he watched farmers set fire to the dead grass across the plains in order to make the land ready for planting. He recalls that sometimes these fires . . .

> . . . would go out of control, and the dry wind would whip them into a ferocious blaze. . . . These roaring winds and fierce fires made a profound impression on me that I remember to this day . . . when I returned to Beijing [after the Cultural Revolution], I came across this poem, written in the new spirit of free expression, that captured my feelings.

> A little spark, Starts a new world.
> What a raging fire, The wilderness becomes a sea of flames!
> . . . The fire is marching forward, Fertilizing the land!
> Quickly sharpening our ploughs, To open up a new era on the land![3] [excerpt]

The above experience inspired Zhou Long to compose the original version of *Future of Fire* for orchestra and children's chorus. In 2008–09 he created a wind version of the piece for the University of Missouri-Kansas City Conservatory of Music Wind Symphony, Steven Davis, conductor.

John Mackey's *Asphalt Cocktail* was commissioned by Howard J. Gourwitz as a gift to Kevin L. Sedatole and the Michigan State University Wind Symphony. Mackey, however, dedicated the piece to his close friend and fellow composer, Jonathan Newman who, during a discussion about the "titling" of the piece, suggested "Asphalt Cocktail." Mackey describes the piece as follows:

[It is] ... a five-minute opener, designed to shout, from the opening measure, "We're here." With biting trombones, blaring trumpets, and percussion dominated by cross-rhythms and back beats, it aims to capture the
grit and aggression that I associate with the time I lived in New York.[4]

Todd Malicoate (b. 1966) lives in Stillwater, Oklahoma, and is a
performer and freelance composer/arranger. He wrote *La Pequeña
Habana* for the Oklahoma State University Wind Ensemble, Joseph
Missal, conductor, to bring attention to the rich cultural heritage
of Miami, Florida's *"La Pequeña Habana"* (Little Havana). Malicoate
explains,

The inspiration for *La Pequeña Habana* ... was a two-day trip to that sub-
division of Miami, Florida in the summer of 1988. Twenty years later, I
find the imagery of this place is still vivid in my mind. This composition
is intended to evoke the memories of experiences in that place from
waking up at sunrise to late night in a Latin dance club. The compositional techniques used in this work range from minimalism to big band
jazz.... *La Pequeña Habana* consists of four major sections performed
without a pause ... "Entrada del Sol" (Entrance of the Sun), "Calle Ocho"
(Eighth Street), "Transción—una caminata en la calle" (A Walk in the
Street) and "Hoy Como Ayer" (Latin nightclub in Little Havana).[5]

As a composer, Scott McAllister (b. 1969) draws on culturally relevant references for inspiration. In *Popcopy* (2009), he quotes from
comedy shows, movies, and television. However, the quotes are not
simply drawn from the media but are ones that have found their way
into everyday language and have gained a life of their own outside
of their original contexts. *Popcopy* is in three movements. The first,
"More Cowbell," is based on a popular *Saturday Night Live* skit featuring Will Ferrell as a fictional cowbell player in the Blue Öyster
Cult band. The second, "One Time at Band Camp," is a catchphrase
from the movie *American Pie* in which an eccentric nerd tells annoy-
ing stories about her band camp experiences. The last movement,
"Serenity Now," is inspired by an episode from *Seinfeld* in which
Frank Costanza, is advised to say "serenity now" aloud every time
his blood pressure is in danger. McAllister scatters multiple "band
quotes" throughout the piece (veiled tributes to Holst, Hindemith,
and Sousa).

Toward Ascending by Wayne Oquin (b. 1977) is an eight-minute
work for solo clarinet and wind ensemble. It was commissioned by

the University of Georgia Wind Ensemble and is dedicated to John Stansberry, the composer's band director at Texas State University. *Toward Ascending* is divided into two equal parts, four minutes of slow music, four minutes of fast music. It's the composer's attempt to musically depict one aspect of urban city life: the construction of a modern skyscraper. Oquin explained,

> Just as skyscrapers are built laying stone upon stone, floor upon floor, so, too, is this music constructed from the bottom up: measure upon measure, phrase upon phrase, rhythm upon rhythm. This ascension is gradual and permeates many dimensions of the music.... Although any skyscraper represents this idea perhaps the one that stood out for me during the composing of this piece is the Freedom Tower. It goes beyond architectural marvel to symbolize the resolve of the American spirit.[6]

Joel Puckett's *Southern Comforts* was commissioned by a consortium of ten college wind ensembles organized by Robert J. Ambrose, conductor of the Georgia State University Symphonic Wind Ensemble. Each movement of the work—"Faulkner," "Ritual: Football and the Lord," "Lamentation," and "Mint Julep"—represents a memory from the composer's childhood in the South. The composer states that he thinks about home constantly.

> I haven't spent more then a week in the south in more than seven years and yet, I know it will always be home. Sometimes it's a phone call from mom or a card from my sister. Sometimes it's the faint smell of a dogwood or an Atlanta Braves box score in the paper. No, I haven't really been there in years but I think about it daily.[7]

UMKC Fanfare by Chen Yi (b. 1953) was commissioned by the University of Missouri-Kansas City Wind Symphony for its 2009 CBDNA Conference program. Chen Yi is married to Zhou Long, whose work, *The Future of Fire* is discussed above. The composer wrote the following comment about her high-energy concert opener:

> ... the pitch material is taken from a Chinese folk tune "Baban," and the texture is taken from a kind of Chinese traditional instrumental ensemble music used in ritual ceremony, which feature blowing instruments suona (shawn, made with wood) and sheng (free-reed mouth-organ, made with gourd). The music is slow to fast, and reaches an extremely fast section in a climax, followed by a strong and short coda in unison. The music presents the images of conflict, struggle, yearning, encouragement, and triumph. It's energetic and celebrating.[8]

The works, below, were among the thirty other recently composed pieces performed at the Conference:

Concerto for Trombone and Band (2008) by James Kazik (b. 1974)
Words of Love (2008) by James Mobberley (b. 1954)
Concerto Logic (2007–08) by Carter Pann (b. 1972)

James Kazik's *Concerto for Trombone and Band* was originally written in 2002, specifically for trombonist Paul Compton and the Myriad Brass Ensemble. Six years later Kazik (b. 1974) re-orchestrated the piece for trombone and concert band. It was premiered by the United States Army Band in March 2008 with Compton as the soloist. The composer commented, "In the *Concerto*, I sought to showcase the elements of Mr. Compton's technique that I greatly admire ... I [used] a primarily tonal idiom, with brief forays into modality."[9]

James Mobberley (b. 1954) composed *Words of Love* for a consortium of college and university wind groups in 2008. Timothy Reynish describes the piece as "... a beautifully constructed eight minute song for soprano and wind ... [a] simple and affecting, absolutely beautiful ... rare few minutes of controlled lyricism."[10] The composer stated that his inspiration for the piece came from the writings of David Mobberley, his father (excerpt below):

My darling
How do I love thee?
The ways of love are countless
countless joys with which you bless my life ...[11]

Concerto Logic for Piano and Wind Symphony by Carter Pann (b. 1972) is a four-movement work that is twenty minutes in length. It was inspired by ancient and contemporary games of chance, logic, and strategy. In 2008, Pann was the piano soloist in the premiere performance of the piece by the Michigan State University Wind Symphony, Kevin L. Sedatole, conductor. In a program note for the piece the composer offered information about the games and the music.

I. *Dogs and Jackals (C-minor Fantasy)* is an ancient Egyptian game from between the ninth and twelfth dynasties.

II. *Ërno Rubik's Magic Cube* is a musical depiction of what it's like to work on the Rubik's Cube until finally, after several days, the last few turns are found and the puzzle is solved. ...

III. *Rondo Capriccio: "Rage over a Lost Pawn"* (piano solo) is an extended concert *cadenza brilliante*.... This cadenza is full of unhinged ragtime and Lisztian sweep....

IV. *Dancing with Caissa* is the largest and most ambitious movement of the work.... [It] came about after studying a legendary game played by Georg Rotlewi and the tactical master Akiba Rubinstein. Rotlewi isn't prepared for the sacrificial onslaught by his opponent and finally breaks under the strain. The final position of the game is a marvel of latent pressure![12]

A number of informative "Break-out Sessions" were also included on the Conference program. Among them were the following:

"Robert Kurka's *The Good Soldier Schweik*: A Performance Edition"— Margaret Underwood (Oberlin College)
"'Sinfonia' from Stravinsky's *Octet*: Back to the Future"—Darrin Thornton (Pennsylvania State University)
"Boris Kozhevnikov's Music for Wind Orchestra"—Patrick Murphy (University of Portland)

* * * * * * * * * *

WASBE held its 14th International Conference in Cincinnati, Ohio, from July 5–11, 2009. It was the third time the Conference was held in the United States. (In 1987 it was held in Boston and in 1999 in San Luis Obispo.) Twelve ensembles from six countries plus the 50-member WASBE International Youth Wind Orchestra (IYWO) (players from ten countries) performed concerts at the Conference. The concert by the IYWO was conducted by Frank L. Battisti, Donald Hunsberger, and H. Robert Reynolds, and consisted of four wind band masterpieces: the Holst *First and Second Suites*, Hindemith's *Symphony in B-flat*, and Grainger's *Lincolnshire Posy*. Included among the new works premiered at the Conference were the *Double Concerto for Oboe and Clarinet* by Gary Carpenter (b. 1951), *The Four Earth Songs* by Marco Pütz (b. 1958), *Icarus* (for large brass ensemble, seven percussion, and two pianos) by Richard Danielpour (b. 1956), and *Contrasten* by Bernard van Beurden (b. 1933–2016).

A presentation by Stephen Budiansky, "The Repertoire *is* the Curriculum: Getting Back to Basics in Music Education," provoked a great deal of controversy and heated debate. As he did in his 2005 article in *The Washington Post* ("The Kids Play Great. But That Music..."), Budiansky was extremely critical of school music programs in which teachers do not introduce students to "real music" composed by "real composers" but instead, have them play "third-rate schlock" produced by unknown music writers/educators which he said was foisted upon them by "for-profit" music publishers. Budiansky urged band directors to ...

> ... stop letting "for-profit" musical merchants dictate curriculum and repertoire.... Publishers are not evil people; they are not the ultimate root of the problem; but their interests are never going to place artistic and educational merit ahead of their bottom line. That's *your* job as educators and directors.... Put educational and artistic goals ... back in the driver's seat.[13]

* * * * * * * * *

On December 9, 2010, Frances Richard, Vice President and Director of Concert Music for the American Society of Composers, Authors and Publishers (ASCAP) and Thomas C. Duffy, President of CBDNA, jointly announced the winner of the fifth bi-annual ASCAP/ CBDNA Frederick Fennell Prize for Young Composers of Concert Band Music. The Prize commemorates the legacy of Frederick Fennell and singles out the most talented young composers writing for wind band. The jury, consisting of composers Eric Ewazen and Jonathan Newman and conductors Jerry Junkin (University of Texas) and Mallory Thompson (Northwestern University), awarded the 2010 Frederick Fennell Prize to Joshua Hummel (b. 1980) for his *Haiku Symphony No. 4*.

Composer Joshua Hummel stated the following about his piece:

> *Haiku Symphony No. 4* is a powerhouse of threes, fives, sevens, and seventeens. These numbers are derived from the formal literary components of a traditional English haiku: three lines of poetry, two lines of five syllables surrounding one line of seven, and seventeen syllables in all. *Haiku 4* works these elements into a bit of a romp that reminds one of sunshine, fragrant flowers, endless childhood memories, the beauty of a summer day. All we need is to take the wind ensemble to a verdant meadow, put dandelions in their hair and have them play barefoot while gamboling about the tall grass.[14]

* * * * * * * * * *

From 2008 to 2010, Robert Boudreau and the American Wind Symphony Orchestra (AWSO) commissioned and premiered fourteen new works.

> *Adagio for Harp and Wind Orchestra* by American Carlos Rivera (b. 1970)
> *Colloquy for Trombone and Wind Orchestra* by American William Goldstein (b. 1942)
> *Concerto for Flute* by Venezuelan Efraín Amaya (b. 1959)
> *Concerto for Guitar and Wind Orchestra* by American Sergei Tcherepnin (b. 1965)
> *Epona's Portal: Concerto for Bassoon and Wind Orchestra* by Efraín Amaya (b. 1959)
> *Festival on the Other Side* by Japanese Masashi Ishida (b. 1979)
> *Goldstein Variations* by William Goldstein (b. 1942)
> *Marahuaka: Concerto for Three Marimbas and Wind Orchestra* by Efraín Amaya (b. 1959)
> *Memorial* by German Rolf Rudin (b. 1961)
> *Nightfall* by Canadian Mattheiu Lussier (b. 1973)
> *Prism-Protonic Constructions II* by Greek Minas Borboudakis (b. 1975)
> *The Art of Seven* by American David Morgan (b. 1957)
> *Toone* by Japanese Kaoru Wada (b. 1962)
> *Vertientes* by Argentinian Javier Giménez Noble (b. 1951)

A facsimile edition of the original holograph score of Mozart's *Gran Partita, K. 361* was published by the Library of Congress in 1976. When all copies had been sold, it was not republished due to a lack of funds. Two decades later, in 2006, the Educational Projects Committee of the American Bandmasters Association contacted the Library of Congress and inquired about the possibility of reprinting and reissuing of the Mozart score. They were told that it would not be reprinted because Congress was no longer allotting funds for this purpose. However, the Library of Congress did express interest in discussing the possible reprinting of the score with the ABA or any other organization. ABA contacted GIA Publications and, after lengthy discussions, decided to collaborate with the Library of Congress in republishing the Mozart score. In April 2008, the facsimile score of Mozart's masterpiece, published by GIA Publications, was once again available.

A year later (May 2009) another book about Mozart's *Gran Partita* was published: *Gran Partita: A book about Mozart's Serenade in B-flat, K. 361 for 12 Wind Instruments and String Bass* by Daniel N. Leeson.[15] Leeson is an authority on Mozart's music, especially on his works for wind instruments. The book contains detailed information about the *Serenade, K.361* and remarkable photographs of historic editions of the work, as well as informative and insightful essays by Mozart scholars Roger Hellyer, Bastiaan Blomhert, and Robert Levin.

* * * * * * * * * *

The 10th anniversary of the founding of the Boston University Tanglewood Institute's Young Artists Wind Ensemble (YAWE) was celebrated with a gala concert in Ozawa Hall on July 30, 2010. The concert was conducted by H. Robert Reynolds and YAWE Emeritus Conductor Frank L. Battisti (program below).

Boston University Tanglewood Institute
Young Artists Wind Ensemble
H. Robert Reynolds, Conductor
Frank L. Battisti, YAWE Conductor Emeritus
Ozawa Hall
Friday, July 30, 2010
7:30 PM

John Estacio (b. 1966)   *Frenergy* (2006)
Transcribed by Fraser Linklater
David Amram (b. 1930)   *Ode to Lord Buckley* (1981)
  II. Taxim; Ayn Adir

Kenneth Radnofsky, saxophone

Jonathan Newman (b. 1972)   *Sowing Useful Truths* (2010)

Commissioned by Boston University for the Tanglewood Institute
Young Artists Wind Ensemble 10th Anniversary

Charles Ives (1874-1954)   *Postlude in F* (1895)
Transcribed by Kenneth Singleton

Charles Ives   *Variations on "America"* (1892)
Transcribed by William Rhoads

Frank L. Battisti, Conductor Emeritus

Intermission

Robert G. Patterson (b. 1957)   *Traffic at Tom Lee Park* (2008)
Frank Ticheli (b. 1958)   *Angels in the Architecture* (2008)
                    Shirley Leiphon, soprano
Michael Daugherty (b. 1954)   *Red Cape Tango* (1999)
Transcribed by Mark Spede

* * * * * * * * * *

The Gotham Wind Symphony Tactical Land Strike Force (GWSTLSF), a smaller version of Michael Christianson's Gotham Wind Symphony, performed its debut engagement on October 16, 2010, at the Tea Lounge in Brooklyn, NY. The Strike Force consists of 5 reeds, 4 trumpets, 1 French horn, 2 trombones, 2 tubas, string bass, guitar, piano, vibes, and percussion. According to Christianson this smaller instrumental group allows the GWS "... to infiltrate and perform in more 'intimate' venues."[16] The ensemble's inaugural performance featured works composed by John Carisi (*Angkor Wat, Moom Taj, Isreal, Sax Quartet No. 1, Piece for 2 Clarinets & Chamber Ensemble, Ballade for Fluegelhorn & Chamber Quintet,* etc.). Carisi (1922–1990) played trumpet, composed, and arranged for numerous big bands including those of Charlie Barnet, Benny Goodman, and Ray McKinley. Many jazz artists, including Miles Davis, Gerry Mulligan, Gil Evans, and Bill Evans, performed and recorded his Carisi pieces.

On January 1, 2010, the first fifty of CBDNA supported segments of *Composers Datebook* was broadcast over the National Public Radio (NPR) network to an estimated 120 million listeners. Each of the segments included an excerpt from a recorded performance of a wind work by a college/university or military band as well as information about the piece and its composer. CBDNA President Thomas Duffy, Richard Floyd, and Frank Battisti worked with the American Composers Forum to develop this series of broadcasts which ran from January 1, 2010 to July 6, 2012. A selective number of them are still being broadcast on the *Composers Datebook*.[17]

Glen Adsit, conductor of the Hartt School Wind Ensemble, organized the National Wind Ensemble Consortium Group (NWECG) in 2004. The objective of the Group was to commission the finest composers—especially those who had not composed a "significant work" for wind ensemble—to write pieces for the medium.

Forty-five colleges, universities, and institutions participated in the NWECG.

The first three composers commissioned by the Consortium Group were Chen Yi, Jennifer Higdon, and Susan Botti. Chen Yi's piece, *Dragon Rhyme*, was premiered in May 2010 by the Hartt School of Music Wind Ensemble, Glen Adsit, conductor. The premiere performances of Jennifer Higdon's piece, *Road Stories,* and Susan Botti's piece, *Terra Cruda*, took place in 2011.

In December 2005, the CBDNA Gender and Ethnic Issues Committee embarked on a project to promote and highlight the accomplishments of underrepresented ethnicities in the classical music field. To that end they decided to commission Valerie Coleman (b. 1970) to compose a piece for the Roma (Texas) High School Band. Roma High School is located on the U. S.-Mexico border and has a predominantly Latino student population. Coleman, flutist and founder of the Imani Winds, is an African-American artist-composer who incorporates elements of African-American heritage and urban culture into her music. This was CBDNA's first commission to an African-American composer, and the first to a black woman.

The Roma High School Band, directed by Dena Laurel, premiered Coleman's piece, *Roma*, on April 9, 2010. Below is the composer's program note for the piece.

> A nation without a country is the best way to describe the nomadic tribes known as gypsies, or properly called, the Romani. Their traditions, their language (*Roma*), legends, and music stretch all over the globe, from the Middle East, the Mediterranean region, the Iberian Peninsula [and] across the ocean to the Americas. *ROMA* is a tribute to that culture, in five descriptive themes, as told through the eyes and hearts of Romani women everywhere: "Romani Woman," "Mystic," "Youth," "Trickster," "History." The melodies and rhythms are a fusion of styles and cultures: Malagueña of Spain, Argentine Tango, Arabic music, Turkish folk songs, 3/2 Latin claves and Jazz.[18]

* * * * * * * * * *

In 2010–11, Cliff Towner conducted a second replication of Acton Ostling's landmark study of 1973–1978, "An Evaluation of Compositions for Wind Band According to Specific Criteria of Serious Artistic Merit," in which he sought to define a repertoire of "serious and artistic merit" for college and university wind bands/ensembles.

In 1992, Jay W. Gilbert undertook the first replication of Ostling's study. Both Ostling's and Gilbert's studies are discussed in Chapters 8 and 9, respectively.

On October 1, 2010, Towner sent email letters to all CBDNA and WASBE members informing them of his intention to replicate Ostling's study and defining the requirements needed to participate in his survey. Towner wrote, "...you must currently be the principal conductor of a professional or collegiate/university wind-band. Current students, composers, and other members of CBDNA and WASBE who do not meet these criteria are asked not to participate. In addition, some participants in this initial phase may be invited to participate in the second phase of the study if they are nominated through this initial survey." All who wished to participate in the project were asked to supply their name, title, institution or ensemble, city, state/province/country in which they resided and answer the following question: "Who, in your opinion, are the ten current wind-band conductors you consider to be the most diligent seekers, and programmers of, music of serious artistic merit for the wind-band medium?[19] The procedure used by Towner to select evaluators deviated from that used by Ostling and Gilbert. Ostling's and Gilbert's studies only involved wind band/ensemble conductors from the United States—Ostling 312 and Gilbert 356. Towner invited all CBDNA and WASBE members to participate in hopes it would result in the selection of evaluators who would be more representative of the larger wind-band world. Unfortunately this did not happen—he only received responses from wind band/ensemble conductors in the United States and Canada. Below are the eighteen conductors selected as evaluators for Towner's study. Only two are non-U. S. wind band/ensemble conductors: Felix Hauswirth from Switzerland and Timothy Reynish from the United Kingdom.

Frank Battisti	Felix Hauswirth	Timothy Reynish
Richard Clary	Gary Hill	Eric Rombach-Kendell
Eugene Corporon	Donald Hunsberger	Tim Salzman
Steven Davis	Jerry Junkin	Kevin Sedatole
Gary Green	John Lynch	Jack Stamp
Michael Haithcock	Steve Pratt	Mallory Thompson

Four of these evaluators (Battisti, Corporon, Hunsberger, and Junkin) participated in Gilbert's study and two (Battisti and Hunsberger) also participated in Ostling's original study.

The foundational core of Towner's 1,680 works to be evaluated included 589 compositions from Ostling's and Gilbert's previous studies, 362 of which had met the "serious artistic merit" criteria in those studies. The evaluators in Towner's study selected 144 compositions, known by at least a majority of the evaluators, as meeting the criteria for "serious artistic merit."[20] Of these 144 compositions, 89 were also included in Ostling's and Gilbert's lists of compositions having "artistic merit." They are listed below in alphabetical order. This deviates from what Ostling and Gilbert did—they listed the works meeting the "serious and artistic merit" criteria in rank order. Towner explained his decision to list them alphabetically: "[The] reasoning behind this was to hinder the direct rankings of [works] from top to bottom by the reader. One of the goals of the study was to identify the works that met the qualifying score based on the criteria of serious artistic merit, which I did. I felt ranking them from 1–144, however, created too much of a competitive bias to the data for the reader."[21]

Composer	Title/Year
Amram, David	King Lear Variations (1967)
Badings, Henk	Concerto for Flute and Wind Symphony (1963)
Bassett, Leslie	Designs, Images and Textures (1966)
Bennett, Robert Russell	Suite of Old American Dances (1949)
Benson, Warren	Concertino (for alto saxophone and wind ensemble) (1954)
Benson, Warren	Symphony for Drums and Wind Orchestra (1963)
Benson, Warren	The Leaves are Falling (1963)
Benson, Warren	The Passing Bell (1974)
Benson, Warren	The Solitary Dancer (1969)
Berg, Alban	Chamber Concerto for Violin, Piano and 13 Wind Instruments, Op. 8 (1925)
Berlioz, Hector	Symphonie Funèbre et Triomphale, Op. 15 (1840)
Bernstein, Leonard	Prelude, Fugue and Riffs (1949)
Brahms, Johannes	Begräbnisgesang, Op. 13 (chorus and wind ensemble) (1858)
Brant, Henry	Angels and Devils (1931)
Bruckner, Anton	Mass No. 2 in E Minor (1882)
Copland, Aaron	An Outdoor Overture (1942)
Copland, Aaron	Emblems (1964)
Dahl, Ingolf	Concerto for Alto Saxophone and Wind Orchestra (1949)

Composer	Title/Year
Dahl, Ingolf	Sinfonietta for Band (1961)
Dello Joio, Norman	Variants on a Medieval Tune (1963)
Dvořák, Antonín	Serenade in D Minor, Op. 44 (1878)
Françaix, Jean	"Sept Dances" from the ballet les Malheurs de Sophie (10 winds) (1972)
Gilmore, Bernard	Five Folk Songs for Soprano and Band (1965)
Gould, Morton	Symphony No. 4 (West Point Symphony) (1952)
Gounod, Charles	Petite Symphonie in B-flat, Op. 90 (1888)
Grainger, Percy	Colonial Song (1918)
Grainger, Percy	Hill Song No. 1 (for wind ensemble of 14 instruments, 7 single string instruments, percussion and harmonium) (1923–24)
Grainger, Percy	Hill Song No. 2 (1907/1948)
Grainger, Percy	Irish Tune from County Derry (1918)
Grainger, Percy	Lincolnshire Posy (1937)
Hahn, Reynaldo	Le Bal de Béatrice d'Este (for piano, two harps and wind orchestra) (1906)
Hindemith, Paul	Concerto for Organ and Wind Instruments: Kammermusik No. 7, Op. 46, No. 2 (1927)
Hindemith, Paul	Konzertmusik, Op. 41 (1926)
Hindemith, Paul	Symphony in B-flat (1951)
Holst, Gustav	Hammersmith (Prelude and Scherzo), Op. 52 (1930)
Holst, Gustav	Suite No. 1 in E-flat (1909)
Holst, Gustav	Suite No. 2 in F (1911)
Honegger, Arthur	Le Roi David (original version) (1921)
Husa, Karel	Apotheosis of this Earth (1971)
Husa, Karel	Concerto for Alto Saxophone and Concert Band (1967)
Husa, Karel	Concerto for Percussion and Wind Ensemble (1970–71)
Husa, Karel	Concerto for Trumpet and Wind Ensemble (1973)
Husa, Karel	Music for Prague 1968 (1968)
Jacob, Gordon	William Byrd Suite (1924)
Kurka, Robert	The Good Soldier Schweik: Suite, Op. 22 (1957)
Mahler, Gustav	"Um Mitternacht" from Aus den Rückert Lieder (1901)
Mendelssohn, Felix	Ouverture für Harmoniemusik, Op. 24 (1826), edited by John Boyd

Composer	Title/Year
Messiaen, Olivier	Colors of the Celestial City (1963)
Messiaen, Olivier	Et Exspecto Resurrectionem Mortuorum (1965)
Messiaen, Olivier	Oiseaux exotiques (for piano solo and small wind orchestra) (1955)
Milhaud, Darius	Suite Française, Op. 248 (1944)
Mozart, Wolfgang	Divertimento No. 3 in E-flat, K166 (1773)
Mozart, Wolfgang	Divertimento No. 4 in B-flat, K186 (1773)
Mozart, Wolfgang	Serenade No. 10 in B-flat, K370a (old K361), "Gran Partita" (1781)
Penderecki, Krzysztof	Pittsburgh Overture (1967)
Persichetti, Vincent	Divertimento for Band, Op. 42 (1950)
Persichetti, Vincent	Masquerade for Band, Op. 102 (1965)
Persichetti, Vincent	Symphony No. 6, Op. 69 (1956)
Poulenc, Francis	Suite Française (for harpsichord and 9 wind instruments) (1935)
Reed, H. Owen	La Fiesta Mexicana (1949)
Reynolds, Verne	Scenes (1971)
Rodrigo, Joaquín	Adagio (1966)
Schmitt, Florent	Dionysiaques, Op. 62 (1914–25)
Schmitt, Florent	Lied et Scherzo, Op. 54 (solo horn and small wind ensemble) (1910)
Schoenberg, Arnold	Theme and Variations, Op. 43a (1943)
Schuller, Gunther	Symphony for Brass and Percussion (1950)
Schuman, William	George Washington Bridge: An Impression for Band (1950)
Schuman, William	New England Triptych: Be Glad Then, America; When Jesus Wept; Chester (1956)
Strauss, Richard	Serenade Op. 7 (1881)
Strauss, Richard	Sonatine in F "Aus der Werkstatt eines Invaliden," AV 135 (1943)
Strauss, Richard	Suite in B-flat, Op. 4 (1884)
Strauss, Richard	Symphonie for Winds "Fröliche Werkstatt," AV 143 (1944–45) ·
Stravinsky, Igor	Concerto for Piano and Wind Instruments (1924)
Stravinsky, Igor	Ebony Concerto (1945)
Stravinsky, Igor	Mass for Chorus and Double Wind Quintet (1948)
Stravinsky, Igor	Symphonies of Wind Instruments (1920)
Stravinsky, Igor	Symphonies of Wind Instruments (revised 1947)

Composer	Title/Year
Stravinsky, Igor	Symphony of Psalms (1930, rev. 1948)
Tippett, Michael	Concerto for Orchestra: First Movement (Mosaic) (1962–63)
Van Otterloo, Willem	Symphonietta for Woodwinds (1948)
Varèse, Edgard	Deserts (1954)
Varèse, Edgard	Hyperprism (1923)
Varèse, Edgard	Intégrales (1925)
Vaughan Williams, Ralph	English Folk Song Suite (1923)
Vaughan Williams, Ralph	Toccata Marziale (1924)
Wagner, Richard	Trauersinfonie (1844) revised by Erik Leidzén
Weill, Kurt	Concerto for Violin, Op. 12 (1924)
Weill, Kurt	Das Berliner Requiem (Tenor, Baritone, Bass soli and wind instruments) (1928)
Weill, Kurt	Little Threepenny Music (1928)[22]

Towner's recommendations for future studies of wind literature, specifically, the replication of Ostling's 1978 research project, include the following:

1. That the evaluation be done every ten years, with the next study commencing during the 2021–22 academic year with a compositional date cut-off of 2020, similar to the timeline used for the United States census.

2. That a one or two-year compositional time buffer be utilized in creating the compositional master lists.

3. That the time frame for the initial survey (nominations for evaluators) be extended to at least two months, with reminders sent every other week. (Note: Towner received the bulk of his responses within short periods after he sent out reminders. He feels the response rate would have been improved if he had sent out more reminders).

ENDNOTES

1   Thomas M. Wallis, "Donald Grantham's *Symphony for Winds and Percussion*: A Description of Compositional Techniques" (M.M. project paper, Ball State University, 2014), 7–8.

2   James Kazik, "Composer's Program Note," Oklahoma State University Wind Ensemble, concert of March 25, 2009.

3   Zhou Long, "Composer's Program Note," University of Missouri-Kansas City Conservatory of Music Wind Symphony, concert of March 27, 2009.

4   "Asphalt Cocktail (2009) for wind ensemble," Osti Music: The Website of Composer John Mackey, accessed June 10, 2018, http://www.ostimusic.com/Asphalt.php.

5   Todd Malicoate, "Composer's Program Note," Oklahoma State University Wind Ensemble, concert of March 25, 2009.

6   Wayne Oquin, "Program Note—Tower Ascending," Wayne Oquin, Composer, accessed June 20, 2018, http://www.wayneoquin.com/works.htm.

7   Joel Puckett, "Southern Comforts: Program Note," Joel Puckett, Composer, accessed June 20, 2018, http://joelpuckett.com/music/southerncomforts/.

8   Chen Yi, "Composer's Program Note," University of Missouri-Kansas City Wind Symphony, concert of March 25, 2009.

9   James Kazik, "Composer's Program Note," Oklahoma State University Wind Ensemble, concert of March 25, 2009.

10 Tim Reynish, "CBDNA 2009 Conference: University Of Missouri—Kansas City Conservatory of Music and Dance Wind Symphony," Tim Reynish, accessed June 20, 2018, http://www.timreynish.com/conferences/cbdna-2009.php.

11 David Mobberley, "Composer's Program Note," University of Missouri-Kansas City Wind Symphony, concert of March 26, 2009.

12 Carter Pann, "Composer's Program Note," Michigan State University Wind Symphony, concert of October 30, 2008.

13 Stephen Budiansky, "The Repertoire is the Curriculum: Getting Back to Basics in Music Education," Stephen Budiansky, author, historian, journalist, accessed June 20, 2018, http://www.budiansky.com/MUSIC_files/budiansky%20wasbe%20journal%202009.pdf.

14 "2010 ASCAP/CBDNA Frederick Fennell Prize Winner Announced," ASCAP, accessed June 20, 2018, https://www.ascap.com/press/2010/1209_ASCAP_CBDNA.aspx.

15 Bloomington, IN: AuthorHouse, 2009. ISBN 9781438980195. https://www.authorhouse.com.

16 Michael Christianson, email to the author, September 21, 2010.

17 Composers Datebook, accessed June 20, 2018, https://www.yourclassical.org/programs/composers-datebook/episodes.

18 Valerie Coleman, *Roma for Concert Band* (Theodore Presser, 2011), 3.

19 Cliff Towner, email to CBDNA and WASBE members, October 1, 2010.

20 Clifford Towner, "An Evaluation of Compositions for Wind Band According to Specific Criteria of Serious Artistic Merit: A Second Update" (D.M.A. diss., University of Nebraska, 2011), ii–iii.

21 Cliff Towner, email to the author, August 8, 2011.

22 Towner, "An Evaluation," 176.

CHAPTER 17

Premiere Performances Galore (2011–2012)

| *2011 CBDNA Conference • 2011 WASBE Conference in Taiwan • Expansion of Wind Works in all Genres* |

Commissioning works for wind bands/ensembles, which began in the middle of the twentieth century, had become a well-established practice by the beginning of the twenty-first century. This practice created a large and eclectic body of literature for wind groups that varied in quality from very low to very high. The ten works, below, were premiered at the 2011 CBDNA National Conference in Seattle, Washington. They provide a panoramic view of the varied kinds/styles of music composed for wind band/ensembles during this time.

Daniel Kellogg	*A Toast to Ben*
Jody Nagel	*As You Like It*
Scott McAllister	*Music from the Redneck Songbook II*
Shawn E. Okpebholo	*This is Africa*
Mark Camphouse	*Reminiscences*
Joel Puckett	*Avelynn's Lullaby*
Jess Langston Turner	*Burning Music*
Mason Bates	*Sea-Blue Circuitry*
Huck Hodge	*from the language of shadows*
Cuong Vu	*Solitary Confinement* (wind ensemble version orchestrated by T. Salzman)

A Toast to Ben by Daniel Kellogg (b. 1976) and *As You Like It by* Jody Nagel (b. 1960) were both premiered by the Ball State University Wind Ensemble, Thomas E. Caneva, conductor. Kellogg is a member of the music faculty at the University of Colorado. *A Toast for Ben,* is a reworking of a piece, entitled *Ben,* that Kellogg wrote in 2005–06 for the Philadelphia Orchestra and the city of Philadelphia's celebration of Ben Franklin's 300th birthday. The composer described the piece as "a raucous toast that incorporates two drinking songs beloved by Franklin." In his program note about the piece the composer wrote:

> ... the piece begins with a verse sung by the ensemble before the music takes off in a fast, celebratory toast. At the midpoint of the piece, the ensemble sings two verses from one of Franklin's ... favorite drinking songs, "The Old Man's Wish," [which Ben sang] thousands of times in his youth, and quoted ... more than once in correspondence.[1]

Jody Nagel, Professor of Composition at Ball State University, had no programmatic ideas in mind when he started to compose *As You Like It.* The William Shakespeare play of the same name is a pastoral comedy replete with the usual array of love triangles and false identities that contains profound metaphors and ethical narratives. The first movement of Nagel's work was originally composed in 1980 for French horn and piano and was given the title, *As You Like It,* purely by mistake. When the composer was asked what the piece should be called, he responded, "You should name it as you like." His words were misheard and reordered to *As You Like It* and the title stuck.

Music from the Redneck Songbook II by Scott McAllister (b. 1969) is a multi-movement work which was inspired by the composers' childhood memories of growing up in the south. Its first movement, "Full Pull," emulates the mechanical precision and power of a tractor pull. The second movement, "In the Pines," is in a variation form and was inspired by the southern folk song "In the Pines," which the composer also used in his *Clarinet Concerto X.* This movement portrays the story of a mother who found her son's head deep in the piney woods near a railroad track, but never found his body. "Wilt," the third movement is inspired by the oak wilt disease that devastated many of the great live oaks in the south. The work's last movement, "Cage Match," was inspired by the old WWF wrestling league of the 1970s and early eighties.

Shawn E. Okpebholo (b. 1981) teaches composition and theory at Wheaton College Conservatory in Illinois. His composition, *This is Africa*, was inspired by an ethnomusicological research trip he took to Nigeria. The composer writes, "[The piece] ... evokes moods, events, and sounds that [I] experienced from the journey, including West African drumming and tribal melodies. One of the primary musical themes of the composition is an adaptation of [a] melody that comes from the Esan people, a small ethnic group in the southern part of Nigeria and the tribe in which I am a part and have rich historical family ties. The text of this poetic language of which the melody is based is chanted [at various moments throughout the work]."

> "Ekine leleyea do obhimen la doeki nalo," which translated means "My investment in you has paid off. Because of your hard work, your future is bright and others will benefit."[2]

Okpebholo dedicated the piece to the memory of Harry Begian. In his program note he wrote, "As an educator, Begian influenced many students who went on to do the same with their students.... As such, the Esan text is fitting, as Begian's investment in his students made the future bright for many musicians."[3]

Like Shawn Okpebholo's piece, Mark Camphouse's *Reminiscences* is dedicated to the memory of Dr. Harry Begian. It was commissioned by Marcellus Brown, conductor of the Boise State Symphonic Winds, who requested that Camphouse (b. 1954) write something "very simple and direct: song-like, with a duration of approximately five minutes." The composer recalled that the timing of the commission was propitious because he was sketching a solo piano piece for a friend, whose father had just passed away, which embodied the same expressive qualities that Brown had requested for his piece. Camphouse immediately recognized the sonic possibilities of a modified version of the piano piece and proceeded to write *Reminiscences*. Included in the work is a brief quote from a hymn sung at his friend's father's memorial service, "It is Well With My Soul."

Joel Puckett's *Avelynn's Lullaby* is a refreshing and gentle eight-minute work for wind ensemble. It was commissioned by ten college and university bands and premiered by the Long Beach Wind Ensemble, conducted by John Carnahan. As is often the case in Puckett's music, this piece evokes a memory—the ritual he and his daughter, Avelynn, went through every night.

Our nighttime routine has become set in stone. I give her a bath, put her in her pajamas, and we read a book or two. And then we [came] to my favorite portion of the routine: the lullabies. Doing my part, I sing her slow lullabies while rocking her, and she does her part, fighting the onset of sleep. By far her favorite lullaby is the one my mother used to sing to me: "Sail Far Away, Sail Across the Sea, Only don't forget to Sail, back again to me." At least, I thought it was the one my mother used to sing to me. I got curious about the rest of the verses and found that the piece was written in 1898, by Alice Riley and Jesse Gaynor and has only a passing resemblance to the song I remember my mother singing to me. Better yet, it has virtually no resemblance to the lullaby I had been singing to Avelynn! So, *Avelynn's Lullaby* is both a journey of daddy trying to coax daughter to sleep and a journey of daughter enjoying the song, fighting sleep, and eventually succumbing to slumber.[4]

Joel Puckett (b. 1977) has the players sing through their instrument at the end of the piece to create a peaceful end to the work, an indication that Avelynn has fallen asleep.

Burning Music by Jesse Langston Turner (b. 1983) deals with the consuming power of fire. It is a chamber ensemble piece for Flute (doubles piccolo), Oboe, Bb Clarinet, Alto Sax (doubles soprano sax), Bassoon, F Horn, C Trumpet, Piano, Harp, Violin I, Violin II, Viola, Cello, Double Bass, Percussion I, Percussion II. The work's fiery imagery conveys the terrifying and destructive force of fire and contains "... several direct allusions to pieces by other composers who also wrote pieces dealing with the nature of fire. One [can] hear references to the 'Ritual Fire Dance' from Manuel de Falla's *El Amor Brujo*, as well as several overt references to Stravinsky's *The Firebird*."[5]

Mason Bates (b. 1977) has pursued a parallel career as a DJ and a performer in clubs around the San Francisco Bay Area. He has also been a composer-in-residence with the Chicago Symphony (2011). Bates's music is often a fusion of traditional acoustical sounds and electronics. However, he has also composed several works for purely acoustic ensembles, *Sea-Blue Circuitry*, a fourteen-minute, three-movement work, is one of them. The composer has written the following about his piece:

The grooves of *Sea-Blue Circuitry* hiccup from measure to measure as rapidly as data quietly flashing on the silicon innards of a computer, yet the piece is entirely unplugged. While some of my recent works fuse orchestral textures and electronica, this piece explores ways of recreating the precision of electronica through the instruments alone.

Breathy flute interjections, chirping trumpets, and even an old typewriter brings to life the quicksilver music of the opening "Silicon Blues." The morphing beat, at the movement's climax, begins to lengthen persistently, and by the time we enter "Marine Snow," a pulsing prepared-piano figure becomes a distant, out-of-tune gong.…

As the marine snow drifts lower, the gentle pulse returns with growing insistence. The prepared low-end of the piano finally presents itself in "Greyhound," a mad dash across bumpy terrain.… By the work's end, we return to a clunkier version of the silicon-based world that began the piece—like an old-fashioned mainframe computer doing a lopsided dance.[6]

Huck Hodge (b. 1977) is Chair of Composition at the University of Washington. His composition, *from the language of shadows*, was inspired by images from F. W. Murnau's 1926 masterpiece of expressionistic cinema, *Faust*. The composer says he was drawn to the images by "the striking and stark blending of bright and dark lighting in the film as well as the angularly dramatic imagery." The movement titles (I. Prologue in Heaven, II. Tenebrae, III. Of signs and erring stars, IV. Inveiglement, V. Epilogue: Now body, turn to air …) are taken from Goethe as well as from Christopher Marlowe's 1604 play *Doctor Faustus*. At the work's premiere, Murnau's 1926 silent film was shown during the performance.

Cuong Vu (b. 1969) is widely recognized by jazz critics as the leader of a generation of innovative musicians. Nate Chinen, in a March 1, 2011, *New York Times* review of one of Vu's CD recordings noted, "The voracious sweep of postmillennial jazz has plenty of exemplars but few truer than the trumpeter Cuong Vu." His composition, *Solitary Confinement*, was orchestrated by Timothy Salzman, conductor of the University of Washington Wind Ensemble. Vu's piece explores new musical directions through its exploration of sound and form as it embraces the undercurrents of underground rock and electronic music.

Symphonie pour Musique d'Harmonie (known in the United States as *Symphony in B-Flat*) by Paul Robert Marcel Fauchet (1881–1937) is a large, thirty-minute, four-movement symphony written in a post-romantic style. It was composed in 1926 for and premiered by France's most prestigious band, *Batterie et musique de la Garde républican*. It is one of the earliest symphonies composed for the band. Music scholar/historian Jon Mitchell wrote the following about Fauchet's work:

> The composer chose to follow in the footsteps of the French symphonists Saint-Saëns and d'Indy rather than take up the newer styles being developed by Schmitt, Ibert, and "Les Six." In an era when composers—particularly those ... in France—were discarding the forms and methods of the past. Fauchet's symphony, while not appearing to be entirely anachronistic in character, has its roots deeply entrenched in the past. A masterpiece of counterpoint and instrumentation, the work is clearly from the pen of a learned music theoretician.[7]

The California State University Long Beach Wind Symphony, John Carnahan, conductor, performed a newly revised edition of Fauchet's *Symphonie*, edited by Michel Etchegoncelay. The new edition includes a full score which did not exist before, and calls for Trumpets, Cornets and Bugles, Alto Horns, Baritones, and Euphoniums which Fauchet used in the work's original instrumentation.

Included among the other works performed at the 2011 CBDNA National Conference was one entitled *An American Soldier's Tale* which is an updated version of Igor Stravinsky's *Histoire du Soldat* with a new libretto by American author Kurt Vonnegut (1922–2007). David Waybright conducted the performance with Jerry Junkin, Stephen Peterson, Sarah McKoin, and John Watkins performing the principal roles.

* * * * * * * *

New works continued to be added to wind band/ensemble literature in 2011. Particularly welcomed were Steven Bryant's *Concerto for Cello and Wind Ensemble* and Anderson Alden's *Winter Concerto for Electric Violin and Wind Ensemble*, which enlarged the pieces available for performances by a solo string instrument and wind ensemble. These and the works listed below are among the varied kinds of compositions written for wind band/ensemble in 2011.

Anderson Alden	Winter Concerto for Electric Violin and Wind Ensemble
James Barnes	Symphonic Requiem (Symphony No. 7)
Andrew Boysen	Symphony No. 6
Steven Bryant	Concerto for Wind Ensemble

Bruce Broughton	In the World of Spirits
Chen Yi	Dragon Rhyme
John Corigliano	The Red Violin Chacone (transcribed for wind ensemble by Benjamin Lorenzo)
Viet Cuong	Sound and Smoke
John M. Davis	First Little Serenade
Avner Dorman	Astrolatry (transcribed for wind ensemble by Corey Pompey)
Donald Grantham	Concerto for Tuba, Orchestra Winds, Percussion and Piano
Jennifer Higdon	Mysterium
Takuma Itoh	Daydreams
Ben Hjertmann	Catclaw Mimosa
Jesse Jones	Beyond the Veil
John Mackey	Foundry
Bryan Morgan	Aaron's Fanfare
Carter Pann	My Brother's Brain—A Symphony for Winds
Nathan Prillaman	Transcontinental
Brian Rhodes	Icefire for Alto Saxophone and Concert Band
Bright Sheng	Shanghai Overture (2007/2011)
Michael Schelle	The End of the World
Kristina Warren	negative one plus three equals two

Both the *Winter Concerto for Electric Violin and Wind Ensemble* by Anderson Alden (b. 1991) and *Transcontinental* by Nathan Prillaman (b. 1991) were premiered by the Yale University Concert Band, Thomas Duffy, conductor, on December 2, 2011. Anderson Alden (b. 1991) is an award-winning composer based in Los Angeles and one of the first Composer Fellows with the Los Angeles Philharmonic. During his sophomore year at Yale, Alden experienced the most severe winter he had ever seen, which led to the writing of the *Winter Concerto for Electric Violin and Wind Ensemble*. He wrote,

> This was the winter I had fantasized about. So I expressed my excitement [in] the way I know best: I wrote music.... I was inspired by how [Jourdan Urbach's] electric violin behaved differently from an acoustic violin.... It sounds at times more aggressive than its acoustic counterpart, and at times sweeter and more pure. This high, mellow timbre blended quite well with the flute in our ensemble, so I started imagining other ways the electric violin could be paired with wind instruments. In the middle of [the piece] you'll hear sounds of ice cracking and shattering, snow crunching, and taps on glass bottles that I have recorded, edited and programmed into a keyboard.[8]

Nathan Prillaman (b. 1991) is a composer and producer of film, classical, and electronic music. He also writes music for dance and musicals and is involved in a variety of other musical projects ranging from DSP design to recording technology consultant. His work required that he travel to various places. The sounds he heard on the train during his journeys gradually ignited ideas that led to the writing of *Transcontinental*.

> I was inspired by the propulsive rhythm of Amtrak's trains, by the sound of wind rushing past the cabin, and most importantly, by the sometimes gradual, sometimes sudden changes in environment one witnesses through the window as the train rumbles on. One moment, you see suburbs, the next, a city, and the next, mountains. These real-world, sensory experiences are inexorably tied to my emotional experience of travel, and as such, I worked to weave them into the musical dialect of [my] piece.[9]

Symphony No. 6 by Andrew Boysen (b. 1968) was composed for conductor Andy Mast and the Lawrence University Wind Ensemble. Boysen intended to compose a concerto in which all the sections of the ensemble would be featured. What he ended up writing was a symphony in which many individual members of the ensemble are featured. Constructed as a one-movement work, it consists of four distinct sections that are similar to the four movements found in traditional symphonies. The composer provided the following information about the *Symphony*:

> ... the symphony is really about transformation and emergence from darkness into light. The opening notes of the introduction begin mysteriously at the very bottom of the ensemble in the contrabassoon and ascend in a sort of primal scream, eventually leading into a threatening, angry, and aggressive first movement. After a transition ... this aggressiveness gives way to a second movement scherzo that is more sarcastic, still angry, but with an edgy humor to it. The second transition section features the alto saxophone over pulsating drums, eventually tapering into the third movement, which really represents the moment of metamorphosis, with the emergence of a melody of hope and love that is initially presented by a lengthy horn solo. The third transition section follows, featuring the flute in a variation on the first transition section. The final movement is triumphant, but not in an overtly happy way; instead, it is a triumph of strength and celebration that brings the symphony to a powerful close.[10]

In 2010 a consortium consisting of cellist Caroline Stinson, the Cornell University Wind Ensemble, and the Ridgewood Concert Band commissioned Steven Bryant to compose a concerto for cello and wind ensemble. Even though Bryant had never been drawn to the traditional concerto form, he knew that an opportunity to write a concerto for Stinson was the "perfect project to dispel [his] hesitation [to do so]." He scored his *Concerto for Cello and Wind Ensemble* for an orchestral wind section plus percussion so that it could be performed by either a symphony orchestra or a wind ensemble. The composer wrote the following words about the work:

> Cast in two movements, the work displays more of my recent fascination with both serialized pitch usage and minimalist rhythmic patterns, while hopefully retaining the drama I strive to imbue in all of my music. The first movement explores a fairly strict serial treatment of a nine-tone pitch row (stated clearly in the first bar), punctuated by a few notable moments of triadic harmony (still melodically related to the row). The second movement exploits the natural harmonics of the Cello, and is thus necessarily in a bright D-major (veering toward A-major) tonality, full of life and joy.[11]

Bryant's *Concerto for Cello and Wind Ensemble* was premiered twice, both times with Caroline Stinson as soloist. The first was on March 25, 2011, by the Ridgewood Concert Band, Chris Wilhjelm, conductor; the second on April 30, 2011, by the Cornell University Wind Ensemble, Cynthia Johnston Turner, conductor.

The Cornell Wind Ensemble and conductor Cynthia Johnston Turner developed a unique "in house" commissioning program. They commissioned DMA students at the University who were studying composition with Roberto Sierra and Steven Stucky. Turner instructed these composers to "push the boundaries of what a wind ensemble can sound like." Included among the works they commissioned were Xi Wang's *Concerto for Piano, Percussion and Wind Ensemble* (2006), Christopher Starks's *Augenblick for Electronics and Wind Ensemble* (2007), Zachery Wadsworth's *Symphony of Glances* (2008), Ryan Gallagher's *Exorcism for death metal drummer and wind ensemble* (2007), and Takuma Itoh's fifteen minute work, *Daydreams*, which was premiered on March 13, 2011, and won the 2012 ASCAP/CBDNA Frederick Fennell Young Composers Competition. Itoh provided the following insightful information about *Daydreams*:

In *Daydreams*, I wanted to create an atmosphere of going in and out of a timeless suspension. To create this feeling, I used indeterminate (ad libitum) notation alongside a more conventional, metered notation: at times, the indeterminate figures creates a suspended atmosphere ... while in other moments [they propel] the music forward with a rapid flurry of notes. The piece gradually builds until the climactic moment when the sounds literally engulf the listeners: a group of musicians who were on stage in the beginning of the piece are now playing from the balconies, creating a reverberant, "surround-sound" effect for the listeners situated within the auditorium.[12]

Chen Yi (b. 1953) employs both Chinese and Western "sounds and practices" in her two-movement work, *Dragon Rhyme*. The first movement marked "Mysteriously-Harmoniously," is lyrical; the second, marked "Energetically," is powerful. The texture of the piece is layered, multidimensional, and rich in color that ranges from transparent and delicate to angular and strong. The composer wrote that "it symbolizes Eastern culture. When it meets the world, it becomes a part of the global family."[13]

Viet Cuong (b. 1990) composed *Sound and Smoke* when he was a student at the Peabody Conservatory. It was his first important work for wind band/ensemble. In 2012, it won the Ithaca College Walter Beeler Memorial Prize for new band compositions. The work's program note, written by the composer, provides a detailed description of the piece (excerpt below).

Both the title and concept of *Sound and Smoke* were derived from a line from Johann Wolfgang von Goethe's play *Faust*, when Faust equates words to "mere sound and smoke" and declares that "feeling is everything. ..."

The first movement, (feudal castle lights), blurs the many different timbres of the ensemble to create a resonant and slowly "smoldering" effect.... The second and final movement, (avalanche of eyes), opens with an alternating unison-note brass fanfare that is then spun out into a fast-paced toccata.[14]

In 2011, Charles Villarrubia, tuba soloist and Professor of Tuba, Euphonium, and Brass Chamber Music at the University at Texas, and Dr. Robert Camochan, Associate Director of Bands at the University of Texas, contacted Donald Grantham about composing a piece for solo tuba and orchestra winds. The result was a *Concerto for*

Tuba, Orchestra Winds, Percussion, and Piano. The composer offers the following information about the piece.

> My Tuba Concerto ... is in three movements. The first movement, marked "Fiery and bold," is a virtuosic workout featuring much interplay between the soloist and percussion, particularly the timpani. The second movement is lyrical and expressive. Formally it is a kind of continuous development ... all the elements combine and interact throughout the entire movement. The third movement is in a much more popular and jazzy vein, and is dedicated to the memory of Tiny Parham, a jazz musician who flourished in Chicago in the 1920s and 1930s and a composer whose music and scoring I particularly admired.[15]

The Emory University Wind Ensemble, Scott A. Stewart, conductor, performed two new works on their April 20, 2011 concert: *Mysterium* by Jennifer Higdon (b. 1962) and *In the World of Spirits* by Bruce Broughton (b. 1945). Higdon's piece is a wind ensemble version of one of her earlier choral pieces, *O magnum mysterium*, which she describes as "... a tribute to the wonderful mystery of how music moves us. Perhaps it is the unexplainable that creates such magic, for both the performer and the listener, but there is no denying the incredible power of a shared musical experience."[16]

Bruce Broughton was inspired to write *In the World of Spirits* by a paragraph from S. C. Gwynne's *Empire of the Summer Moon* which depicted the rise and fall of the Comanches. In his book Gwynne describes the life of the Plains Indian as "a world ... of pure magic, of beaver ceremonies and eagle dances, of spirits that inhabited springs, trees, rock, turtles, and crows ... where ... ghosts were alive in the wind ... where nature and divinity became one."[17] The piece is based on two main themes. The first, a short burst of repeated notes followed by numerous leaping phrases; the second, a much more declamatory and pompous theme. The interaction of these two themes creates a fast–slow–fast rhapsodic structure.

Ben Hjertmann (b. 1985) is a composer and vocalist based in Boone, North Carolina. He composes and sings with the avant-folk trio Grant Wallace Band, and surrealist-pop band Kong Must Dead. *Catclaw Mimosa*, the title of his first piece for wind ensemble, is also the name of an invasive species of shrub that infested areas of the American Southwest. The composer wrote this about *Catclaw Mimosa*:

The piece begins with short groove—slowly expanding outward. The opening material heard in the saxes and low brass as a composite is repeated many times, but always with a slightly varied metrical context. Meanwhile, cliché 4/4 Rock patterns appear in a false tempo in the drum set. Like the invasive species, the motives in my piece begin as tiny seed-motives, interjected in the texture. Slowly they accrue and multiply until the ensemble is overtaken and forced into a sort of temporal wasteland.[18]

Catclaw Mimosa was the winner of the 2013 Grade VI Frank Ticheli International Composition Contest.

John Mackey's *Foundry* was commissioned by a consortium of three middle/junior high school and five high school bands. In 2011, it won the CBDNA Young Band Composition Contest. Mackey said his intention in writing *Foundry* was to create "... a piece that celebrated the fact that percussionists have [the] ability to make just about anything into an "instrument."[19]

In some cases, I was specific about what instrument [was to be played] (timpani, xylophone, etc.) ... [However, in] many of the parts ... I only described what *sound* I wanted (ex. play a "clang" ... sound) and allowed the percussionist to be creative in finding the best "instrument" to produce the sound I described.[20]

Carter Pann's *My Brother's Brain: A Symphony for Winds*, is scored for a large ensemble and is in three movements: Movement I. The Inventions—to my brother's uncompromising craft; Movement II. Demonsphere—on my brother's struggle; Movement III. The Hymn of Forgiving—to my brother's unwavering empathy. The piece was commissioned in 2011 by a consortium of twenty-seven ensembles and is the composer's tenth work for wind ensemble. Pann wrote the following program note for the piece:

There is no one person on the planet I resemble more closely in mind, soul, and general human rhythm, than my younger brother Alex ... We keep in touch with a somewhat waning regularity. Growing up together (5 years his senior) I was a typical older brother, exercising my greater strength and cunning on a kid who would inevitably grow up to eclipse me with his sheer brainpower, and ultimately forgive my well-aimed indiscretions. I look back on his mental feats often from our younger years and swell with silent pride ... that I had the privilege to grow in close parallel with him into our adulthoods. *My Brother's Brain, A Symphony for Winds* is a triptych of sound paintings describing the man as I remember him in our earlier years together.[21]

Bright Sheng (b. 1955) composed the *Shanghai Overture* in 2007 for the eightieth anniversary celebration of the Shanghai Conservatory of Music. In 2011, he created a symphonic band version of the piece for the University of Michigan Symphony Band's tour to China. The inspiration for the *Overture* came from two very different traditional Chinese compositions, *General Degree* and *Purple Bamboo*— one grand and powerful the other light and elegant. Sheng explained what he was trying to achieve in writing the piece.

> In Western music, the term neo-Classicism primarily refers to a movement in music composition prevalent in the 1920s and 1930s.... the main aesthetics of the style [emphasized] ... textural clarity, light orchestration and formal balance.... I always wondered what the result would be if I [applied] ... similar ... neo-Classical [techniques] ... to traditional Chinese classical or folk music.... I took the opportunity to explore [this] idea when I was asked to write a short composition for The Shanghai Conservatory of Music.[22]

The End of the World by Michael Schelle (b. 1950) was commissioned by a consortium of thirty-five university and professional wind bands/ensembles. The inspiration for the piece was the notorious cataclysmic end-of-the-world prophecy of Nostradamus (scheduled for late December 2012) and the Mayan calendar's end-of-time prediction (also, according to some, on the immediate horizon). Schelle's intention was to compose a "serious" Nostradamus-related piece, but fate interceded. In March 2011 a great earthquake and tsunami leveled much of northern Japan. He explained, "As I began work on the music in Spring 2011, I was heartbroken by the fear, disbelief and sadness on the face of my Japanese wife, composer/pianist Miho Sasaki, as she sat paralyzed by her emotions, watching televised images of her homeland's devastation. So my piece took its shape and inspiration from this disaster."[23] *The End of the World* won the 2012 National Band Association William D. Revelli Composition Contest.

* * * * * * * * * *

The 2011 WASBE Conference was held in Chiayi City, Taiwan. The logistical challenges involved in traveling to this location resulted in a smaller than expected attendance and a program of performances dominated by Asian wind bands/ensembles/orchestras. Listed below are the ensembles that performed at the Conference. Seven of them are from Asian countries.

Taiwan Military of National Defense Symphonic Wind Orchestra
China Youth Corps Wind Orchestra
Tom Lee Hong Kong Youth NeoWinds Orchestra
Norwegian Wind Orchestra
The Philharmonic Winds Singapore
Uniao Filharmonica do Troviscal
United States Coast Guard Band
Osaka College of Music Wind Orchestra
Taiwan Wind Ensemble
National Youth Wind Ensemble of Great Britain
Southern Illinois University at Edwardsville Wind Symphony
Tokyo Kosei Wind Orchestra
WASBE Youth Wind Orchestra

Timothy Reynish in his review of the Conference wrote:

Many of the programmes were neatly balanced between orient and occi-dent, there were a number of masterpieces from the 18th, 19th and 20th centuries to complement the contemporary music, and the Asian bands played to a very high standard. A colleague wrote to me recently sadly commenting that for many groups good playing seems to mean fast and loud, and of course this is encouraged by the repertoire. The excellent hall had a very lively acoustic, misjudged by many conductors who per-haps came to us fresh from an open-air concert for 3,000 people....

Unfortunately, much of the Taiwanese and other Asian music was of limited or no interest, consisting of repetitious short-winded pen-tatonic phrases, little melodic or harmonic development, sometimes poorly orchestrated and often naive in the extreme. There were pieces from other parts of the globe, also offering poverty stricken ideas. The WASBE Artistic Planning Committee, while preserving WASBE as an all-embracing umbrella, must avoid the trap of selecting a band or pro-gramming a piece just because it comes from an area of the world not frequently featured in WASBE conferences. [24]

* * * * * * * * * *

In 2012, composers continued to write works that expanded and enriched the wind band/ensemble medium. In *Point Blank*, Paul Dooley explores the interaction between computer-generated musical material and the human performer. Alexandre Lunsqui's concerto-like piece, *Ubehebe*, is a work for an unusual "duo" of soloists—a flutist and percussionist—and Steven Bryant integrates recordings of individual players in *Solace* to augment the timbre and expressive power of the wind ensemble.

These works, and those below, exemplify the broad spectrum of styles found in works that enlarged wind band/ensemble literature in 2012.

Daniel Basford	*Partita in D*
Laurence Bilensky	*Fearsome Critters*
Mark Camphouse	*Elegy, Prayer, and Hymn*
Tyler Capp	*Cryptogram*
John Corigliano	*Elegy* (1965, transcribed 2012)
Cody Criswell	*The Awesome Machinery of Nature*
Joseph Curtis	*Thornbriar Rhadsody*
Costas Dafnis	*Parliament in Flight*
Christopher Dietz	*Chrysanthemum*
Michael Gandolfi	*Flourishes and Meditations on a Renaissance Theme*
Amil Gilutz	*this is not a march*
Patrick Harlin	*Rapture* (2011, revised 2012)
James Lee III	*Ancient Words! Current Realities*
John Mackey	*Sheltering Sky*
Kristopher Maloy	*SPIN*
John Mayrose	*Bending Light*
Scott McAllister	*Gone*
Scott McAllister	*Mercury on the Moon*
Marc Mellits	*Requiem for a Hummingbird*
Jonathan Newman	*Blow it Up, Start Again* (2011, transcribed 2012)
Narong Prangcharoen	*Anātman, a work for Cello And Wind Ensemble*
Daniel Bernard Roumain	*The Order of an Empty Place*
Gerard Schwarz	*Above and Beyond*
Zach Stanton	*Concerto for Piano and Wind Ensemble*
Frank Ticheli	*Songs of Love and Life*
Travis Weller	*Romance for Winds*
Eric Whitacre	*Rumor Mill*
Michael Young	*Concerto for Alto Saxophone, Op. 123*

Solace by Steven Bryant was commissioned by the University of North Carolina at Greensboro and a consortium of twelve universities. The work was premiered on October 9, 2012, by the above ensemble, conducted by Kevin Geraldi. The piece is scored for a standard wind ensemble plus electronics, in which the composer transforms recordings of individual players to augment the timbre of the ensemble. "*Solace* [illuminates] the experience of seeking, and perhaps finding, consolation."[25]

Christopher Dietz (b. 1977) is a professor of composition at Bowling Green State University. *Chrysanthemum*, his first work for wind band/ensemble, was written in 2012 and premiered on April 12, 2013, by the University of Michigan Symphony Band, Michael Haithcock, conductor. The composer offers the following insight into the inspiration for his work.

> Among the vast and varied species of the world's flowering plants, the chrysanthemum seems rather common in appearance. Its name, derived from Greek, sounds exotic to the ear but is merely the plainest of descriptions—*golden flower*. Despite this, or perhaps because of it, mankind has adopted the chrysanthemum over the millennia to represent and accompany a variety of human experiences.... Does this piece of music describe a chrysanthemum? Not necessarily. The music, like the flower, is an opportunity to experience something beautiful and different. It is defined by those who engage it. Music too can be ascribed diverse symbolic associations and is also variable in its shapes, colors and configurations as it continues to be cultivated and hybridized into contemporary derivations and varieties.[26]

Paul Dooley's piece, *Point Blank*, exists in three versions: one for large chamber ensemble (2010), one for full orchestra (2011), and one for wind ensemble (2012). Dooley (b. 1983) often blends Western classical traditions with other musical traditions. The composer wrote the following about his piece:

> *Point Blank* is inspired by the sounds and rhythms and virtuosity of the New York City-based new music ensemble *Alarm Will Sound*.... Featuring synthetic sound worlds and tightly interlocking percussion ideas ... the ensemble [is whirled] through an array of electronically inspired orchestrations.... *Point Blank* is a central processing unit of floating point tremelos, discrete pizzicatos, multi-threading scales and random access modulations.[27]

Flourishes and Meditations on a Renaissance Theme by Michael Gandolfi (b. 1956) was commissioned by "The President's Own" United States Marine Band. It received its premiere performance on March 4, 2011, at the American Bandmasters Association Convention in Norfolk, Virginia, and was awarded the Sousa/Ostwald Composition Award in 2012. This is Gandolfi's second piece for wind ensemble.

His first, *Vientos y Tangos*, was also premiered by the U. S. Marine Band. *Flourishes and Meditations on a Renaissance Theme* is a set of seven variations on a Renaissance melody titled "Spagnoletta" that is derived from a popular melody titled "Españoleta" or "Little Spanish Tune." The composer commented on his relationship with the melody and his use of it in his piece.

> I first knew this melody as quoted by Joaquín Rodrigo in his *Fantasia para un gentilhombre* for guitar and orchestra. I also found this tune in the 1970s in a collection of Renaissance songs for classical guitar, and I have played it in that form countless times over the years.... The beauty and elegance of the original tune resides in its simplicity, so I chose to present it at the outset of the piece in a clear and streamlined orchestration. The basic nature or character of each variation is revealed in the labels that are placed in the score:
>
> (Theme)
> Variation I. (A Cubist Kaleidoscope)
> Variation II. (Cantus in augmentation: speed demon)
> Variation III. (Carnival)
> Variation IV. (Tunes in the round)
> Variation V. (Spike)
> Variation VI. (Rewind/Fast Forward)
> Variation VII. (Echoes: a surreal reprise)[28]

This is not a march for wind ensemble and electronics by Amit Gilutz (b. 1983) is another work Cynthia Johnston Turner commissioned from DMA composition students at Cornell University. Gilutz spent part of his childhood on a military base in Israel and often would attend military ceremonies and parades with his family in which he encountered both the roar of jet planes and a marching band playing its repertoire of marches and songs. He was very attracted to the "Hercules" airplane which was the largest vehicle he had ever seen and which gave off deafening noises and flames from its jets. The playing of the marching band was always an insignificant background sound to the spectacular display of air power and technology. The composer stated:

> In [*this is not a march*] I am exploring the gap between the sterile representation of wars and technology in the mainstream media and culture and the realities of those conflicts.... I went back to the official march of the Israeli military and electronically stretched and manipulated it, trying to symbolically reveal a certain truth it held and which was hidden.

It became an austere and dysfunctional slow piece ... perhaps a funeral march.... The original recording of the march is played through speakers towards the end of the piece, but it is framed within the larger piece in a way that is alienating and distancing. The players [in the ensemble] do not participate in the playing of the march. *this is not a march* is an attempt to refract the relationship of the wind ensemble and its militaristic history.[29]

James Lee III is a professor of composition/theory at Morgan State University in Baltimore. He was inspired to write *Ancient Words! Current Realities* in 2012 by biblical text from Luke 21:26-28:

Men's hearts failing them for fear, and looking after those things, which are coming on the earth: for the powers of heaven shall be shaken. And then shall they see the Son of man coming in a cloud with power and great glory. And when these things begin to come to pass, then look up, and lift up your heads; for your redemption draweth nigh.

Commenting on the piece, Lee wrote:

I have tried to provide a musical commentary on these verses that include the elements of delicate dissonances, relative security, and a world engulfed with pleasure and revelry. As the music continues, there are harsh dissonant chords that evoke the panic and strife for some people as the result of the global financial crisis and extreme weather conditions.... From time to time delicate dissonances transform into beautiful, gorgeous sonorities evoking nostalgia for a time of more youthful innocence and a carefree world of ease.[30]

Composer Alexandre Lunsqui (b. 1969) considered his camping in Death Valley to be one of the most incredible experiences of his life. Among the impressive sights in Death Valley National Park is Ubehebe, a volcanic crater composed of colorful layers of sediments that have undergone a continuous process of transformation and renewal over thousands of years. When Lunsqui was asked to write a piece for Due East (a duo consisting of Erin Lesser, flute and Greg Beyer, percussion) and the Lawrence University Wind Ensemble, he decided to compose one that would pay homage to this fantastic place and titled it *Ubehebe*. The collaboration of a duo of flute and percussion with a wind ensemble makes *Ubehebe* a very unique work.[31]

Sheltering Sky is a striking departure from the high energy and virtuoso style music usually composed by John Mackey. Commissioned by the Traughber Junior High School Band (Rachel Maxwell, director) and Thompson Junior High School Band (Daniel Harrison, director), Mackey's piece is very simple and serene. Like Percy Grainger, who wrote an original folk-like tune for his *Colonial Song*, Mackey also creates original folk-like tunes for his composition (however, there are "hints of the contours and colors of 'Danny Boy' and 'Shenandoah'"). Jake Wallace, program note author, comments on the piece:

> Mackey avoids traditional triadic sonorities almost exclusively, instead choosing more indistinct chords with diatonic extensions (particularly seventh and ninth chords) that facilitate the hazy sonic world that the piece inhabits. Near cadences, chromatic dissonances fill the narrow spaces in these harmonies, creating an even greater pull toward wistful nostalgia. Each new phrase begins over the resolution of the previous one, creating a sense of motion that never completely stops. The melodies themselves unfold and eventually dissipate until at last the serene introductory material returns—the opening chords finally coming to rest.[32]

Narong Prangcharoen (b. 1973) is a Thai composer whose compositions have won him international acclaim and numerous awards including the prestigious $15,000 2013 Barlow Composition Prize. He is recognized as one of Asia's leading composers. On April 26, 2012, the University of Missouri-Kansas City Wind Symphony, Steven Davis, conductor, premiered *Anātman*, a work for Cello and Wind Ensemble. Prangcharoen provided the following words about the piece:

> A Sanskrit word, Anātman is usually referred to as the notion of "selflessness" or "self-illusion." In the doctrine of Buddhism, the word Anātman is commonly used in a context to teach that all things perceived by the senses are not actually "me" or "mine" so one should avoid attaching oneself to them.... The solo cello symbolizes a soul and self against distractions around it presented by the ensemble.... The music is mainly divided into three sections. The first begins with a chanting-like melody focusing on the main note "E". The music moves around the central note as if the mind is trying to find a real soul. The second mainly focuses on a melodic idea derived from an old lullaby of Northeastern Thailand.... The last section is fast and vigorous, using the same material as the first section but in a different manner.... The piece concludes with fast and loud music with the re-emphasis of E, the principal note of the entire piece.[33]

Zach Stanton (b. 1983) was encouraged to write a piano concerto by his teacher, Dan Welcher, and a friend, Dr. Damon Talley. They reminded him that the number of concerto-type works for wind ensemble was considerably less than those for orchestra and that wind ensemble conductors would welcome a new piano concerto for their medium. In 2012 Stanton acted upon their suggestion and composed his *Concerto for Piano and Wind Ensemble.* Cast in a traditional three-movement form, the work's first movement has three distinct themes: a stately fanfare-like theme, a fast scherzando theme, and a chorale.... The second movement is a simple slow Romantic movement that recalls the slow movements of Shostakovich, Barber, and Ravel piano concertos. The final movement is a knuckle-buster for the soloist, with fistfuls of notes from beginning to end. It finds its inspiration in jazz/rock, bringing the concerto to a close on a very loud and very high note.[34]

* * * * * * * * * *

Gerard Schwarz (b. 1947), for many years music director/conductor of the Seattle Symphony Orchestra, conducted the U. S. Marine Band in the premiere performance of his first work for wind band/ensemble, *Above and Beyond*, on March 12, 2012. Gwyn Parry-Jones, in his review of the work wrote,

> ... [the piece] develops into a really fine and rather thrilling work, skillfully scored for the forces available. This is not surprising in that Schwarz is an experienced and distinguished conductor of this type of repertoire. There is a surprisingly thoughtful ending, the woodwind winding the music down over rumbling percussion, with occasional snarls from muted brass. This is a work I'd commend strongly to music directors of wind bands, with the proviso that it's not only technically pretty demanding, but also requires a very fully 'staffed' band. A real find.[35]

ENDNOTES

1   Daniel Kellogg, "Composer's Program Note," Ball State University Wind Ensemble, College Band Directors National Association, National Conference 2011, concert of March 23, 2011.
2   Shawn E. Okpebholo, "Composer's Program Note," Boise State Symphonic Winds, College Band Directors National Association, National Conference 2011, concert of March 24, 2011.
3   Ibid.

4   Joel Puckett, "Avelynn's Lullaby: Program Note," Joel Puckett, Composer, accessed June 20, 2018, http://joelpuckett.com/music/lullaby/.

5   Jess Langston Turner, "Burning Music: Overview," Jess Langston Turner, accessed June 20, 2018, http://jesslturnermusic.com/music/burning-music.

6   "Sea-Blue Circuitry for orchestra or wind ensemble: Program Notes," Mason Bates, accessed June 20, 2018, http://www.masonbates.com/work/work-seabluecircuitry.html.

7   Jon C. Mitchell, "Paul Robert Marcel Fauchet: Symphonie pour Musique d'Harmonie (Symphony in B-Flat)." *Journal of Band Research* 20 (1985): 11–12.

8   Anderson Alden, "About Tonight's Music," Yale Concert Band, concert of December 2, 2011.

9   Nathan Prillaman, "About Tonight's Music," Yale Concert Band, concert of December 2, 2011.

10   "Symphony No. 6 (manuscript)," Andrew Boysen Jr., Composer, accessed June 20, 2018, http://www.andrewboysenjr.com/about1-c1z4h.

11   "Concerto for Cello," Steven Bryant: Composer/Conductor, accessed June 1, 2018, https://www.stevenbryant.com/music/catalog/concerto-for-cello.

12   "Daydreams (2010) for Wind Ensemble. Program Notes," Takuma Itoh, Composer, accessed June 20, 2018, http://www.takumaitoh.com/music/daydreams.html.

13   Chen Yi, *Dragon Rhyme For Symphonic Band*, Theodore Presser Company, accessed June 20, 2018, https://www.presser.com/shop/dragon-rhyme-104534.html.

14   "Sound and Smoke for wind band. Program Notes," Viet Cuong, Music, accessed June 20, 2018, http://vietcuongmusic.com/sound-and-smoke.

15   "Commissions: Donald Grantham Commission," Charles Villarrubia, accessed June 20, 2018, http://www.charlesvillarrubia.com/commissions#!home/mainPage.

16   "Wind Ensemble & Band Works: Mysterium. Program Notes," Jennifer Higdon, accessed June 20, 2018, http://jenniferhigdon.com/pdf/program-notes/Mysterium.pdf/.

17   "Program Note," Emory University Wind Ensemble, concert of April 20, 2011.

18   "Catclaw Mimosa (2011)," Ben Hjertmann, Composer, accessed June 20, 2018, http://www.benhjertmann.com/catclaw-mimosa.

19   Jake Wallace, "Foundry (2011) for concert band with 'found' percussion," Osti Music: The Website of Composer John Mackey, accessed June 10, 2018, http://www.ostimusic.com/Foundry.php.

20   Ibid.

21   Rickey Hauoli-Deponte Badua, "The Maverick: An Analytical Study of Carter Pann's *Symphony for Winds: My Brother's Brain (2011)*." (D.M.A. diss., University of Georgia, 2014), 13–14.

22   "Shanghai Overture," Bright Sheng: Composer, Conductor & Pianist, accessed June 20, 2018, http://brightsheng.com/programnotes/Shanghaioverture.html.

23   "The End of the World: Program Note," Michael Schelle, Composer, accessed June 20, 2018, http://schellemusic.com/8.html.

24   "WASBE 2011 Conference Concert Reviews," Tim Reynish, accessed June 20, 2018, http://www.timreynish.com/conferences/wasbe-2011-conference-concert-reviews/.

25 Steven Bryant, "Solace: Wind Ensemble + Electronics (2012)" (Steven Bryant/ Gorilla Salad Productions, n.d.) Perusal Score, accessed June 20, 2018az, https://www.stevenbryant.com/music/catalog/solace-band.

26 "Program Notes," University of Michigan Band, concert of April 12, 2013.

27 "Point Blank: Program Notes," Paul Dooley, accessed June 20, 2018, https:// www.pauldooley.net/works/pointblankband.

28 *Flourishes and Meditations*, United States Marine Band, Michael J. Colburn, director, USMB CD-27, 2011, Liner notes by Michael Gandolfi.

29 "Commissions and Premieres: *this is not a march*—Amit Gilut," *CBDNA Report* (Spring 2012): 4.

30 "Program Note," St. Olaf Band [St. Olaf College, Northfield, Minnesota], concert of March 21, 2013.

31 "Program Note," Lawrence University Wind Ensemble, concert of March 21, 2013.

32 Jake Wallace, "Sheltering Sky (2012) for concert band," Osti Music: The Website of Composer John Mackey, accessed June 10, 2018, http://ostimusic.com/ ShelteringSky.php.

33 "Anātman for Cello and Wind Ensemble: Quick Overview," Theodore Presser Company, accessed June 20, 2018, https://www.presser.com/shop/ anatman-98313.html.

34 "Concerto for Piano and Wind Ensemble," Zack Stanton, Composer, accessed June 20, 2018, http://www.zackstantonmusic.com/news/2016/5/12/ concerto-for-piano-and-wind-ensemble-mvt-i.

35 Gwyn Parry-Jones, review of *Above and Beyond*, "The President's Own" United States Marine Band/Gerard Schwarz (Naxos Wind Band Classics 8.573121) MusicWeb International, http://www.musicweb-international.com/ classrev/2014/Jul14/Above_beyond_8573121.htm.

CHAPTER 18

Advancing—Old and New Voices (2013)

> *2013 CBDNA Conference • Cancellation of 2013 WASBE Conference • A Klezmer Piece • Concertos for Tuba, Bassoon, Clarinet, Saxophone, Saxophone Quartet, and String Quartet*

CBDNA President Stephen Peterson, writing in the Spring 2013 issue of CBDNA *Report*, commented on the evolution of wind band/ensemble literature during the previous three decades.

> When considering all of the music we've heard in the past twenty years at [CBDNA] conferences, certain trends appear. Wind music seems to be moving through "phases" as time moves forward. These phases are reflective of the times, as art should be. As we might hope, the music we heard last month [at the March 2013 CBDNA Conference] sounds different from much of that heard ten, twenty, or thirty years ago. While we still have work to do in the area of repertoire development, we have made huge strides, and can thank the leaders of the past twenty years (and before) who have piqued the interest of many of today's top-shelf composers, and brought our own sound world closer to the discussions about classical music in other realms.[1]

The instrumentation used by composers of the better wind band/ensemble works written between the 1990s and 2010s, often included instruments that were not employed by earlier composers (i.e., electronic and non-Western instruments). Augmenting the wind band/ensemble's instrumentation and sound resources expanded the timbre, textural, and expressive capabilities of the medium.

Ten new works were premiered at the CBDNA National Conference which was held in Greensboro, North Carolina, on March 20–23, 2013.

Steven Bryant	*Solace*
Brett William Dietz	*Spiritual: Concerto for Alto Saxophone and Wind Ensemble*
James Lee III	*Ancient Words! Current Realities* (2012)
Scott Lindroth	*Alarm Calls*
Alexandre Lunsqui	*Ubehebe*
John Mackey	*The Frozen Cathedral*
John Mayrose	*Bending Light*
Mike Mower	*Concerto Maxo Mosso*
Joel Puckett	*Short Stories*
John Fitz Rogers	*Narragansett*

Steven Bryant's *Solace*, Brett William Dietz's *Spiritual: Concerto for Alto Saxophone and Wind Ensemble*, James Lee III's *Ancient Words! Current Realities*, John Mayrose's *Bending Light*, and Alexandre Lunsqui's *Ubehebe* were all composed in 2012. However, they did not receive their premiere performance until the 2013 CBDNA National Conference. (Read about Bryant's and Lunsqui's works in Chapter 17.)

Scott Lindroth (b. 1958) wrote *Alarm Calls* for the University of North Carolina at Greensboro Wind Ensemble, John Locke, conductor. The composer offered the following comment about the piece:

> *Alarm Calls* is an urgent call to action. The music continually repeats an insistent melody that suggests an emergency or threat that never appears. The mood is unsettled and unstable, with stark contrasts between transparent textures and sudden eruptions from the full ensemble. Even when the music takes on a more sustained or lyrical character, the ticking percussion figures remind us of the earlier agitated music. The ending recasts the opening section in more heroic terms.[2]

John Mackey (b. 1973) composed *The Frozen Cathedral* in 2012. John Locke, conductor of the University of North Carolina at Greensboro Wind Ensemble and a member of the commissioning consortium, asked Mackey to dedicate the piece to the memory of his late son, J. P., who had a particular fascination with Alaska, especially the scenery of Denali National Park. Mackey agreed—and immediately found himself grappling with two problems. The first was how to write a concert closer, "making it joyous and exciting and celebratory, while also acknowledging, at least to myself, that this piece is rooted in unimaginable loss: The death of a child?" The second was "... connecting the piece to Alaska—a place I'd never seen in person." Mackey comments on how his wife came to his rescue.

> I kept thinking about all of this in literal terms, and I just wasn't getting anywhere. My wife, who titles all of my pieces, said I should focus on what it is that draws people to these places. People go to the mountains—these monumental, remote, ethereal and awesome parts of the world—as a kind of pilgrimage. It's a search for the sublime, for transcendence. A great mountain is like a church. "Call it *The Frozen Cathedral*," she said.[3]

A program note by Jake Wallace describes Mackey's piece.

> ... The initial sonic environment is an icy and alien one, a cold and distant landscape whose mystery is only heightened by a longing, modal solo for bass flute ... and [made] more insistent by the eventual addition of alto flute, English horn, and bassoon.... Just as it seems their wailing despair can drive no further, however, it shatters like glass, dissipating once again into the timbres of the introductory percussion.
>
> The second half of the piece begins ... remarkably similar to the first.... the bass flute takes up the long solo again, it resonates with far more compatible consonance.... Now, instead of anger and bitter conflict, the melody projects an aura of warmth, nostalgia, and even joy.... [A] new chorale, led in particular by the trombones, is a statement of catharsis, at once banishing the earlier darkness in a moment of spiritual transcendence and celebrating the grandeur of the surroundings. A triumphant conclusion in E-flat major is made all the more jubilant by the ecstatic clattering of the antiphonal percussion, which ring into the silence like voices across the ice.[4]

Concerto Maxo Mosso by Mike Mower (b. 1958) is a virtuoso two-movement work for saxophone quartet and wind orchestra. It was commissioned by the Osland Saxophone Quartet and the University of Kentucky Wind Symphony. The composer stated that since the Osland Quartet "sits comfortably between jazz and classical music, [I decided] to give the piece a jazz tinge with some Samba and Partido

Alto rhythms interjecting here and there. The first movement is in the shape of an arch which creeps in and faces away. Odd time signatures creep into the second movement, jostling for importance against the Latin groove."[5]

Short Stories: Concerto for String Quartet and Wind Orchestra by Joel Puckett (b. 1977) was premiered by the University of North Carolina at Greensboro Wind Ensemble, Kevin Geraldi conductor, with members of the Melver Quartet as soloists. It is a twenty-two minute long work that consists of eight short movements that are grouped into three distinct parts. The opening and closing movements of the piece serve as a "frame" for the three pairs of linked movements in each of the three parts.

Part I:
      1. Somewhere near the end [tutti]
      2. Introit [quartet]
      3. The Priests [viola and cello duet]
Part II:
      4. Recitative [quartet]
      5. mother and child [violin duet]
Part III:
      6. sonno agitato [ensemble alone]
      7. The Bridge [cadenza] [quartet]
      8. Ma Fin [tutti]

In a program note for the piece, Jacob Wallace wrote:

> What makes the construct of the short story itself so unique among other literary devices is the demands placed on the author to create a meaningful narrative. They must describe the relationships between characters, present a conflict, and resolve it in a remarkably short span.... . Joel Puckett's *Short Stories* is a study in structure. On the surface, it bears the appearance of eight vignettes strung together into a concerto for solo string quartet and wind ensemble. Upon listening, however, the work's movements reveal themselves as inextricably linked through a layered thematic language that plays out through a sort of "game of pairs."[6]

The music of John Fitz Rogers (b. 1963) has been performed in many major concert venues and by ensembles such as the Pittsburgh New Music Ensemble, Albany, Louisville, Charleston, and Tulsa Symphony Orchestras, and the Eastman Wind Ensemble. The inspiration for *Narragansett* came about as the result of Rogers's visit to the picturesque New England town of Narragansett, Rhode Island, to attend a friend's wedding. The music reflects "... the sometimes quiet, sometimes crashing surf; the bright autumn colors and beautiful blazing sun; the dramatic, rocky coast; the tranquility of ... tidal shallows."

Included in the fifty-eight works performed at the 2013 CBDNA Conference was *Elegy*, a short piece originally composed in 1965 for orchestra by John Corigliano (b. 1938). It is a very nostalgic and intimate work composed in a Neo-Romantic American style and is dedicated to Samuel Barber. Christopher Anderson created the wind band version of the piece in 2012.

Listed below are more works that were premiered in 2013. Composers continued to explore the expressive potential and sound resources found in the wind band/ensemble.

Susan Botti	*sull'ala* (Concerto for Saxophone and Wind Ensemble)
Andrew Boysen	*This is the Drum*
Michael Daugherty	*Labyrinth of Love for Soprano, Winds, Piano, Contrabass and Percussion*
Mohammed Fairouz	*Symphony No. 4, "In the Shadow of No Towers"*
Adam Gorb	*Love Transforming*
Kenneth Hesketh	*Autumn's Elegy*
Stephen Gryc	*Six Romances after Mendelssohn*
David Maslanka	*Requiem*
Scott McAllister	*Gone*
Kevin Puts	*Network*
Donald Grantham	*Let Evening Come*
James Stephenson	*A Dialogue of Self and Soul* (Concerto for Bassoon and Wind Ensemble)
John Williams	*For "The President's Own"*
Dana Wilson	*Concerto for Tuba and Wind Ensemble*

Susan Botti's eclectic background and experiences are reflected in her music. Theatre and the visual arts play an important role in the aesthetic of her work. Her music encompasses traditional, improvisational, and non-classical composition and singing styles. *Sull'ala* (Concerto for Saxophone and Wind Ensemble) is a twenty-eight minute, three-movement work (1. Propulsion—murmuration 1; 2. Torque—murmuration 2; 3. Aloft) which was premiered on October 5, 2013, by the Hartt Wind Ensemble, Glen Adsit, conductor, and Carrie Koffman, saxophone soloist. Botti (b. 1962) provided the following information about *sull'ala*:

Sull'ala (on the wing) is inspired by flight. Some of the different physical properties of flight suggested to me different musical expressions
of rhythm, harmony, texture … The relationship of soloist to ensemble
reflects the individual flier's relationship to surrounding elements. The
murmurations are small bridge movements for the soloist and sax sextet. A *murmuration* is a group of starlings, whose mesmerizing group
acrobatics fill the sky in sweeping clouds.[7]

On March 31, 2013, at the Japan Wind Ensemble Conductors Conference (JWECC), a special "super" band (consisting of nineteen individual bands) premiered *This is the Drum* by Andrew Boysen (b. 1968).
According to the composer, the inspiration for this piece came from an
interview Bruce Duffie did with Morton Gould in 1988. Boysen stated
that he was struck by how much he agreed with Gould's words.

He was discussing what makes some pieces succeed and others fail, and
he spoke of the way that certain works seem to have a visceral impact
on the listener. He said, "This is the drum," referring to the ability of
drums to immediately connect with us. I have chosen to honor Morton
Gould by attempting to create a piece which makes that visceral impact
and features the drum in many ways. The basic material for the piece
comes from the opening motive of Gould's most famous work, *American
Salute*. The piece also includes the use of a marching machine, famously
used by Gould in his *Symphony for Band*.[8]

The Times of London has called Michael Daugherty (b. 1954) a
"master icon maker." "His idiom bears the stamp of classic modern-
ism, with colliding tonalities and blocks of sound. At the same time,
his melodies are infectious, and the rhythmic structures are driving
and energetic."[9]

Daugherty very often derives his works from popular culture figures ranging from American icons Elvis and Superman to Jacqueline
Kennedy and artists like Diego Rivera and Frieda Kahlo. The world
premiere of the wind version of the *Labyrinth of Love for Soprano,
Winds, Piano, Contrabass and Percussion* took place on October 6,
2016, in Coral Gables, Florida, and was performed by the University
of Miami Wind Ensemble, Gary D. Green, conductor, with Hila Plitmann as soprano soloist.

The composer provided the following information about his piece:

Labyrinth of Love is inspired by the love poetry and prose by eight women:
Sappho (612 BC–570 BC; Greek), Lady Mary Wroth (1587–1653; British),

Juana Ines de la Cruz (1651–1695; Mexican), Mary Shelley (1797–1851; British), Elizabeth Barrett Browning (1806–1861; British), Emily Dickinson (1830–1886; American), Elizabeth Taylor (1932–2011; American), and Anne Carson (b. 1950; Canadian). The texts I have selected, and the musical landscape I have created, is full of bitterness, desire, longing, ecstasy, irony, tenderness, despair, hope, sadness and humor.[10]

Mohammed Fairouz (b. 1985) in his first major work for wind ensemble, *Symphony No. 4, "In the Shadow of No Towers,"* grapples with the aftermath of the terrorist attack of September 11, 2001. His piece is inspired by the provocative 2004 graphic novel *In the Shadow of No Towers* by Art Spiegelman. Spiegelman, reacting to Fairouz's symphony stated, "I'm moved by [this] scary, somber and seriously silly symphony.... I'm honored that the composer found an echo in my work that allowed him to strike a responsive chord and express his own complex responses to post 9/11 America."[11]

Fairouz's thirty-eight minute *Symphony* evokes the cataclysm of 9/11 and its repercussions—from the personal to the national—over the following years. It is a deeply emotional piece which was premiered by the University of Kansas Wind Ensemble, Paul W. Popiel, conductor, in Carnegie Hall on March 26, 2013.

Two new works, both ten minutes in length, were premiered at the Royal Northern College of Music in Manchester, UK, on March 9, 2013, to celebrate the seventy-fifth birthday of Timothy Reynish. The first, *Love Transforming* by Adam Gorb (b. 1958), is a work of great intensity that makes use of spatial effects with pairs of trumpets in side balconies and a pair of saxophones in the rear of the hall. It is built from a number of small motifs, each featuring a different section of the ensemble, with a central chorale marked *pppp*. The critic of the *Manchester Evening News* described it as "both evocative and a model of how to write clearly and imaginatively for unusual textures." The second work, *Autumn's Elegy* by Kenneth Hesketh (b. 1968), is a work in "slow 4/4 time, luxuriously scored with a series of lyrical themes emerging from the textures."[12] Timothy Reynish is a conductor and self-appointed critic and reviewer of worldwide wind band/ensemble music, recordings and conferences. His comments can be read on his website, http://www.timreynish.com.

Stephen Gryc (b. 1949), besides being Professor of Composition and Theory at the Hartt School of Music in Hartford, Connecticut, has also been Director of the Hartt Contemporary Players, the Institute for Contemporary American Music, and Co-Director of the Center for Computer and Electronic Music. His wind piece, *Six Romances after Mendelssohn*, was commissioned by the University of New Mexico and premiered by its Wind Ensemble, Eric Rombach-Kendall conducting, on May 1, 2013. The composer harbors a great admiration for Mendelssohn's music, especially the "luminous instrumental colors and haunting lyricism" found in his orchestra music.

> [My *Six Romances after Mendelssohn*] is based on the opening tune of the composer's third symphony, the *Scottish Symphony*, which features the same ten wind instruments employed in my romances. This music is Mendelssohn at his moody, melodious best. The romances of the title of my piece refer not only to love stories but also to tales of heroism, exoticism and fantasy.[13]

Requiem by David Maslanka (1943–2017) was commissioned by a consortium of twelve ensembles and premiered by the Brooklyn Wind Symphony, Jeff W. Ball, Conductor and Artistic Director, on June 15, 2013. A relatively short single-movement instrumental fantasia, it is Maslanka's response to a single Holocaust event in World War II—the death of a one year-old baby. The composer stated,

> It is not possible truly to grasp the deaths of millions of people, but the death of one, in this case a year-old baby—brought me face-to-face with the horror and revulsion of the whole. We think that history is past, and nothing can change it. But the effects of such things as the Holocaust are still immediately with us; the open wound has not been healed. It is my feeling that music can bring closure, and it is my hope that *Requiem* will serve in this capacity.
>
> [My] ... *Requiem* is not a Mass, but serves a parallel function—the need to lay to rest old things in order to turn the mind and heart toward the new.... I do believe that we are in a major transitional time, and that this transition happens first in each of us. My *Requiem* is both for the unnamed dead of all wars, and for each person making their own inner step, saying goodbye in order to say hello.[14]

All adventurous clarinetists are familiar with the works of composer Scott McAllister (1969). His *X Concerto* and *Black Dog* have become standard pieces in the repertoire for the instrument. McAllister's *Gone* is a transcription of the sixth movement of his sixty-minute long concerto for clarinet, the *Epic Concerto*. The composer penned the following words about the piece:

Each movement of the [*Epic Concerto*] relates to different pillar moments of my life as a clarinetist. In 1994, my playing career was ended in an automobile accident. *Gone* is about loss and the emotions and process of healing and learning to move on after a life-changing event.... [The inspiration for the piece] was the death of my mentor James Croft, and the wonderful influence he was in my life with his encouragement to never forget about writing for band.[15]

A concert performed by the University of Texas Wind Ensemble on October 27, 2013, featured premiere performances of two new works: a wind transcription of an orchestra work by Pulitzer Prize winner Kevin Puts (b. 1972) and a new composition by Texas faculty member Donald Grantham. Puts's work, *Network*, was originally written for the California Symphony. It was transcribed for wind ensemble by Ryan Kelly, a DMA conducting assistant at the University of Texas. Puts provided the following comment about his work:

Network is a short, explosive fanfare that uses a recurring eight-voice canon of busy sixteenth notes to generate all the music in the piece. It is as if this "network" of melodic lines is always happening in the background, but only pieces of it are actually played at any given moment by the instruments in the orchestra.... [The work] wasn't inspired by anything in particular. It is driven by the pure enjoyment of chords and rhythm and orchestral sounds.[16]

Donald Grantham's work, *Let Evening Come*, is a setting of Jane Kenyon's beautiful and descriptive poem of the same name. Originally composed as a choral piece in 2009, it is a beautiful, serene work of richly woven melodic and harmonic lines in slow tempo that is "atmospheric in its impact."

James Stephenson (b. 1969) came late to full-time composing. After graduating from high school, he studied trumpet at the New England Conservatory (NEC) and played in the Wind Ensemble, which I conducted. Following his graduation from NEC, Stephenson spent the next seventeen years playing trumpet in the Naples (Florida) Philharmonic before embarking on his career as a composer. Largely self-taught, Stephenson writes music that is fresh, energized, and attractive to audiences.

His *A Dialogue of Self and Soul, Concerto for Bassoon and Wind Ensemble* was inspired by a poem of the same name by William Butler Yeats. Stephenson said he never intended a Yeats poem to shape his concept for a bassoon concerto. However, he recalls that he was "...

directed by happenstance to the Yeats poem, and [was] very taken by its meaning." *A Dialogue of Self and Soul* is a twenty-minute long work in two contrasting movements with a solo bassoon part that is "intended to be accessible [by] almost all levels of player; not too difficult for the young player, but also musically rewarding and stimulating for the seasoned professional."[17]

Stephenson's piece was premiered on April 1, 2014, by bassoonist Norbert Nielubowski and the University of Minnesota Wind Ensemble, Craig Kirchhoff, conductor. One of the unique features of the work is an optional solo voice part (text from Yeats's poem) which can be inserted at the end of the second movement.

John Williams's close relationship with the Marine Band began in 2003, when he conducted them in a concert of his music celebrating the Band's 205th anniversary at the Kennedy Center in Washington, D. C. In 2005, when he was informed that he was to receive a Kennedy Center Honors award, he requested that the Marine Band be invited to perform at the awards program. In 2013, Williams composed a piece, *For "The President's Own"*, and presented it to the band as a token of his high esteem for the Band and in celebration of the Marine Band's 215th anniversary. The piece is a virtuosic mixture of intertwining lines, playful themes and bright fanfares that captures the many colors and textures that are characteristic of Williams' inimitable music.

Dana Wilson (b. 1946) has composed numerous concertos for wind instruments and wind ensemble. In 2012, inspired by the artistry and technique of tubist Aaron Tindall, he wrote his *Concerto for Tuba and Wind Ensemble* which was premiered by Tindall and the Ithaca College Wind Ensemble, Stephen Peterson, conductor, on March 1, 2013. The composer shared his ideas about writing a piece for tuba.

> So many of the traditional works featuring the tuba emphasize its humorous and very low capabilities. In recent decades, performers and their corresponding literature have featured the lyrical, mid-range warmth of the instrument. My *Concerto for Tuba* certainly draws upon this latter evolution, but is also designed to exhibit the many dramatic and virtuosic abilities of the great contemporary tuba soloists by placing the soloist in three very distinct musical settings, one in each movement. The movements are linked by common thematic material in order to create an organic whole.[18]

* * * * * * * * * *

Hankus Netsky's composition, *Nonantum Bulgar,* is the four-teenth work in the American Composers Forum's *BandQuest* series. It was premiered by the 5th–8th grade students in the Newton All City Band, under the direction of Gary Fox and Elaine Ropi. Netsky (b. 1955) is a multi-instrumentalist, composer, ethnomusicologist, and founder/director of the Klezmer Conservatory Band, an interna-tionally renowned Yiddish music ensemble. The composer provided the following background information about the piece:

> Since my local middle school (F. A. Day) is located in close proximity to Nonantum, the oldest area of Newton, MA, I decided to imagine the dedication of the Adams Street Shul, our city's oldest synagogue, which took place around a hundred years ago (December 15, 1912). According to the Yiddish and English poster announcing the dedication, the event featured a prominent Boston cantor, a choir and a klezmer orchestra leading a 'Grand March' down Adams Street The piece tries to re-create what the klezmer band might have played on that occasion. A "Bulgar" is a Romanian Jewish Dance that was very popular among Jewish immi-grants at the beginning of the twentieth century.[19]

* * * * * * * * * *

During the 2011 International WASBE Conference in Chiayi City, Taiwan, President-Elect Odd Terje Lysebo (Norway) announced to the Board of Directors that, due to financial difficulties, the con-ference organizing committee in Pécs, Hungary, had withdrawn its commitment to host the 2013 International Conference. When Terje Lysebo became president, at the end of the conference, he immedi-ately began working with Board member Rafael Sans-Espert (Spain) to re-schedule the 2013 International Conference in Valencia, Spain. After a great deal of effort, the negotiations with Valencia fell apart. In lieu of the cancelled conference, the WASBE Board of Directors did meet on July 18 and 19, 2013, in Kerkrade, The Netherlands, to discuss the challenges confronting the Association and its future.

ENDNOTES

1   Steve Peterson, "From the Podium," *CBDNA Report* (Spring 2013): 1.

2   "Program Notes," Michigan State University Symphony Band, concert of October 27, 2015.

3   Jake Wallace, "The Frozen Cathedral (2013) for wind ensemble," Osti Music: The Website of Composer John Mackey, accessed June 10, 2018, http://ostimusic.com/Cathedral.php.

4   Ibid.

5   "Program Note," University of Kentucky Wind Symphony, concert of March 22, 2013.

6   Jacob Wallace, "Short Stories: Program Note," Joel Puckett, Composer, accessed June 20, 2018, http://joelpuckett.com/music/shortstories/.

7   "sull'ala (Concerto for Saxophone and Wind Ensemble)," Susan Botti. Composer/Performer, accessed June 20, 2018, http://www.susanbotti.com/works/sullala.html.

8   "This is the Drum (manuscript)," Andrew Boysen Jr., Composer, accessed June 20, 2018, http://www.andrewboysenjr.com/about1-c1frk.

9   "Program Note," University of Michigan Symphony Band, concert of March 11, 2016.

10 "Labyrinth of Love for Soprano, Winds, Piano, Percussion and Strings (2013): Program Note," Michael Daugherty, accessed June 20, 2018, http://www.michaeldaugherty.net/index.cfm?id=180&i=20&pagename=works.

11 "Symphony No. 4, 'In the Shadow of No Towers' (2012): Note from Art Spiegelman," Mohammed Fairouz, accessed June 20, 2018, http://mohammedfairouz.com/work/symphony-no-4-in-the-shadow-of-no-towers/.

12 "Commissions and Premieres: Autumn's Elegy—Kenneth Hesketh," CBDNA Report (Spring 2013): 4.

13 "Program Note," University of Michigan Symphony Band, concert of March 15, 2016.

14 "Requiem: Description [and] Program Note," David Maslanka, accessed June 20, 2018, http://davidmaslanka.com/works/requiem-2013-11/.

15 Andy Pease, "Gone by Scott McAllister," Wind Band Literature: A Conductor's Perspective, 2012, accessed June 20, 2018, http://windliterature.org/2014/05/03/gone-by-scott-mcallister/.

16 "Works: Network for orchestra (1997)," Kevin Puts, Composer, accessed June 20, 2018, http://www.kevinputs.com/program/network.html.

17 Jim Stephenson, "A Dialogue of Self and Soul: Notes from the Composer," Stephenson Music, accessed June 20, 2018, https://composerjim.com/works/a-dialogue-of-self-and-soul-bassoon-concerto-piano-reduction/.

18 Dana Wilson, email to the author, January 18, 2018.

19 Hankus Netsky, "Editorial Reviews," Amazon.com, accessed June 20, 2018, https://www.amazon.com/BandQuest-Nonantum-Bulgar-Concert-Composed/dp/B00PCKZAOO.

CHAPTER 19

More Composers Discover the "String-less" Band (2014)

More Third Stream and Crossover Works • Literary Inspired Works for Winds • André Previn's "Music for Wind Orchestra" (No Strings Attached)

The 2014 CBDNA Eastern Division Conference was held at the New England Conservatory (NEC) from March 6–8. Entitled "Crossing Over—Wind Music Created from a Diverse Musical World," it focused on the influence and core inspiration of a variety of different styles/kinds of music: ethnic, jazz, commercial popular music, etc., on wind band/ensemble literature. Charles Peltz, conductor of the NEC Wind Ensemble and Conference host, articulated the purpose of the Conference.

> The world of music grows smaller as sounds from all corners of the globe are brought to us with breathtaking immediacy. With each generation, the interest of musicians in other music grows as does resistance to the constraints of genres. The mission of this conference is to introduce ideas and music, to initiate thinking and start conversations about how the world of wind music engages with this larger world. It does not attempt to answer all questions or address all issues. Rather, it attempts to clarify the challenges and highlight the rewards when embracing the larger world of music, and moreover, to envision the place of wind music in that larger world.[1]

The opening concert of the Conference on March 6, 2014, was performed by the NEC Wind Ensemble and Symphonic Winds, Charles Peltz and Bill Drury, conductors. Entitled, "Headwaters of the Third Stream," it included premiere performances and repertoire recollections of the origins of the crossover movement, ranging from Babbitt's *All Set* (1957) to Schuller's newest work in the genre, *From Here to There* (see program below).

NEC Symphonic Winds
William Drury, director

Solar Return Suite	Guillermo Klein

Jerry Bergonzi, Tenor Sax

Sarah Vaughan/Count Basie Song Book	arr. Sammy Nestico
Concerto for Bass Trombone and Orchestra	Chris Brubeck

Matthew Erickson, Bass Trombone

Intermission

NEC Wind Ensemble
Charles Peltz, director

All Set	Milton Babbitt
From Here to There	Gunther Schuller

World Premiere

Half Mast Inhibitions	Charles Mingus
Dog Breath Variations	Frank Zappa

Steve Elman, in his review of Schuller's piece for *The Arts Fuse* (Boston's online Arts magazine), wrote,

> [*From Here to There* is] a thrilling, powerful experience as contemporary classical music, and a very welcome addition to Schuller's Third Stream library. *From Here to There* navigates a new current in Schuller's Third Stream. The convergence here is not an engagement between living performers of jazz and classical, but an homage from a living master of composition to a deceased master of improvisation. Schuller's description from the program explains that he wanted to write a piece for winds that would begin very simply and build to a "totally chaotic ending." Simultaneously, he wanted to memorialize his friend Dave Brubeck, who had died in December 2012. Brubeck's work gave Schuller a working concept: he noted that some of the Brubeck solos he most admired "started very simply and calmly and then grew incrementally

into gigantic climax[es], so rhythmically and harmonically complex that one thought that this pianist had suddenly acquired more than ten fingers." Schuller transcribed and orchestrated one of these, from a 1999 performance of *Take Five*, and then "camouflaged Dave's solo behind a curtain of other sounds," and, as he self-effacingly describes the process, "surround[ed] it with some typical Schuller." This hardly does justice to the result—a piece that begins and ends in the most intimate way, at first bluesy and at the conclusion elegiacally, and in between erects a great ascending mountain of sound, punctuated by Brubeck's signature swing-feel 5/4.[2]

Other ensembles performing concerts at the Conference were:

UMass Amherst Symphony Band, James Miller, conductor
Gotham Wind Symphony, Michael Christianson, conductor
Hartt School Wind Ensemble, Glen Adsit, conductor
The College of New Jersey Wind Ensemble, David Vickerman, conductor
Temple University Chamber Winds, Emily Threinen, conductor
West Chester University Wind Ensemble, Andrew Yozviak, conductor.

Included among the works performed by these ensembles were:

Louis Andriessen (b. 1939)	*M is for Man, Music and Mozart* (Hartt School Wind Ensemble)
Mason Bates (b. 1977)	*Mothership* (The College of New Jersey Wind Ensemble)
Gunther Schuller (1925–2015)	*Headin' Out, Movin' In* (Temple University Chamber Winds)
James Syler (b. 1961)	*Minton's Playhouse* (West Chester University Wind Ensemble)
Jeff Tyzik (b. 1951)	*Riffs* (UMass Amherst Symphony Band)

One of the highlights of the Conference (and there were many) was a conversation-interview between composers David Amram and Gunther Schuller, which was moderated by Thomas Duffy of Yale University. Both composers have lived lives dedicated to championing, creating, and producing music without boundaries. The remarks delivered by Amram were particularly poignant and are quoted in full, as follows:

I am not a "Cross Over" composer or a "Third Stream" composer any more than Bartók, Tchaikovsky, Borodin, Vaughn Williams, Mendelssohn (see his *Scotch Symphony*), Beethoven, or Mozart (see their Turkish marches), Bach (see the German hunting and drinking songs which he incorporated at the end of his Goldberg Variations) or ANY of the acknowledged masters who used in their work music from other parts of the world as well as folkloric music from their own neighborhoods that they LOVED to hear and wanted others to hear and honor.

All the idioms, which SOMETIMES appear in my written out compositions, are musics which I have learned to PLAY and SING and have over the years become part of my life, long before I included them as the basis for SOME of my compositions.

So when I occasionally include these idioms in my written down work, I am not "crossing over." I am already THERE!!!!

I am not a tourist "slumming." I am already at home!! And I have more than one hometown.

Just as we can learn to speak more than one language and eat more than a steady diet of hamburgers and fries, or whatever is convenient and easy to obtain, ALL the sincere musics of the world are valid, strong, and VITAMINS FOR THE SOUL, since they survived for centuries, and also are often of historical value to show what it was like to be there in the environments where the composers created music often inspired by these forms of roots music. And they are worth spending a lifetime in kindergarten, in order to learn the fundamentals of these endless varieties of musical treasures.

So what I do is not "Crossover."

These forms of music have become PART OF MY LIFE, just as the music of Haydn and Brahms are part of my life.

I never leave Palestrina and Bach chorales as the basis for what I do.

And the sonata, theme and variations, and rondo forms are always great help in creating something that has STRUCTURE and FORM so that neither the performers nor the audience need 25 pages of instructions to know what the music is about.

I am simply INCLUDING others forms of sincere and heart-felt music which have become part of what I have learned to be at home with through a lifetime of being open to LEARN MORE of whatever touches my heart, rather than being enslaved by what I am told is the hip new thing and cutting edge flavor of the month.

Today's fashion is usually guaranteed to end up in tomorrow's landfill. A thing of beauty IS a joy forever. And the world contains an infinite treasure chest of beautiful music to inspire composers.[3]

A number of masterclasses, clinics and presentations rounded out the Conference schedule. Among them were the following:

1. "What Makes It Ethnic?" presented by Hankus Netsky, one of the world's experts in Klezmer and other ethnic musics. His presentation dealt with "authentic performances" of music from other cultures.

2. "Sounds as Written." Frederick Harris, conductor of the MIT Wind Ensemble, presided over a panel of three composers— Michael Gandolfi, John Mackey, and David Sanford—who discussed how they wrote music that they first heard as improvised.

3. "Tango!" Pablo Aslan, bassist and tango musician, led a coaching session on various aspects of the tangos in Michael Gandolfi's *Vientos y Tangos*.

In 2014, more composers joined the long list of those who had already discovered the fulfillment and profitability of writing music for the "string-less" band. Below is a list of works that are representative of the various styles of music composed at the time.

Robert Beaser	The End of Knowing
Steven Bryant	all stars are love
Steve Danyew	Alcott Songs, for Soprano and Chamber Winds
Paul Dooley	Coast of Dreams
Michael Gandolfi	Winding Up/Winding Down, for Clarinet and Wind Ensemble
John Mackey	Wine-Dark Sea: Symphony for Band
Clint Needham	Concerto for Wind Ensemble
André Previn	Music for Wind Orchestra (No Strings Attached)
Gunther Schuller	From Here to There
Shuying Li	Slippery Slope
Peter Van Zandt Lane	Hivemind
Chelsea Williamson	Dreams of Another Time

The End of Knowing, a song-symphony for soprano, baritone, and wind ensemble, was commissioned by a consortium of twenty-seven bands/wind ensembles. Composer Robert Beaser (b. 1954) uses the poetry of Seamus Heaney, Alfred Noyes, Joseph Brodsky, Gjertrud Schnackenberg, Chidiock Tichborne, Theodore Worozbyt, and James

Joyce to create a twenty-eight minute long dramatic meditation on the connection of religion, politics, and the delicate human condition. The piece was premiered on September 25, 2014, by the Michigan State University Wind Symphony, Kevin Sedatole conducting, with Lindsay Kesselman and Benjamin Park as soloists.

Steven Bryant (b. 1972) composed the original version of *all stars are love* (setting of a poem by E. E. Cummings) as a surprise gift for his wife, Verena, for their wedding in Austria in 2010. Later, fellow composer and friend, Eric Whitacre, suggested he consider doing an instrumental version of the piece. A commission offer from the Colorado University Wind Ensemble afforded Bryant the opportunity to do so. When working on the piece Bryant found it necessary to recompose large portions of the work. Thus, the wind ensemble version of *all stars are love* contains much new music although the expressive shape and harmonic progression at the core of the original version of the piece remain intact.

Steve Danyew (b. 1983) is the recipient of numerous national and international awards. His *Alcott Songs* (for Soprano and Chamber Winds) is a witty and whimsical song cycle consisting of six short pieces with clever, playful texts by the nineteenth century American author Louisa May Alcott. The songs are organized so as to depict a carefree summer day. They begin with a light, dance-like song and end with a soft, dreamy lullaby.

Coast of Dreams by Paul Dooley (b. 1983) was commissioned by a consortium of wind ensembles organized by the State University of New York at Fredonia, Paula Holcomb, conductor. The fifteen-minute, two movement work (1. "Flowers of Our Lost Romance"; II. "Velocity Festivals") is a musical tribute to early Los Angeles. In his program note, Dooley wrote about the inspiration for the piece.

> Inspiration came when I visited El Alisal, a rustic home built by Charles Lummis in the late 1800s, located in Arroyo Seco in Northeast Los Angeles. Lummis was a *Los Angeles Times* journalist, an Indian rights activist, a historian, photographer, and all around Southern California guru. When at El Alisal, I discovered one of the first Southern California lifestyle magazines, *Land of Sunshine*, published by Lummis beginning in the late 19th century. I began to hear a composition in two movements as an emotional, cultural and musical exploration of this romantic vision of Southern California.[4]

Winding Up/Winding Down by Michael Gandolfi (b. 1956) was commissioned by a consortium of twenty ensembles. It is a ten-minute, single movement serenade for clarinet and wind ensemble which was generated by an audio crosswalk signal that Gandolfi heard in Harvard Square on his way home in Cambridge, Massachusetts. He stated,

> The rhythmical phasing of two of these signal-beacons is quite striking, so I decided to build this pulsed dance into an elaborate passage that provides the introductory (and main) material for the piece. There are many sections in the work, featuring the clarinet in virtuosic as well as lyrical guises and accompanied by various instrumental groupings, all of which are placed in an overall form that is suggestive of a condensed, introduction-fast-slow-fast-coda, concerto design."[5]

Gandolfi dedicated *Winding Up/Winding Down* to William Wrzesien who he describes as "… an extraordinary clarinetist, brilliant musician … whose artistry I was fortunate to observe during my developmental years as an NEC student.[6]

When John Mackey (b. 1973) was commissioned to compose a piece for the 100th anniversary of the Sarah and Ernest Butler School of Music at the University of Texas, Austin, wind ensemble conductor Jerry Junkin requested that he write a piece of approximately thirty minutes in length. Mackey's immediate reaction to this request was "How can I put together a piece that large?" Abby, his wife, provided him with an idea—"why not write something programmatic and let the story determine the structure." Mackey took her advice and turned to Greek mythology for ideas and inspiration. He decided to write a piece that traced Odysseus's epic journey home after the Trojan War as told by Homer in the *Odyssey*. His wife wrote a truncated version of this story and Mackey set about setting it to music. The result was *Wine-Dark Sea: Symphony for Band* which was premiered by Jerry Junkin and the University of Texas Wind Ensemble at the Texas Music Educators Association convention in San Antonio, Texas, on February 13, 2014. The three movement work (I. "Hubris"; II. "Immortal thread, so weak"; III. "The attentions of souls") is a musical portrayal of Odysseus's arduous journey home over an ocean that Homer called a "wine-dark sea."[7]

The *Concerto for Wind Ensemble* by Clint Needham (b. 1981) won the 2014 Walter Beeler Memorial Prize. The piece was commissioned by the Baldwin Wallace Conservatory Symphonic Wind Ensemble and premiered by the ensemble on March 28, 2014, with Dwight Oltman conducting. It is a virtuosic tour-de-force piece that challenges every performer in the ensemble. The composer offered the following comment about the piece:

> Cast in three continuous movements, the first ... opens with a musical flourish that contains the musical DNA for everything that follows ... [the] movement is quite propulsive and often employs a rhapsodically darker tone than the other movements.
>
> The second movement is a calm balance to the frenetic energy to the first. [It is] a slow-moving musical tapestry where textural and harmonic changes occur organically....
>
> The final movement begins with an extended section devoted to the percussion.... A great deal of musical material used in this movement is suggestive of both jazz and rock genres.
>
> To link each movement together, an electronic track [was] created that takes on the energy of the music at hand. The only non-segue electronic music is found at the very end of the work, which is added to enhance the already wild and hectic environment as the music sprints to the end![8]

Music for Wind Orchestra (No Strings Attached) was composed by André Previn (b. 1929), one of the world's most celebrated, distinctive, and varied contemporary musicians. It was premiered at a concert titled "Celebrating André Previn at 85" which was held at the Eastman School of Music on October 10, 2014.

Music for Wind Orchestra (No Strings Attached) is a large three-movement work (marked "fast, slow, fast," respectively) for full wind band/ensemble instrumentation. The score received by conductors in the commissioning consortium contained minimal markings/ instructions concerning tempo, dynamics, articulation, and phrasing. (When Previn was asked about the absence of this information, he replied, "You'll figure it out.") The lack of this information made for varying interpretations and realizations of Previn's piece. Charles Peltz, conductor of the New England Conservatory Wind Ensemble and one of the first consortium conductors to conduct the piece, wrote the following program note about Previn's piece.

> The first movement, in a three part A B A' form, opens boldly with a starter's pistol of percussion followed by a sound wall of formidable bitonal chords. This dense brilliance leads into transparent yet energetic

Eastman Wind Ensemble
Celebrating André Previn at 85
Mark Davis Scatterday, Conductor
Friday, October 10, 2014
Kilbourn Hall, 8 PM

Music of André Previn

Triolet for Brass (1985)
  Opening
  Very still
  Fanfare
  Waltz
  Interlude 1
  Interlude 2
  From a Distance
  Chubbs

Trio for Oboe, Bassoon, and Piano (1994)
  Lively
  Slow
  Jaunty

Octet for Eleven (2010)
  1. = 92
  11. = 42
  111. = 132

INTERMISSION

Award of the Honorary Doctor of Music Degree to André Previn
Joel Seligman, President
University of Rochester
Jamal J. Rossi
Joan and Martin Messinger Dean, Eastman School of Music

Vocalise for Soprano, Cello, and Winds (1995)
arranged by Mark Davis Scatterday
                    Megan Moore, soprano
                    Alexa Ciciretti, cello

Music for Wind Orchestra (No Strings Attached)
  1. Tempo 1
  II. Slow
  111. Fast

World Premiere

phrases of melody—lyrical but often gymnastic—supported by the major 7th and 9th chords, altered chromatically, which will be a harmonic base for the piece. A shadow of sonata form is recognized as an exact recapitulation brings back the opening heraldic music, ending then with brass hammers in a final cadence.

The second movement begins as dark and reflective as the first movement began brilliantly and impetuously. This slow second is the soloist's movement with every voice getting a moment to comment in miniature ariettas. Surprise measures of quasi-aleatoric trumpet and clarinet duet exclamations serve as the center point of this meandering movement. The music wanders into the distance as the trumpet asks a fading question.

The third movement is all dance and capriciousness. Mixed meters, syncopations, gestural glissandos and slides call the players and listener to be free and to dance. A nod to the British band tradition is found in a rugged country dance middle passage—done up right with a modal melody in striding low brass. It all comes to a final conclusion with a B major chord—a brilliant half step up from the oft-used band key of B-flat. In that half step rise Previn concludes his own contribution by lifting up the wind orchestra by an inspired step.[9]

Composer Shuying Li (b. 1989) grew up in China. After the completion of her freshman year at the Shanghai Conservatory of Music she traveled to the United States and studied at the Hartt School of Music and the University of Michigan. Her compositions have been performed by the Seattle Symphony Orchestra as well as ensembles in the Netherlands, Finland, Romania, Canada, and Italy. *Slippery Slope*, Li's two-movement work for winds, was commissioned and premiered by the Hartt School Wind Ensemble, Glen Adsit, conductor, on February 7, 2014. Later that year the piece won the ASCAP/ CBDNA Frederick Fennell Prize. Shuying Li wrote the following about the piece:

> The first note of *Slippery Slope* was put to paper only after I had the whole second movement in mind—at that time, this was [the] one and only movement. And it was not until I had almost finished the movement that I developed ideas about the third movement, and the first, chronologically.
>
> While the second movement, or the main movement explores various relationships between two different musical personalities (one rigid and angular, the other lyrical and emotional), and constrains every possible growth from developing into a final climax until the very last

moment, the third movement offers the audience straightforward and undisguised excitement with the partially humorous, partially passionate journey as it takes so much effort to arrive at the peak (the second movement is indeed the longest) before slipping down the slope. Consider the first movement as a mystifying preparation interrupted by several "trailers"—fragments from the subsequent two movements, that either reveal or obscure what will happen next.[10]

Peter Van Zandt Lane (b. 1985) is an American composer and bassoonist who performs regularly in the Boston area. He composed *Hivemind* when he was in residence at the MacDowell Colony in the spring of 2014. It was commissioned by the Sydney Conservatorium Wind Symphony (Australia), John P. Lynch, conductor, for their inaugural Estivo Festival in Verona, Italy. It is a fast-paced, energetic piece in which the composer explores the idea of consensus building:

> Scattered themes and fragments gradually come together into more cohesive units. Melodies emerge from buzzing textures, trying to make sense of conflicting harmonies. Instruments imitate each other in different ways, until they finally agree on how the music goes, in the more climatic moments of the piece. The ensemble is grounded by two percussionists ... who constantly bounce rhythms back and forth ... (until they, also, coalesce into unity).[11]

Chelsea Williamson (b.1989) was a DMA composition student at the University of Oklahoma when she composed *Dreams of Another Time*. The idea of incorporating klezmer music into a piece came to her after hearing clarinetist Martin Fröst play a piece entitled *Klezmer Dances*. "Hearing that piece sparked a strong interest in this music and a desire to try writing my own." *Dreams of Another Time* began as work for a modified klezmer ensemble (clarinet, soprano saxophone, violin, cello, trumpet, trombone, and electric bass) and orchestra and then became a piece for wind ensemble in which solos pass throughout the group during its three movements. The composer derives much inspiration and understanding from the music of J. S. Bach. "I began to play with the idea of melding a chorale with klezmer. The chorale that resonated deeply with me was "Christ Lag in Todesbanden" (Christ Lay in the Bonds of Death).... it appears in the first and third movements blended with klezmer [and creates] a beautiful tension between the two.[12]

* * * * * * * * * *

On August 31, 2014, Glen Adsit announced the formation of ASPIRE, the Institute for Advancement of Secondary and Primary Instrumental Repertoire Excellence. The objective of the institute is to commission works for high and middle school instrumentalists from excellent composers who have never written music for these groups. In an email message announcing the formation of ASPIRE Adsit wote:

> I am seeking a 5-year ($1,250.00 total) commitment from at least two high schools and two middle schools in every state. With 200+ schools participating, I think we could commission three or four composers each year to write a 4–10 minute work. I propose that every year, we commission two composers to write a grade 3 work. The third composition would be a grade 4 and the fourth a grade 5. In this way we would end up with ten grade 3 compositions, five grade 4 compositions and five grade 5 compositions. Of course if we have greater participation than expected we could commission more works. If we have fewer we will only commission a couple of pieces a year.

For their first round of commissions, ASPIRE commissioned works from William Bolcom, Steven Bryant, Jennifer Jolly, and Kristin Kuster.[13]

* * * * * * * * * *

At their 2014 convention, the American Bandmasters Association announced they would collaborate with the U. S. Navy Band to produce a DVD about Karel Husa's *Music for Prague 1968*. This DVD was produced and released in 2018, the 50th anniversary of the premiere performance of *Music for Prague 1968*. It includes a video of Husa conducting rehearsals and a performance of *Music for Prague* with the Navy Band, a video of the composer talking about his piece, and a discussion about the historical significance of Husa and *Music for Prague* by five ABA members closely associated with Husa: Mark Scatterday, Thomas Duffy, Terry Austin, Dennis Zeisler, and Frank Battisti.

ENDNOTES

1   Charles Peltz, College Band Directors National Association Eastern Division Conference, Program Book (March 6–8, 2014), 1.

2   Steve Elman, "Fuse Concert Review: NEC Winds Play Mingus, Schuller, Babbitt (and More)," *The Arts Fuse* (March 12, 2014), http://artsfuse.org/102460/fuse-concert-review-nec-winds-play-mingus-schuller-babbitt-and-more/.

3   David Amram, "Eastern Division CBDNA Conference, Opening Remarks," *WASBE Journal* 21 (2014): 138–139.

4   Paul Dooley, "Coast of Dreams (2014) for Wind Ensemble/Paul M Dooley [notated music]: Summary," The Library of Congress, Performing Arts Databases, accessed June 20, 2018, http://memory.loc.gov/diglib/ihas/loc.music.ismn.49908/default.html.

5   Michael Gandolfi, *Winding Up/Winding Down for Bb Clarinet and Wind Ensemble* (M51 Music, 2014), [Full score] Program notes.

6   Ibid.

7   "Wine-Dark Sea: Symphony for Band (2014) for wind ensemble," Osti Music: The Website of Composer John Mackey, accessed June 10, 2018, http://ostimusic.com/WineDarkSea.php.

8   Clint Needham, *Concerto for Wind Ensemble*, Theodore Presser Company, accessed June 20, 2018, https://www.presser.com/shop/concerto-for-wind-ensemble.html?SID=bb861bc751c745efff86c0e9ead84631.

9   Charles Peltz, "Programme Note: André Previn, *Music for Wind Orchestra (No Strings Attached)* (2014), Music Sales Classical, accessed June 20, 2018, http://www.musicsalesclassical.com/composer/work/49709.

10 "2014 ASCAP/CBDNA Frederick Fennell Prize Winner Announced," ASCAP, accessed June 20, 2018, https://www.ascap.com/press/2015/0115-2014-ascap-cbdna-frederick-fennell-prize-winner.aspx.

11 "Hivemind: Program Note," Peter van Zandt Lane, Composer, accessed June 20, 2018, http://www.petervanzandtlane.com/work-hivemind.html.

12 "Program Note," University of Central Oklahoma Wind Symphony, concert of October 11, 2015.

13 Glen Adsit, email to the author, August 31, 2014.

CHAPTER 20

Towards 2020 (2015)

National and International Conferences • The Expanding Number of Commissioned Works • Gender and Ethnicity issues

Unlike the concerts at the 2009, 2011, 2013 CBDNA National Conferences, in which at least ten new works were premiered each year, there were only three new works premiered at the 2015 Conference.

1. Mason Bates: "Chicago, 2012" from *Alternative Energy* (2014) (version for wind ensemble and electronica) premiered by the Florida State University Wind Orchestra, Richard Clary, conductor.

2. John Mackey: *Fanfare for Full Fathom Five* (2015) premiered by the Columbus State University Wind Ensemble, Jamie L. Nix, conductor.

3. Stephen Andrew Taylor, arranger: *Spirituals* (2014) premiered by the Illinois Wind Symphony, Linda R. Moorhouse, conductor; Ollie Watts Davis, soprano

"Chicago, 2012" is an extract from Mason Bates's *Alternative Energy* (2014), an "energy symphony" spanning four movements and hundreds of years. Beginning in a rustic Midwestern junkyard in the late 19th Century, the piece travels through ever greater and more powerful forces of energy—a present-day particle collider, a futuristic Chinese nuclear plant—until it reaches a future Icelandic rainforest, where humanity's last inhabitants seek a return to a simpler way of life.[1] Bates (b. 1977) spent a whole year composing, editing, proofing, and mixing at Skywalker Studios to create *Alternative Energy*, which he dedicated to Maestro Riccardo Muti and the Chicago Symphony. Muti and the Symphony premiered the piece on February 2, 2014.

In "Chicago 2012" Bates juxtaposes the brash sounds of a jazzy brass section with the pops, hisses, and whooshes of the particle accelerator FermiLab, a huge facility that searches for energy's secrets by spinning and smashing atoms.

Fanfare for Full Fathom Five by John Mackey (b. 1973) is scored for 6 trumpets, 6 horns, 6 trombones (3 tenor, 3 bass; or 3 tenor, 2 bass, 1 contrabass), 2 tubas, and 4 percussionists, with optional organ. The title of the piece is taken from Shakespeare's play, *The Tempest*, where Shakespeare's text refers to a drowning during a storm and shipwreck in about five fathoms (30 feet) of water. Jake Wallace, in his program note for the piece, wrote:

> The orchestration and architecture of the piece is designed to be analogous to Richard Strauss' *Wiener Philharmoniker Fanfare*, but where Strauss' fanfare is emotionally straightforward with bounds of unstoppable heroism, Mackey's is more complex, taking the traditional fanfare rhythms and motifs and blurring them with a whirlwind of dissonance through chromaticism and murky glissandi that present the whole in a darker and more sinister context. All of the typical hallmarks of the future genre are present: vibrantly articulated triplets in the trumpets, soaring horn lines, and brash pedal points in the low brass (doubled colorfully by the organ). The harmonic language is one of abrupt shift; the blustery opening seems to clearly establish B-flat major as the home key, but each time it seems to reaffirm this notion, it veers wildly into unexpected territory. The piece ends triumphantly in E-flat.[2]

Stephen Andrew Taylor (b. 1965) often explores boundaries between art and science in his music. His first orchestra piece, *Unapproachable Light*, was inspired by images from the Hubble Space Telescope and the New Testament. *Spirituals* was derived from a four-movement piece Taylor originally wrote in 2014 for string quartet and soprano. The composer said this about *Spirituals*:

If there is a single source, or wellspring, of American music, it must be the spirituals: They are so deep and powerful, full of history, suffering and joy. Their profound simplicity terrifies and inspires me. As an American musician, I have always felt like I should offer up something to this great repertoire.... So these arrangements are both an homage to this deep current of American music, and to two great composers, teachers and musicians—Hall Johnson (1888–1970) and Betty Jackson King (1928–1994).[3]

The majority of pieces performed at the Conference concerts were composed between 2000–2015. However, a number of pieces composed during the twentieth century were also performed, including Paul Hindemith's *Symphonic Metamorphosis on Themes of Carl Maria von Weber* (arr. Wilson) (1943), Vincent Persichetti's *Psalm for Band* (1952) and *Symphony No. 6* (1956), Aaron Copland's *Emblems* (1964), David Amram's *King Lear Variations* (1967), Don Freund's *Jug Blues and Fat Pickin'* (1986), and John Harbison's *Three City Blocks* (1991).

The numerous "breakout sessions" during the Conference were informative and stimulating. Included among them were the following:

"Stanislaw Skrowaczewski's *Music for Winds*"—Adam V. Fontana
"Vincent Persichetti at 100: An Examination of the Man, His Music, and His Contributions to the Wind Band"—Andrew Mast
"Pedagogy for Musical Expression: Perspectives from Professional Wind Instrumentalists and Conductors"—Brian Gibbs
"Rediscovering Nineteenth-Century Transcriptions for Winds: Beethoven's *Symphony No. 1* and *Wellington's Sieg*"—Jonathan Caldwell
"A Conductor's Analysis of Kurt Weill's *Concerto for Violin and Wind Orchestra*, Op. 12"—Gerard Morris
"Music Education from the Podium"—Mark Fonder and Elizabeth Peterson

* * * * * * * * * * * * *

The works listed below, written in 2015, were composed by an ethnically diverse group of composers who were inspired by a variety of subjects including architecture, ancient Chinese music, global warming, a revolutionary painting, civil rights, and Negro slave music.

James Barnes	Symphony No. 8
William Bolcom	Inventing Flight (transcribed by Jason Nam)
Chen Yi	Ba Yin (The Eight Sounds), for Saxophone Quartet and Chamber Winds

Nigel Clarke	A Richer Dust (Symphony No. 1 for Speaker and Wind Orchestra) (libretto by Malene Sheppard Skærved)
Michael Daugherty	Reflections on the Mississippi for Tuba and Symphonic Band
Michael Daugherty	Winter Dreams
Paul Dooley	Masks and Machines
David Gillingham	Vital Signs of Planet Earth
Michael Kurek	Monument
Steven Mackey	Songs from the End of the World
Michael Markowski	Monk by the Sea
Carter Pann	The High Songs for Amplified Cello and Chamber Winds
Narong Prangcharoen	Lokuttara
Marco Pütz	Time for Outrage
James Stephenson	Song of Myself for Soprano and Wind Ensemble
James Syler	Congo Square for African Drum Quartet and Wind Ensemble
Dana Wilson	Concerto for Contrabass and Wind Ensemble
Dana Wilson	Concerto for Trombone and Wind Ensemble

Michael Daugherty (b. 1954) composed *Reflections on the Mississippi* for tuba and symphonic band in memory of his father, Willis Daugherty (1929–2011). It was commissioned and premiered by the University of Michigan Symphony Band, Michael Haithcock, conductor, with Carol Jantsch (Philadelphia Orchestra) as tuba soloist on February 6, 2015. The concerto is a musical reflection on family trips taken to the Mississippi River near McGregor, Iowa, during the composer's childhood. In July and October 2012, Daugherty returned to the Mississippi River to make two road trips along the "Great River Road." He recalled "[exploring] small river towns and [snapping] photographs of scenic river vistas. Local boat owners also guided me to the secluded wildlife havens and murky backwaters of the Mississippi River. All the while I was collecting sounds, musical ideas and emotional framework for my tuba concerto." He concluded,

> Much as the tuba plays a central role in Zydeco and Second line music of New Orleans, the tuba soloist in my concerto leads a "second line" of syncopated rhythms that propels the concerto to a virtuosic conclusion.[4]

Masks and Machines by Paul Dooley (b. 1983) was commissioned by a consortium of wind bands to honor Gary Green on his retirement from the Frost School of Music at the University of Miami. The early twentieth century works of Bauhaus artist Oskar Schlemmer, as well as the Neoclassical music of Igor Stravinsky inspired the work. The composer stated that he admired "the simplicity of shapes and color in Schlemmer's works such as the *Bauhaus Stairway* and *Triadic Ballet* as well as the renaissance and baroque musical influences in Stravinsky's *Pulcinella*. *Masks and Machines* contains three contrasting character pieces featuring renaissance brass music, Baroque *fortspinnung* in virtuosic mallet percussion, lush oboe, clarinet, and bassoon solos, and machine-like flute rips."[5] *Masks and Machines* was the co-winner of the 2015 William D. Revelli Composition Contest.

Chen Yi (b. 1953) composed the wind version of *Ba Yin* for the Prism Quartet and the University of Missouri-Kansas City Wind Ensemble, Steven Davis, conductor. Its instrumentation includes flute, oboe, clarinet, bassoon, French horn, trumpet, trombone, and 2 percussionists.

The original version of the piece was premiered by the Rascher Saxophone Quartet and the Stuttgart Chamber Orchestra on October 27, 2001, in Stuttgart, Germany. The composer wrote the following about the piece:

> In ancient China music was played with eight kinds of instruments made of or with metal, stone, silk, bamboo, gourd, clay, leather and wood. It was then called "The Eight Sounds:" (Ba Yin). In my [piece], I use a saxophone quartet and a string orchestra [later a wind ensemble] to recall my impression of what I have heard in China, the music played by villagers on old traditional instruments in various ensembles. The first movement is entitled "Praying for Rain." It's inspired by the music played in the ritual ceremony, featuring blowing instruments suona (shawm, made with wood) and sheng (free-reed mouth-organ, made with gourd).
>
> The second movement is called "Song of the Chu" (name of a country in Zhou Dynasty, located in the middle of China). It's influenced by a traditional Chinese instrumental solo piece with the same title, featuring the sound of xun (blowing instrument, made from clay).... "Shifan Gong-and-drum," the title of the third movement, is taken from the name of the ensembles of "silk-and-bamboo with gong-and-drum" in the Southeast.[6]

Vital Signs of Planet Earth is a concerto for bass trombone and wind ensemble composed by David Gillingham (b. 1947). It was premiered by the Central Michigan University Symphonic Wind

Ensemble, John E. Williamson, conductor, on February 19, 2015, with George Curran, bass trombonist of the New York Philharmonic, as the soloist. The piece is an expression of the composer's concern about the effects of global warming. Each of its three movements portrays a crisis brought on by global warming: Heat Wave, Glacial Retreat and Deluge. "Heat Wave" depicts the "undulating waves of heat [through conflicting] half step movement, timpani and trombone glissando, and edgy clusters in the low brass." "Glacial Retreat" "reflects the dichotomy of the awe and beauty of the glacier and the concern over the dire effects of their retreat." The final movement, "Deluge," portrays the devastation brought on by "'walls' of water."[7] Throughout the piece the solo bass trombone reacts and provides commentary to each of these three events.

Songs from the End of the World is a twenty-one minute long song cycle by John Mackey (b. 1973), with text by A. E. Jaques, for soprano and chamber wind ensemble (Flute/Alto Flute, Oboe/English Horn, 2 B-flat Clarinets, Bass Clarinet/Contrabass Clarinet, 2 Bassoons, Double Bass, Harp, Piano, and 3 Percussion). It was commissioned by a consortium of fourteen universities and premiered by the University of North Carolina at Greensboro Wind Ensemble, Kevin Geraldi, conductor, with Lindsay Kesselman as soprano soloist, on November 19, 2015.

> "The cycle [was] inspired by a passage in the *Odyssey* [Mackey's *Wine-Dark Sea: Symphony for Band* was also inspired by Homer's *Odyssey*] in which Odysseus, shipwrecked and near death, washes up on the shore of an island belonging to the nymph Kalypso. Homer's telling treats the ensuing interlude as just another bit of exotic travelogue, one of many adventures on Odysseus's long journey home; these three songs imagine what it meant to Kalypso herself, and are sung in her voice."[8]

Monk by the Sea by Michael Markowski (b. 1986) was commissioned by ten universities/colleges in Arkansas. It was inspired by a German Romantic landscape painter, Caspar David Friedrich (1774–1840), whose revolutionary painting, *Der Mönch am Meer (The Monk by the Sea)*, was deemed shocking and controversial when it was painted. Now it is considered to be an excellent example of early abstract painting. It depicts a lone man "cloaked in black [standing] on a barren outcropping [meditating on] a dark expanse of choppy waters that recedes into a murky grey mass of clouds." Jacob Wallace, who penned the program note for *Monk by the Sea* wrote,

> Markowski . . . certainly includes several overt foreground references to images included in Friedrich's work. An oscillation in the lowest register of the piano has the sensation of unstill waters, while an inventive series of sliding artificial harmonics on contrabass mimics the cries of seagulls. The similarities, however, are not limited to sound effects. The lush harmonic language is one of mysterious nostalgia, more reminiscent of mid-20th century neoromantic composers like Howard Hanson and Miklós Rózsa than of more contemporary styles.[9]

The High Songs for Amplified Cello and Chamber Winds by Carter Pann (b. 1972) was premiered on October 11, 2015, by the University of Central Oklahoma Wind Symphony, Brian Lamb, conductor, with Tess Remy-Schumacher as the cello soloist and the composer playing piano. Pann stated that soon after beginning work on the piece he realized that the high tessitura of the cello would be featured throughout and that he would actually be writing songs for the instrument. "Nepenthe," the calm opening of the suite calls attention to the sedative nature of this calming elixir. In "Moto Perpetuo" the music barrels forward in a big-band style. "Passacaglias" casts the cello in a bel canto role, and "Adjusting the Torque" is a nod to fellow composer Michael Torke. The suite ends with a simple "Song for Heidi," which features a piano duet.

Narong Prangcharoen (b. 1973) wrote *Lokuttara* on a commission awarded by the Barlow Endowment for Music Composition at Brigham Young University. It was written specifically for the United States Marine Band, Brigham Young University Wind Symphony, and Florida State University Wind Orchestra. "Lokuttara" means Ultramundane [which] is the power that enables the mind to transcend beyond the world, or beyond the limits of our system. . . . [The] texture and timbre [is] inspired by chanting and praying . . . imitating the rhythm of speech or the singing of words or sounds, called 'reciting tones,' as in a [Tibetan] chant or a prayer. . . . *Lokuttara* consists of three main sections divided fast—slow—fast. Although the material is from the same pitch collection, the music in each section transforms into many different forms."[10]

Time for Outrage! by Marco Pütz (b. 1958) was commissioned by the Luxembourg Military Band and Frënn vun der Militärmusek a.s.b.l., and premiered by the Band at Luxembourg Philharmonic Concert Hall on March 26, 2015. The sixteen-minute long work is in three movements: 1. Breaking Silence, 2. Troubled—attacca—3. Rock the Culprits! Pütz describes the piece as being "… an expression of my personal aversion against all the current crises and injustice of any kind in the world."

> I am aware that I cannot alleviate or even eradicate these crises with my music, but as a free citizen I believe I have the right to express my indignation through music. As in *Meltdown* (1992), a protest against … nuclear power, in *Time for Outrage!* I try to cover up my weakness in this hopeless struggle with a pinch of sarcasm.
>
> Thus, the perpetrators in the third part (Rock the Culprits!) are not punished, but 'rocked' …
>
> If you are not outraged, you are not paying attention. In other words: if you are not indignant about what is happening anywhere in the world, you walk with blinkers.[11]

James Stephenson's *Song of Myself for Soprano and Wind Ensemble* and Dana Wilson's *Concerto for Trombone and Wind Ensemble* were both premiered on April 26, 2015, by the University of Minnesota Wind Ensemble under the direction of Craig Kirchhoff. Thomas Ashworth, trombone professor at the University, was the soloist in the concerto and contemporary music artist Lucy Shelton was the soprano soloist in *Song of Myself*. This was Craig Kirchhoff's final concert as Director of Bands at the University of Minnesota before retiring at the end of the 2014–15 academic year.

The University of Maryland Wind Orchestra, Michael Votta, conductor, premiered James Syler's *Congo Square for African Drum Quartet and Wind Ensemble* on February 27, 2015, at the University of Maryland. It was included in a trilogy of pieces, all composed by Syler, performed under the title *Three Places in Jazz* (the other two were *Storyville* and *Minton's Playhouse*). *Congo Square* is a twelve-minute composition commissioned by a consortium of twelve universities. It takes its inspiration from Congo Square in New Orleans, where in the 18th and 19th centuries Negro slaves were freed on Sunday afternoons to make music and dance. Syler uses the three musical styles associated with Congo Square in his piece: West African drumming, Creole, and early jazz.

Dana Wilson's *Concerto for Contrabass and Wind Ensemble* was composed "with deep admiration" for bassist and Ithaca College professor, Nicholas Walker. The Ithaca College Wind Ensemble, Stephen Peterson, conductor, with Walker as soloist, premiered the piece on April 12, 2015. The composer provided the following information about the work:

> When Nicholas Walker first approached me about writing a bass concerto for him, I became concerned. How could I get such a low instrument to project within the context of a large ensemble? How could this instrument, whose strings are so long and relatively slow to speak, generate the enormous musical energy that an entire concerto requires? Then, of course, I thought about Nicholas' special approach to the instrument and his excitement about its possibilities. What resulted was a piece that I hope matches his and others' musical sensibility while also exploring boundless technique. During this journey, the bass became for me a truly unique voice. The movement titles reflect this. They are adapted, respectively, from three of my favorite poems: *Song of Myself #25* by Walt Whitman; *Holy Spirit* by Hildegard von Bingen; and a variation on *Sailing to Byzantium* by W. B. Yeats.[12]

* * * * * * * * * * * *

By the second decade of the twenty-first century many university, college, and school wind bands/ensembles, large and small, were commissioning composers to write works for them. The majority of these groups participated as members of a consortium which made it possible for ensembles with limited budgets to participate in this important work. A select group of wind bands/ensembles possessed the financial resources needed to commission works independently. Included among these ensembles were the University of Kansas Wind Ensemble, University of Michigan Symphony Band, University of Texas Wind Ensemble, Michigan State University, University of Miami (Florida), Yale University and others. Following is a list of compositions commissioned independently and/or as a member of a consortium by the University of Kansas Wind Ensemble, University of Michigan Symphony Band, and the University of Texas Wind Ensemble, along with the date each of the works were premiered.

University of Kansas Wind Ensemble

Kevin Walczyk—*Songs of Paradise*	12/3/2011
Joni Greene—*Event Horizon*	11/2/2012
Michael Torke—*Mojave*	2/4/2012
James Barnes—*Anniversary Fanfare*	10/22/2013
Kip Haaheim—*Concerto for Bassoon, Electronics, and Winds*	10/22/2013
Michael Torke—*Bliss* (revised version)	10/6/2013
Forrest Pierce—*Ravenkind*	4/23/2013
Mohammed Fairouz—*Symphony No. 4, "In the Shadow of No Towers"*	3/26/2013
William Bolcom/arr. Frenkel—*Radical Sally and Over the Piano*	10/6/2014
James Barnes—*Concerto for Flute and Wind Orchestra*	4/15/2014
James Barnes—*Citadel, Op. 150*	11/12/2015
James Barnes—*Serenade, Op. 149*	4/19/2015
Mohammed Fairouz—*Sadat*	4/19/2015
Joel Puckett—*Knells for Bonnie*	4/18/2016
Nathan Jones—*Metropolis Triptych*	2/23/2016
Kevin Walczyk—*Symphony No. 5, Freedom From Fear*	4/29/2018

University of Michigan Symphony Band

Scott Lindroth—*Spin Cycle*	3/8/2002
Charles Young—*Concerto for Alto Saxophone*	4/13/2003
Joel Puckett—*Ping, Pang, Pong*	11/1/2004
Joshua Penman—*The Pilgrimage of Fire and Earth*	4/15/2005
Roshanne Etezady—*Anahita*	9/30/2005
Matthew Tommasini—*Three Spanish Songs* (wind version)	12/9/2005
David Little—*East Coast Attitude* (wind version)	4/7/2006
Andrew Mead—*Concerto for Winds*	10/25/2006
Elizabeth Kelly—*Jolt!*	12/6/2006
Evan Premo—*Concertino for Bass Fiddle*	12/8/2006
Eliza Brown—*oh lord, lay down my soul*	4/15/2007
Daron Hagen—*The Banner of My Purpose* (for solo baritone voice)	10/26/2007
Jeff Myers—*Organ-Tambura*	4/4/2008
Stephen Eddins—*Why I Live at the P.O.* (operetta)	10/12/2009
Michael Udow—*Moon Shadows* (for solo percussion)	10/23/2009
Daniel Pesca—*Forking Paths*	4/9/2010
Subaram Raman—*Madhavi's Dance at the Royal Court*	4/14/2010
Evan Hause—*Tango Variations*	10/23/2010
Bright Sheng—*Shanghai Overture* (wind version)	4/8/2011
Kristin Kuster—*Two Jades*	4/8/2011
Lembit Beecher—*Three Poems on the Sounds of the Human Heart*	10/21/2011
Christopher Dietz—*Chrysanthemum*	4/12/2013
Patrick Harlan—*Rapture* (wind version)	3/14/2014
Michael Daugherty—*Reflections on the Mississippi* (wind version)	2/6/2015
William Bolcom—*Circus Overture* (wind version)	3/13/2015

Karl Ronneburg—*blue-green*	9/28/2017
James Stephenson—*The Storyteller* (wind version)	9/28/2017
William Bolcom—*Concerto for Trombone* (wind version)	11/21/2017
Carlos Simon—*AMEN!*	11/21/2017
Judy Bozone—*Spilled Orange* (wind version)	11/16/2018
Jeremy Kittel—TBA (violin, cross-over artist)	Fall 2019
Kristin Kuster—New Piece	Calendar year 2020

University of Texas Wind Ensemble
Commissioned as part of a consortium

David Maslanka—*Concerto for Alto Saxophone and Band* (1999)	5/3/2000
Kenneth Amis—*Driven!* (2002)	10/30/2002
Steven Bryant—*Concerto for Wind Ensemble* (2007–10)	10/27/2010
Steven Bryant—*Concerto for Trombone and Wind Ensemble* (2016)	2/19/2016

Commissioned (not as part of a consortium)

Leonard Mark Lewis—*The Tall Extraordinary Light* (1999)	3/29/2000
Frank Proto—*Paganini in Metropolis for Clarinet and Wind Symphony* (2001)	2/21/2002
Jeffrey Nytch—*Acclamations* (2002)	10/2/2002
Donald Grantham—*Come, memory . . .* (2002)	10/2/2002
David Del Tredici—*In Wartime* (2003)	4/30/2003
HyeKyung Lee—*Sonatina for Soprano Saxophone and Wind Ensemble* (2002)	10/1/2003
John Corigliano—*Circus Maximus*, Symphony No. 3 (2004)	2/16/2005
Dan Welcher—*Symphony No. 4 "American Visionary"* (2005)	11/10/2005
Donald Grantham—*Concerto for Tuba* (2012)	4/28/2013
John Mackey—*Wine-Dark Sea: Symphony for Band* (2013–14)	2/13/2014
Bruce Pennycook—*The Giant's Tomb* (2014)	10/26/2014
Andrew Boss—*Tetelestai* (2014)	11/23/2014
Casey Martin—*The Autonomy of Machines* (2016)	1/19/2016
Christopher Rouse—*Supplica* (2016)	2/19/2016
Rob Deemer—*Pillars of Creation* (2015)	4/3/2016
Michael Barry—*Boomba* (2015)	10/23/2016
Adam Schoenberg—*Symphony No. 2* (2016)	3/18/2017
Jennifer Jolley—*The Eyes of the World Are Upon You* (2017)	3/18/2017
Casey Martin—*Ashen Skies of a Timeworn World* (2017)	4/30/2017
Dan Welcher—*Symphony No. 6, Three Places in the East* (2018)	4/29/2018

Commissioned Transcription/Edition

John Corigliano—*"Tarantella" from Symphony No. 1* (1990) (trans. Gershman)	10/31/2001
Kevin Puts—*Millennium Canons* (2001) (arr. Spede)	12/5/2001

John Corigliano—*Mr. Tambourine Man: Seven Poems of Bob Dylan* (2003) (trans. Mösenbichler)	3/27/2009
John Adams—*The Chairman Dances* from "Nixon in China" (1985–7) (trans. Cannon)	10/30/2011
John Corigliano—*Red Violin Chaconne* (1997) (trans. Lorenzo)	3/25/2012
Kevin Puts—*Network* (1997) (trans. Kelly)	10/27/2013
J. S. Bach—*Passacaglia and Fugue in c minor, BWV 582* (c. 1708) (arr. Stokowski, ed. Sosnowchik)	3/30/2014
Giovanni Bottesini—*Fantasia on Themes from "La Sonnambula"* (c. 1840) (arr. Kelly)	4/27/2014
John Corigliano—*Clarinet Concerto* (1977) (trans. Davis)	2/20/2015
Osvaldo Golijov—*Three Songs for Soprano and Wind Ensemble* (2002) (trans. Sosnowchik)	3/31/2015
Mason Bates—*White Lies for Lomax* (2015) (trans. Marinello)	11/22/2015
Aaron Jay Kernis—*Overture in Feet and Meters* (2015) (trans. Knight)	11/22/2015
Avner Dorman—*Astrolatry* (2011) (trans. Pompey)	4/3/2016
Sergei Prokofiev—*Visions Fugitives* (1915–1917) (trans. Missal)	2/19/2017
Derek Bermel—*Migration Series* (2017) (trans. Marinello)	2/19/2017
Adam Schoenberg—*Finding Rothko* (2006) (trans. Sample)	12/10/2017

* * * * * * * * * * * * *

Composer, conductor, French horn player, author, teacher, and wind band/ensemble friend and advocate Gunther Schuller (1925–2015) died on June 21, 2015. He was probably best known as the composer who coined the term "Third Stream" to describe music drawn from both classical and jazz forms and resources. Schuller began his musical career at age 15 (1943) as a French horn player with the American Ballet Theatre. From 1943–45, he was principal horn player with the Cincinnati Symphony Orchestra and, from 1945–59, with the Metropolitan Opera Orchestra. During his years at the Met he also performed with the Goldman Band and played and recorded with such jazz greats as Dizzy Gillespie and John Lewis.

Schuller stopped playing French horn in 1959 so he could devote all his time to composition, teaching, and writing.

In the 1960s and 1970s, Schuller served as president of the New England Conservatory (and founder of the New England Conservatory Ragtime Ensemble). He held a variety of postions at Tanglewood, the Boston Symphony Orchestra's summer home, from 1965 to 1984 serving as director of new music activities (1965–1969) and as artistic director of the Tanglewood Music Center (1970–1984).

Many of Schuller's best works are scored for selective and/or unusual instrumental combinations. His early *Symphony for Brass and Percussion* (1950) explores the capabilities of brass instrument performance and is one of his most widely performed works. *Spectra* is a study in orchestral color in which the orchestra is split into seven distinct groups that are deployed separately on the stage so that each can be heard independently or in combination with the others. He also composed *Five Pieces for Five Horns* (1952) and quartets for four double basses (1947) and four cellos (1958). His more than twenty concertos include showpieces for the double bass (1968), the contra-bassoon (1978), and the alto saxophone (1983), as well as a *Grand Concerto for Percussion and Keyboards* (2005). In all, he composed almost 200 compositions.

Schuller's participation and involvement with wind bands/ensembles included playing in the Goldman Band in New York City, conducting performances and delivering important keynote addresses at CBDNA and WASBE Conferences, as well as composing a number of significant works for the medium, among them the following:

Meditation (1963)
Diptych for Brass Quintet and Concert Band (1964)
Study in Textures (1967)
Tre Invenzioni for Chamber Ensemble (twenty-five players divided into five groups of five players each) (1972)
Eine Kleine Posaunenmusik for Trombone (1980)
Symphony No. 3: "In Praise of Winds" (1981)
On Winged Flight: A Divertimento for Band (1989)
Song and Dance for Violin and Large Wind Ensemble (1990)
Festive Music (for orchestra winds in quadruple with percussion, harp, piano doubling celesta) (1992)
Blue Dawn into White Heat for Concert Band (1997)
Nature's Way (2006)

Composer Augusta Read Thomas, speaking at the presentation of the MacDowell Award to Schuller in August 2017, stated, "he has inspired generations of students, setting an example of discovery and experimentation." Also included among those Schuller inspired was a generation of wind band/ensemble conductors.

* * * * * * * * * * * *

The 16th WASBE International Conference, held in San Jose, California, from July 12–18, 2015, was in the opinion of many of the delegates, the finest in the 34-year history of the Association. Seventeen concerts, five repertoire sessions, and numerous presentations filled the weeklong conference schedule. Below are the wind bands/ensembles that performed at the Conference. They included eleven from the United States, two from Canada, and one each from Israel, Germany, and Japan, as well as the WASBE Youth Wind Orchestra.

> San Francisco Wind Ensemble, Martin Seggelke, conductor
> University of Maryland Chamber Winds, Michael Votta, conductor
> Brooklyn Wind Symphony, Jeff Ball, conductor
> Temple University Wind Symphony: Chamber Winds, Emily Threinen, conductor
> University of Wisconsin-Milwaukee Wind Ensemble, John Climer, conductor
> University of Louisville Wind Ensemble, Frederick Speck, conductor
> Lone Star Wind Orchestra, Eugene Migliaro Corporan, conductor
> San Jose Wind Symphony, Ed Harris, conductor
> Dallas Winds, Jerry Junkin, conductor
> University of Houston Moores School Wind Ensemble, David Bertman, conductor
> Pacific Symphonic Wind Ensemble, David Branter, conductor
> New Edmonton Wind Sinfonia, Raymond Baril, conductor
> University of Saskatchewan Wind Orchestra, Darrin Oehlerking, conductor
> Israel National Youth Wind Orchestra, Motti Miron, conductor
> Landesblasorchester Baden-Württemberg, Björn Bus, conductor
> Showa Wind Symphony, Shintaro Fukumoto, conductor
> WASBE Youth Wind Orchestra, José Rafael Pascual-Vilaplana, conductor

Ninety works were performed on conference programs, 34 of which were composed by U. S. composers, 12 by Canadian composers, 5 by Japanese composers, and 4 by UK composers. The other fifty-five works were written by composers from the Netherlands, Austria, Spain, Russia, Korea, Thailand, France, Estonia, and Argentina. Included among the American works performed at the conference were Bernard Gilmore's *Five Folksongs for Soprano and Band* (1963), Charles Ives's *Country Band March* (c. 1903) (arr. James B.

Sinclair), John Mackey's *The Frozen Cathedral* (2012), David Maslanka's *Requiem* (2011), Scott McAllister's *Gone* (2013), Ron Nelson's *Aspen Jubilee* (1984), Kevin Puts's *Millennium Canons* (2001/03) (trans. Mark Spede), H. Owen Reed's *La Fiesta Mexicana* (1949), Joseph Schwantner's *Luminosity: Concerto for Wind Orchestra* (2015), and Frank Ticheli's *Concerto for Alto Saxophone and Wind Ensemble* (2014).

A highlight of the conference was a concert performed by the Temple University Chamber Winds conducted by Emily Threinen.

Temple University Wind Symphony: Chamber Winds
Emily Threinen, conductor
World Association for Symphonic Bands and Ensembles International Conference
July 15, 2015
"Homage to Mozart"

Overture to The Marriage of Figaro	Wolfgang Amadeus Mozart, arr. Wendt
Hommage à l'ami Papageno	Jean Françaix
Figures in the Garden	Jonathan Dove
Mozart new-look	Jean Françaix
Serenade in c minor, K. 388/384a	Wolfgang Amadeus Mozart

Mozart new-look, composed in 1981 by Jean Françaix (1912–1997) is a delightful "petite" fantasy for double bass and wind instruments. "While the double bass plays an aria from *Don Giovanni*, Françaix [interjects] an aria from *Carmen* with a wink. A true 'Musique pour faire plaisir!'"[13]

Cynthia Johnston Turner (USA) moderated a panel discussion that attempted to define quality in repertoire and program planning. Panel members included conductors Eugene Corporon (USA), Marcelo Jardim (Brazil), Jerry Junkin (USA), Glenn Price (Canada/USA), Alberto Roque (Portugal), and Frederick Speck (USA). The panel also discussed gender and diversity disparity in the band profession. This was particularly poignant given the make-up of the members of the panel.

The Conference also included eleven presentations by scholars and conductors on a variety of topics, three of which were:

"Appoggiaturas, Nachschlags, and other Forgotten Terms: Ornamentation & Articulation in the Mozart Wind Serenades" by Dr. Jeffrey Boeckman.

"*Uni Phillipiana* and *A Day on the Farm*, Two Unpublished Works for Band by Ferde Grofé" by Dr. Robert J. Cesario.

"Giya Kancheli's *Magnum Ignotum for Wind Ensemble*: Composing in the Present without Compromising the Past" by Dr. Jason Caslor.

* * * * * * * * * * * *

In the fall of 2015, Andrew Pease assembled a consortium of thirteen ensembles to commission Oliver Caplan (b. 1982) to compose a piece having the same instrumentation as Stravinsky's *Octet for Wind Instruments*. On April 17, 2016, Caplan's *Krummholz Variations* was premiered by Sun Valley Chamber Winds, Andrew Pease conducting, on a program entitled "Stravinsky Alone No More." *Krummholz* is the German word for "crooked wood," twisted trees that serve as gateways to the alpine zone and mountaintop sentinels. "[Caplan's] tone poem … recalls aspects of life in the alpine zone, expressed through a set of short, connected variations: Dawn, Marmots, Alpine Meadow, Ptarmigan, The Summit, Headwaters, Cloudburst, and Dusk."[14] A second work on the program, *Chamber Symphony* by Christopher Lamb (b. 1989), also employed the same instrumentation as used in Stravinsky's *Octet*. Lamb's work is based on a collection of famous paradoxes. "Each movement borrows the feel and setting of the statements behind the paradoxes and explores the feeling they conjure."[15]

* * * * * * * * * * * *

In 2015, the North Hills High School Band of Pittsburgh, Pennsylvania, Leonard Lavelle, director, celebrated the 50th anniversary of its Commissioned Works Project by commissioning and premiering Michael Daugherty's *Winter Dreams*. Daugherty's eight-minute composition "evokes the bleak winter scenes of rural Iowa depicted in Grant Wood's paintings and lithographs of the 1930s–1940s."[16] The Band's Commissioned Works Project began in 1965 and is the longest running commissioning series of any high school band in the United States. So far nearly fifty pieces have been commissioned including works by James Barnes, James Curnow, Elliott Del Borgo, Norman Dello Joio, Frank Erickson, David Holsinger, Robert Jager, Joseph Wilcox Jenkins, Anne McGinty, Vaclav Nelhybel, Alfred Reed, and Dana Wilson.

* * * * * * * * * * * * *

All "alphabet soup" organizations such as ASBDA, NBA, CBDNA, ACB, ABC, CMS, and NASM initiated projects to address Gender and Ethnicity issues during the early part of the twenty-first century. The National Band Association (NBA), College Band Directors National Association (CBDNA), and Music for All (MFA) joined together and formed the Music Education Alliance to support bands in underserved communities. One of the Alliance's first initiatives was the Dr. William P. Foster Project. Dr. Foster was the legendary Director of Bands at Florida A & M University from 1946 until his retirement in 1998. The Foster Project presents an "Award of Excellence" to quality band programs serving historically disadvantaged student populations. It also conducts a Mentorship program in which a network of peer consultants work with and support teachers who direct band programs in underserved schools. The third component of the Project, entitled "Best Practices," assembles and distributes a collection of articles and videos for use in teaching and band directing.

The American Bandmasters Association also has a mentorship program in which their members work with school band directors, especially those teaching in minority populated schools.

In 1999, CBDNA began presenting grants to young minority conductors. Each recipient received up to $300 (now $500) to defray the cost of traveling to a Summer Conducting Seminar in which their registration fee was also waived by participating institutions. In 2018, there were forty-eight applications for the twelve grants, which are now called Mike Moss Conducting Grants. Myron "Mike" Moss initiated the grant program and was a passionate advocate for gender and ethnicity equity in the wind band/ensemble profession.

CBDNA's Gender and Ethnic Committee, renamed the Diversity Committee, commissioned Valerie Coleman to compose a piece for the Roma (Texas) High School Band which has a predominantly Latino student population. The commission was the association's first to an African-American composer and the first to a black woman. (Note: this commission is discussed in greater detail in Chapter 16, page 312).

CBDNA also hosted a group of diverse and underrepresented composers at its 2011 and 2013 national conferences. These composers had been successful in writing music for other mediums but had no understanding of the wind band/ensemble. During the conferences they attended concerts, met other composers, and networked with university wind band/ensemble conductors. It was hoped that this experience might kindle their interest in writing music for the wind band/ensemble.

ENDNOTES

1   "Alternative Energy for orchestra & electronica: Program Notes," Mason Bates, accessed June 20, 2018, http://www.masonbates.com/work/work-alternativeenergy.html.

2   Jake Wallace, "Fanfare for Full Fathom Five (2015) for brass and percussion, with optional organ," Osti Music: The Website of Composer John Mackey, accessed June 10, 2018, http://www.ostimusic.com/FullFathom.php.

3   "Program Note," University of Illinois Wind Symphony, concert of March 28, 2015.

4   "*Reflections on the Mississippi* for tuba and orchestra (2013): Program Note," Michael Daugherty, accessed June 20, 2018, http://michaeldaugherty.net/index.cfm?id=157&i=2&pagename=works.

5   "Masks and Machines: Program Notes," Paul Dooley, accessed June 20, 2018, https://www.pauldooley.net/works/masksandmachinesband.

6   Chen Yi, email to the author, February 21, 2018.

7   "Vital Signs of Planet Earth (piano reduction): Program Notes," C. Alan Publications, accessed June 20, 2018, http://c-alanpublications.com/vital-signs-of-planet-earth-piano-reduction/.

8   A. E. Jacques, "Songs from the End of the World (2015) for soprano and chamber ensemble," Osti Music: The Website of Composer John Mackey, accessed June 10, 2018, http://www.ostimusic.com/Songs.php.

9   Jacob Wallace, "Monk by the Sea (2015): Program Note," Michael Markowski, Composer, accessed June 20, 2018, http://www.michaelmarkowski.com/music/monk-by-the-sea/.

10 "Lokuttara for Wind Ensemble," Theodore Presser Company, accessed June 20, 2018, https://www.presser.com/shop/lokuttara.html?SID=68fda8c761c87699fc37e711d7d6d4f0.

11 http://www.ongehoord.live/programma/time-for-outrage. (accessed 2015).

12 "Program Notes," Ithaca College Wind Ensemble, concert of February 21, 2015.

13 "Mozart new-look," Schott, accessed June 20, 2018, https://en.schott-music.com/shop/mozart-new-look-no37587.html.

14 Andy Pease, "Krummholz Variations by Oliver Caplan," Wind Band Literature: A Conductor's Perspective, May 13, 2016, accessed May 15, 2018, http://windliterature.org/2016/05/13/krummholz-variations-by-oliver-caplan/.

15 Andy Pease, "Chamber Symphony by Chris Lamb," Wind Band Literature: A Conductor's Perspective, May 13, 2016, accessed May 15, 2018, http://windliterature.org/2016/05/13/chamber-symphony-by-chris-lamb/.

16 "Winter Dreams for Concert Band by Michael Daugherty," SheetMusicPlus, accessed June 20, 2018, https://www.sheetmusicplus.com/title/winter-dreams-sheet-music/20207343.

PART II

The American School Band Movement and Other Wind Band/Ensemble, Music Education Issues

CHAPTER 21

The American School Band and Music Education

History and Development of American School Bands • Selecting School Band Literature • Music Education and Bands in the 21st Century

History—Early School Band Development

Music education in the United States began in 1838 with Lowell Mason teaching singing to students in the Boston schools. However, it was not until the twentieth century that bands and instrumental music instruction were added to school music education programs. In the classically oriented curricula of nineteenth century schools, bands were not considered a proper activity.

There was a rapid growth in enrollment in American public schools during the last two decades of the nineteenth century "as a result of compulsory school attendance laws, stricter child labor laws, and an increase in the income of the general populace, attributable to the industrial revolution. As a result of children spending more years in school, activities that had been the domain of the home and church became public concerns."[1] Orchestras began to be organized in high schools about 1900. Their instrumentation generally resembled that of a "pit orchestra." A few years later, bands were organized in Rockford, Illinois (1907), Connorsville, Indiana (1908), and Richland Center, Wisconsin (1909). Edward Bailey Birge, writing about bands of this era, stated, "Though often associated with the orchestra, either as an adjunct [or] source of supply for wind instruments, and though the same boys frequently played in both organizations, this activity more often started independently of the orchestra, the prevailing motive in many cases being to capitalize on the irresistible appeal which bands, especially in uniform, make to the adolescent boy, and thus turn it into educational channels."[2] Early school bands, such as the Boston Farm and Trade School Band, met outside of school time and received no academic credit.

Starting in 1913, school systems in Oakland, California, Grand Rapids and Detroit, Michigan, Pittsburgh, Pennsylvania, and Cleveland, Ohio, began acquiring instruments for the purpose of offering instrumental class instruction and developing bands and orchestras. In 1927, the national convention of school superintendents, meeting in Dallas, Texas, urged "all American schools to place music on a par with the three Rs as one of the fundamentals of education in the country."[3]

A report issued by the U. S. Bureau of Education in 1919–1920 revealed that orchestras outnumbered bands in every state and that the Central states were the areas where instrumental music programs were the strongest. Mark Fonder, speculating about the possible reasons for this, states that "many instrument manufacturers were based in this region and perhaps they promoted their wares more intensely in their home areas ... [also] certain ethnic and cultural traditions found in the Midwest strongly favored instrumental music education. In 1922, there were an estimated 60,000 pupils in approximately 200 school bands and orchestras."[4] In 1929, C. M. Tremaine, in the article "As We Go Marching," estimated that there were "15,000 to 25,000 bands and 25,000 to 35,000 orchestras."[5] By 1938, approximately 2 million students were participating in bands and orchestras throughout the United States and by 1941 there were over 50,000 school and university bands.[6]

The 1930s saw the decline of professional bands in America, the result of public interest shifting to newer forms of entertainment such as moving pictures and the phonograph record. Communities began to enlist school bands to provide music for civic events such as parades, holiday celebrations, etc. Following the end of World War I and the disappearance of the military band market, musical instrument manufacturing industries began to promote instrumental music and especially band development in hundreds of towns and cities across the United States. The teachers and band directors needed for these new and developing school music programs were found among the veterans who were trained and played in military bands during World War I.

Edwin Franko Goldman, in a commencement address at Philips University in 1934, stated that "despite the general business depression of the last few years and despite the fact that in some instances music has been eliminated from some of the public schools, the cause of bands and band music is going forward with greater momentum than ever before ... while the professional band has, unfortunately, been [traveling] the downward path for the last few years, the amateur bands, particularly the high school and college bands, have been surging forward and the strides they have made have been simply phenomenal."[7]

Soon band contests became an important factor in the development of school instrumental music and bands throughout the country. Among the first states to organize contests were North Dakota and Oklahoma in 1919 and Michigan and Wisconsin in 1920. Eventually state band contest activity led to the organization of the first national band contest, which was held in Chicago in 1923, attracting thirty bands, fifteen of which were from the immediate Chicago area. The Fostoria (Ohio) Band, directed by John Wainwright, won the initial contest and was awarded a prize of $1,000. By 1932 there were 1,150 bands competing in forty-four states.

In 1924, the National Bureau for the Advancement of Music (NBAM), an advisory group sponsored by the manufacturers of instruments and the Music Supervisors National Conference (MSNC) decided to hold regional elimination contests in order to insure that all sections of the country would be represented. Due to the lack of a sufficient number of regional contests, no national contests were held in 1924 and 1925. The national contest was resumed in 1926 in Fostoria, Ohio, and the Joliet Township High School Band of Joliet, Illinois, was selected as the best band. National band contests continued to be held between 1926 to 1936 in Iowa, Illinois, Colorado, Michigan, and Oklahoma.

Band contests created strong and cohesive community spirit. One of the best examples occurred in Hobart (Indiana) during the Depression year of 1930, the year William D. Revelli's Hobart High School Band won the National Band Contest. Revelli recalled, "The band's success was the source of what was probably the greatest community pride that Hobart ever developed. Hobart became famous and respected. The community responded by providing the moral and economic support necessary for the band to develop into and remain the best. The expense was great, and it is an indication of the community's pride that it supplied significant financial support for equipment, music, and travel during the Great Depression, when money for food was often scarce."[8] Even when the community was forced to close its schools due to the lack of money, Revelli's rehearsals continued so that the high school band could be prepared for state, regional, and national contests.

Adjudicators for all contests through 1931 were instructed to evaluate and rank bands, the best band first, followed by the second, third, etc. In 1932 the National School Band Association (NSBA) discontinued the use of the competitive ranking system and adopted a "competitive festival" format based on group ratings. When A. R. McAllister, director of the Joliet (Illinois) Township High School Band and president of the NSBA, announced the decision to initiate the new competition-festival format he stated, "everyone gains something by taking part." In the ranking system "few win and many lose."

The 1933 contest, held in Evanston, Illinois, attracted the largest number of bands, seventy-four. Below is the Concert and Recital program presented at the 1934 National High School Band Contest in Des Moines, Iowa. It consists of performances by solo players, small ensembles and bands.

Part I
Baton Twirling, Philip Burman, Drum Major, University of Illinois Bands
Cornet solo, (representation of 1st Division)
Saxophone solo, (representation of 1st Division)
Accompanied Trio, (representation of 1st Division)
Trombone Solo, (representation of 1st Division)
Saxophone Sextet, (representation of 1st Division)

Part II
Joliet Township High School Band
A. R. McAllister, Conductor

1. March, Purple Carnival	Alford
2. Rhapsodie Norvegienne	Lalo
3. Ballet Suite, Enchanted Lake	Tchaikovsky
4. Tone Poem, Carnival in Paris	Svendsen
5. Descriptive March, Third Alarm	Goldman

Part III
Joliet Township High School Band and Des Moines East, Lincoln, North and Roosevelt High School Bands

1. Iowa Corn Song	Arr. by Beeston

John T. Beeston, Conductor

2. Grand March, University	Goldman

Edwin Franko Goldman, Conductor

3. Grand Promenade at the White House, from *Tales of a Traveler*	Sousa
4. Finale from the Tone Poem, *Pines of Rome*	Respighi
5. The Stars and Stripes Forever	Sousa

Frank Simon, Conductor

By 1938, the national contest had grown too large to manage and was replaced by ten regional contests. Fonder credits the contest movement for "stimulating the growth, standardization, and improvement of school musical groups, especially bands ... Joseph E. Maddy declared that the radical changes in instrument manufacturing, band publications, and improved performance standards ... would have taken one hundred years to accomplish had it not been for the contest movement."[9] Robert T. Stroker, in an article entitled "The American Band Contest Movement 1875–1940," wrote, "The school band movement became an important phase of the expanding program of instrumental music education in the public schools. The contest in many communities often became the reason for the school band, driven more by the spirit of competition than the spirit of music making. However misguided this may seem, the contests did awaken the community's interest to the cause of public music education."[10]

By the beginning of World War II (1941) the contest movement had (1) attracted public attention and support for school music, (2) influenced thousands of young people to study instrumental music and participate in school bands, and (3) improved the performance level and instrumentation of school bands. From the mid-1930s through 1940, thousands of students participated in city, district, state, and regional band contests. In 1940 alone, four hundred and thirty-six bands (26,617 students) and eighty-eight orchestras (13,468 students) participated in regional festivals.[11] Competition festivals remained popular until World War II when wartime travel restrictions curtailed travel to such activities. When the war was over most contest festival activity was confined within each state.

End of World War II to the End of the Twentieth Century—Literature And Repertoire

Starting in the mid-1940s, good quality original literature for school bands became an important issue. Arnold Schoenberg and Darius Milhaud (both important, world-class composers) were commissioned by their publishers in 1943 and 1944, respectively, to write pieces specifically for American high school bands. The results were Schoenberg's *Theme and Variations, Op. 43a* and Milhaud's *Suite Française, Op. 248*, both interesting, exciting, and challenging pieces. Band directors and publishers both realized that if the quality and quantity of original compositions for school wind groups were to be improved, major composers would have to be persuaded to write music for them. The first important composers commissioned to write pieces for band in the 1950s were William Schuman, Vincent Persichetti, and Howard Hanson. Their works, listed below, were immediately embraced by bands at all levels and performed thousands of times, quickly becoming part of the standard band repertoire.

1950	Schuman, William	George Washington Bridge: An Impression for Band
1952	Persichetti, Vincent	Psalm for Band
1953	Persichetti, Vincent	Pageant
1954	Hanson, Howard	Chorale and Alleluia
1957	Schuman, William	Chester (Overture for Band)
1959	Schuman, William	When Jesus Wept

Below is a program performed by the Greensboro (North Carolina) Senior High School Band on November 3, 1955. Two of the new works, listed above, by Vincent Persichetti (*Pageant*) and Howard Hanson (*Chorale and Alleluia*) are included on the program. Dr. Edwin Franko Goldman was the guest conductor on the second half of the concert. This was the last concert he conducted before his death.

Greensboro Senior High School Band
Herbert Hazelman, Director
Dr. Edwin Franko Goldman, Guest Conductor
November 3, 1955

Howard Hanson	Chorale and Alleluia
Vincent Persichetti	Pageant
Frank Perkins	Fandango
Fred Kepner	Cuban Fantasy—Suite for Band

Intermission

Edwin Franko Goldman	Grand March, International Accord
Jean Sibelius	Finlandia
J. S. Bach	Come, Sweet Death
	Jesu, Joy of Man's Desiring
George F. Handel	Slow March from Scipio
Edwin Franko Goldman	Illinois March
	Anniversary March

Among the high school bands beginning to commission pieces during the 1960s were:

Batavia, New York High School Band
Clarence, New York High School Band
Greensboro, North Carolina High School Band
Grimsley High School Band, Greensboro, North Carolina
Ithaca, New York High School Band
Mason City, Iowa High School Band
North Hills High School Band, Pittsburgh, Pennsylvania

As school bands continued to grow (there were an estimated 3 million instrumentalists playing in 50,000 bands by 1960) so did concerns about the quality of music education students were receiving in band programs. William Moody, president of the National Band Association in 1968, noted, "The musical and educational significance of the school band movement needs critical evaluation

… Too little time is now being given by most directors to the general music background of band students. Most students are graduating from high school after more than six years of band, with very little knowledge of music history and music theory, and very little familiarity with the compositions of the great composers. School bands should be primarily *musical* and *educational*, with most functional and entertaining activities limited to school events."[12] Moody urged band directors to change "rehearsing/drilling" band experiences into experiences that provided students with opportunities to create, understand, and appreciate music as an art. Moody's thoughts reflected the values and objectives included in the new music education doctrine of "aesthetic education" being advocated by Charles Leonhard, Harry Broudy, James Mursell, and especially Bennett Reimer. The core of "aesthetic" music education was the study and performance of music of exceptional quality. In the 1960s and 1970s the music educators above called on music teachers/band directors to develop programs that focused on basic music skill development, acquisition of musical knowledge, and musical growth through performance.

Below is a selection of wind band/ensemble pieces that were composed between 1960 and 1975 and performed by the better high school bands.

1960	Bernstein, Leonard/Beeler	Overture to *Candide*
1961	Chance, John Barnes	Incantation and Dance
1962	Dello Joio, Norman	Variants on a Medieval Tune
1962	Erb, Donald	Space Music
1963	Schuller, Gunther	Meditation
1964	Shostakovich, Dmitri/Hunsberger	Festive Overture, Op. 96
1964	Grainger, Percy/Goldman	The Sussex Mummers' Christmas Carol
1964	Lo Presti, Ronald	Elegy for a Young American
1964	Nelhybel, Vaclav	Prelude and Fugue
1965	Benson, Warren	Remembrance
1965	Chance, John Barnes	Variations on a Korean Folk Song
1965	Childs, Barney	Six Events for 58 Players
1965	Hartley, Walter	Sinfonia No. 4
1966	Bassett, Leslie	Designs, Images and Textures
1966	Bielawa, Herbert	Spectrum

1966	Nelhybel, Vaclav	Symphonic Movement
1966	Dello Joio, Norman	Scenes from "The Louvre"
1967	Erb, Donald	Stargazing
1968	Arnold, Malcolm/Paynter	Four Scottish Dances
1968	Pennington, John	Apollo
1969	Benson, Warren	The Solitary Dancer
1971	Tull, Fisher	Sketches on a Tudor Psalm
1972	Broege, Timothy	Sinfonia III
1972	Chance, John Barnes	Elegy
1972	Zdechlik, John	Chorale and Shaker Dance
1974	Ives, Charles/Elkus	Old Home Days (Suite for Band)
1975	Husa, Karel	Al Fresco
1975	Paulson, John	Epinicion

The MENC Committee on Creativity in Music Education, supported by a grant from the Ford Foundation, inaugurated a Young Composers-in-Residence Program in the 1960s. This program placed young composers in selective school systems throughout the United States to write pieces for student ensembles and nurture a greater receptivity and appreciation for contemporary music in young people. Among school systems selected for participation in this program were those in Oshkosh, Wisconsin, and Ithaca, New York. Below is a program featuring works by Jack Jarrett, MENC Ford Foundation composer-in-residence in the Oshkosh Public Schools, performed by the Oshkosh Senior High Concert Band, A Cappella Choir, and Symphonette at the 1967 North Central Divisional Meeting of the MENC.

Oshkosh Senior High Concert Band, A Cappella Choir and Symphonette
April 15, 1967
Cobo Hall
Detroit, Michigan

Jack Jarrett   Choral Symphony on American Poems (1965–66)

The Oshkosh High School
A Cappella Choir and Concert Band
Fred Leist, Conductor

Jack Jarrett   Serenade for Small Orchestra (1957, 1967)

The Oshkosh High School Symphonette
James Croft, Conductor

Jack Jarrett   Missa Pro Tempore Mortis (1967)

The Oshkosh High School
A Cappella Choir and Concert Band
James Croft, Conductor

The MENC Ford Foundation Composer-in-Residence in the Ithaca City School District was David Borden. His piece, *All-American; Teenage; Lovesongs*, was one of four works premiered on a program of seven contemporary works performed by the Ithaca High School Band at Ithaca College's Ford Hall on May 17, 1967. The other premiered works were composed by Vincent Persichetti, Robert Ward, and Warren Benson.

Ithaca High School Band
May 17, 1967
Frank L. Battisti, Conductor
Frederick Fennell, Guest Conductor
Harvey Phillips, Guest Soloist

Prisms	Herbert Bielawa
Turn Not Thy Face *	Vincent Persichetti

Premiere Performance

All-American; Teenage; Lovesongs *	David Borden #

Premiere Performance

Fiesta Processional *	Robert Ward

Premiere Performance

Helix *	Warren Benson

Harvey Phillips, Tuba
Ithaca, NY Premiere Performance

Lincolnshire Posy	Percy Grainger

Frederick Fennell, Guest Conductor

The Leaves Are Falling	Warren Benson

Note: * indicates Ithaca High School Band commissioned work.
# indicates CMP Composer-in-Residence in Ithaca City School District

In 1986, Brian Norcross undertook a study to determine what literature was being performed by high school bands in the following northeastern states: Connecticut, Delaware, District of Columbia, Massachusetts, Maine, Maryland, New Hampshire, New Jersey,

New York, Pennsylvania, Rhode Island, Vermont, and Virginia. One thousand one hundred high school band directors were asked to submit programs performed between the years of 1980–85. He received responses from 63 directors representing 83 bands. In total, Norcross surveyed 2,449 performances of 1,412 compositions by 593 composers.[13]

The composers receiving the highest number of performances were:

Composer	Number of Performances
Anderson, Leroy	84 performances of 12 compositions
Sousa, John Philip	83 performances of 24 compositions
Bach, Johann Sebastian	57 performances of 27 compositions
Reed, Alfred	55 performances of 21 compositions
Grundman, Clare	50 performances of 17 compositions
Swearingen, James	46 performances of 11 compositions
Erickson, Frank	45 performances of 19 compositions
Lowden, Robert	45 performances of 21 compositions
Ployhar, James	41 performances of 30 compositions
Holst, Gustav	39 performances of 8 compositions[14]

Norcross concluded that there was not a specific repertoire for high school bands, as no school band performed a work by each of the four top composers in the overall survey. However, he did state that the survey shows that there is a broad group of composers whose works make up the majority of the repertoire being performed.[15]

In 1989, *The Instrumentalist* published three articles I wrote under the title, "My View of the Wind Repertoire." I received numerous letters about the articles. One of the most interesting and troubling came from a school instrumental music supervisor who expressed frustration regarding the repertoire being published and performed by school bands. In his letter he wrote:

> I want to register a concern for the quality of music being written for the elementary, junior and high school band. As the person in charge of instrumental music in my school system, I attend many concerts in schools and with our All-City program.
>
> Each spring our All-City Concert Band (grades 5 and 6), and our All-City Symphonic Band present a final concert for the year (about two hours in length). I can tell you that after about forty minutes of listening the individuality of the music being played simply melts into

a kind of "aural mush." I am subjected to an endless stream of tertian harmonies, trite melodic material (many times of a quasi-pop nature), and the inevitable ABA form—always fast—slow—fast. The harmonies and melodies are virtually interchangeable between pieces.

With very few notable exceptions the quality of music being written for the concert band at the levels with which I deal is appalling, surely our students deserve better. As well, I find that this mediocrity of material only serves to stigmatize the band in the eyes of colleagues in the orchestral and choral areas. It also increases the resistance of students to new harmonic material or even harmonies and dissonances considered mainstream twentieth century.

I think it a serious problem. I know I find myself going back to repertoire from the 50s and 60s out of sheer frustration.[16]

In 1991, composer W. Francis McBeth expressed concern about the scarcity of good quality literature for junior/middle school bands. He stated that perhaps the greatest challenge in band music education was retaining more junior high players. "I think we would be shocked if we knew students' reactions to much of the music that is played: they are really quite bored with it, and I don't blame them … If composers do not write some exciting concert music for junior high students, we will lose them … I think many composers take the wrong approach to junior high music … [They] should be writing more musically challenging music [and] tailoring it to the ease of fingerings and the characteristics of each instrument: in other words, simplicity of mechanics as opposed to simple music." McBeth added the following about band literature in general, "I am not pleased with much of the present literature [1991] …. We are still in our paper plate period—using a piece once and throwing it away—but that will change. History will change it, and history will determine our repertoire, not the compilation of lists today."[17]

The Book of Proceedings of the 1994 American Bandmasters Association Conference contains a 1993–94 Task Force Committee Report on "Strategic Planning for Instrumental Education." Bobby Adams, Director of Bands at Stetson University (Florida) and a member of the Task Force Committee, discussed "How Should Band Directors Deal with School Reform?" He stated,

The Leadership in our profession must redefine the mission of music education and preach that mission to the band director first. The biggest problems in music education have been caused by the music teachers themselves. Those problems have to do with too much "activity" and not enough emphasis on the study of serious literature. As we all know, the strength of any academic discipline is in its subject matter. Obviously, our subject matter is the literature we teach and perform. The quality of our literature must be equal to, if not better than, the subject matter of math, science and the language arts.[18]

Frederick Fennell, who in addition to being a conductor was also an editor/arranger and a person very involved in music publishing, offered the following comment on school band music being published at the time. "So many publishers in the business ... are printers who don't care about the quality, but only about what will sell."[19] Allen Britton, a past president of the MENC, in his essay, "American Music Education: Is It Better Than We Think? A Discussion of the Role of Performance and Repertory, Together with Brief Mention of Certain Other Problems," observed, "... we learn to play in order to learn repertory. Playing is fun, but playing remains only fun unless we play something worth playing."[20]

Much of the literature composed, published, and performed by school bands during the latter part of the twentieth century emphasized the commercial and popular elements of American society—television theme music, movie theme music, rock music, and so on. Even most of the best-selling original concert band pieces were trite, contrived, and calculated to make the band "sound good." Band libraries are filled with "best-sellers-of-the-day"—pieces that were played once and never performed again. Music of this caliber offers few opportunities for students to develop a deeper understanding and appreciation of high quality musical art. Zoltán Kodály, one of the twentieth century's important composers and music educators, stated that, "Children should be taught with only the most musically valuable materials. For the young, only the best is good enough. They should be led to masterpieces by means of masterpieces."[21] The development of good musical values and appreciation is linked directly to the quality of music students create, recreate, hear, and consume.

Below is a program performed by the J. J. Pearce High School Band of the Richardson Independent School District in Texas at the Morton H. Meyerson Symphony Center in Dallas on May 15, 1998. The works on the program are varied in styles and composed by excellent composers.

J. J. Pearce High School Bands
Peter J. Warshaw, Symphonic I; Lynne Jackson, Symphonic II;
Jeff Bridges, Concert Band, Conductors
Richard L. Floyd, Guest Conductor
Morton H. Meyerson Symphony Center
May 15, 1998

Symphonic I Brass

Paul Dukas	Fanfare to *La Peri* (1927)

Concert Band

John Philip Sousa	The Belle of Chicago (1892)
Aaron Copland	Down a Country Lane (1962)
Pierre LaPlante	American Riversongs (1991)

Symphonic II

John Philip Sousa	In Darkest Africa (1896)
Norman Dello Joio	Scenes from *The Louvre* (1966)
Percy Grainger	Shepherd's Hey (1918)

Symphonic I

Leonard Bernstein/Beeler	Overture to *Candide* (1955)
Gustav Holst	Hammersmith, Prelude and Scherzo (1930)
Frank Ticheli	Amazing Grace (1994)

Richard L. Floyd, Guest Conductor

John Philip Sousa	The Glory of the Yankee Navy (1909)

In the 1990s, the Belmont (Massachusetts) High School Symphonic band was an inclusive, non-select group of wind and percussion students. Their Spring Concert on March 20, 1996, featured the premiere of a new work commissioned by the Band, *Blue Dawn into White Heat*, written by Pulitzer Prize winning composer Gunther Schuller.

Belmont High School Band
Fred Harris, Conductor
Gunther Schuller, Guest Conductor
March 20, 1996

Symphonic Band

Gustav Holst	First Suite in E-flat for Military Band (1909)
Kenneth L. Amis	A tonal fanfare (1996)

In Tribute to Gunther Schuller's Seventieth Birthday

Gunther Schuller	Meditation (1963)
Scott Joplin/Schuller	Combination March (1896)

Ragtime Ensemble

Scott Joplin/Schuller	The Ragtime Dance (1906)
Scott Joplin/Schuller	The Easy Winners (1901)

Wind Ensemble

Gunther Schuller	Blue Dawn into White Heat (1996)

World Premiere
Gunther Schuller, Guest Conductor

Music Education and Bands in the Twenty-First Century

At the mid-point of the second decade of the twenty-first century, the government, some educational institutions, and most of the general public do not consider music and the other arts to be of prime importance. This is nothing new. Music and the arts have always been regarded as "soft subjects—add ons—extras." Music, as an art, doesn't fit into current educational practice which is obsessed with standardized testing and objective measurement of students in subjects deemed "important" by educational VIPs. Music teachers, band directors, concerned parents, and all who consider music to be an indispensable component in the education of young people, must resist all attempts to downgrade or eliminate music in school curriculums.

High school teenagers love music. However, the majority of them do not participate in school bands or any large ensemble. Among the reasons given for their non-participation is the quest for high grades, scheduling conflicts, block schedule problems, or the need to work and make money. However, the main reason might be that they find the music and music making in these groups to be uninteresting and limited.

A student's musical experience in a traditional high school band is primarily a re-creative musical experience. Seldom do students have opportunities to create their own music or attend a live musical performance. Future band programs should provide opportunities for students to create, re-create and consume music in a variety of styles and genres. The music they study and play should be of excellent musical quality and meaningful and relevant for them.

School Band Literature and Repertoire

School band directors/teachers today who are concerned about the lack of quality music for school bands should take a cue from 1950s–60s school band directors who faced the same dilemma and did something about it. They began commissioning major composers to write pieces for their bands (the same composers who were writing music for major professional ensembles and artists)—Vincent Persichetti, Warren Benson, Leslie Bassett, Robert Ward—"real composers" who wrote "real music."

A student's potential for developing high musical taste, values, and appreciation is much greater when he/she studies, performs, and consumes high quality music and not "junk food" quality music. Teachers who teach English Literature have their students read novels written by the best authors in the English language (Shakespeare, Dickens, Faulkner, Twain, etc.). Likewise, school music teachers/band directors should have their students play pieces written by the best composers of music, such as Bach, Ives, Gershwin, Ellington, Copland, Sousa, Joplin, Piazzolla, Schuller, Williams, etc. Below are some guidelines that can be used in the selection of music.

1. Select pieces that are interesting; that are imaginative in development of some or all of their musical elements—melody, harmony, texture, rhythm, form, etc. The pieces should provide opportunities for the teaching of musical concepts such as form/construction, style, etc.
2. As much as possible, select pieces that have interesting individual parts. Students like to play pieces that allow them to be "part of the action." Tubas like to play melodies as well as bass lines; French Horns like to play more than off-beats. Choose music that will help each student grow musically and technically (examine the individual parts).
3. Select pieces that fit the instrumentation of the ensemble. However, if a conductor-teacher wants to perform an excellent work that requires an instrument (or two) that they do not have in their ensemble, they should consider performing it if a reasonable

substitution can be made for the missing instrument(s) that doesn't violate the musical integrity of the piece. (Note: Creating a fully instrumentated ensemble should be a priority objective for all band directors since most of the medium's important works require a fully instrumentated ensemble.)

4. Select pieces in which the elements of music are integrated and developed creatively and have the potential for evocating feelings and conveying expressive meaning to the students.

5. Avoid selecting pieces in which the technical demands are excessive. This creates the need to expend excessive amounts of time "drilling the notes" and hinders the truly "collaborative music-making" experiences students should have. Excessive technical demands also can prevent students from achieving a "high plateau of expressiveness" in their performances.

6. Select pieces that encompass a variety of styles—contemporary, avant-garde, Renaissance, Baroque, Romantic, Jazz, Popular, etc. This makes the teaching of history and musical styles possible.

7. Select pieces that have a variety of textures ranging from thinly scored passages (solo and small group instrumentation) to those scored for the full ensemble.

Pieces selected should include some that are familiar and comfortable and some that are unfamiliar and uncomfortable (music that will "challenge and take students to places they have never been"). All pieces provide opportunities for students to develop technical skills and musical knowledge. However, only the study and performance of excellent quality music (music of artistic merit) provide opportunities for students to discover and feel the expressive power of music.

The kinds and quality of music students study, perform, and consume truly matters and influences what they grow up to like and consume. ("We are what we eat/consume.") If the goal of music education is to help students understand and appreciate music as an expressive art, band directors must select and use music of artistic merit in a variety of genres.

It is interesting to note that the Declaration emanating from the Tanglewood Symposium in 1967 called for "music to be placed in the core of the school curriculum." The Tanglewood Symposium was a gathering of scientists, sociologists, labor leaders, educators, representatives of corporations, musicians, and people involved with other aspects of music who came together to discuss and define the role of music education in contemporary American society and to make recommendations to improve the effectiveness of music instruction. Most of their recommendations are as relevant today as they were five decades ago especially the five below.

1. Music serves best when its integrity as an art is maintained.
2. Music of all periods, styles, forms, and cultures belongs in the curriculum. The musical repertory should be expanded to involve music of our time in its rich variety, including currently popular teenage music and avant-garde music, American folk music, and the music of other cultures.
3. Schools and colleges should provide adequate time for music programs ranging from pre-school through adult or continuing education.
4. Instruction in the arts should be a general and important part of education in the senior high school.
5. Greater emphasis should be placed on helping the individual student to fulfill his/her needs, goals, and potential.

At the Symposium's conclusion, MENC President Louis Wersen gave the following charge to music educators:

> In an era of protest, irritation, and rapid change, when students tell us that the music we teach and the methods we use are irrelevant and ineffectual; music educators cannot simply sit back with eyes closed and ears tuned backward. Clearly each music teacher's responsibility is to become increasingly aware of the aesthetic needs of not only all his/her students but also the entire community in which he/she serves. His/her teaching must relate to these needs. To a large extent the musical future will be what all of us, working together, make it. Let us put our minds and our talents to that task.[22]

A Selection of Programs Performed by Four Exemplary High School Bands/Wind Ensembles (1992–2016)

Wando (South Carolina) High School Symphonic Band
Scott B. Rush, conductor
March 23, 1992

Gumsucker's March	Percy Grainger
"Nimrod" from *Enigma Variations*	Edward Elgar/Slocum
Divertimento for Band	Vincent Persichetti

Toccata	Girolamo Frescobaldi/Slocum
The Solitary Dancer	Warren Benson
March from *Symphonic Metamorphosis*	Paul Hindemith/Wilson

Foxboro (Massachusetts) High School Wind Ensemble
Stephen C. Massey, conductor
January 30, 2003

George Washington Bridge	William Schumann
Children's March	Percy Aldridge Grainger
Down a Country Lane	Aaron Copland
Sketches on a Tudor Psalm	Fisher Tull

Westlake (Texas) High School Band
Kerry Taylor, conductor
April 9, 2008

March from *Symphonic Metamorphosis*	Paul Hindemith/Wilson
Dionysiaques	Florent Schmitt/Duker
J'ai été au bal	Donald Grantham

Spring (Texas) High School Wind Ensembles
Gabe Musella, conductor
May 9, 2016

Geschwindmarsch	Paul Hindemith
Russian Christmas Music	Alfred Reed
Sketches on a Tudor Psalm	Fisher Tull
"Jupiter, Venus, & Uranus" from *The Planets*	Gustav Holst/Patterson

ENDNOTES

1   Mark Leslie Fonder, "An Investigation of the Origin and Development of Four Wisconsin High School Bands." (Ed.D. diss., University of Illinois at Urbana-Champaign, 1983), 18.

2   Edward Bailey Birge, *A History of Public School Music in the United States* (Oliver Ditson, 1928), 182–183.

3   Joseph E. Maddy, "The School Orchestra and Band Movement," in *Who is Who in Music* (Lee Stern Press, 1941), 387.

4   Fonder, "An Investigation," 24.

5   C. M. Tremaine, "As We Go Marching," *School Musician* (December 1929): 6–9.

6   Peter Buys, "Bands in the United States," in *Who is Who in Music* (Lee Stern Press, 1941), 560.

7   Edwin Franko Goldman, "A Talk on Bands," *The Instrumentalist* 48 (September 1993): 112.

8   Michael L. Marks, "William D. Revelli: Portrait of a Distinguished Career," *Journal of Band Research* 16 (Fall 1980): 9.

9   Fonder, An Investigation," 35–36.

10 Robert T. Stroker, "The American Band Contest Movement, 1875–1940,"
    Journal of the World Association of Symphonic Bands and Ensembles 3 (1996): 38.

11 Jere T. Humphreys, "An Overview of American Public School Bands and
    Orchestras Before World War II," *Bulletin of the Council for Research in Music
    Education* No. 101 (Summer 1989): 58.

12 William Moody, "Tradition and the Band's Future," *The Instrumentalist* 23
    (November 1968): 80.

13 Brian Norcross, "The High School Band Repertoire, 1980–85" (Unpublished
    document, New England Conservatory, 1986), 1–2.

14 Ibid., 4–5.

15 Ibid., 49.

16 Correspondence with the author.

17 Roger Rocco, "Band Music and the Paper-Plate Mentality: An Interview with W.
    Francis McBeth," *The Instrumentalist* 46 (December 1991): 12–14.

18 Bobby Adams, "How Should Band Directors Deal with School Reform?" *Book
    of Proceedings*, 61st American Bandmasters Association Convention (March
    22–27, 1994), 39.

19 Frederick Fennell, interview with the author.

20 Allen Britton, "American Music Education: Is it Better Than We Think? A
    Discussion of the Role of Performance and Repertory, Together with Brief
    Mention of Certain Other Problems," in *Basic Concepts in Music Education II*, ed.
    Richard Colwell (University Press of Colorado, 1991), 180.

21 Zoltán Kodály, *The Selected Writings of Zoltán Kodály*, Ferenc Bónis, ed. (Boosey
    & Hawkes, 1974).

22 Louis G. Wersen, "Tanglewood's Lessons for Music Education," in *The
    Tanglewood Symposium: Music in American Society* (Music Educators National
    Conference, 1968), 57–58.

CHAPTER 22

What Music to Play and How to Program It

| *Repertoire, Programming, Concert Presentation, and the Audience* |

What Is a Repertoire?

A repertoire is a collection of works that have earned the respect and appreciation of conductors, players, and audiences and are played over and over. John Philip Sousa's *The Stars and Stripes Forever* is a solid fixture in the wind band's repertoire because it has been performed hundreds of times, by hundreds of bands, in hundreds of different environments since it was premiered in 1897. Audiences know the piece, like the piece, and enjoy hearing it performed. Works that are repeatedly performed in the same environment (for the same listeners) can increase the audience's awareness, understanding, appreciation, and enjoyment of them. A quote by composer/conductor André Previn, supports this point, "If people could hear out-of-the-way pieces as much as they hear Tchaikovsky five, they would become fans of these pieces."[1] The majority of works included on orchestra and chamber music programs consist of a body of pieces that have been and continue to be played over and over. Audiences know these works, like them, and attend concerts to hear them played again and again.

By contrast, wind bands/ensembles do not play a select body of works over and over—they do not have a repertoire. Their programs consist primarily of newly written works by composers that the general public is not acquainted with and know little or nothing about. The lack of a repertoire—repeat performances of a select body of works—is a detriment to the public's discovery, understanding, and appreciation of wind band/ensemble music.

Selecting a Repertoire—Programming—Expansion of the Audience's Awareness, Understanding, and Appreciation of Wind Band Music

Wind band/ensemble conductors past and present have faced the challenge of developing audiences that appreciate their music and attend their concerts. Edwin Franko Goldman, over seven decades ago (1942), stated that there were two hurdles that had to be overcome concerning wind band literature and audiences: first, the small repertoire of original band music, and second, the size of audiences that attend band concerts, which in large part is "made up of people who have little musical knowledge, training, or appreciation." Goldman concluded that "... we could work half-heartedly with what we have, or [with patience and planning,] develop, side by side, both the repertory and the audience's understanding of music."[2]

Happily, much progress has been made regarding Goldman's "first hurdle." There is now a sizable and significant body of original literature for wind band/ensemble composed by some of the best composers of the world. However, the development of an audience that appreciates wind band/ensemble music still has not been realized. Can anything be done to improve this situation? Below is a suggestion.

> Every conductor should identify a body of exceptional wind band/ensemble works that he/she feels needs to be played over and over (a personal repertoire). The number of pieces selected should not exceed

twenty. Fifty per cent of the music included on their concerts should be pieces from the conductor's selected body of works (repertoire). The remaining fifty per cent should be "new pieces"—new in the sense that they would be works receiving their first performance in that location. Thus, in a concert containing sixty minutes of music, thirty minutes would consist of works from the conductor's personal repertoire and the other thirty, works receiving their first performance in that location.

The repeated performances of a body of works could potentially help audiences: 1. become better acquainted with wind band/ensemble literature and, 2. over a period of time develop an appreciation and enthusiasm for the music.

Concert Presentation

Frederick Fennell, in a letter to the author dated February 6, 1995, commented on the presentation of the wind ensemble's contemporary repertoire. "We copied standard concert procedures without thought that this might not have been the best way to introduce new music by a new version of an old group. Programming Husa next to Owen Reed might have been orchestral and chamber [ensembles'] way, but they had such an informed audience in comparison to ours—one that had heard so much music, whereas those who came to us had been fed band pap, and all the rest. Perhaps we should have set up a completely new shop, with informative lectures, explanations, come-ons, different dress, change the set...."[3] Was Fennell suggesting that conductors should think "outside the box" and be creative in the presentation of their concerts?

If wind bands/ensembles are to become a significant component in American culture and society, the music they play must be appreciated, valued, and embraced by people. Formulating programs that can attract audiences is the key to audience expansion. Concerts that include pieces by composers such as Bernstein, Copland, and Gershwin as well as works by Schuller and Husa will attract a larger audience than a concert having only works by Schuller, Husa, Bassett, and Dahl. It would be wise for conductors to heed the advice of Vladimir Horowitz concerning the formulation of programs, "Remember the audience."

ENDNOTES

1 André Previn, "A View from Two Continents," *The Instrumentalist* 42 (February 1988): 17.
2 Edwin Franko Goldman, "Facing the Music" (typescript document, 1942), 270.
3 Frederick Fennell, letter to the author, February 6, 1995.

CHAPTER 23

What Leaders Think

❚ *Responses to Six Questions* **❚**

Chapter 18 in the original version of *The Winds of Change* includes the reflections of ten conductors who played important roles in the development of wind bands/ensembles during the last half of the twentieth century. They commented on what had been achieved and accomplished and what still needed to be done. For this second edition of the book I have again asked a group of leading conductors to share their thoughts about the current state of wind bands/ensembles in America. The conductors are:

Brendan Caldwell, Director, Wind Ensembles, Baldwin Wallace University Conservatory

Steven Davis, Director, Bands and Wind Ensembles, University of Missouri–Kansas City Conservatory

Michael Haithcock, Director of Bands, University of Michigan

Cynthia Johnston Turner, Director of Bands, University of Georgia

Charles Peltz, Director of Wind Ensemble, New England Conservatory

Stephen Peterson, Director of Bands, University of Illinois

Mark Scatterday, Conductor, Eastman Wind Ensemble

Kevin Sedatole, Director of Bands, Michigan State University

Mallory Thompson, Director of Bands, Northwestern University

Each conductor was asked to respond to the following questions.

1. Do you think the wind band/ensemble has advanced as a vehicle for artistic expression in the past two decades? If so, in what ways?

2. What in your opinion are the most significant works composed for the wind band/ensemble since 2000?

3. What are the greatest challenges now facing:
   a. The wind band/ensemble
   b. The art of music in our society

4. Are band directors/associations commissioning the greatest composers in the world to write pieces for the wind band/ensemble? If not, why do you think this is not being done?

5. List composers, who have never written a piece for wind band/ensembles, that you feel should be commissioned to write a work for the medium.

6. Is what is happening in the best university/college wind band/ensemble programs affecting what is occurring in American high school bands as well as its directors? If so, how; if not, why not.

Note: Each conductor below is identified by the letters of their first and last name: Brendan Caldwell (**BC**), Steven Davis (**SD**), Michael Haithcock (**MH**), Cynthia Johnston Turner (**CJT**), Charles Peltz (**CP**), Stephen Peterson (**SP**), Mark Scatterday (**MS**), Kevin Sedatole (**KS**), Mallory Thompson (**MT**)

Question No. 1. Do you think the wind band/ensemble has advanced as a vehicle for artistic expression in the past two decades? If so, in what ways?

MH: Most Definitely! The amount of repertoire composed by major composers who in previous decades would not have given the wind band the time of day is a prime indicator. Bolcom and Corigliano are two exemplary cases. The number of young composers of high quality who are starting their professional lives with works for band as opposed to us having to chase them is a second, but equally important, indicator. These young composers are not pedagogically contracted composers but people who view the band through the lens of their own experience as a vehicle for a high level of artistic expression.

I also think the types of pieces being written elevate the genre: longer, more substantive works; more concertos and song cycles; more mixed media; and multiple operas with wind accompaniment.

All of these elements point to the continued growth and evolution of the medium.

MS: The wind ensemble movement in the past two decades has certainly seen a significant advancement in the training and education of wind conductors, which has become more diverse, comprehensive, and thorough.... Our ensembles have become more malleable in their size and instrumentation. The repertoire has become more diverse in its styles.... While we certainly need to seek out more continued artistic enlightenment, we have seen the wind ensemble far outpacing the growth of the orchestra in the past two decades, and that trend only appears to be increasing.

CJT: Yes, and no. The commissioning wave has not waned, in fact the wave has gained momentum. The wind ensemble as a medium is in love with the new.... We are "the friend of the living composer." We are celebrated for innovation and in some ways, we are (slowly) leading the way in diversity programming (female composers/composers of color). But, we don't seem to be re-programming the works that we have commissioned over the years—the works that we deem as significant. There are some exceptions to this, of course, but good new works tend to have a shelf life "of a few years.... We keep commissioning, and that's fine, but we won't grow a standard repertoire until we establish one.

If we define "success" as an acceptance of the wind band in the art world at large, we have not succeeded. Many living composers laud the wind band and encourage their students to write for the medium. They know their music will be performed, rehearsed, and taken seriously, and they also know that academic ensembles are getting better and better. Perhaps we just need to keep on [doing what we're doing] and be patient.

MT: I would love to be able to give an unequivocal positive response to the question, but I can't. I think that the level of individual "playing" has advanced, particularly in terms of technique and the pedagogy that is used to train musicians.... As a result, I believe that the potential for artistic expression has improved over the past twenty years.

Positive: Repertoire continues to challenge boundaries of style (beyond just technique) and preconceived limitations of what a wind band/ensemble "IS."

Negative: There seems to be an increased focus on advanced technical playing and loud dynamics.... This is a ... huge negative.

BC: There is little doubt in my mind that our medium has continued to advance in the first two decades of this new millennium. [There is continuous growth] in the quantity and quality of well-trained conductors.... The finest composition teachers in the world [are encouraging] their students to write for the medium.... World-class recordings are coming from ensembles across the globe

CP: No, not really. But I wonder what academic musical endeavors (at any level) have done so? I do think some directors have become aware of how the individual musician can be enticed/inspired to be more expressively involved in ensembles. But there are those who might be unconnected to the transcendence of art in general. It seems as if sometimes the director is more engaged in an exercise which creates a product, albeit often an exceptionally good one. But the creation of this product is not in itself an expressive accomplishment. Some of this lack of expression is inherent in the music itself, there is often too great an emphasis on energy, gesture, and effect. There is too little demand for a repertoire (including the reclaiming of older repertoire) which has a wider rhetoric of nuanced narrative or sustained, thoughtful expression.

SP: I believe the wind ensemble has advanced as a vehicle for artistic expression to the extent that we seem to have a larger number of highly proficient ensembles than we did twenty years ago.... Unfortunately, [these] ensembles remain, by and large, in the academic/collegiate arena, so whatever inroads we have achieved remain largely unnoticed by those outside our field of influence. Beyond the quality of performances themselves, we have been more successful at attracting more ... composers to our medium, though there is still much work to do here.

KS: There is no question that the wind ensemble has advanced in the last twenty years. I think the most significant qualifier of this is the attraction of world-renowned composers. The response to the medium by composers such as John Corigliano, William Bolcom, [and] David Del Tredici have influenced so many more.... Additionally, I believe the flexibility of the ensemble instrumentation/personnel has given freedom to composers to write what they want.

SD: We have advanced while also not advancing, and, even moving backwards, in some instances. Numerous people are leading consortia that are beneficial to the art by commissioning such composers as Skrowaczewski, Beaser, Corigliano, and Zhou Long. However, the field gets bogged down with other composers that are mediocre in their artistic merit. It is not that these composers are not appreciated for their efforts, they are. But I would rather see other new composers write for the medium, instead of ten (or twenty) pieces from the same composers. Once we have a couple of pieces from a composer, we should commission other world-class composers (those who have not written a wind ensemble piece) to write for our ensembles—Reich, Glass, Adams, etc. Many of the pieces we now have certainly exploit loud, visceral, and pop driven devices. I would rather see effort spent on soliciting chamber music pieces and one-act chamber operas with chamber wind ensembles.

Question No. 2. What in your opinion are the most significant works composed for the wind band/ensemble since 2000?

MH: Bolcom — *First Symphony for Band* (2009)
Botti — *Cosmosis* (2005)
Corigliano — *Symphony No. 3 "Circus Maximus"* (2004)
Daugherty — *Labyrinth of Love* (2013)
Skrowaczewski — *Music for Winds* (2009)

MS: Skrowaczewski — *Music for Winds* (2009)
Maslanka — *Symphony No. 8* (2008)
Beaser — *The End of Knowing* (2014)
Bryant — *Concerto for Wind Ensemble* (2009)
Corigliano — *Symphony no. 3 "Circus Maximus"* (2004)
Previn — *Music for Wind Orchestra* (2014)

CJT: In this context, I'm assuming "significant" means "advancing the medium" or "pushing the boundaries."
Skrowaczewski — *Music for Winds* (2001). There are moments in this work where he would have failed an orchestration class, but because of that he's created incredible new colors.
Corigliano — *Circus Maximus* (2004). A feat of excess and brilliantly conceived.
Likhuta — *Scraps from a Madman's Diary* (2016). A secular oratorio with an important message. Provides a wonderful addition to the repertoire for wind band and singers. Audience reactions are consistently overwhelming.
Mackey — *Frozen Cathedral* (2013). Architecturally beautiful. Every climax is deserved. Audiences are inspired by it.

MT: This is a very difficult question for me to answer, because there are many additional works and composers whose music I believe in.... Each [of the pieces below] brings a unique point of view, creates a distinct and transformative sound world, and offers limitless opportunities for expression and reflection.
Corigliano — Symphony No. 3, "*Circus Maximus*" (2004)
Bryant — *Concerto for Wind Ensemble* (2009)
Skrowaczewski — *Music for Winds* (2009)
Pann — *My Brother's Brain: A Symphony for Winds* (2011)
Puckett — *that secret from the river* (2015)

BC: Ticheli — *Songs of Love and Life* (2011)
Needham — *Resolve* (2018)
Maslanka — *Give Us This Day: Short Symphony for Wind Ensemble* (2005)
Daugherty — *Bells for Stokowski* (2002)
Pann — *My Brother's Brain: A Symphony for Winds* (2011)

CP: Lindberg — *Gran Duo* (2000)
Skrowaczewski — *Music for Winds* (2009)
Ticheli — *Songs of Love and Life* (2012)
Henze — *L'heure bleue* (2001)

SP: Skrowaczewski — *Music For Winds* (2009)
Corigliano — *Symphony No. 3, "Circus Maximus* (2004)
Bryant — *Concerto for Wind Ensemble* (2009)

KS: Corigliano — *Symphony No. 3, Circus Maximus* (2004)
Bolcom — *First Symphony for Band* (2009)
Bryant — *Concerto for Wind Ensemble* (2009)
Schoenberg — *Migration* (2017)

SD: Skrowaczewski — *Music for Winds* (2009)
Beaser — *The End of Knowing* (2014)
Bolcom — *First Symphony for Band* (2009)
Botti — *Cosmosis* (2005)
Corigliano — *Symphony No. 3, "Circus Maximus"* (2004)
Others: Zhou Long — *Ancient Echoes*, Mobberley — *Words of Love*, Magnus Lindberg — *Gran Duo*

Question No. 3. What are the greatest challenges now facing:
a. The wind band/ensemble
b. The art of music in our society

MH: Part a. Make the ensemble about the music! Cultivate the best new music possible and "filter" the available repertoire as time goes on. Pieces that were stalwarts of the repertoire when I started in 1978 are now somewhat on the back burner. Persichetti works for example. All that has replaced it might not be better, but much of it is.

MS: Part a & b. Probably the biggest challenge is how we can improve the wind ensemble's reputation and function as a serious medium for the performance of art music.... We need to commit to commissioning ... but we also need to follow-through from our end and program ... works often enough that they become part of our repertoire.... We must ... attract and engage audiences ... we need to be innovative, creative, and adapt to the changing tastes and consumption habits of modern audiences.... the more we can do to connect our art to society, the community, and human beings, the more connected to society our art will become.... Worldwide, we face marginalization. Live music is confronted with decreasing audience appeal and performing arts education continues to decline in many countries. Staying in touch with society's needs and wants can lead to more creative artistic connections.

CJT: Part a. Ourselves. There are too many collegiate wind conductors more interested in advancing their own careers (to what end?) instead of advancing the medium, or caring for the students in front of them to the best of their ability.

The more we focus on the competition or judged performance in band, the fewer consumers of music we will have in the future. I don't think we are teaching our students to appreciate quality. We aren't defining it well enough. We criticize well ... we're really good at that, but we don't establish criteria for defining good music. That's harder, isn't it?

Music education (CMS) is leaning toward diversity in higher education curriculum models and there is a perceived (if not real) threat to large ensembles in the curriculum.

Part b. The digitized world is often perceived as a challenge to the attention span and/or presence of an audience for art making in our society. But I don't think that's the case. Technology has always been a force for good or for bad depending on the user. Many arts organizations are using AR and VR to enhance the consumer experience and it's working. Music is perceived by many as peripheral to the real concerns of society, which is why music making with a social justice or activism is gaining more popularity.

MT: Part a. & b. My answers to both a. and b. lie in the following questions:

Why do we exist?

What are we trying to express?

Are we providing substantial and meaningful fuel for our students and audiences?

Can we do a better job of reflecting the actual makeup of our society in our membership, audiences, and the composers we perform?

Part b. I think that a looming issue has to do with the immediate access technology provides to almost everything. While technology offers many positives, I believe that the negatives will ultimately influence our ability to reflect on or express large-scale ideas or simply sit with or BE WITH an art that evolves slowly in real time.

BC: Part b. In our society, the practice of sustained, focused perception is becoming increasingly rare. Through the advent of social media, our society has replaced literature with quotations and meaningful dialogue with sound bites. For the art of music, this is both an existential challenge ... and a profound opportunity (as subsequently, music education holds an essential role in the survival and enlightenment of our species).

CP: Part a. The wind band/ensemble's non-contemplative music is ... too reliant on a program or an idea which compels (allows) composers to rely on the "idea" and not the demands inherent in the writing of absolute music—the artful manipulation of tones.

Part b. The culture [in our society] is abandoning the communal partaking of things. As such, the idea of a temporal, communal/shared artistic moment is becoming less understood and desired by many. The abandonment of the "ideal" in art elevates the banal and reduces the aspirations of a culture to something higher.

SP: Part a. One of the biggest challenges for the band/wind ensemble is maintaining its relevancy.... The band is seen as old fashioned, deeply embedded in only western European culture, incapable of allowing individual creativity, and rife with self-serving authoritarian conductor/teachers. These criticisms are not without merit, though, I believe they are greatly exaggerated.

There seems to have been a shift whereby listening to music has, for most, become a passive activity—no longer an active consumer endeavor. We must figure new ways to engage our audiences ... that are meaningful [so] that they will return to our concerts over and over again.

SD: Part a. Wind ensembles function primarily on academic campuses. They need to move into communities and make themselves "indispensable."

Part b. Music in society is more disparate than ever. This means that there are many silos. How can we join hands and make our music environment more "together?"

Question No. 4. Are band directors/associations commissioning the greatest composers in the world to write pieces for the wind band/ensemble? If not, why do you think this is not being done?

MH: As much as possible, I think this is happening. Money flows toward what is available. John Adams has not been willing to accept a commission, so he has not written an original piece since *Grand Pianola Music*. Is that our fault? I don't think so, lots of effort has been expended. The amount of money is sometimes staggering and the "greatest composers" are not always willing to [accept a commission from] a large consortium. There are many factors. I don't think effort or awareness is lacking.

MS: In some cases, we are, but in large part we are not. We tend to [commission] certain composers who write a majority of their works (if not exclusively) for winds and continue to commission [them]. While many great works come out of this practice, and it feels safe to go to a reliable, predictable source, we need to do better [and] commission [other] composers. Perhaps the main constraint to commissioning the "greatest" composers in the world is a financial one; the higher the demand of a composer, the more exorbitant the cost of a commission. With most programs facing [tighter] budgets, it makes sense to participate in more affordable consortiums. We may need to change the way we organize these ... commissioning projects and involve more entities [in order to] successfully engage the world's most in-demand composers.

CJT: No. Of course not. Why is this not being done? One, [because] we're not paying attention. We tend to focus on those who are already writing for wind band and go there. Two, American conductors focus on American composers and play American music. There are several composers doing interesting, even "incredible" things around the world, but we don't pay that much attention or do the research to find out.

MT: We are doing a good job of identifying composers and trying to build relationships with them, so to a degree, yes. If composers don't write for us it is probably because of money, lack of composer interest, timing, and because there are vastly more ensembles ... that are commissioning now.

BC: While I applaud (and still participate with) conductors pooling their resources together to commission projects too expensive for any one institution, I have found the process of personal collaboration with a composer to be much more meaningful to all those bringing the premiere to life. Please don't get me wrong, consortia commissioning projects are wonderful—and I thoroughly believe our profession should continue to "gather resources" to bring great art to life. But I also assert that commissioning projects become more meaningful in equal measure to the extent that the conductor and performing musicians get to engage with the composer in meaningful dialogue regarding the intention and development of the premiere.

SP: Band directors and associations have done a much better job in recent years at commissioning some of the great composers. There are, however, many more we need to commission but it seems like we are making progress. We need to pursue composers who have never written for the wind band/ensemble as well as underrepresented women and African-American composers. The world's major composers are paid large sums of money for their works. We must find the financial resources so we can commission them. We should also establish a major band composition prize similar to major international composition prizes that [would hopefully] entice the world's great composers to write pieces for us.

SD: No, I do not. We need to come up with substantial dollars—through consortia—that will allow us to commission the finest composers and idea-makers. We need a person, hired full time, to oversee our consortia operations. The administrative aspects of commissioning are substantial. If we raised $100,000 a year we could commission a substantial, large-scale piece? If we did that, annually, for five years, we [potentially] could have five substantial pieces. The "hit parade"—$10,000 consortiums—provides very little, long term benefit and do not really advance the wind band/ensemble, beyond hype and hysterics. The first thing we need to do is identify the finest 5–10 living composers who haven't written for the wind band/ensemble and then come up with a plan to get them to do so.

Question No. 5. List composers, who have never written a piece for wind band/ensembles, that you feel should be commissioned to write a work for the medium.

MH: John Adams is at the top of the list. There are so many young composers who are emerging. Caroline Shaw is an example, but she has rejected overtures to this point.

MS: Michael Nyman
Giya Kancheli
John Adams
Philip Glass
Thomas Adès
Kaija Saariaho
Esa-Pekka Salonen
Steve Reich
Hans Abrahamsen
Missy Mazzoli
Daníel Bjarnason
Arvo Pärt
Caroline Shaw
John Luther Adams

CJT: I love this question. All you have to do is Google the Pulitzer Prize winners/nominees for the last several years. Kate Soper, Henry Threadgill, John Zorn, John Luther Adams, Caroline Shaw, Julia Wolfe, Julia Adolphe, Bruce Adolphe ... but also, wouldn't it be cool to ask, Randy Newman, Billy Joel, Chanda Dancy, AnthonyR.Green, Maria Schneider, Daniel Kidane, Björk, Betsy Jolas, Wolfgang Rihm, Olga Neuwirth, Unsuk Chin ... You may note that I've included mostly women and/or composers of color. More white men need to commission and champion these composers.

MT: Glass, Muhly, Sondheim (why not? it would be great to have a musical for winds, percussion and synthesizers), Puts, Wolfe, Soper. Plus I would LOVE to have a new work by John Adams.

BC: Dan Redfield
Osvaldo Golijov
Missy Mazzoli
Phillip Glass
John Luther Adams

CP: Maria Schneider
Esa-Pekka Salonen
James MacMillan

SP: John Adams
Missy Mazzoli
Caroline Shaw
Wynton Marsalis
Shulamit Ran
Andrew Norman
Julia Wolfe
Steve Reich
George Crumb
Maria Schneider
Arvo Pärt
Georg Friedrich Haas

KS: John Adams
Philip Glass
Robert Beaser

SD: In no particular order:
Mark Anthony Turnage, Anna Cline, Missy Mazzoli, Du Yun, Shulamit Ran, Nico Muhly, Arvo Pärt, Morten Lauridsen (an original piece), Reich, Glass, John Adams, John Luther Adams, Andrew Norman, Julia Wolfe, George Crumb, Sam Adams (John's son), Tan Dun, Caroline Shaw

Question No. 6. Is what is happening in the best university/ college wind band/ensemble programs affecting what is happening in American high school bands as well as its directors? If so, how; if not, why not.

MH: Yes. I think YouTube and recordings are serving as models for the level of performance and a gateway into discovering composers that rise beyond the pedagogical contract composers.

CJT: I like to think that what is happening at the University of Georgia is affecting what is happening in Georgia schools. But that's partly because I visit a lot of schools and am trying to forge good relationships with our excellent music educators in the state. I think there has been a fundamental mistrust or miscommunication between high school band directors [and] our best higher education wind ensemble programs—the proverbial "ivory tower." High school directors see many of us as elitist and out of touch, which in some cases is true. Again, that's partly because many higher education conductors are more ... career focused instead of student and/or music focused.

I'm not sure the best higher education ensemble programs SHOULD affect what is happening in high school bands. If you mean repertoire (Why aren't higher ed ensembles playing music my high school band can play so they can model excellence?), then I'm not sure that's good.... I think the institutions have different missions. But they all should be focusing on QUALITY music and teaching a love for music, not just band, or competition, or trophies, or marching.

MT: Positive influences: there are more commissions and greater interest in creating new music at all levels, more composers of university-level [works] are also writing for school ensembles, more teachers are working to improve their conducting skills by attending conducting symposia, some districts are sponsoring their own in-service events which focus on conducting or rehearsal techniques.

Negative influences: too much focus on value or status of playing technically difficult music. Conducting well [and] looking good seems to eclipse understanding the score and having something musical to express.

BC: There are some aspects of distinguished university programs that are affecting high school programs. One such example is the culture of commissioning new compositions that seems to have baked itself into the very DNA of what it means to be a wind band conductor.... As high school band directors tend to mimic their collegiate mentors, so too does the process of performance driven pedagogy tend to under-nurture a more comprehensive approach to music education that seeks to develop "music lovers."

CP: One can't make a general statement here, which is the temptation. But in so many ways the cultures are completely different [and] not just musically. From school discipline issues ... to the popular music today, there is a vast gulf between the focused formality and (attempted) sophistication required in college music study and the opposite of these (even the disdain for these) often embraced in many levels and places in secondary education. I don't see how secondary school art music study survives in the current culture. Except in ... schools ... led by the rare, unique person who rejects most of the shallow contemporary and embraces the enduring. And that strikes damagingly at the heart of an equal society.

The embrace of "Toscanini over Sousa" has had unintended consequences. It has made the conducting of music more important than the teaching of it. It has elevated the visual affects over the sonic essentials. The error was in not recognizing that Arturo had professionals who did not need to be taught. Most wind band conductors have students desperately in need of a person for whom teaching is at the ever-present forefront of their thinking. To think that we could have both Arturo Toscanini and Walter Beeler was in itself an assumption that required more thought.

SP: It is difficult if not impossible for most high school bands to perform much of the literature [composed for the better university bands]. Without a shared repertoire, I suspect that college programs have less effect on high school programs than in the past. Beyond that ... I fear that [the] daily pressures felt in the public high school, along with the all too prevalent lean toward making high school band an activity as opposed to a vehicle for learning about music, have pulled these two essential parts of the band ... world apart from each other.

SD: This question would require an entire book to answer. I feel that the disconnect between university and school bands has never been greater than it is at the present time.

* * * * * * * * * * *

A review of the conductor responses above reveals that there was general agreement on some issues and a variety of opinions on others. Most conductors thought the wind band/ensemble "had advanced as a vehicle of artistic expression" since 2000. However, Steven Davis pointed out that the continuous commissioning of "composers that are mediocre in their artistic merit" has "bogged down" the advancement of the medium.

Stanislaw Skrowaczewski's *Music for Winds* and John Corigliano's *Symphony No. 3 "Circus Maximus"* were on almost everyone's list of significant wind works composed since 2000.

There was general agreement that wind bands/ensembles had to improve their relationship and connection with people, communities and society at large. Cynthia Johnston Turner stated that concerts associated with social justice or activism were growing in popularity and attracting listeners. Steven Davis pointed out that wind groups needed to leave their academic environments, move into the larger community, and make themselves "indispensable."

Five of the nine conductors believed that the reason for not commissioning "the best composers in the world" was because of the "staggering" amount of money needed to do so. Stephen Peterson and Cynthia Johnston Turner recommended that more commissions go to women and African-American composers.

Topping the list of important world composers that should be commissioned to write a wind band/ensemble piece were John Adams, Caroline Shaw, and Philip Glass.

A majority of conductors felt that the relationship between university/college wind bands/ensembles and high school bands was "not as strong as it used to be" and that university/college band directors did not exert as much influence on school band directors as they once did. Stephen Peterson stated that the loss of a shared repertoire was a significant factor in the weakening of this relationship. However, Michael Haithcock did point out that performances of college/university wind bands/ensembles on YouTube and CD recordings were being used by school band directors to motivate students.

CHAPTER 24

Coda—An Agenda for the 2020s and Beyond

Below are some suggestions regarding the future of wind bands/ensembles and the teaching of the art of music.

1. Every wind band/ensemble association (CBDNA, ABA, NBA, ASBDA, ACB, WASBE, etc.) has objectives dedicated to advancing the wind band/ensemble and the professional development of its conductor/director membership. All organize and hold conferences/conventions and undertake various projects. Often these projects and initiatives overlap and/or duplicate each other. I would suggest that these associations join together and develop initiatives that would benefit the entire wind band/ensemble community. Advocacies undertaken and supported by an alliance of all wind band/ensemble associations would, I believe, be more effective and successful than those undertaken by separate associations.

2. Strategies must be developed to ensure that funds are available to commission "the best composers in the world." These composers should be commissioned to write works for all levels of wind bands/ensembles and not just for advanced and/or professional level groups. Igor Stravinsky and Béla Bartók both wrote music for young and professional level musicians.

3. Most works programmed on wind band/ensemble concerts for the past four decades have consisted primarily of new or recently composed works written by composers that are, for the most part, unknown to the general public. This practice has limited the performances of excellent older works, some of which were composed by master composers. It has also restricted opportunities for audiences to hear works often enough to become acquainted with them. People generally attend concerts to hear music they know, appreciate, and enjoy. They are not attracted to concerts that consist of pieces they do not know, written by composers completely unknown to them. Expanding audiences at wind band/ensemble concerts should be a top priority of everyone associated with wind groups. Repeated performances of a select group of pieces (repertoire) would help listeners become familiar and, hopefully, appreciate them. This strategy, I believe, could potentially lead to increased audiences for wind band/ensemble music.

4. Conductors need to experiment with new means of "presenting" wind band/ensemble music to the public. Developing imaginative and new "presentation formats" might attract people, who have no interest in attending a "traditional wind band concert," to attend one. For example, at a concert performed by a small wind ensemble, the audience could be seated on stage where they could both listen to the music and also observe the interaction between the conductor and players and between players. Full ensemble performances could be enhanced through the use of appropriate videos that complement the music being performed.

5. All new technological devices and instruments should be used to promote wind bands/ensembles and their music. Every iPhone and iPad is a concert hall.

6. Wind band/ensemble conductors in the United States should take a greater interest in works written by composers beyond their borders. Several of these composers have written extraordinary pieces for the medium. An increase in the performance of works by non-American composers could

transform the American wind band/ensemble from a nationally focused music group into a more international/global musical ensemble.

7. The practice of continuously commissioning the same composers should be abandoned. This practice stymies the growth and enrichment of wind band/ensemble literature. For a medium to develop and grow as an expressive sonic vehicle, its literature must be continually fueled and expanded through contributions of new creative voices. Commissioning important world composers, those who write music for a diverse spectrum of performers and ensembles, is the best way to ensure that this happens. Wind band/ensemble conductors, ensembles, and professional associations should retreat from continuously commissioning the same composers and instead, commission the best composers in the world (including women and African-American composers) to compose music for the medium.

8. The preparation and education of future music teachers/wind band/ensemble directors needs to be revised. Much more emphasis should be placed on the artistic development of these future music teachers. In striving to become a better musician—"an artist musician"—these students discover and feel the richness and excitement of the "musical experience"—they grow to "love music!" As "artists" who also want to teach, their focus will be on helping students become "music lovers." Presently most colleges and universities do not prepare future music educators to be "artist teachers." Instead, they prepare them to become organizers, administrators, and supervisors of "activities" in which music "is used." Unfortunately, most of those "activities" have not (and will not) nurture a genuine "love of music."

Postscript

Every once in a while we have feelings so deep and so special that we have no words for them. Music names them for us, only in notes instead of in words. It's all in the way music moves—we must never forget that music is movement, always going somewhere, shifting and changing, and flowing, from one note to another; and that movement can tell us more about the way we feel than a million words can.

Leonard Bernstein, composer and conductor
(*Young People's Concerts*, CBS-TV, 1960)

... when [I and] one hundred men[/women] share feelings exactly, simultaneously, responding as one to each rise and fall of the music, to each point of arrival and departure, to each little inner pulse—then there is a human identity of feeling that has no equal elsewhere ....

Leonard Bernstein, composer and conductor
(*The Joy of Music*, 1959)

I think some young people want a deeper experience. Some people just wanna be hit over the head and, you know, if then they [get] hit hard enough maybe they'll feel something. You know? But some people want to get inside of something and discover, maybe, more richness. And I think it will always be the same; they're not going to be the great percentage of the people. A great percentage of the people don't want a challenge. They want something to be done to them—they don't want to participate. But there'll always be maybe 15% maybe, 15%, that desire something more, and they'll search it out—and maybe that's where art is, I think.

Bill Evans, jazz musician
(Interview: *The Bill Evans Web Pages*, 1980)

The experience of art ... is an experience through which we can gain an insight into what it means to be free in emotional response, and free in the choice of ideas. The experience of art is a way of enriching the quality of human experience, and of reaching a precision in the choice of values. It is a particular kind of experience which requires for its fulfillment a discipline, freely undertaken, a knowledge firmly grasped, a heightened consciousness, and an intensity of interest in the creative and imaginative aspects of human life. It is not an experience which takes the [individual/]artist out of the material world or out of the context of his[/her] society, but an experience which moves through contemporary reality into newer levels of awareness of what human society is.

Harold Taylor, philosopher and educator
(*Art and Intellect*, 1960)

APPENDIX 1

Chronology of Selected Wind Band/Ensemble Literature 2011–2015

Note: Each composition is listed either in the year of its completion or première performance date. A chronology of selected wind band/ensemble literature from 1900–1999 included in *The Winds of Change*, and a similar chronology covering the years 2000–2010, from *The Winds of Change II* can be found at http://www.sheetmusicdirect.com/go/the-winds-of-change-chronology-of-works.

2011

Anderson Alden	*Winter Concerto for Electric Violin*
James Barnes	*Symphonic Requiem (Symphony No. 7)*
Mason Bates	*Sea-Blue Circuitry*
Andrew Boysen	*Symphony No. 6*
Bruce Broughton	*In the World of Spirits*
Steven Bryant	*Concerto for Wind Ensemble*
Mark Camphouse	*Reminiscences*
Chen Yi	*Dragon Rhyme*
John Corigliano	*The Red Violin Chacone* (trans. B. Lorenzo)
Viet Cuong	*Sound and Smoke*
Cuong Vu	*Solitary Confinement* (trans. T. Salzman)
John M. Davis	*First Little Serenade*
Avner Dorman	*Astrolatry* (trans. Pompey)

Donald Grantham	*Concerto for Tuba, Orchestra Winds, Percussion and Piano*
Jennifer Higdon	*Mysterium*
Ben Hjertmann	*Catclaw Mimosa*
Huck Hodge	*from the language of shadows*
Takuma Itoh	*Daydreams*
Jesse Jones	*Beyond the Veil*
Daniel Kellogg	*A Toast to Ben*
David Lang	*cheating, lying, stealing*
John Mackey	*Foundry*
Scott McAllister	*Music from the Redneck Songbook II*
Bryan Morgan	*Aaron's Fanfare*
Jody Nagel	*As You Like It*
Shawn E. Okpebholo	*This is Africa*
Carter Pann	*My Brother's Brain: A Symphony for Winds*
Joel Puckett	*Avelynn's Lullaby*
Nathan Prillaman	*Transcontinental*
Brian Rhodes	*Icefire for Alto Saxophone and Concert Band*
Michael Schelle	*The End of the World*
Bright Sheng	*Shanghai Overture (2007/2011)*
Jess Langston Turner	*Burning Music*
Joseph Turrin	*Equinox*
Kristina Warren	*negative one plus three equals two*

2012

Daniel Basford	*Partita in D*
Laurence Bilensky	*Fearsome Critters*
Steven Bryant	*Solace*
Mark Camphouse	*Elegy, Prayer, and Hymn*
Tyler Capp	*Cryptogram*
John Corigliano	*Elegy (1965, trans. 2012)*
Cody Criswell	*The Awesome Machingery of Nature*
Joseph Curtis	*Thornbriar Rhapsody*
Costas Dafnis	*Parliament in Flight Animation*
Brett William Dietz	*Spiritual: Concerto for Alto Saxophone and Wind Ensemble*
Christopher Dietz	*Chrysanthemum*
Paul Dooley	*Point Blank*
Michael Gandolfi	*Flourishes and Meditations on a Renaissance Theme*

Amil Gilut	*this is not a march*
Patrick Harlin	*Rapture* (2011, rev. 2012)
James Lee III	*Ancient Words! Current Realities*
Alexandre Lunsqui	*Ubehebe*
John Mackey	*Sheltering Sky*
Kristopher Maloy	*SPIN*
John Mayrose	*Bending Light*
Scott McAllister	*Gone*
Scott McAllister	*Mercury on the Moon*
Marc Mellits	*Requiem for a Hummingbird*
Jonathan Newman	*Blow it Up, Start Again*
Narong Prangcharoen	*Anātman, a work for Cello And Wind Ensemble*
Andrew Rindfleisch	*American Scripture*
Danield Bernard Roumain	*The Order of an Empty Place*
Gerard Schwarz	*Above and Beyond*
Zach Stanton	*Concerto for Piano and Wind Ensemble*
Frank Ticheli	*Songs of Love and Life*
Travis Weller	*Romance for Winds*
Eric Whitacre	*Rumor Mill*
Michael Young	*Concerto for Alto Saxophone, Op. 123*

2013

William Bolcom	*Circus Overture*
Susan Botti	*sull'ala (Concerto for Saxophone and Wind Ensemble)*
Andrew Boysen	*This is the Drum*
Michael Daugherty	*Labyrinth of Love for Soprano, Winds, Piano, Contrabass and Percussion*
Mohammed Fairouz	*Symphony No. 4, "In the Shadow of No Towers"*
David Gillingham	*Bright Gleams a Beacon*
Adam Gorb	*Love Transforming*
Donald Granthem	*Let Evening Come*
Stephen Gryc	*Six Romances after Mendelssohn*
Kenneth Hesketh	*Autumn's Elegy*
Scott Lindroth	*Alarm Calls*
John Mackey	*The Frozen Cathedral*
John Mackey	*The Soul Has Many Motions*
Christopher Marshall	*Glimpses of Love*
David Maslanka	*Requiem*
John Mayrose	*Bending Light*

James Mobberley	*A Crowd of Stars*
Mike Mower	*Concerto Maxo Mosso*
Hankus Netsky	*Nonantum Bulgar*
Joel Puckett	*Short Stories*
Kevin Puts	*Network*
John Fitz Rogers	*Narragansett*
Nathan Stang	*Undertow*
James Stephenson	*A Dialogue of Self and Soul*, for Bassoon and Wind Ensemble
Christopher Theofanidis	*Glimpses of Love*
Christopher Theofanidis	*Concerto for Marimba and Wind Sinfonietta*
Michael Torke	*Bliss*
John Williams	*For "The President's Own"*
Dana Wilson	*Concerto for Tuba and Wind Ensemble*
Kerwin Young	*Inescapable (Concerto for Contrabass and Wind Symphony)*

2014

Robert Beaser	*The End of Knowing*
William Bolcom	*Concerto for Clarinet and Band*
Steven Bryant	*all stars are love* (wind band version)
Steven Bryant	*Concerto for Alto Saxophone*
Chiayu Hsu	*Jie Ching (Festivals)*
Steve Danyew	*Alcott Songs* (for Soprano and Chamber Winds)
James David	*All Dark Is Now No More*
Paul Dooley	*Coast of Dreams*
Paul Dooley	*Masks and Machines*
Michael Gandolfi	*Winding Up/Winding Down* (for Clarinet and Wind Ensemble)
John Mackey	*Wine-Dark Sea: Symphony for Band*
Clint Needham	*Concerto for Wind Ensemble*
André Previn	*Music for Wind Orchestra (No Strings Attached)*
Gunther Schuller	*From Here to There*
Shuying Li	*Slippery Slope*
Peter Van Zandt Lane	*Hivemind*
Dan Welcher	*Downshifting*
Chelsea Williamson	*Dreams of Another Time*

2015

James Barnes	*Symphony No. 8*
Mason Bates	"Chicago, 2012" from *Alternative Energy*
William Bolcom	*Inventing Flight* (trans. Jason Nam)
Chen Yi	*Ba Yin (The Eight Sounds) (Saxophone Quartet and Chamber Winds)*
Nigel Clarke	*A Richer Dust (Symphony No. 1 for Speaker and Wind Orchestra)*
John Mackey	*Fanfare for Full Fathom Five*
John Mackey	*Ohm*
Michael Daugherty	*Reflections on the Mississippi for Tuba and Symphonic Band*
Michael Daugherty	*Winter Dreams*
Paul Dooley	*Masks and Machines*
David Gillingham	*Vital Signs of Planet Earth*
Michael Kurek	*Monument*
Steven Mackey	*Songs from the End of the World*
Michael Markowski	*Monk by the Sea*
Carter Pann	*High Songs for Amplified Cello and Chamber Winds*
Narong Prangcharoen	*Lokuttara*
Marco Pütz	*Time for Outrage*
James Stephenson	*Song of Myself for Soprano and Wind Ensemble*
James Syler	*Congo Square (for African Drum Quartet and Wind Ensemble)*
Stephen Andrew Taylor (arr.)	*Spirituals*
Dana Wilson	*Concerto for Contrabass and Wind Ensemble*
Dana Wilson	*Concerto for Trombone and Wind Ensemble*
Kevin Wilt	*Concerto for Saxophone Quartet, Winds, and Percussion*

APPENDIX 2

Wind Band/Ensemble Composition Awards and Prizes in the Twenty-First Century

American Bandmasters Association/Ostwald Award

2000	Donald Grantham	*Southern Harmony*
2001	No winner.	
2002	Peter Graham	*Harrison's Dream*
2003	No contest held.	
2004	No contest held.	
2005	John Mackey	*Redline Tango*
2006	No contest held.	
2007	Michael Daugherty	*Raise the Roof*
2008	No contest held.	
2009	John Mackey	*Aurora Awakes*
2010	No contest held.	
2011	Yo Goto	*Songs for Wind Ensemble*
2012	Michael Gandolfi	*Flourishes and Meditations on a Renaissance Theme*
2013	Aaron Perrine	*Pale Blue on Deep*
2014	Steve Bryant	*Concerto for Alto Saxophone*

2015	Aaron Perrine	*Only Light*
2016	Paul Dooley	*Masks and Machines*
	John Mackey	*Wine-Dark Sea*
2017	Christopher Lowry	*A Cypress Prelude*

Barlow International Competition (Wind Ensemble Compositions)

2007	David Rakowski	*Cantina*
2014	Narong Prangcharoen	*Lokuttara*

National Band Association/Merrill Jones Composition Contest

2001	Samuel Hazo	*Novo Lenio*
2003	Jonathan Newman	*Moon by Night*
2005	Brett Dietz	*shards of glass*
2007	Ryan Main	*The Clash*
2009	No award made.	
2010	Jack Hughes	*After Rain*
2012	Jess Turner	*Exultant Heart*
2014	David Faleris	*Of Chivalry and Valor*
2016	Joshua Hummel	*Fanfare for the Appalachians:1–77*

National Band Association/William D. Revelli Composition Contest

2000	David Kechley	*Restless Birds Before the Dark Moon*
2001	Joseph Spaniola	*Escapade*
2002	Dean Roush	*Illuminations*
2003	David Dzubay	*Ra!*
2003	Samuel Hazo	*Perthshire Majesty*
2004	Joseph Turrin	*Illuminations*
2005	Philip Sparke	*Music of the Spheres*
2006	Frank Ticheli	*Symphony No. 2*

2007	Steven Bryant	*Radiant Joy*
2008	Steven Bryant	*Suite Dreams*
2009	John Mackey	*Aurora Awakes*
2010	Steven Bryant	*Ecstatic Waters*
2011	Scott Lindroth	*Passage*
	Kevin Walczyk	*Epitaphs Unwritten*
2012	Michael Schelle	*The End of the World*
2013	Oliver Waespi	*Audivi Media Nocte*
2014	Wayne Oquin	*Affirmation*
2015	Paul Dooley	*Masks and Machines*
	John Mackey	*Wine-Dark Sea*
2016	Philip Sparke	*A Colour Symphony*
2017	James Stephenson	*Symphony No. 2, "Voices"*

Walter Beeler Memorial Commission Series/Prize

2000	David Dzubay	*Myaku*
2002	Michael Djupstrom	*Homages*
2004	John Mackey	*Redline Tango*
2006	No winner.	
2008	Kathryn Salfelder	*Cathedrals*
2010	Jess Langston Turner	*Rumpelstilzchen: A Fairy Tale for Wind Ensemble*
2012	Viet Cuong	*Sound and Smoke*

ASCAP/CBDNA Frederick Fennell Prize

2002	Michael Djupstrom	*Homages*
2004	Yotam Haber	*Espresso*
2006	Matthew Tommasini	*Three Spanish Songs*
2008	Kathryn Salfelder	*Cathedrals*
2010	Joshua Hummel	*Haiku Symphony No. 4*
2012	Takuma Itoh	*Daydreams*
2014	Shuying Li	*Slippery Slope*
2016	Nathan Stang	*Undertow*

College Band Directors National Association Young Band Composition Contest

1999	Greg Danner	*Walls of Zion*
2001	Christopher Tucker	*Americans Lost*
2003	Christopher Tucker	*Twilight in the Wilderness*
2005	Anthony Suter	*Dancing at Stonehenge*
2007	John Carnahan	*And the Antelope Play*
2009	No winner.	
2011	John Mackey	*Foundry*
2012	Clifton Jones	*Rondo Picoso*
2013	Andrew Boysen	*Snowflakes Dancing*
2014	Erika Svanoe	*The Haunted Carousel*
2015	Haley Woodrow	*And It Begins*
2016	James Syler	*Wu Xing*
2017	Aaron Perrine	*Temperance*

The Pulitzer Prize for Music

No work specifically composed for wind band/ensemble has yet won a Pulitzer Prize.

The Grawemeyer Award

No work specifically composed for wind band/ensemble has yet won a Grawemeyer Award.

Index

441

About the Author

Frank L. Battisti

Frank L. Battisti is Conductor Emeritus of the New England Conservatory Wind Ensemble. He founded and conducted the ensemble for thirty years (1969–99). Today the NEC Wind Ensemble is recognized as one of the premiere ensembles of its kind in the United States and throughout the world. Its performances and recordings have earned high critical praise and accolades.

Performances by the NEC Wind Ensemble have been broadcast over National Public Radio (NPR) and other classical music radio stations throughout the United States and world. Battisti was Principal Guest Conductor of the Longy School of Music Chamber Winds, Cambridge, Massachusetts, from 2000–2008 and founder and Music Director of the Tanglewood Institute's Young Artists Wind Ensemble from 2000–2004. In 2005 he became the Ensemble's Conductor Emeritus.

Dr. Battisti is responsible for commissioning and premiering over sixty works for wind ensemble by distinguished American and world composers including Warren Benson, Leslie Bassett, Robert Ceely, John Harbison, Robin Holloway, Witold Lutosławski, William Thomas McKinley, Vincent Persichetti, Michael Colgrass, Daniel Pinkham, Gunther Schuller, Robert Selig, Ivan Tcheripnin, Sir Michael Tippett, William Kraft, Robert Ward, and Alec Wilder. Critics, composers, and colleagues have praised Battisti for his commitment to contemporary music and his outstanding performances.

Battisti has guest conducted numerous university, college, military, professional, and high school bands/wind ensembles and served as a visiting teacher/clinician throughout the United States, UK, Europe, Middle East, Africa, Scandinavia, Australia, China, Taiwan, Canada, South America, South Korea, Iceland, and the former U.S.S.R.

Past President of the U.S. College Band Directors National Association (CBDNA), Battisti is also a member of the American Bandmasters Association (ABA) and founder of the National Wind Ensemble Conference, World Association of Symphonic Bands and Ensembles (WASBE), Massachusetts Youth Wind Ensemble (MYWE), and New England College Band Association (NECBA). He has also served on the Standard Award Panel of American Society for Composers, Authors and Publishers (ASCAP) and the National Foundation for Advancement of the Arts Recognition and Talent Search Panel (ARTS).

Considered one of the world's foremost authorities on wind music literature, Battisti has written numerous articles on wind ensemble/band literature, conducting, and music education for national and international professional journals and magazines (*The Instrumentalist, WASBE Journal, WINDS, MENC Music Journal*, etc.). He is the author of *The 20th Century American Wind Band/Ensemble* (1995), *The Winds of Change* (2002), *On Becoming a Conductor* (2007), *The Best We Can Be* (2010), *Winds of Change II: The New Millenium* (2012), *The Conductor's Challenge* (2016), and co-author of *Score Study for the Wind Band Conductor* (1990), *Lead and Inspire* (2007), and *Sourcebook for Wind Band and Instrumental Music* (2014). Battisti has also served as editor for various music publishing companies and is currently a consulting editor for *The Instrumentalist* magazine.

In 1986 and 1993, Dr. Battisti was a visiting fellow at Clare Hall, Cambridge University, England. He has received many awards and honors including Honorary Doctor of Music degrees from Ithaca College in 1992, Rhode Island College in 2010, New England Conservatory of Music in 2012; the Ithaca College Alumni Association Lifetime Achievement Award in 2003, New England Conservatory Alumni Association Lifetime Achievement Award in 2008, the first Louis and Adrienne Krasner Excellence in Teaching Award from the New England Conservatory of Music in 1997, the Lowell Mason Award from the Massachusetts Music Educators Association in 1998, the New England College Band Association's Lifetime Achievement

Award in 1999, Midwest International Band and Orchestra Clinic's Medal of Honor in 2001, and the National Band Association's AWAPA in 2006.

Officially retired, Battisti maintains a very active guest conducting, teaching and writing career. He lives in Leverett, Massachusetts with his wife of 63 years, Charlotte.